M000275623

Property, Liberty, and
Self-Ownership in
Seventeenth-Century
England

Property, Liberty, and Self-Ownership in Seventeenth-Century England

L O R E N Z O   S A B B A D I N I

McGill-Queen's University Press

Montreal & Kingston · London · Chicago

© McGill-Queen's University Press 2020

ISBN 978-0-2280-0168-3 (cloth)
ISBN 978-0-2280-0169-0 (paper)
ISBN 978-0-2280-0303-8 (ePDF)
ISBN 978-0-2280-0304-5 (ePUB)

Legal deposit third quarter 2020
Bibliothèque nationale du Québec

Printed in Canada on acid-free paper that is 100% ancient forest free
(100% post-consumer recycled), processed chlorine free

We acknowledge the support of the Canada Council for the Arts.

Nous remercions le Conseil des arts du Canada de son soutien.

Library and Archives Canada Cataloguing in Publication

Title: Property, liberty, and self-ownership in seventeenth-century
    England / Lorenzo Sabbadini.
Names: Sabbadini, Lorenzo, 1986- author.
Description: Includes bibliographical references and index.
Identifiers: Canadiana (print) 20200224301 | Canadiana (ebook)
    20200224395 | ISBN 9780228001690 (softcover) | ISBN 9780228001683
    (hardcover) | ISBN 9780228003038 (PDF) | ISBN 9780228003045 (EPUB)
Subjects: LCSH: Liberty. | LCSH: Political science—Philosophy. | LCSH:
    Philosophy, English—17th century.
Classification: LCC JC585 .S23 2020 | DDC 323.44—dc23

For Mascha

Contents

FOREWORD
Quentin Skinner

Lorenzo Sabbadini's book started life as a PhD dissertation I supervised at Queen Mary University of London. As with almost every graduate student I have had the good fortune to teach, Lorenzo arrived with a clear project in mind and needed very little in the way of guidance to bring it to a successful conclusion. His highly impressive study centres on the important but elusive concept of self-ownership. As he demonstrates, the idea was first articulated in the radical political writings of the Levellers in the English Revolution and was subsequently taken up and developed by John Locke in his *Two Treatises of Government*. Sabbadini begins by examining the debates between the Parliamentarians and the Levellers out of which the concept arose, and his book culminates in a strikingly original exploration of the role played by self-ownership in Locke's analysis of individual liberty and legitimate government.

Of recent times there has been a widespread revival of interest in ideas about self-ownership among political philosophers as well as intellectual historians. A generation ago, a number of Marxist commentators – most notably C.B. Macpherson – suggested that the emergence of the concept mirrored the growth of a fully market society in England. Macpherson argued that, if someone can be said to be the owner of their own body, it follows that they must be able to alienate their labour-power and place it in the service of others. The acceptance of this possibility was taken to be proof that an ideology of "possessive individualism" had already taken hold before the end of the seventeenth century.

More recently, a number of libertarian political philosophers have found a strongly contrasting reason for taking an interest in Locke's theory of self-ownership. The classic statement of their case can be found in Robert Nozick's *Anarchy, State, and Utopia*. According to Nozick, Locke's underlying aim is to defend an absolute right to private property. Locke is telling us that, if you take away the fruits of someone's labour, you are contravening their fundamental right to the ownership of whatever their bodily powers enabled them to appropriate. He is thus recruited as a defender of the view that any attempt to tax or redistribute private property must amount to an unjust act of confiscation and hence an affront to liberty.

One of Sabbadini's most significant contributions is to clear this rubbish out of the way. He shows that both these interpretations fail to grasp the nature of the ideological debates out of which the concept of self-ownership arose and fail, in consequence, to identify the problem that the concept was introduced to solve. We need to begin, he argues, by considering the attacks on the monarchy mounted by the protagonists of Parliament at the outbreak of the English Civil War in 1642. More specifically, we need to begin with the most important of the Parliamentarian propagandists, Henry Parker, about whom Sabbadini writes in his opening chapter with exceptional perceptiveness. Parker maintains in his *Observations* of 1642 that sovereignty lies with the whole body of the people. As he concedes, however, the people obviously constitute a body too large to be capable of assembling and making decisions on their own behalf. They have therefore entrusted these tasks to the representative body of Parliament, whose actions can be taken to count as those of the people as a whole.

The Levellers responded that, on this account, the power of Parliament confronts each citizen in the form of a unitary will to which they are all subject and, hence, as an arbitrary form of power. But as Richard Overton most emphatically objected, this is to overlook the importance of personal liberty. Every individual, Overton insists, is the possessor of certain fundamental rights and liberties that any legitimate government is under an obligation to respect, and one of the most basic of these is freedom from dependence or servitude.

At this stage it becomes vital to Sabbadini's argument to stress that the Levellers espouse what has recently come to be known as the "republican" theory of civil liberty. This label is potentially misleading, if only because some of the most prominent early modern defenders of the "republican" ideal, including John Locke, would have been horrified to find themselves described as republican in their political allegiances. I would myself prefer to speak (as Sabbadini sometimes does) of the neo-Roman understanding of liberty, in an allusion to its juristic provenance. But whatever description we use, Sabbadini's point is that we are referring to a theory very different from the currently prevailing view that freedom consists in an absence of interference with the exercise of our powers. The distinctively neo-Roman contention is that, in speaking of individual freedom, we are referring to the possession of a certain status as a citizen, that of not being subject to the arbitrary will and power of anyone else. Freedom is thus taken to reside in a body of fundamental rights fully protected from any possible acts of interference.

It was in connection with this view of liberty that the argument about self-ownership originally made its appearance. If you are to count as a free person, Overton proposed, it must be possible to say that you own yourself. Your body, that is, must not be under the control of anyone else's will. To be rendered subject to any such form of arbitrary power – even that of a Parliament claiming to act in your name – is to forfeit the status of a free person and fall into the condition of a slave. The enjoyment of personal liberty thus came to be equated with self-ownership.

By focusing on this line of argument, Sabbadini is able to make a new and fertile contribution to understanding the political theory of the English Revolution. But he is able at the same time to make a valuable addition to recent discussions about the nature and merits of the neo-Roman view of civil liberty. So far, protagonists of this view have tended to concentrate on the relations between individual citizens and the powers of the state, arguing that to live in subjection to the mere will of a sovereign is to suffer a form of servitude. To this argument Sabbadini adds that freedom from subjection can no less easily be undermined by relations of domination and dependence within civil society, and especially by living in economic dependence on the goodwill of others. As he rightly emphasizes in his thought-provoking Conclusion, such unequal relationships are among the most insidious enemies of individual liberty in contemporary democracies. As a result, to understand Sabbadini's historical argument is not merely to learn something new about the English Revolution; it is also to equip ourselves with a vocabulary and a set of insights powerfully relevant to the moral improvement of our contemporary world.

Acknowledgments

During the many years it has taken me to complete this study, I have had the good fortune to be supported by some extraordinary people, and it gives me great pleasure to acknowledge some of them here. I would like to begin by expressing my most heartfelt gratitude to Quentin Skinner, who supervised with unfailing dedication, enthusiasm, and kindness the PhD dissertation from which this book has emerged. I cannot imagine a more inspirational or supportive *Doktorvater*, and I am enormously grateful for his continuing generosity and friendship. I would also like to thank my examiners, David Armitage and Jason Peacey, both for the stimulating discussion during the *viva* and for their extremely insightful examiners' reports, which have provided a point of departure in the manuscript's journey from dissertation to book.

I am profoundly indebted to the experts who have read and commented on my manuscript at various stages. I feel especially grateful to James Tully, whose thoughtful observations on my chapter on Locke helped refine my interpretation and sharpen my argument. My sincerest thanks also to Georgios Giannakopoulos, Elliott Karstadt, John Miller, Joad Raymond, Markku Peltonen, Evangelos Sakkas, and the anonymous reviewers at McGill-Queen's University Press for their helpful feedback. Finally, I would like to register my gratitude to Richard Baggaley, my editor at the press, for his advice about revising the manuscript for publication and, more generally, for the professional way in which he steered the project from start to finish.

My academic work has been immeasurably enriched by conversation with teachers, scholars, and friends. I would like to acknowledge in particular Richard Bourke, Annabel Brett, the late James Campbell, Nicholas Davidson, Signy Gutnick-Allen, Bob Harris, Felicity Heal, Peter Heather,

Maurizio Isabella, Jeremy Jennings, Melissa Lane, Giorgio Lizzul, Eric Nelson, Julia Nicholls, Joanne Paul, Philip Pettit, John Robertson, Miri Rubin, Sophie Smith, Gareth Stedman Jones, Georgios Varouxakis, and Hanna Weibye.

Since finishing my PhD, I have begun a new career as a government lawyer at HM Treasury. I would like to pay tribute to Peter King, James Neilson, Muhammad Saley, and other colleagues at the Treasury for making this such a welcoming and stimulating place in which to work. My thanks to them also for being so accommodating when I needed to take time off for writing this book.

The unwavering affection and support of my parents, Andrea and Laura, have been invaluable in bringing this book to fruition, as in so much else. I am also thankful to Marta and Tom for all they have done over the years. Among the friends who provided encouragement, or simply a welcome distraction, as I worked on this project, I am particularly grateful to Adam Back, Tamerlane Camden-Dunne, Laurence Doering, Dylan Grainger, Paul Humpherson, Ilona Mannan, Joseph Popper, Josh Segal, Lee Solomons, and Amelia Walsh.

My warmest thanks are reserved for Mascha Gerasimenko, whom I met just before embarking on my doctoral studies and who has supported me in my writing with generosity of spirit, lightheartedness, and tenderness. I dedicate this book to her, with love.

Notes on the Text

Bibliography. The bibliography lists only those primary and secondary sources referred to in this book; I have not attempted to provide a full list of works relating to my subject. Anonymous sources are listed alphabetically by title. Where a text is issued anonymously but a widely accepted attribution exists, I provide the author's name in square brackets. I do not follow this practice, however, when quoting from a modern edition of a text originally published anonymously (e.g., Locke's *Two Treatises of Government*). For sources published pseudonymously whose author has not been identified, the pseudonym is provided in inverted commas.

Editions. I use modern editions where these are reliable and readily available; otherwise my preference is for original editions. For the pamphlet literature of chapters 1 and 2, I have opted to use the original editions contained in the Thomason Collection at the British Library, even though in a few cases an acceptable modern text exists. The only exception is Winstanley's pamphlets, for which I have availed myself of the critical edition published by Oxford University Press.

Transcriptions. My general rule is to preserve the spelling, punctuation, capitalization, and italicization of the texts from which I quote. However, I normalize the long "s," alter "u" to "v" and "i" to "j" and vice versa in accordance with modern usage, and adjust the case of initial letters when inserting quotations into my text. I apply this rule also to titles, except for works widely known in a modernized form. Thus *An Essay concerning Human Understanding*, not *An Essay concerning Humane Understanding*.

Translations. When quoting from non-English sources, my general practice is to use a modern English translation, providing excerpts from the original in square brackets where this is deemed necessary. When quoting from an English source with the occasional passage in a foreign language, I have preserved the original and included my own translation in square brackets. Titles are provided in the original language, except in the case of works commonly referred to in English (e.g., Aristotle's *Politics*).

Property, Liberty, and
Self-Ownership in
Seventeenth-Century
England

INTRODUCTION

I

This book is about the conjunction of property and liberty in a number of distinct but related debates in a period stretching from the English Civil War to the Glorious Revolution. It explores this relationship with a particular focus on the concept of self-ownership, tracing its complex history over the course of this period. Much has been written about ideas of liberty and freedom[1] in this period and, in particular, what has variously been referred to as the "neo-Roman" or "republican" concept,[2] according to which liberty describes not the absence of interference but the status of not being subject to arbitrary power. The protagonists of this study almost invariably thought of liberty in these terms, although rival accounts of liberty were also put forward in this period, most notably that of Thomas Hobbes.[3] What has largely been missed in the recent work on republican liberty is the distinctive role played by ideas of property, and self-ownership in particular. In the chapters that follow, I seek to remedy this situation, showing how economic forms of dependence were as much a concern for republican theorists as political forms, and that it was within this context that the concept of self-ownership emerged.

The starting point for this study is the articulation by supporters of Parliament of a new and distinctive language of liberty during the so-called paper war of the early 1640s. There had been a long tradition in England of invoking the subject's liberty – or, more often, "liberties" – to counterbalance the king's prerogative, but in the debates of the 1640s the language of liberty began to be deployed in more far-reaching ways: not to protest against specific acts of interference by the king but to make broader claims about his possession of arbitrary power and its consequences for the status of his subjects. Issues of property were central because one of the major grievances against Charles I was that he was attempting to raise revenues from his subjects without having first obtained Parliament's consent and, as such, was acting arbitrarily. Concerns such as these continued to animate debates in the following decades, whose participants variously appropriated, rejected, or re-elaborated ideas first put forward in the 1640s. For these writers, there was a fundamental relationship between liberty and property that went to the heart of what it means to be a free-man: freedom was, for them, not merely a political condition but also an economic one.

While the protagonists of this book were all in some way engaging with the question of how to conceptualize the relationship between liberty and property, I do not wish to suggest that they were all intervening in precisely the same debate, still less that taken together their works articulate a single, coherent theory of liberty and property. Some of the writers were engaged in a conversation with one another, others self-consciously appropriated the ideas of their predecessors, and others still may have been influenced in less direct ways. Yet the texts discussed in this study constituted discrete interventions in particular debates, and there is considerable diversity in terms of their polemical intentions, the sources upon which they drew, and the conceptual contribution that they sought to make.

Nevertheless, two broad ways of thinking about the relationship between property and liberty may be detected. The first, in which ideas of self-ownership were central, was that the secure enjoyment of one's property was in some sense a manifestation of one's status as a free-man, such that to interfere with established property rights was to undermine liberty. This was undoubtedly the most common way of thinking about the nexus between liberty and property, being the dominant strand in the writings of the Parliamentarian pamphleteers, the Levellers, Interregnum republicans such as John Milton and Marchamont Nedham, and John Locke. The second approach – central to the writings of the Diggers, Harrington, and the neo-Harringtonians, and hinted at in several of the authors mentioned above – was to argue that freedom required all men (or at least all men considered worthy of being citizens) to be property holders.[4] Whereas for Harrington this was still fundamentally an argument about private property, for the Diggers private property and the covetousness that it engendered were themselves the greatest obstacles to freedom. Several other writers in this period emphasized the dangers of excessive riches, while nevertheless defending the fundamental right to private property.

In the chapters that follow, I seek to reconstruct a variety of arguments about liberty and property that emerged in the period from the Civil War to the Glorious Revolution. I attempt to locate them within their historical context, while also drawing out some points of connection between authors who are not conventionally grouped together. My aim in doing so is to provide a fresh perspective on republican thought in one of the crucial moments in its development. The focus in much contemporary republican scholarship on what constitutes arbitrary power in the political sphere has precluded engagement with some of the vital questions thrown up by the authors of the seventeenth century. If the condition of the slave is that of being the property of somebody else, what does it mean to be self-owning? What is the relationship between popular sovereignty and individual liberty? In what sense does interference with property in external goods undermine property in the self? Does private property itself, and the economic inequality to which it gives rise, create relationships of dependence that are incompatible with freedom? What is the relationship between property in the self and property in external goods? By bringing these questions to the fore, this study aims to recast the republican tradition in a new light and thereby to bring into sharper relief some of its most valuable insights.

II

I would like to begin with a brief survey of the republican concept of liberty as it has been "excavated" by political theorists and intellectual historians such as Philip Pettit and Quentin Skinner.[5] According to these scholars, the neo-Roman theory is predicated on a dichotomy, originating in Roman law, between the free-man and the slave. As such, freedom is not principally concerned with the performance of actions but with the status of persons.[6] Although there are differences between Skinner's and Pettit's accounts of slavery, both present freedom as the condition of non-subjection to arbitrary power.[7] As they point out, if the slave is fortunate to have a benevolent master, he may be able to go about his daily business unmolested, but according to the neo-Roman theory he is nevertheless existentially unfree because the master retains the power at any moment to compel him to perform or forbear from performing a given action. A second feature of the republican concept is the idea that the condition of servitude breeds servility.[8] The mere knowledge of one's dependence, of one's liability to be interfered with at any moment upon the master's whim, leads to abstention and self-censorship. Not knowing where he stands, the slave will be inclined to play it safe and avoid doing anything that might result in the master's coercive interference. The master need not even lift a finger to bend the slave's will to his own: the slave's internalization of his condition of dependence will have already done the necessary work. However, as Skinner points out, the slave's liberty is not curtailed only insofar as he restricts his own behaviour in this manner.[9] A reckless slave may rarely choose to modify his behaviour in this way, but he would be unfree all the same because he remained subject to his master's will.

Republican freedom is often thought of as a third concept of liberty, distinct from both positive and negative liberty as set out in Isaiah Berlin's seminal essay, "Two Concepts of Liberty."[10] It differs from the former in that it does not posit a normative conception of human nature in whose attainment liberty is taken to lie. One particularly influential version of the positive concept of liberty in the early modern period was the Aristotelian notion of freedom as man's self-realization through active participation in the *polis*.[11] By contrast, participatory politics in the republican tradition is important only for instrumental reasons: it may be viewed as a necessary condition for the avoidance of arbitrary power.[12] The republican concept of freedom also differs from conventional accounts of negative liberty as absence of interference. According to the republican position, the logical antithesis of freedom is not coercive interference but dependence or domination: one can be interfered with and yet still be free, provided that the interference does not result in dependence; conversely, one can be unfree without suffering any interference at all since the mere *capacity* of another to interfere creates a relationship of domination.[13] Freedom is thus, in Pettit's most synthetic formulation, not a condition of non-interference but of "non-domination."[14]

The principal point of divergence between Skinner and Pettit – and the aspect of the republican concept of freedom that has generated most controversy – regards the nature of arbitrary power. In Pettit's account, at least as expressed in *Republicanism: A Theory of Freedom and Government*, this appears to have two separate dimensions.[15] According to the first, one is free if one is not subject to arbitrary interference, that is, interference that does not track one's "interests and ideas."[16] This way of setting up the argument is problematic not so much because – as Pettit's critics argue[17] – it "moralizes" the republican concept of liberty but because it undermines what I take to be its key insight: that certain structures of power, irrespective of the way they are used, are contrary to freedom. To describe non-arbitrary power merely in terms of whether it is in accordance with the aspirations of those subject to it would seem to have the effect – contrary to Pettit's intentions – of lending support to enlightened despotism, where power is exercised in the interests of those subject to it but only because this happens to coincide with the ruler's preferences.

However, Pettit's second argument makes it clear that such a regime could not possibly be consistent with republican freedom. In this analysis the mere *capacity* of a ruler to interfere with his people on an arbitrary basis – that is, once again, in a way that does not follow their interests and ideas – would already undermine freedom.[18] In order to deprive rulers of the capacity for arbitrary interference, what is required is not that the people should necessarily be in a position to consent to the laws to which they are subject but that they should be able to *contest* them.[19] This way of expressing the argument is not only more compelling but also more in line with the spirit of the Roman and neo-Roman tradition to which Pettit appeals. Yet the force of Pettit's argument is undermined by his definition of arbitrary power in terms of whether or not it promotes the interests and ideas of those subject to it. Pettit appears to have recognized this problem with his discussion of republican liberty in *Republicanism* and in later works has abandoned it in favour of a more procedural way of understanding arbitrary – or "uncontrolled" – power.[20] In his latest book on republican liberty, *Just Freedom: A Moral Compass for a Complex World*, he describes an act of interference as being non-dominating if and only if "the people affected by the interference share equally in controlling the form that it takes."[21]

Skinner manages to avoid such difficulties by conceptualizing arbitrary power in a different way. In *Liberty before Liberalism* and other early works on neo-Roman liberty he draws on the metaphor of the body politic and the view that, just like natural bodies, states are liable to have their freedom taken away if they fall into a condition of dependence. This, Skinner claims, can arise in two ways: first, if the body politic becomes subject to a foreign power, for example through conquest; second, if an individual or group within it is able to wield unchecked, discretionary power.[22] To the extent that the political body is dependent on neither a foreign nor an internal power, it can be said to be self-governing and therefore free from arbitrary power. To be a free person is simply the condition of living in such a "free-state."[23]

In later writings Skinner has tended to move away from this formulation and argue that individual liberty is taken away by arbitrary power, where arbitrary power is understood as the capacity to interfere with somebody else at will, regardless of whether any interference actually takes place.[24] However, as Skinner has recently stressed, there is not in his mind a distinction between political and individual liberty, for it is with the potential for arbitrary power in the political sphere that he is principally concerned.[25] It remains his view that to avoid arbitrary power and therefore to be free is to be a citizen of a self-governing political community. The question whether the power under which one lives tracks one's interests and ideas is irrelevant to Skinner since it is the way in which the power is constituted that makes it arbitrary, not the use to which it is put.[26] Given the possibility that arbitrary power may be exercised in an unobtrusive way, Skinner has eschewed Pettit's vocabulary of non-domination, with its overtones of domineering behaviour, preferring to characterize liberty as the condition of not living in dependence on others, or – most recently – as autonomy of choice.[27]

Something that is largely missing from the conventional account of republican liberty is the issue of property. The reason contemporary republicans have tended to marginalize the question of property, Knud Haakonssen suggests, is not that they are unaware of its importance to the early modern republican tradition but that they are embarrassed by the claim that only propertied males could be capable of liberty.[28] As Pettit acknowledges, part of the reason for the triumph of liberalism in the nineteenth century was the extension of citizenship to include those who were not property owners, which made it clear that "freedom would have to be reconceived in less demanding terms."[29] In their attempt to challenge the hegemony of liberalism and to highlight the relevance of republicanism to contemporary debates, republican scholars have been anxious to jettison what they might be tempted to view as the most backward-looking aspect of their heritage.

One work that does give due weight to the role of property in the republican theory is Eric MacGilvray's *The Invention of Market Freedom*. According to MacGilvray, early modern republicanism stipulated that "the free man must be economically independent, so that he does not rely on others for his livelihood and is not obliged either to ask for or to accept favors."[30] Liberty within this tradition was not an ideal with a universal application but the description of the status enjoyed by a particular class of propertied men. MacGilvray stresses that it was precisely this aspect of the republican theory that resulted in its decline over the course of the eighteenth century, as the rise of commercial society and the extension of the franchise led to the development of a new concept of freedom centred on the institution of the market. MacGilvray's purpose in tracing this narrative is not to revive republican liberty but to put forward a new way of thinking about freedom based on the contrast between republican and market freedom; it is perhaps because he is not himself a proponent of republicanism that he has been more ready than others to discuss the issue of property.

It might be protested that the attempt to make use of republican liberty as part of a defence of private property is merely an application of the theory and not integral to it. It is true that there are other aspects of early modern republican thought that contemporary republicans can overlook without betraying its spirit. The gendered language of citizenship that is so characteristic of early modern republicanism, for example, can be dropped without any loss to the basic structure of the theory. In other words, there is nothing inherent in the concept of the "free-man" that could not apply to women as well as men.[31] But I do not think the same is true of property. Some of the authors discussed in this book may have presented interference with property as an *instance* of arbitrary power, but for most of our authors the question of political liberty as described by Pettit and Skinner did not even arise unless certain conditions obtained within the economic domain. Property arrangements were viewed by these authors as a vital condition of independence and therefore as constitutive of liberty. It is this shortcoming in the received account of the republican theory that I hope to remedy in the chapters that follow and that I should now like to highlight in a preliminary way.

III

The term "property" or "propriety" – the two were generally used inter-
changeably³² – had a range of overlapping senses in the seventeenth
century.³³ First, it could be used to describe that which is "proper" to somebody, either in the morally neutral sense of the attributes of a particular
agent or in the normative sense now captured by the term "propriety." Second, property could serve to denote a right to something, usually but not
exclusively a material good or estate. This notion of property is connected
with, and to an extent may be viewed as translating, the Latin concept of
suum, the sphere around each individual that encapsulates all that is properly his own.³⁴ Third, property could refer to the object of this right, the
possession or parcel of land that belongs to the bearer of the property right.

To distinguish these senses of property is not to suggest that they can always be disentangled in the texts under examination. The term is indeed
characterized by indeterminacy and fluidity, which may have been part of
its appeal. As James Tully points out, "The word 'property' had a broader
reference than today: it included personal rights, especially religious and
civil liberties."³⁵ Discussions of property in the seventeenth century show
little trace of what are now widely regarded as some of its most vital ing-
redients.³⁶ Most notably, the notion that to have a property in something
must include the right to alienate it is either absent or expressly denied. But
the term property did have particular connotations of ownership; it was
not merely a synonym of "liberty" or "right." John Lilburne, for example,
distinguishes between the "Liberty of my Person" and "Propriety, or goods"
(although his point in doing so was to draw a connection between the
two).³⁷ When John Wildman claimed that the king does not have a "property in all the Townes of England,"³⁸ he was not arguing that the king does
not have any kind of right in the towns (which of course he did) but, rather,
that he does not own them in the way that one owns one's possessions, the
polemical point being that that was precisely how the king treated them.
The term property thus evoked ideas of possession, ownership and occupation,³⁹ while being capable of being applied in a broader context than
discussions of estates or material goods.

It is the polyvalence of property that made it possible for the language
of self-ownership or property in the person to develop.⁴⁰ The idea that every
individual has a "selfe propriety" was first put forward by the Levellers in

order to affirm the liberty of the individual in the face of what they regarded as the increasingly absolutist stance being adopted by Parliament.[41] This "individualist" notion of self-ownership subverted the Parliamentarians' discourse of popular sovereignty, in which the people's innate power was treated as a form of property that was "entrusted" (rather than donated) to the king. Both the Parliamentarians and the Levellers were preoccupied with the problem of arbitrary power, whether in the hands of the king or Parliament. Self-ownership may be seen as restating in positive terms the Roman law understanding of freedom as not being the property of another.[42] Subsuming the individual into the corporate body of the people, the Parliamentarians had sought to challenge the king's arbitrary measures, while justifying Parliament's no less questionable actions by appealing to its representative nature. The Levellers' individualist notion of self-ownership enabled them to resist this argument: to say that an individual had a property in himself was to say that he could not be the property of anybody else and, therefore, that no person or institution, even one claiming a unique capacity to represent the corporate body of the people, could exercise arbitrary power over him.

The particular appeal of this vocabulary was that it drew a direct parallel between freedom (property in oneself) and property in external goods. One of the central anxieties about arbitrary power shared by most of the authors discussed in this book was its fundamental threat to the institution of private property. If being free was defined as the condition of not being the property of somebody else, then holding one's private property securely could be viewed as an indispensable feature of one's liberty. At first glance, this appears to be something of a non sequitur, and indeed (with the notable exception of Locke) the connection between property in the person and in external goods is not always clearly delineated. But it appears that our authors were generally relying on the following argument. A ruler who was able to tax his subjects at will could, if he wished, take away all of their property; as such, subjects could enjoy their property only at the whim of their rulers and so did not have any real property rights at all.[43] And if an individual was deprived of his property rights, then he was also deprived of his property in himself, which was as much as to say that he was deprived of his liberty. The idea of self-ownership thus made it possible to marshal the rhetorically powerful language of liberty in defence of private property.

It is within this mode of thought that Locke's famous assertion that "every Man has a *Property* in his own *Person*" emerges.[44] Locke's predecessors had failed to tackle head on the question of why interference with property in external goods necessarily undermined property in the person, beyond the vague and often implicit idea that interference with private property undermines property rights and therefore also property in the self. Locke sought to provide an answer to this question with his argument that property in the person makes possible, through the act of mixing labour with natural resources, the individuation of private property. Locke's argument is more ambitious and theoretically sophisticated than that of his predecessors, but it is motivated by a broadly similar concern with resisting the arbitrary interference with property on the grounds that it is incompatible with liberty.

My reading of the seventeenth-century discourse of self-ownership thus diverges from the influential interpretation put forward by C.B. Macpherson in his classic work, *The Political Theory of Possessive Individualism*. Macpherson argues that the idea of self-ownership as expressed by both the Levellers and Locke underpinned a theory of "possessive individualism" that, in legitimating a society built around self-interested, competitive market relations, provided the ideological foundations of an emerging "possessive market society."[45] Central to Macpherson's thesis is the idea that one's property in one's person, like any other kind of property, must be alienable. For Macpherson, the attempt to define freedom as a function of the property one has in one's person and capacities served to explain how a market society with vast inequalities of wealth that resulted in some members having nothing to sell but their labour was nevertheless compatible with individual liberty. If to be free is to have a property in one's person and capacities, and if the right of alienation is a fundamental feature of a property right, then it follows that alienating one's labour is merely an expression of one's freedom, even where this amounts to "wage slavery."

There is certainly both a possessive and an individualist quality to the language of self-ownership. It was fundamentally concerned with protecting the individual from arbitrary power, and in its initial formulation by the Levellers was intended to challenge what could be described as a "corporatist" notion of self-ownership. It is also clear that the language was deployed as part of a defence of private property, though many of its proponents did express anxieties about excessive riches that sit uneasily with Macpherson's view that it served to legitimate uncontrolled capitalist accumulation. However, self-ownership was not thought of as being alienable: to the extent that such a possibility was contemplated at all, it was expressly rejected. The Leveller Richard Overton argued that self-ownership could not entail the right to give away one's property in oneself but only to entrust one's rulers to use it for one's benefit, for "he that gives more, sins against his owne flesh; and he that takes more, is a Theife and Robber to his kind."[45] Locke believed that man's property in his person was subordinate to God's property in his creation and that man was under an obligation under natural law to further God's plan for the universe through preserving himself and others. Therefore, although Locke accepted that, in the state of nature, man has an "uncontroleable Liberty, to dispose of his Person or Possessions," this did not mean that he could alienate his property in himself absolutely since he lacks the "Liberty to destroy himself, or so much as any Creature in his Possession."[46] Far from enabling the kind of voluntary servitude envisaged by Macpherson, Locke's notion of self-ownership was intended to prevent it.

The crucial point that I hope will emerge from this study is that self-ownership should be viewed as a republican concept that is fundamentally concerned with the way in which arbitrary power, and arbitrary interference with private property in particular, undermines liberty. By creating a bridge between liberty and property, the idea of self-ownership that emerged in seventeenth-century England constituted a significant contribution to republican thought. Yet, as I now wish to show by examining some of the principal Roman and common law sources, while the precise vocabulary of self-ownership was new, the underlying idea of freedom as not being the property of another had deep roots.

IV

The neo-Roman concept of liberty was juristic in origin.[47] Although it was taken up by historians and moralists such as Cicero, Livy, and Sallust, who played a significant role in transmitting it to the early modern period, there is no doubt that it is in the Roman law itself that the concept was articulated most clearly. The principal source of Roman law for early modern theorists of neo-Roman liberty – much as for contemporary theorists – was the *Digest*, a compendium of juristic writings compiled by order of Emperor Justinian in the sixth century AD. The division of persons between free and slave that it sets out has been extensively discussed by historians of political thought. However, what has not been sufficiently highlighted is the role played by ideas of property in framing this division. Not only does the *Digest* define freedom as the condition of not being the property of somebody else, but it is the establishment of property that gives rise to the institution of slavery – and with it the means to conceptualize freedom.

The main rubric dealing with the juridical status of persons in the *Digest* is *De statu hominum*. This rubric appears to be putting forward two rival definitions of liberty. In the first freedom is described simply as "one's natural power of doing what one pleases, save insofar as it is ruled out either by coercion or by law,"[48] a loose formulation broadly consistent with a modern notion of pure negative liberty that certainly could not sustain the kind of republican analysis found in the works of contemporary theorists such as Pettit. It is the second way of thinking about liberty that provides the inspiration for the neo-Roman argument. Freedom is defined here as the antonym of slavery, which is in turn described as "an institution of the *ius gentium*, whereby someone is against nature made subject to the ownership of another [*dominio alieno*]."[49] Slavery is then understood in terms of a property relationship: the slave is the person who is the property of somebody else and, as such, is in a position where he can be used and abused purely for the benefit of another.

When seen in these terms, the Roman law concept of slavery appears to have more in common than is generally appreciated with the Aristotelian understanding of the slave as "a living possession" who "wholly belongs" to his master, such that the master-slave relationship is "exercised primarily with a view to the interest of the master."[50] There remains, however, a major difference between the concept of slavery in the two traditions. Whereas for Aristotle slavery is a natural institution, deriving from the slave's inability to govern himself, in Roman law it is described as having been established "against nature" by the *ius gentium*. It is therefore surprising that in the account of the *ius gentium* found earlier in the *Digest*, no mention is made of the institution of slavery. With the establishment of the *ius gentium*, we are told, "wars were introduced, nations differentiated, kingdoms founded, properties individuated, estate boundaries settled, buildings put up, and commerce established, including contracts of buying and selling and letting and hiring."[51] If slavery is introduced by the *ius gentium*, it can only be as a further consequence of one or more of these developments.

Such a conclusion is confirmed by the *Digest*'s account of the two ways in which slavery can come about. In the first instance, slavery is said to arise as a consequence of war or, more specifically, of the generals' "custom of selling their prisoners and thereby *preserving* rather than killing them."[52] The introduction of war by the *ius gentium* is thus inadvertently responsible for slavery since without it there would be no prisoners for generals to sell into bondage. Moreover – and of greater interest for our purposes – it would be impossible for prisoners of war to be made slaves if the *ius gentium* had not also introduced property. It is because of this institution that an individual could be conceived of as belonging to somebody else, as a commodity to be bought and sold on the market.

The second way in which slavery can come into being gives even greater prominence to property. It appears to be a later development for it is described as arising only after the civil laws have been instituted, but it, too, is entirely dependent on the introduction of private property by the *ius gentium* and the institution of buying and selling. This form of slavery is said to arise "voluntarily" when an individual decides to sell himself into bondage.[53] The free person, according to this analysis, is the proprietor of himself and hence is entitled to dispose of that property by enslaving himself and thus becoming the property of somebody else. Self-ownership is then the condition of liberty but also the precondition for slavery since it requires having the ability to sell oneself into bondage. While the first proposition was an important point of departure for the discourse of self-ownership that emerged in seventeenth-century England, the second proposition was, as we have seen, either not considered or explicitly rejected.[54]

If we turn to the rubric that comes immediately after *De statu hominum*, entitled *De his qui sui vel alieni iuris sunt*, we find a second division of persons, much emphasized by Skinner, between those who are *sui iuris* and those who are "within the jurisdiction of someone else."[55] This rubric is again principally concerned with contrasting the status of free-men and slaves, but the condition of being in the jurisdiction of another is not presented as definitional of slavery for there is another class of persons – children – who also fall within this category.[56] Although all slaves are subject to the *ius* of another person, this is merely a contingent fact deriving from the still more unfortunate predicament of being their property.

The distinction between these two ways of conceptualizing the relationship between the free-man and slave should not be exaggerated. The term *dominium* used in the *Digest* in relation to the slave has been translated here as "property," but it also has connotations of "power" or "jurisdiction."[57] Moreover, whether we think of the slave as the property of his master or as subject to his *ius*, the upshot remains that he is subject to the master's discretionary power. But it seems to me important to highlight the way in which the Roman law concept of slavery was underpinned by ideas of property, not least because by doing so we are in a better position to understand the influence of this way of thinking about liberty in seventeenth-century England.

From the point of view of the authors discussed in this book, the attraction of thinking about slavery as the condition of being the property of another was, as we have seen, that it enabled them to make a further claim about the connection between freedom and property in external goods. Although Roman sources such as the *Digest* provided plenty of material for a robust defence of private property,[58] they did not offer any guidance on how to frame the relationship between property in the person and in possessions or estates. Indeed, the account of the connection between property and slavery found in the *Digest* points towards the contrasting conclusion that securing freedom might actually involve abolishing property: without this, it would be impossible to claim ownership of somebody else and thus slavery would at one stroke be eradicated.

The attempt to make property ownership integral to republican liberty was essentially an innovation of seventeenth-century England. Yet it is possible that our authors received some encouragement from an alternative idiom, one in which many of them were trained and in which all were conversant: English common law. The idea of freedom that is found within this tradition should not be seen as entirely distinct from that of Roman law, as has too often been the case.[59] It is true that the ideal of the "ancient constitution" to which many common lawyers in the seventeenth century appealed points to a different way of thinking about liberty. According to this tradition, England had, since time immemorial, attained a unique balance between the prerogative powers of the king and the "liberties" of subjects, conceived of essentially as a range of exemptions from the royal prerogative.

This differed from the neo-Roman concept not only in its tendency to think of liberties as rights governing specific spheres but also in that freedom was held to be compatible with, indeed to depend on, the presence of extensive arbitrary powers in the hands of the king.

However, the ideal of the ancient constitution was not the only contribution that the common law made to seventeenth-century discussions of freedom. If we look at two of the most widely read common law sources, we find a discussion of freedom that is entirely consistent with, and indeed draws extensively on, the Roman tradition. Perhaps the most influential of all common law texts was Henry de Bracton's *De legibus et consuetudinibus Angliae*, probably written in the first half of the thirteenth century.[60] What is immediately striking about this work, or at least about the section entitled *De personis*, is how closely it follows the *Digest*. Taking up the Roman law view that "the first and shortest classification of persons is this, that all men are either free or bond [*servi*]," Bracton's formal definition of the two is an almost word-for-word restatement of the *Digest*: "Freedom is the natural power of every man to do what he pleases, unless forbidden by law or force," whereas "servitude is an institution of the *ius gentium*, by which, contrary to nature, one person is subjected to the dominion of another."[61] Bracton – again closely tracking the *Digest* – also offers a "second classification" of persons, according to which "every man is either in his own *potestas* or another's."[62] Those who are *alieni iuris* include not only slaves but also children, though Bracton attempts to distinguish between the two by describing children as being subject to "parental" *potestas* and slaves to "seigneurial."

The principal linguistic innovation in *De legibus* is that, in addition to speaking of the *servus*, Bracton has at his disposal the terms *villanus* and *nativus*, both generally translated into English as "villein" or "villain." Yet, from a conceptual point of view, this does not appear to constitute a major break with the Roman tradition, for Bracton seems to use *servus* and *villanus/nativus* interchangeably. This can be seen, for example, in the following discussion:

> He is born a bondsman [*servus*] who is procreated of an unmarried neif [*nativa*] though of a free father, for he follows the condition of his mother, as though conceived at large. Also he who is begotten of a free father who has connexion with a neif [*villana*] established in a villein tenement [*villenagium*], whether married or not. Conversely,

if a villein [*villanus*] has connexion with a free woman in a free tene-
ment, their offspring will be bond [*servus*].[63]

The fluidity with which Bracton moves between the terms *servus, villanus,*
and *nativus* suggests that these do not constitute separate categories of
analysis; they are indeed, quite literally, part of the same family. *Villanus*
and *nativus* are, for Bracton, antonyms of freedom no less than *servus,* and
all three denote the condition of being the property of somebody else.

The semantic overlap between the categories of villein and slave in Bracton undermines the neat division between the two proposed by Skinner in
his article "Classical Liberty, Renaissance Translation, and the English Civil
War." Although Skinner has often been careful to emphasize that the neo-
Roman and common law accounts of liberty are not incompatible,[64] in this
article he attempts to distance them, albeit recognizing that in practice they
were often put forward by the same people.[65] Skinner argues that the villein
of the common law tradition is a fundamentally different creature from the
servus of Roman law since it is "only his property, not his person, which is
sub potestate domini."[66] He thus sets up a conceptual distinction between
the criticisms of the king's violation of his subjects' property rights that
began to be voiced in the early Stuart Parliaments and the more full-blown
attack, emerging slightly later, on the royal prerogative, in which the neo-
Roman concept of freedom was first invoked.[67] However, not only were the
categories of villein and slave blurred, but, as I hope to show in the pages
that follow, anxieties about the king's infringement of subjects' property
rights were inextricably bound up with concerns about their persons becoming subject to the king's arbitrary power.

For Johann Sommerville, the absence of a clear distinction between
the villein and the slave demonstrates that the neo-Roman theory "is in
fact an English theory, rooted in the common law ideas" and owes nothing at all to the Roman heritage.[68] But to make this claim is to ignore the
extent to which the common law had itself absorbed the basic categories
of analysis of Roman law.[69] Whether the authors discussed in this book
were drawing primarily on Roman or English sources is in a sense beside
the point; what is important to note is that they were putting forward a
concept of freedom that had at its heart the Roman law division of men
into free and slave.

It would be wrong, however, to claim that the common law simply restated the Roman concept of freedom without contributing anything new. Common law texts such as Bracton's were not abstract treatises of political theory but handbooks for lawyers, designed to assist them in their day-to-day practice. The simple dichotomy of the free-man and the slave did not adequately describe the myriad relationships of dependence and semi-dependence that existed in medieval and early modern English society, nor did it account for the ways in which structures of landownership could impose obligations on those who otherwise enjoyed the status of free-men. What we therefore find in the common law tradition is an attempt to apply the broad analysis of freedom found in the Roman sources to the realities of feudal and post-feudal England.

This concern with landholding may be seen towards the end of the rubric *De personis*. Inserting a passage that has no precedent in the *Digest*, Bracton upsets the neat division of persons into free and bond by suggesting that some juridically free persons may appear to lead the life of slaves:

> There were also there at the Conquest free men, who held their tenements freely by free services or free customs, who, after they had been ejected by the more powerful and had returned, took their same tenements up again to hold in villeinage, by doing thence servile, but certain and specified, works. These men are called *glebae ascripticii*, and, none the less, free men, for though they do servile works they do them not by reason of their persons but of their tenements.[70]

What Bracton is indicating here is that property arrangements have a bearing on the extent of an individual's freedom, even if the services that they entail, being "certain and specified" and therefore not determined by the unbridled will of the lord, do not go so far as to alter his juridical status. While the common law retains the conceptual distinction that is to be found in Roman law between the free-man and the slave, it recognizes that, in practice, the situation is more complex, owing to the different forms of dependence deriving from feudal property relations.

Such arguments feature still more prominently in another common law text, Sir Thomas Littleton's *Treatise on Tenures*, composed in the second half of the fifteenth century and published for the first time in English in 1594.

Here the concept of villeinage receives a less classicizing treatment than in Bracton and is more closely related to feudal property arrangements:

> Tenure in villenage is most properly when a Villein holdeth of his Lord (to whom he is villein) certaine lands and tenements after the custome and manor, or els at the will of his Lord, and to do his villein service, as to beare, bring, and carry out, the donge and filth of the Lord unto the land of his Lord, there to lay it, cast it, & spread it abroad upon the land, and to do such other maner of service.[71]

The villein is thus somebody who is in a relationship of dependence specifically by virtue of the nature of his tenure, and who is as a result "at the will of his Lord," suggesting that the latter has the power to dictate the terms of the tenure and to extract from the villein whatever services he desires.

Like Bracton, Littleton recognizes a difference between holding a tenure in villeinage and actually being a villein. As he is careful to point out, "some free tenants hold their tenements after the custome of certain manors by such service, and their tenure is called tenure in villenage, and yet they be no villeines, for no land holden by villenage, or villeine lands, or any custome rysing of the land, shall never make a free man villein."[72] While freedom is bound up with the question of landholding, there appears to be a juridical category of the "free-man" that remains in some sense independent of it.

These canonical texts of the common law may have demonstrated the potential for ideas of property to become enmeshed within a neo-Roman discussion of liberty, but they left a great deal to the theorists discussed in the following chapters to work out for themselves. The particular proposition that almost all of these authors were anxious to defend was that, if being free was defined as not being the property of somebody else, then owning property was a fundamental feature of liberty. This study examines the various ways in which this argument was framed, focusing on the idea of self-ownership. I should now like to bring these introductory remarks to a close by offering a brief summary of the argument put forward in this book.

V

Anxieties about arbitrary forms of taxation had a long history in England, becoming particularly acute from the early seventeenth century in response to a range of extra-parliamentary levies. The most significant of these, and the point of departure for this book, was ship money. Chapter 1 begins by considering the arguments put forward to oppose this measure, first in the law courts and then in Parliament. These were framed to a large extent in the language of the ancient constitution: the problem with ship money, it was alleged, was that it undermined the traditional balance between the subject's liberties and the king's prerogative. Although it was accepted that in times of national crisis the king could tamper with his subjects' property rights, it was widely argued that no such danger presented itself in the 1630s and that, therefore, ship money was contrary to the principles of the ancient constitution.

This language was never entirely abandoned, but in the pamphlet literature of the early 1640s a new argument began to emerge. This was first put forward in Henry Parker's *Observations upon some of His Majesties late Answers and Expresses* (1642). Whereas in the earlier tradition Parliament had been viewed merely as supplying the people's consent to the king's subsidies, Parker sought to provide a justification for Parliament's own increasingly assertive stance. The difficulty of presenting Parliament as the custodian of individual property rights was that, as the Royalist pamphleteers delighted in pointing out, Parliament was itself guilty of the very transgressions it had been accusing the king of perpetrating. In order to defend Parliament's actions, Parker introduced a theory of popular sovereignty, using this to make the claim that the corporate body of the people owned itself and all the material goods in the land. The king was a mere trustee of the people's power and property, such that even what appeared to be his own private possessions actually belonged to the people. Through a theory of "virtual" representation, Parliament was treated as though it were a physical manifestation of the abstract entity of the people; it did not merely have the power to act on the people's behalf but was, in an almost mystical sense, taken to "re-present" them. Measures such as ship money could thus be resoundingly condemned as affronts to freedom, whereas whatever Parliament did could be justified as the actions of a sovereign, property-owning people.

It was in response to this argument – chapter 2 claims – that the Levellers introduced the individualist language of self-ownership. Like the Parliamentarian pamphleteers, they took up the neo-Roman idea that freedom consists in not being the property of another person; where they differed was in their determination to use this insight to oppose not only the king's interference with his subjects' property but also that of Parliament. It was the individual who owned himself, not the corporate body of the people, which in any case could not be equated with Parliament in the way Parker had suggested. That is not to say that the Levellers denied the existence of such a thing as "the people," nor that they denied that Parliament could play a significant role in defending their liberty. But what they wanted to resist was the subordination of the individual to the collectivity, and of the collectivity to Parliament in its current form. The authority exercised by Parliament derived from the inherent power of each self-owning individual whom it was taken to represent, and, consequently, its attempts to deprive subjects of their property were unjust. Interference with an individual's property rights by any institution, least of all one that was as unrepresentative of the population as the English Parliament as then constituted, called into question the individual's ownership of himself and hence his status as a free person.

In contrast to the staunch defence of private property that is to be found in the writings of leading Levellers such as Overton, Lilburne, and John Wildman, there were figures on the fringes of the movement who made a very different argument about the relationship between private property and freedom. Like the mainstream Levellers and Parliamentarians, these writers tended to think of freedom in neo-Roman terms and to treat the condition of non-domination as arising not merely from political relations between ruler and ruled but also from property arrangements. Whereas the authors we have so far been discussing viewed the secure possession of private property as a bulwark of one's self-ownership, for these more radical theorists the greatest threat to the independence of the people was the institution of private property itself and the gross economic inequalities that it engendered. The solution was consequently the implementation of agrarian laws to break up excessive concentrations of wealth or, in the extreme case of the Diggers, the wholesale abolition of private property and the communitarian cultivation of the earth.

Chapter 3 turns to the republican literature of the Interregnum, with a particular focus on John Milton and Marchamont Nedham. These authors, it is claimed, owed considerably more to their Parliamentarian and Leveller predecessors than is generally acknowledged. The polemical purpose for which they wrote had changed considerably, enabling a profound engagement with the classical republican tradition that had not previously been possible. But their opposition to hereditary forms of government was framed according to the familiar view that these amounted to a claim of ownership over the people and, as such, undermined their freedom. This argument was coupled with a defence of private property, based on the claim that it served to guarantee citizens' independence from their rulers. Yet alongside this position there was a contrasting preoccupation, derived principally from Sallust and Machiavelli, with the dangers attendant upon "luxury." Private property was a constituent feature of liberty, but there was the risk that, if individuals were allowed to amass excessive riches, they would be in a position to subject others to their will or even become themselves enslaved to their wealth. However, committed as they were to the idea of self-ownership, Milton and Nedham could not bring themselves to support the kinds of redistributive measures that would have been necessary to prevent property undermining liberty in this way.

In chapters 4 and 5, I argue that, in part as a result of the problems faced by these republicans, the language of self-ownership was dropped, and alternative ways were found to establish a connection between property and freedom. The key figure here was James Harrington, who argued that liberty required not that existing property holders should necessarily enjoy their property securely but that property should be in the hands of the people. This was because freedom was understood as the condition of living in a particular kind of state, the "commonwealth," which could only be established, according to the doctrine of the balance, if most of the landed wealth was in the hands of the people. Harrington believed that this requirement had been met in contemporary England and that therefore a unique opportunity presented itself for the establishment of a genuinely free state.

The authors discussed in chapter 5, writing after the Restoration, had no such illusions. Henry Neville took up the basic structure of Harrington's theory, seeking to adapt it to the altered circumstances in which he found himself. He continued to eschew the language of self-ownership, presenting

the popular ownership of property as the precondition for the kind of state
that alone could guarantee the freedom of its inhabitants. The principal
difference from Harrington lay in his willingness to identify such a state
with the ancient constitution, a calculated attempt to present Harringtonian theory in a guise more palatable to the monarchical realities of the
Restoration. The other author discussed in chapter 5 is Algernon Sidney.
His analysis had more in common with that of Milton than Harrington,
and his preoccupation was once again with defending established property
arrangements. Yet he, too, sought to avoid the language of self-ownership.
Freedom for him was not defined with reference to economic considerations but – in a more conventionally republican sense – as the condition
of living only under laws to which one had consented. Private property
was not an integral feature of this account of freedom, but the consequence
of living in this kind of state – and one of its principal advantages – was
that one could rest assured that one's property would not be taken away
on an arbitrary basis.

One of the most striking features of John Locke's *Two Treatises of Government* is that the all but forgotten language of self-ownership is not only
reinstated but placed at its very core. The role of self-ownership in Locke's
theory is in the first instance to provide an explanation for the origins of
private property, which is said to derive from the natural property right
that every individual has in his "person." Self-ownership is thus brought to
bear on questions raised by interlocutors such as Hugo Grotius, Samuel
Pufendorf, and Sir Robert Filmer that were largely absent from the works
discussed in the previous chapters. Yet Locke was also engaging with the
question of how to express the relationship between property and liberty,
and attempting to find a solution to some of the problems raised by his
predecessors. He did so by presenting private property as the pivot between
man's natural and political conditions, and hence as the means by which
he can retain something of his natural liberty in spite of having submitted
to government. As such, I claim, Locke's theory of property is best viewed
within the context of an English tradition of thought in which discussions
of property were intimately connected with republican ideas of liberty.

As this brief narrative suggests, the chapters that follow group together
a number of authors who are not generally regarded as having much in
common. Although these writers were intervening in different political
debates, and were drawing on diverse languages to do so, the role played by

property in their discussions of liberty constitutes a significant but neg-lected common thread in their thought. By foregrounding the issue of prop-erty and thus highlighting certain continuities between these authors, this book aims not only to enrich our understanding of seventeenth-century discussions of liberty but also to suggest new ways of thinking about their relevance to contemporary debates.

1

PROPERTY, SHIP MONEY, AND THE PAPER WAR

The idea that the period leading up to the outbreak of the Civil War in 1642 was characterized by ideological conflict, once taken for granted, is now widely disputed. The Whig narrative of the Civil War as an epochal struggle between the forces of progress – as later embodied in nineteenth-century parliamentary democracy – and absolutism was first supplanted by Marxist historians, who regarded the constitutional issues as at best a surface manifestation of a deeper class conflict,[1] before being dealt a near fatal blow by so-called revisionists from the 1970s.[2] Historians who went by this label constituted a broad church and emphasized a number of different, often overlapping, causes of the Civil War – Charles I's character flaws, the British dimension, religious divisions – but all shared a common rejection of the notion that long-term constitutional tensions played any significant role in bringing Englishmen to fight each other in 1642.

The revisionist orthodoxy has not gone entirely unchallenged, and some important work by historians such as Johann Sommerville and Glenn Burgess has given a renewed prominence to the constitutional debates of the first half of the seventeenth century.[3] Yet in their desire to stress the long-term roots of the ideological conflict between Parliamentarians and Royalists – in Sommerville's case a conflict between constitutionalism and absolutism, in Burgess's between rival interpretations of the ancient constitution – these historians have been insufficiently attentive to the shifts that took place, particularly in the immediate run-up to the outbreak of civil war. Focusing on the issue of property, this chapter argues that the Parliamentarians of the 1640s, while drawing extensively on the ideas of their predecessors, ultimately came to embrace a more radical stance, one that moved away from the traditional language of the ancient constitution and towards a theory of popular sovereignty.[4]

THE DEBATES ABOUT PROPERTY AND LIBERTY IN THE
EARLY STUART PARLIAMENTS

Since the start of the seventeenth century, the question of property had been a major source of tension between the Stuart kings and their Parliaments. The occasion for the debates surrounding this issue was provided by the various extra-parliamentary sources of revenue implemented by James I and Charles I. These included impositions (import duties on specific luxury items such as tobacco and currants, which James extended to most goods), tonnage and poundage (levies on imports traditionally granted to kings for life, which Charles raised without parliamentary authority), and the forced loan of 1626.[5] Measures such as these provoked widespread opposition across the country and contributed to the rambunctious nature of many early Stuart Parliaments, resulting in Charles's eleven-year period of Personal Rule.

The view, central to the Parliamentarian opposition of the 1640s, that extra-parliamentary and hence arbitrary forms of de facto taxation undermined freedom was already being voiced earlier in the century. It was widely invoked in the Parliament of 1610 over the course of the heated debates surrounding James's impositions, and nowhere more forcefully than in Sir Thomas Hedley's famous speech.[6] Hedley begins his attack on impositions by simply asserting that "the king cannot alter the property of lands or goods of any of his free subjects without their consent."[7] The reason is that, if this were permitted, the English people would be bereft of their liberty. Hedley frames his argument according to the common law ideal of balancing the king's prerogative and the subject's liberties, declaring that "to sovereignty, the law alloweth many prerogative rights of a large spread and many free exemptions, and to the subjects such ingenuity and freedom as maintains him in spirit and courage and yet contains him in all duteous subjection." These various prerogatives and liberties can, however, be reduced "to that point wherein I take them chiefly to consist. The sovereignty of the king hath his existence principally in matter of honor or government, the liberty of the subject in matter of profit or property."[8]

Freedom is defined in relation to property, a point that Hedley then elaborates through a comparison between the free-man and the villein as defined in Magna Carta:

The quality of the *liber homo* is plainly described and differenced from the *nativus*, and that only or especially in matter of profit and property, for in other things the bound and freemen are almost alike. In case of life or member, there is little or no difference; for if the king of his absolute power command his *villain* to be slain or maimed, an appeal will lie for the villein or his heir against him that doth it by the king's commandment; in case of liberty as little, for as no action lieth for the imprisonment of a villein by the king's commandment, neither doth there for a freeman for upon suggestion of matter or secret of estate he is not bailable by law neither can he have an action of false imprisonment … But now in point of profit or property of lands and goods, there is a great difference betwixt the king's free subjects and his bondmen; for the king may by commission at his pleasure seize the lands or goods of his *villain*, but so can he not of his free subjects.[9]

An interference with the subject's property such as impositions was therefore not merely an inconvenience but a fact of such profound moral significance as to be incompatible with freedom: "Take away the liberty of the subject in his profit or property and you make a promiscuous confusion of a freeman and a bound slave."[10]

Hedley concludes his speech by warning the House about the dangerous implications of permitting such a transformation to take place. His argument is the Machiavellian one that, if a people is not maintained in liberty, it will become debased and unfit for war, rendering it impossible for the state to achieve glory. In words that would be echoed in Francis Bacon's essay "Of the True Greatness of Kingdoms and Estates" (1612, enlarged 1625), Hedley argues that, if the Englishman's "lands and goods are only in the power of his lord," this will "so abase his mind, even the lack of liberty in this point, that he is neither fit to do service to his country in war nor peace." A "drooping dismayedness" will overcome the English commoners and they will become "poor and base-minded like to the peasants in other countries, which be no soldiers nor will be ever made any, whereas every Englishman is as fit for a soldier as the gentleman elsewhere."[11] By turning free-men into villeins, Hedley claims, James I is depriving himself of the material on which England's military greatness rested.

A similar set of ideas was also voiced in the 1628 Parliament, which once again focused on the Crown's extra-parliamentary charges, in this case tonnage and poundage and the forced loan. A point repeatedly made by those

MPs who spoke out against Charles's extra-parliamentary charges was that, if the Crown retained the right at any moment to deprive subjects of their property, this was as much as to say that they lacked property altogether. Sir Francis Seymour asked the House: "If his Majesty be persuaded by any to take from his subjects what he will and when it pleaseth him, I would gladly know what we have to give?"[12] Property rights were simply incompatible with the kind of arbitrary power being exercised by the king.

As in 1610, MPs were quick to draw the conclusion that to be so dispossessed and hence to lack fundamental property rights was to be deprived of one's freedom. For Sir John Elliot, the issue being debated was not "monies, or the manner how to be levied, but the propriety of goods, whether there be a power in the law to preserve our goods," something that "reflects on all that we call ours, those rights that made our fathers free men, and they render our posterity less free."[13] Sir Edward Coke, the leading common lawyer and most vociferous opponent of the forced loan in the 1628 Parliament, expressed a similar sentiment:

> Loans against the will of the subject are against reason and the franchises of the land, and they desire restitution. What a word is that "franchise." Villeins *in nativo habendo*, their lord may tax them high or low, but this is against the franchise of the land for freemen. "Franchise" is a French word, and in Latin it is liberty.[14]

Finally, we find Sir Dudley Digges, a diplomat and politician – and the father of the Royalist Dudley Digges, whom we shall meet later in this chapter – echoing the thought with which Hedley had concluded his speech of 1610. Drawing on his experience from his "employments abroad," Digges refers his audience on the question of "the propriety of goods and of liberty" to "the mischief of the contrary in other nations." In Muscovy, he claims, "one English mariner with a sword will beat five Muscovites that are likely to eat him. In the states where there are no excises, as in trades, they are most free and noble. If these be brought, the King will lose more than he gains."[15] The apparent gains made by Charles I through the forced loan are thus illusory, for the consequent loss is a free and virile people capable of bringing him glory.

The ideas put forward by MPs such as Digges were immortalized in one of the most important constitutional documents of the seventeenth century, the Petition of Right. Here it is declared that the forced loan is "against reason and the franchises of the land" and that "your subjects have inherited this freedom, and they should not be compelled to contribute any tax, tallage, or aid, or other like charge not set by common consent in parliament."[16] As we shall see, these ideas and the document in which they were enshrined would become a point of departure for a new generation of politicians and pamphleteers, who moved beyond the confines of the ancient constitution to mount a still more formidable challenge to the powers of the king.

THE CASE OF SHIP MONEY

The tensions between the Stuarts and their Parliaments were merely put on hold during the Personal Rule: when Charles was eventually forced to recall Parliament in April 1640 to raise revenues for his campaign against the Scots, the old grievances immediately resurfaced. Chief among these was ship money, a charge intended for the defence of coastal towns in times of war that Charles had effectively transformed into an extra-parliamentary tax on the whole population. As tensions in Westminster spilled out onto the streets in the early 1640s, this became a major battleground of the "paper war" that erupted between Parliamentarian and Royalist sympathizers.[17]

A further source of tension arose in early 1642, when Parliament passed the Militia Ordinance and thus declared itself capable of legislating without royal assent, bypassing the king's prerogative of the negative voice.[18] While this crisis engendered fierce constitutional debates about the proper balance between monarchical and parliamentary power, it was also in a sense a dispute about property. The context of the Militia Ordinance was Sir John Hotham's seizure of the arsenal at Hull and his refusal – following parliamentary orders – to let Royalist forces enter the city. The debates generated by this controversy dealt extensively with questions of property: Was the king or the people the true proprietor of England's towns, ports, and other assets? Did Hotham's actions amount to a defence of property or did they set a dangerous precedent for the arbitrary expropriation of subjects' goods?[19]

Even in the absence of Parliament as a focal point for opposition to Charles's policies, the issue of property continued to stir up passions, and other vehicles could be found for challenging the legality of Charles's policies.

From 1636, when ship money began to be levied on inland areas, a number of influential figures refused payment in order to trigger a test case in the law courts. The man eventually chosen was John Hampden, a Buckinghamshire landowner and future MP, whose case was heard in 1637 before all twelve judges of the Court of Exchequer Chamber.[20]

Hampden's Case was a momentous event in the run-up to the Civil War, which – as those present at the trial recognized – touched on some fundamental constitutional principles. In spite of this, the case that was initially put forward by Oliver St John, Hampden's counsel, played down the theoretical rift between the two sides.[21] St John accepted that "the Subject's goods sometimes without their consent may be taken from them" and that not only the king but "every man that hath power in his hands" may, in times of war, do anything that "conduce[s] to the safety of the kingdom, without respect to any man's property."[22] His point was simply that the situation England faced in the mid-1630s did not amount to a crisis of the kind that would warrant property to be "resolved into the common principles of nature" (col. 904). The question of the legality of ship money had to be decided on the basis of the principles that applied in ordinary circumstances, and St John's view was that the king did not have the right to alter his subjects' property without their consent.

In putting forward this argument, St John made an unexpected concession to the supporters of ship money. One of the principal sources of revenue available to the king, which made him perfectly capable of fulfilling his royal duties without having recourse to ship money, was his "Tenure of Lands" and the right to claim dues from his tenants. Appealing to a feudal understanding of landownership rarely adopted even by the most uncompromising Royalists, St John argued that "all the lands within the realm are held mediately or immediately of the crown" and that, in order for kings to be able to carry out their duty of defending the realm, the law has "trusted them with the reservation of such Tenures, as might serve for that purpose" (col. 865).[23] The corollary was that, "in transferring these lands to the several inhabitants, we see … that the care and provision of the law was, that all should by tenure of the crown be made liable to the defence of the kingdom" (col. 867). This was a surprising position for St John to adopt: if all lands were ultimately the property of the king, it would seem that in raising ship money Charles was merely acting as a landlord collecting rent from his tenant-subjects and was thus perfectly within his rights.

Yet, St John emphasizes, in ordinary circumstances the king can only place levies on his subjects' property according to the "law" and not on an arbitrary basis, meaning that all taxes are to be raised with Parliament's consent. Not only is this institution ideally placed to give an accurate assessment of the subjects' estates, but it is also "fittest for the preservation of that fundamental propriety which the subject hath in his lands and goods; because each subject's vote is included in whatsoever there is done" (col. 883). Although the king is the landlord of his realm, he cannot prime the pump of his estates even when he finds himself in financial straits but must rely on Parliament to do this on his behalf. If the king were granted the right to charge an individual twenty shillings for the defence of the realm, St John argues, there would be nothing to stop him charging twenty pounds. "And so *ad infinitum*; whereby it would come to pass, that if the subject hath any thing at all, he is not beholden to the law for it, but is left entirely in the mercy and goodness of the king" (col. 886). The consequence would be to reduce the subject to the condition of the villein, the figure characterized earlier by St John as one who had freedom neither in person nor in property, being liable to be taxed "de haut et de bas" (col. 871).

A similarly moderate and concessive line of argument was put forward by Sir Robert Holborn, Hampden's other counsel.[24] While maintaining that the English people had "an absolute property in their goods and estates" (col. 975), Holborn nevertheless accepted that, in times of necessity, not only the king but also any subject could seize another's property (cols. 1011–12). Like St John, Holborn argued that, in ordinary circumstances, kings lacked the right to charge their subjects "without parliament," for "a king intending to do nothing by his policy without parliamentary assistance, he may, if he would so declare, charge at pleasure, on no necessary occasion, or beyond all proportion" (col. 975). The opposition to ship money was framed according to the terms of the ancient constitution, which this extra-parliamentary levy was regarded as violating. The king was entitled to certain prerogative powers, including the right in times of crisis to raise levies at will; the crucial question was how to balance such prerogatives with the subjects' liberties.

Although Hampden ultimately lost the case, several judges were persuaded by his lawyers' arguments. Sir Richard Hutton, for instance, agreed that, although "in the time of war, when there is an enemy in the field, the king may take goods from the subject," the threat of piracy that England allegedly faced in the 1630s did not constitute such an emergency (col. 1198). Echoing the opposition MPs of the 1610s–20s, Hutton argued that "the subjects of England are free men not slaves, free men not villains. Here is no apparent necessity of any invasion; therefore by law, they cannot be thus compelled to part with their interest in their goods" (col. 1201). Because, the institution of villeinage having been abolished, all English subjects were legally free-men, and because free-men could not in ordinary circumstances be deprived of their property without their consent, ship money was an illegal measure.

The judge who argued most forcefully against ship money was Sir George Crooke. Declaring the levy to be "against the common law of the land, which gives a man a freedom and property in his goods and estate, that it cannot be taken from him, but by his consent in specie, as in parliament, or by his particular assent" (col. 1129), Crooke insisted that "no charge ought to be imposed, but by [the subjects'] common consent" (col. 1132). Unlike his colleagues, Crooke rejected the notion that the king retained a right over his subjects' goods, albeit one that did not justify ship money. There were simply no circumstances in which property could be taken away or altered without subjects' consent, for they were not "bondmen, whose estates are at their lords will and disposition" but, rather, "freemen, whose property none may invade, charge, or unjustly take away but by their own free consent" (col. 1147). To interfere with subjects' property on an arbitrary basis was, for Crooke, to deprive them of their liberty.

If Hampden's lawyers and the judges sympathetic to them often made an effort to reach out to the other side, so too did their opponents. To be sure, there were some absolutist pronouncements. Sir John Banks, the attorney general, who alongside Sir Edward Littleton put forward the case for the Crown, believed that the king of England is "an absolute monarch; and that by the common law of England, all those 'iura summae maiestatis,' are inherent in his person."[25] It followed that "all the land that any subject holdeth, it is derived from the crown" (col. 1964). Raising ship money was, according to Banks, simply a right that the king enjoyed by virtue of his status as an absolute prince and landlord of England. However, views such as these, originating in feudal theories of landholding, were surprisingly rare among supporters of ship money.

The dominant position was that the common good – and not any "private" claims on the part of the king – would justify overriding principles of private property. Michael Mendle has provocatively described this line of reasoning as "republican,"[26] but it may be more helpfully understood as echoing the Aristotelian idea that "property should be private, but the use of it common" or the scholastic notion that in certain circumstances principles of private property established by the *ius gentium* might give way to the natural communistic order.[27]

It was generally accepted by supporters of ship money that subjects were endowed with property rights but that these could be suspended in times of emergency. Sir Robert Berkeley insisted that the question "whether the king may at all times, and upon all occasions, impose charges upon his subjects in general, without common consent in parliament" was not relevant to the debates at hand, for it was clear that the king enjoyed no such right. This was because "the people of the kingdom are subjects, not slaves, freemen, not villains, to be taxed *de alto et basso*" (col. 1090). Like Crooke, Berkeley believed that subjects "have in their goods a property, a peculiar interest, a 'meum et tuum'" and that "no new laws can be put upon them; none of their laws can be altered or abrogated without common consent in parliament" (ibid.). He differed only in making the Aristotelian point that "the ships and arms to be provided are to continue to the subjects own in property: The king doth not assume the property of them to himself; he only commands them to be made and used for the common defence" (col. 1096). Ship money was lawful not because the king had an absolute right over his subjects' property but because principles of public interest required that, in times of necessity, private property be used for the greater good.

The main difference between the two sides was that, whereas the opponents of ship money viewed arbitrary taxation as a necessary evil that was in tension with private property, its supporters regarded it as complementary to it. Littleton, the solicitor general, believed that "the levying of a debt or duty public or private, upon any subject, is so far from destroying the property, that it doth confirm it. He hath as good property that payeth debts to the king, as he that doth not" (cols. 924–5). Even if such levies undermined "private interest," this was "very well repaired by the public utility that comes to the kingdom" (col. 927). Likewise, Sir Thomas Trevor believed that ship money "is for the general good, for the safety of the whole kingdom: the subjects are not prejudiced by it, either in their dignities, or properties in their goods: the king's prerogatives protect the people's liberties, and the subject's liberty the king's prerogative" (col. 1127). Finally, John

Finch argued that, while "the subject hath an absolute property in his goods and estate, and that the king cannot take them to his own use," there might be situations where such principles would be overridden by the public interest (col. 1231). Answering the "great objection" that "the liberty of the subject is lost, and the property is drowned which they have in their estate" if ship money is allowed, Finch maintained that "all private property must give way to the public ... and though every man hath a property in his goods, yet he must not use them to the detriment of the commonwealth" (ibid.). Under no circumstances do men have the right gratuitously to destroy their property, and if they do so they can be punished by common law, because "the public property must take place" (ibid.). Finch's argument is not merely that necessity may justify charges such as ship money but that at all times the commonwealth has a claim upon private property: while property is in the hands of individuals, they must use it in ways that advance the common good.

In the end arguments such as these prevailed and, by the narrowest of margins, the judges upheld the legality of ship money, albeit always insisting that it was a charge extracted in times of emergency and not a tax.[28] Although in the short term this judgment may have enabled Charles I to continue to raise his unpopular levy, in the end it served to galvanize and radicalize the king's opponents, providing them with an issue on which to focus their attention and a language in which to express their grievances.

THE PARLIAMENTARIANS' DEFENCE OF PRIVATE PROPERTY

If the debates in the Court of Exchequer Chamber were restrained, outside passions ran high. When Parliament was recalled in April 1640, ship money was prominent on the MPs' list of grievances, and the Court's judgment was the object of intense criticism. The chief instigator of the furore surrounding ship money was none other than St John – now sitting in the House of Commons as the Member for Totnes – who on 4 May pushed to have the judgment in Hampden's Case overturned by a vote in Parliament. Although Charles's dissolution of Parliament the following day prevented this from happening, St John was at hand to place the unresolved issue of ship money firmly on the agenda when the Long Parliament met in November.

Perhaps the most heated debate on ship money took place on 7 December, when St John's committee for ship money reported to the Commons chamber, leading the MPs to resolve unanimously that "the charge imposed upon the subjects for the providing and furnishing of ships, and the assessments for raising of money for that purpose, commonly called ship money, are against the laws of the realm, the subjects' right of property, and contrary to former resolutions in parliament and to the petition of right."[29] A number of MPs spoke out against ship money, but the most forceful attack undoubtedly came from St John himself. No longer concerned with technicalities such as whether England was then in a state of emergency, St John maintained that "it is not that Ship-money hath beene levied upon us, but its that right whereby Ship-money is claymed, which if it be true, is such, as that it makes this payment of Ship-money the gift and earnest penny of all wee have."[30] If the king were granted the right of arbitrary taxation, all property would be vulnerable to his claims, which was as much as to say that subjects would have no property rights at all.

Moreover, St John argued, "its not that our persons have bin imprisoned, for not payment of Ship-money, but that our persons, and as it is conceived, our lives too, are upon the same grounds of Law delivered up to bare will and pleasure." The upshot was that "our birth-right, our ancestrall right, our condition of continuing free subjects is lost, that of late there hath bin an endeavour to reduce us to the State of Villanage, nay to a lower." The English people were in a worse position than villeins because, although "the Lord might tax his Villaine, *de haut & de Basse*," resulting in his having "no property against his Lord," "the Villaines life was his own, and not his Lords: the Law secured him that." By contrast, St John claimed, "as the Law stands now declared, its disputable, whether it doth so much for us."[31] The dangerous consequence of the Court's judgment in Hampden's Case was that "there is a surrender made of all our legall defence of property; that which hath beene preacht, is now judged, that there is no *meum & tuum* between the King and the People; besides that which concerns our persons."[32] Without private property rights, the English people are deprived of their liberty, even if they retain their property rights in their person.

The recall of Parliament in November 1640 not only offered a platform for opponents of the king's policy to voice their opinions within the Commons chamber but also helped to generate an unprecedented wave of pamphleteering.[33] The paper war erupted in full force in the winter of 1641–42, as the prospect of armed conflict began to seem increasingly unavoidable. Of the earlier pamphlets, perhaps the most significant is *The Case of Shipmony briefly discoursed*, issued anonymously in November 1640 by Henry Parker, a member of a prominent Sussex family and a lawyer by training, who would emerge in 1642 as the most influential spokesman for the Parliamentarian cause.[34] As we shall see, Parker's later writings would bring about a shift in Parliamentarian ideology from the ancient constitutionalism that had characterized earlier debates to a theory of popular sovereignty.[35] In 1640, however, Parker was content to take up and rework the ideas of St John and others, arguing that ship money undermined principles of private property and hence deprived subjects of their liberty.

Making it clear from the outset that he is interested not so much in ship money itself as in the broader issues that lie behind it, Parker argues that this levy is simply "incompatible with popular liberty," for "if wee grant Shipmoney upon these grounds, with Ship-money wee grant all besides."[36] The point Parker emphasizes throughout is that "the Law hath setled a property of goods in the subject, and it doth not stand with that property, that the King may demand them without consent."[37] It is therefore not true, as was held in Hampden's Case, that the king may "compell aid" by virtue of a "naturall allegeance" that subjects would owe him.[38] Parker's fear is that, if the king were allowed to levy ship money, it would be left "to his sole indisputable judgement" to place further charges on his subjects "as often and as great as he pleases." The consequence would be that "he may in one yeare draine all the Kingdome of all its treasure, and leave us the most despicable slaves in the whole world."[39] For to be compelled to pay ship money is to be subject to "the utmost of Tyranny," a tyranny which "hath a controlling power over all Law, and knowes no bounds but its owne will."[40]

The question of how such unbounded power is exercised is largely irrelevant to Parker: even if one were fortunate enough to live under a benevolent monarch, the risk of his abusing his position would remain. And "if wee must presume well of our Princes, to what purpose are Lawes made? and if Lawes are frustrate and absurd, wherein doe we differ in condition from the most abject of all bondslaves?"[41] Whereas Charles I is the "uncontroleable Master of all we have," Parker looks back nostalgically to a time when kings were "so circumscribed by law, that they could not command the goods of their subjects at pleasure without common consent."[42] Unless such principles are restored, Parker warns, there will be an "overthrow [of] all liberty and propriety of goods."[43]

Another early pamphlet that echoes some of the themes raised during the ship money controversy is William Hakewill's *The Libertie of the Subject*. Based on a speech delivered in the Parliament of 1610 in the context of the debates about impositions, it was first published in July 1641 in order, as Hakewill put it, "to prove that the just Prerogative of our Kings never warranted them to raise monies at their pleasure, by laying a charge on Merchandize to bee Exported or Imported, without assent of Parliament."[44] What is crucial for Hakewill in establishing just principles of taxation is that there should be "certainty": in all interactions between the king and his subjects, it is "requisite that bounds of limitation and certainty be set," most of all "where the Common-Law giveth the King a perpetuall profit or revenue to be raised out of the interest and property of his poor Subjects estate, either in lands or goods."[45] Although one benefit of this certainty is that it ensures that the king will not have to "depend upon the good will of his Subject for his revenue," much the most important is that "the Subject may not be under the Kings absolute power to pay what the King pleaseth, which may perhaps extend to the whole value of the Merchandize."[46]

Hakewill offers little detail regarding what the principle of "certainty" involves in practice. He does not, for instance, specify whether revenues should be raised primarily through a subsidy or through import duties and other such measures, nor does he indicate what the rate should be. The single principle that he stresses is that, whether the levy consists in "Impositions, Tallages, or Taxes (for I hold them all in one degree) or any other burden whatsoever," it should not be raised "without the Subjects free and voluntary assent, and that in Parliament":

> If it were otherwise, you see how it were to the utter dissolution and destruction of that politike frame & constitution of this Commonwealth, which I have opened unto you; and of that excellent wise providence of the Common-Law, for the preserving of property, and the avoydance of oppression.[47]

For Hakewill, consent alone provides "certainty," ensuring that, even as subjects renounce a portion of their goods, their property rights remain intact.

Hakewill concludes by discussing and then refuting the opposing view that the king has the right to tax his subjects at will because of his status as the supreme landlord of the realm. Given his pamphlet's origins in the debates about impositions, Hakewill is particularly anxious to refute the notion that the king's alleged ownership of England's ports entitles him to set whatever conditions he wishes on the import and export of goods. While Hakewill concedes that there might be a sense in which not only the ports but also the towns, cities, streets, and highways belong to the king, he does not accept the conclusion that the king therefore has the right to do with them as he wishes. Even "the gates of the Kings owne house," which are "his in a farre neerer degree then any of these," cannot be shut arbitrarily by the king.[48] The reason for this is that "the King is a person publike, and his Subjects ought to have accesse to him … For the law hath given the King power over these things, for the good of the Common-wealth, and not thereby to charge and burden the Subject."[49] There are some common resources that are not allocated to subjects in the form of private property, but even these cannot be exploited by the king for his private ends since his public capacity obliges him to use them for the common good.

HENRY PARKER'S THEORY OF POPULAR SOVEREIGNTY

To a large extent the opponents of ship money found that they could recycle the arguments of the 1610s and 1620s, but as the crisis intensified in the first half of 1642 a new and more radical line of argument began to emerge.[50] Two events were of particular significance. The first was the Militia Ordinance, which the two Houses of Parliament issued in March 1642, declaring the militia to be in Parliament's hands and implicitly proclaiming for the first time the power to legislate without the king's assent. The second was the Siege of Hull of April 1642, in which Charles I attempted, unsuccessfully, to gain access to a large arsenal established in the town during the second bishops' war and seized by Parliament in January 1642. Both of these crises placed severe strains on Parliament's claims to be acting to safeguard the subject's private property as part of its wider defence of the ancient constitution.

The polemicist chiefly responsible for the shift in Parliamentarian ideology was Henry Parker. His most influential pamphlet, *Observations upon some of His Majesties late Answers and Expresses*, issued anonymously in July 1642, offered a new way of thinking about Parliament and its relationship to the king. It was written in reply to *His Majesties Answer to the nineteen Propositions*, a document penned by Lord Falkland and Sir John Culpepper in June, which took the remarkable step of proclaiming England to be a mixed constitution in which sovereignty was shared between the king and the two Houses.[51] Parker's response was to abandon the language of mixed government, whether in the more common ancient constitutionalist form or in the classical version adopted in the *Answer*, and to declare sovereignty to reside exclusively in the people as represented in Parliament.[52]

The bold statement that lies at the heart of Parker's political thought is that "Power is originally in the people, and it is nothing else but that might and vigour which such or such a societie of men containes in it selfe."[53] In earlier tracts Parker had – with some reservations[54] – followed fellow Parliamentarians in arguing from history and legal precedent. Now he invoked natural jurisprudential arguments about the underlying source of political power, which Parker probably absorbed from his reading of the French monarchomachs.[55] It was on the basis of this principle that Parker believed the strongest case could be made for Parliament's right to stand up to the king and, in the last resort, assume the powers of government wholly in its own hands. Parker viewed Parliament as the direct bearer of the people's innate power, for "the whole Kingdome is not so properly the Author as the essence it selfe of Parliaments."[56] It was not simply a representative institution that could be taken to act on the people's behalf, in the way a lawyer might be said to represent his client; it was in a far more fundamental sense taken to be an actual manifestation of the corporate body of the people. It was therefore not merely one of the three estates, as the *Answer* had claimed, but "vertually the whole kingdome it selfe."[57]

By conceptualizing the power of Parliament in these terms, Parker did away with the ancient constitutionalist notion of balancing the king's prerogative with the subject's liberties.[58] The people's freedom required nothing more than that their innate sovereignty should be allowed to express itself unchecked through Parliament. So absolute was Parliament's power that it might even be thought of as "arbitrary," though to attack it on these grounds was wholly to miss the point:

> That there is an Arbitrary power in every State somewhere tis true, tis necessary, and no inconvenience follows upon it; every man has an

absolute power over himself; but because no man can hate himself, this power is not dangerous, nor need to be restrayned: So every State has an Arbitrary power over it self, and there is no danger in it for the same reason. If the State intrusts this to one man, or few, there may be danger in it; but the Parliament is neither one nor few, it is indeed the State it self.[59]

Parker was thus able to respond to those who condemned policies such as the Militia Ordinance as an instance of arbitrary power no less deplorable than Charles's extra-parliamentary levies. By identifying Parliament entirely with the people, its apparently arbitrary measures turned out merely to be acts of self-government.

Parker does not offer a detailed discussion of the philosophical basis for his understanding of the nature of Parliament's power. He remarks, rather feebly, that "we have ever found enmity and antipathy betwixt the Court and the countrey, but never any till now betwixt the Representatives, and the Body, of the Kingdome represented."[60] Later, however, he recognizes that something more is required, and it is to Parliament's role in supplying the people's consent to government that he duly turns: "We see consent as well as counsel is requisite and due in Parliament and that being the proper foundation of all power (for *omnis Potestas fundata est in voluntate* [all power was founded in consent]) we cannot imagine that publique consent should be any where more vigorous or more orderly than it is in Parliament."[61]

Parker accepts that Parliament does not constitute a mirror image of the corporate body of the people, but he believes that it is only through this institution that the people can act within the political sphere:

The whole community in its underived Majesty shall convene to do justice, and that this convention may not be without intelligence, certaine-times and places and formes shall be appointed for its regliment, and that the vastnesse of its owne bulke may not breed confusion, by vertue of election and representation: a few shall act for many, the wise shall consent for the simple, the vertue of all shall redound to some, and the prudence of some shall redound to all.[62]

In addition to elevating Parliament to this lofty position, Parker questions conventional views about the basis of monarchical power. He does so by invoking the equitable doctrine of trust, whereby property is held by one person (the legal owner) on behalf of another (the beneficial owner). Although the king has a role to play in the constitution, his power derives entirely from the people. Moreover, it is not a "meere donation" but held by way of trust and hence "conditionate and fiduciary."[63] In order to fulfill his duties as trustee, the king must ensure that he is not "potent over his subjects" but "Potent in his subjects." In particular, as the language of trust implies, kings must promote their subjects' economic well-being: they must not "ecclipse themselves by impoverishing" their beneficiaries but, rather, "magnifie themselves by infranchising their Subjects." Otherwise all they are doing is "trampl[ing] upon the most contemptible vassells."[64]

The king's duty, as a mere trustee, to increase his subjects' prosperity might in itself have served as a powerful argument against policies such as ship money, but Parker had a still more fundamental line of attack:

> If our Kings receive all royalty from the people, and for the behoofe of the people, and that by a speciall *trust* of safety and libertie expressly by the people limited, and by their owne grants and oathes ratified, then our Kings cannot be sayd to have so unconditionate and high a proprietie in all our lives, liberties and possessions, or in any thing else to the Crowne appertayning, as we have in their dignity, or in our selves.[65]

Power is conceptualized as a form of property in persons and things, and belongs exclusively to the corporate body of the people. Everything, including the king himself, is subject to this property right; the king may enjoy some form of property, but it is strictly subordinated to that of the people. The traditional common law understanding of the English constitution as a delicately poised balance between the king's prerogative and the subject's liberties is thus rejected in favour of a theory of popular sovereignty, expressed in terms of the people's absolute ownership of itself.

The danger of presenting the case in these terms, as will become clear in the following section, is that, if popular sovereignty is conceived of as a form of property, it could be presented as alienable and thus serve to legitimate the arbitrary powers it was designed to oppose. Recognizing this, Parker insists that it is "unnaturall" for a people to "give away its owne proprietie in it selfe absolutely, and to subject it selfe to a condition of servilitie below men."[66] What this entails in practice is that Parliament should be the supreme power in the realm. Ship money was to be rejected not only because it confiscated individual subjects' possessions but also because, lacking parliamentary sanction, it undermined the people's ownership of itself.

THE ROYALIST CHALLENGE

The radicalism of Parker's argument was immediately recognized by the Parliamentarians' opponents, who put forward a range of powerful counterattacks. The most extreme of these – though not necessarily the most effective – was to reject the very foundation of the Parliamentarian case by denying the possibility that subjects could own property. There are three main ways in which this contention could be fleshed out.

The first was the feudal notion that the king is the ultimate landlord of the realm and that, since all property rights are subordinate to his, he is fully within his rights to charge his tenant-subjects at will. This line of reasoning features prominently in William Ball's *A Caveat for Subjects* (1642), where subjects' rights are presented as deriving from the benevolence of the king.[67] A landowner, Ball maintains, may wish to grant his tenants "certain Franchises" to enable them to "live in a more free state and condition then they did in the first purchasers dayes."[68] Subjects may thereby acquire certain rights against their lord, but it would be absurd to claim that the landlord would derive his own rights from his tenants. Yet, Ball claims, this is precisely the point made by the "Observator" with regard to the rights of the king of England. Parker fails to recognize that the king's power derives from his ancestor's conquest, who, coming "as a Purchaser of the Kingdome of England for himself and his heires for ever," was entitled to rule his people however he wished.[69] Although he chose to impose only minor hardships and "his successors afterwards did immune and ease the people from such grievances, so that they lived, and live at more liberty, and enjoy more securely their liberties and properties," this did not make the people sovereign: "Doe therefore such immunities granted to the people, cause the King to derive his power and right from the people? The lawes and customes of all Nations and Kingdomes that live under Monarkes, tell us no."[70]

The second line of argument was the patriarchal one, most forcefully put forward in Sir Robert Filmer's *Patriarcha*, probably written between 1629 and 1642, and published posthumously in 1680.[71] Filmer's theory involves conflating "economical" (or domestic) with "political" power, which he claims "differ

no otherwise than a little commonweal differs from a great one."[72] Absolute
power in the domestic sphere is in the hands of the father and is passed down
from Adam, the first father, to the current king of England.

If the king is styled as a manager of household affairs, the political community over which he rules is said to emerge not with the creation of Adam
but with the latter's individuation of "*property* and *community* of goods."[73]
Property rights established at the origin of society are not held absolutely
but on the condition that property holders perform certain duties. In particular, they are "bound" to use their property to allow the king "royal maintenance by providing revenues for the crown, since it is both for the honour,
profit and safety of the people to have their king glorious, powerful and
abounding in riches."[74] The king will not use his right over his subjects'
property to deprive them of everything they have for "the multitude of
people and the abundance of their riches ... are the only strength and glory
of every prince," and, therefore, "if not out of affection to his people, yet
out of natural love to himself, every tyrant desires to preserve the lives and
protect the goods of his subjects."[75]

However, Filmer is clear that it is entirely within the king's power to do
whatever he pleases with his subjects' property. Subjects contemplating the
legitimacy of a tax should not concern themselves with the question of
"what the law of the land was, or whether there was any statute against it,"
or even "whether the tribute were given by an act of parliament."[76] All property emanated from the king, and in levying taxes he was merely doing what
was required of him as the landlord of the estate of the kingdom.

The third and most radical approach was that of Thomas Hobbes, whose
Elements of Law, circulating in manuscript from May 1640, and *De cive*,
published in Paris in November 1642, may be viewed in part as interventions
into the debate over the legality of ship money and other forms of extra-
parliamentary taxation.[77] Hobbes's theory of property is founded on his
account of the state of nature as one in which "*all things belong to all men*"
and in which "*Mine* and *Yours* (whose names are *dominion* and *property*)
have no place."[78] Defining the right of nature as the right to do whatever
one deems necessary for one's preservation, Hobbes argues that "every man
by nature hath right to all things."[79] If this is so and if, as Hobbes believed,
men in the state of nature are fundamentally equal with one another, "that
right of all men to all things, is in effect no better than if no man had right
to any thing. For there is little use and benefit of the right a man hath, when

another as strong, or stronger than himself, hath right to the same."[80] As a result, the state of nature is a state of war, all violence proceeding from "controversies that arise between men concerning *meum* and *tuum*, right and wrong, good and bad, and the like, which men use every one to measure by their own judgments."[81] It is to escape this condition that men, driven by natural law to seek self-preservation, covenant each with each to transfer their natural right to an individual or assembly, in which their disparate wills are united into a single will. In doing so, men accept that the distribution of goods will be determined entirely by the sovereign.[82] Thus it was Hobbes's view that "property and commonwealths came into being together."[83]

This account of the genesis of property appears to have the purpose of vindicating any form of taxation by the sovereign, and certainly to legitimate ship money. This is undeniably Hobbes's position when he turns to discuss the "body politic by acquisition": the community of master and servants or slaves,[84] which arises when an individual, having defeated another in war, chooses to spare his life, thus acquiring "property or dominion" over his "person."[85] The master may then "say of his servant, that he is *his*" and may also dispose "of all the person could dispose of; insomuch as though there be *meum* and *tuum* amongst servants distinct from one another by the dispensation, and for the benefit of their master; yet there is no *meum* and *tuum* belonging to any of them against the master himself, whom they are not to resist, but to obey all his commands as law."[86] One might be tempted to regard the subjection of servants to their master as qualitatively different from that of subjects to the sovereign. But Hobbes is clear that "the subjection of them who institute a commonwealth amongst themselves, is no less absolute, than the subjection of servants," the only difference being that a "freeman" – the term Hobbes uses here to refer to a subject of a commonwealth by institution – "may expect employments of honour, rather than a servant."[87] Free-men who have established political society through the covenant no less than servants would therefore be the property of the sovereign, with all their goods held at his mercy.

However, when Hobbes comes to describe the principles upon which property would be organized in a commonwealth by institution, a more nuanced picture emerges. One of Hobbes's main preoccupations, as indicated by the frontispiece of *De cive*, is to emphasize the benefits of *Imperium* over *Libertas*, of civil society over the state of nature. The first advantage is, of course, security, but there are also "other benefits which pertain not to their safety and sufficiency, but to their well and delightful being, such as are superfluous riches."[88] It is a mistake to suppose that the sovereign and subject are engaged in a competition over resources, as the debates about ship money might suggest. The sovereign's riches are also his subject's and vice versa:

> For the riches and treasure of the sovereign, is the dominion he hath over the riches of his subjects. If therefore the sovereign provide not so as that particular men may have means, both to preserve themselves, and also to preserve the public; the common or sovereign treasure can be none. And on the other side, if it were not for a common and public treasure belonging to the sovereign power, men's private riches would sooner serve to put them into confusion and war, than to secure or maintain them. Insomuch, as the profit of the sovereign and subject goeth always together.[89]

Whereas Hobbes had earlier described the servant and all his goods as the property of his master, he now speaks of the sovereign as having a property in his property-owning subjects. Determining how goods should be allocated is a prerogative of the sovereign, but to reduce subjects to a condition in which they can no longer provide for themselves would be contrary to reason and hence natural law, "the Dictate of right reason about what should be done or not done for the longest possible preservation of life and limb."[90]

Moreover, even discounting the injury suffered by the sovereign, gratuitously impoverishing subjects would be contrary to natural law since "the duty of a sovereign consisteth in the good government of the people," and when the acts of the sovereign "tend to the hurt of the people in general, they be breaches of the law of nature."[91] This duty includes not just the preservation of life but also the "benefit and good" of subjects, which is defined as a thriving population, commodity of living, internal peace, and defence against foreign powers. In order to promote the second of these, it is the sovereign's duty to secure the "liberty" and the "wealth" of his subjects, which involves above all ensuring "that there be no prohibition without necessity of any thing to any man, which was lawful to him in the law of nature," that is to say, no restraint except where "necessary for the good of the commonwealth."[92] The duty to promote the subject's liberty and wealth also includes guaranteeing "that a man may have commodious passage from place to place" and "the well ordering of trade, procuring of labour, and forbidding the superfluous consuming of food and apparel."[93] Hobbes may have thought of subjects and their goods as the property of the sovereign, but the ownership of this property would appear to entail some fairly extensive obligations.

In spite of these significant caveats, Hobbes is resoundingly clear that subjects do not have the right to resist the sovereign in case of any perceived breaches of duty. Mistaken views regarding subjects' property rights are, Hobbes claims, among the most significant causes of the dissolution of commonwealths. The belief that "uncertainty of *meum* and *tuum*" constitutes an "inconvenience" of subjection is dismissed as being "in appearance only."[94] It is based on the misapprehension that there could be such a thing as property in the absence of the sovereign, whereas in fact "without such sovereign power, the right of men is not propriety to any thing, but a community."[95] Since property is "derived from the sovereign power," Hobbes insists, "those levies therefore which are made upon men's estates, by the sovereign authority, are no more but the price of that peace and defence which the sovereignty maintaineth for them."[96]

These levies ought to be raised equitably, for "there is nothing so aggravateth the grief of parting with money, to the public, as to think they are over-rated, and that their neighbours whom they envy, do thereupon insult over them; and this disposeth them to resistance, and (after that such resistance hath produced a mischief) to rebellion."[97] Yet these remarks are merely intended as prudential advice for rulers, not to inform subjects of their rights or to legitimate resistance. The failure to understand this and the belief that "subjects have their *meum, tuum,* and *suum,* in property, not only by virtue of the sovereign power over them all, distinct from one another, but also against the sovereign himself" lead subjects to "pretend to contribute nothing to the public, but what they please," with the resulting social unrest.[98] It was Hobbes's hope that, by explaining to his fellow subjects why they were under an obligation to provide whatever contributions their sovereign demanded, the dissolution of the English body politic might be averted.

In his views about property, as in much else, Hobbes was on the extreme fringes of the Royalist camp: most of the king's supporters were prepared to accept that subjects had full property rights in their lands and possessions.[99] The turn of events of 1642–43 furnished more moderate Royalists with an alternative and more appealing line of attack, one that involved not so much refuting the Parliamentarians' arguments as turning them to their own advantage.[100] By seizing the arsenal at Hull and passing the Militia Ordinance in the early months of 1642, Parliament was – or so it was argued – violating the very principles of private property that it had claimed to stand for.[101] The argument, as it was parodied in one Parliamentarian pamphlet, was: "*Why may not the Houses of Parliament that have already invaded the prerogative of the King, proceed to doe the like unto the property and liberty of the subject (i.) of themselves?*"[102] To make matters worse, Parliament had from early 1643 begun to extract levies of its own from the populations under its control in order to fund its war effort, often stoking opposition no less fierce than that which Charles had faced in 1637. These included a voluntary and then forced loan, a weekly assessment (essentially a replacement of the subsidy), and an excise tax (an additional customs levy). In their efforts to win the Civil War, Parliament's leaders were making it increasingly difficult for its propagandists to win the paper war.

Unsurprisingly, the Royalists were quick to exploit the Parliamentarians' awkward position and draw attention to their hypocrisy. As one popular satire had it, the Parliamentarians' logic was:

> To secure men their lives their liberties and estates
> by an Arbitrary power, as it pleases the fates
> to take away taxes by imposing great rates
> and to make us a plaister by breaking our pates.[103]

Henry Ferne complained in a similar vein that "right and just subverted property and liberty [are] exposed to the will and power of every one that is pleased to conceive his Neighbour a Malignant," with the result that "at this day we feel and groan under the evils brought upon us through this power of resistance, the Law silenced, the Property and Liberty of the Subject every where invaded."[104] Parodying a Parliamentarian petition, one Royalist satire suggested that the Parliamentarians would stop at nothing short of overthrowing Charles I:

Now if you will make *Hull* your owne,
There's one thing more we must set downe,
   Forgot before.

Sir *John* shall then give up the Towne,
If you will but resigne your Crown,
   We'l ask no more.[105]

However, the Royalists were also able to go beyond satire and invective. Dudley Digges's *An Answer to a Printed Book* of November 1642 draws on the events of 1642 to unpick Parker's theory of popular sovereignty. Responding to Parker's claim that "*our Kings cannot be said to have so unconditionate and high a propriety in all the subjects lives, liberties, and Possessions, or in any thing else to the crown appertaining, as subjects have in the Kings dignity*," Digges protests that "the King pretends not to have any unconditionate proprietie in the subjects lives, liberties, and possessions, he would only be allow'd it in his own."[106] The view that subjects might have a property in the king's "dignity" is scorned as something that "surpasses my understanding" and entails "this wicked doctrine, that subjects may dispose of the Soveraingnty as they please."[107] Digges does not follow Ball, Filmer, and Hobbes in claiming that no property is immune to the claims of the king; his point is simply that the king too has property rights and that these should not be violated in the way they had been at Hull.

Digges seems to take it for granted that some things are the property of the king and others of his subjects, not stopping to consider what happens when the property claims of the two parties come into conflict. A more detailed picture of the relationship between the two emerges in John Bramhall's *The Serpent Salve*, issued in May or June 1643.[108] Taking the same passage from the *Observations* as his point of departure, Bramhall – an Anglican theologian who would become an interlocutor of Hobbes – makes a distinction between "dominion" and "possession": "The propriety which His Majesty hath in our Lifes, Libertyes, and Estates, is of publicke Dominion not of private Possession: His interest in things apperteining to the Crown is both of Dominion and Possession."[109] The king does not own his subjects or their goods, but he does retain a right of dominion over them. The subjects' right in respect of their king is one not of "Dominion over him" but of "Protection from him and under him," and it is precisely

because of this right that the king is said to have dominion over his subjects.[110] Thus the subject's rights are not in tension with the king's but
complementary to them.

What Bramhall means by "things apperteining to the Crown," over which
kings have rights of both dominion and possession, is not immediately obvious. On the one hand, he may be referring to those material goods that
the king owns in his private capacity. Yet if this is so, it is unclear in what
sense the king would have dominion over, as well as possession of, these
goods. The fact that Bramhall speaks here of the "Crown," which denotes
the king in his political capacity, also raises problems for this interpretation.
It would seem, then, that Bramhall has in mind a category of goods that
both belong to the king as a private man and are subject to his dominion
as a public person.

Bramhall does not specify what kinds of goods fall into this category, but
a later discussion suggests that he is thinking of something quite specific:
the town of Hull. Bramhall agrees with Parker's view that the king's "interest" in Hull is not as extensive as in "*other moveables*" since "he hath not the
same right of property or possession to sell it, or give it." But the king retains
a "right of Dominion, and Soveraignty, & protection, which is altogether
inconsistent with his exclusion or shutting out of *Hull*."[111] The king would
thus seem to enjoy the same kind of right over his towns as he does over
his subjects, a political right of dominion but not a right of private possession. Yet the king has "another interest in *Hull* beside that of Dominion":

> Other Townes are indebted to the King for their Protection, but this
> Town for its very Foundation. The Crown purchased it when it *was*
> *capable of nothing but heards of Cattell and flocks of sheepe*, The Crown
> builded it, the Crown indowed it with Privileges & Possessions, made
> it a distinct County and able to support such a Dignity, the Crown
> fortified it and made it so strong as it is ... The proper name of it is
> not *Hull*, but *Kingston* upon *Hull*. The Observer doth well to decline
> the right name, for according to his notions, it may be called *Kingston*
> *per Antiphrasin*, because it is none of the Kings Town.[112]

It is unclear whether Hull is unique in this regard or whether there are other
apparently public entities over which the king has a private interest in parallel to a right of dominion. But by distinguishing between these two kinds
of right, Bramhall is able both to tow a more conciliatory line than Ball,

Filmer, or Hobbes and to respond to the Parliamentarians' claims that the king has no right to interfere with his subjects' property.

SOME PARLIAMENTARIAN RESPONSES

The developments of early 1642 not only supplied Royalists with ammunition to fire at their Parliamentarian enemies but also pushed the Parliamentarians in an increasingly radical direction. It is true that the traditional argument to the effect that Parliament was defending subjects' property against arbitrary interference by the king continued to be voiced. For the anonymous author of *A Briefe Discourse upon Tyrants and Tyranny* (1642), "tyranny may justly bee esteemed the greatest calamity, because it is in opposition to the chiefest felicity which lies in liberty, and the free disposition of that which God and our own industry hath made ours."[113] Likewise, in *A Discourse or Dialogue between the two now Potent Enemies* (1642), the army is said to be undermining "the liberty of the subjects" by using their "tyrannical power" to ensure that "whatsoever they possessed should be subject unto your mercy, and upon any present humour, if you send for their goods or for money, they must deliver them up, and be glad to be undone."[114] Another pamphlet proclaimed that "the roote of all these wrongs" that were leading England towards civil war consisted in "an arbitrary power pretended to be in his Majesty, of taxing the subject and charging their estates without consent of *Parliament*."[115]

However, the more radical line of argument rooted in the concept of popular sovereignty that was initially put forward by Parker soon began to gain ground. Perhaps the most significant of the many works penned in support of the "Observator" was John Goodwin's *Anti-Cavalierisme* (1642).[116] Attacking the Cavaliers as "that Legion of Devils ... who now possesse the Land, and after the mannor of Devils indeed, seek all to rent and teare it in pieces,"[117] Goodwin argued that they had begun to treat the English people as their property, who were thus reduced to the condition of slavery as defined in Roman law.[118] They were not merely used by their masters but *consumed* by them: the Cavaliers, Goodwin lamented, "eat up my people as they eat bread":

> They injure, vex, and consume them with no more remorse, regret, or touch of conscience, then they eat and drinke to preserve their

naturall lives: as if such men as these, the people of God, were made
for the same end and purpose to them that bread is, *viz.* to be eaten
up and devoured by them.[119]

Unsurprisingly, Goodwin believed that those acting in this way had "no
lawfull authority" to do so, for not even the king could entrust them with
the power to "take away the lives, or goods, of those that are innocent and
have not transgressed the Law."[120]

Another pamphleteer who took up Parker's arguments was the Independent minister William Bridge. In *The Wounded Conscience Cured* (1643)
Bridge argued, echoing Parker, that kings held their power not as a result
of a donation or sale but in the form of a trust. Whereas when we give
something away or sell it we irrevocably lose our right to it, "if a thing bee
disposed of by way of trust, then if the fiduciary or trusted shall not dis-
charge his trust, it is in the power (at least of the trusting) to look to the
matter himselfe."[121] Bridge could thus challenge Hobbes's view that subjection to political authority entailed a complete renunciation of one's right
and that therefore property titles were determined by the sovereign. For
Bridge, the king was not the proprietor of the kingdom but merely its
trustee, charged by the people with the task of managing their affairs in
their own interest; should he deviate from the terms of his trust, the people
retained the right to depose him and restore power in their own hands.

If Bridge appears to be conflating the king's political power over his subjects with his property rights in their goods, elsewhere he insists that a distinction must be drawn between them. In *The Truth of the Times Vindicated*
(1643) he seeks to resist the implications of the Hobbesian argument by distinguishing between "jurisdiction" on the one hand and "dominion" or
"propriety" on the other. Maintaining that only the latter is "*a power of disposing of any thing that is a mans owne to his own profit,*" Bridge argues that
the king's power is one of jurisdiction and not of propriety.[122] The problem,
Bridge explains, is that some have "mistaken" the one for the other, leading
them to dangerous conclusions about the power of kings. They have consequently attributed "so much power to the Prince, in regard of Townes,
Castles and Forts, as if he had therein dominion or propriety, which breeds
much confusion in mens apprehensions, and doth bias their thoughts into
state errors."[123] Bridge is thus able to rebut the radical Royalist position on
Parliamentarian terms by arguing that his opponents have misunderstood

how kings acquired their political authority and what exactly it consisted in. Kings cannot take away their subjects' property arbitrarily, in the first place because the transfer of rights in the original contract to establish government is revocable and, in the second, because the rights that kings thereby acquired are the purely political powers of jurisdiction and have nothing to do with property.

The most pressing problem for Parliament's supporters was not, however, responding to Hobbesian theories of sovereignty. As Bridge's pamphlets suggest, an effective – if not philosophically watertight – rejoinder was already present in Parker's notion that the people merely entrusted their innate power to the king and that anything more than this would be "unnatural." A greater anxiety for the Parliamentarian pamphleteers was finding a convincing justification for the increasingly radical stance adopted by Parliament from early 1642 and thus meeting Digges's and Bramhall's charge that it had contravened the very principles for which it professed to stand.

Not all pamphleteers, it should be stressed, lent their pens to this cause. For the moderate Presbyterian Philip Hunton, there could be no justification for the House of Commons' attempts arbitrarily to encroach upon individuals' property rights. This was because, "though the house of Commons is chosen by the people, and they represent the people, yet the representation doth not give them a power which was not in the people."[124] A prime example of such a power was that of "opening and shutting the Purse of the Kingdome," which if allowed would undermine the whole "coordination" between the three estates in Parliament on which Hunton's theory rested: "If it be in one or two of the Estates, without the third, then they by that power might necessitate that other to doe any act, or disable it from its owne defence."[125] Hunton therefore insisted that the Commons had no more right than the king to control the public purse but that this must be placed in the hands of all three estates according to the principles enshrined in the ancient constitution.

Most polemicists did, however, look to legitimate Parliament's unprecedented position. One approach was to invoke the idea that the king enjoyed his rights merely by way of trust to deny that Parliament's actions at Hull constituted an affront to private property. *Maximes Unfolded* (1643), sometimes attributed to William Bridge,[126] sought to discredit the "strange Logicke" of the Royalists, according to which "*what right any man hath in his land or house, that the King hath in his Towne of Hull.*" The absurdity of this view is that it "makes not *Hull* to be the Kings by trust, but by revenue," whereas in fact the whole kingdom is merely entrusted to the king, who is thereby but a "fiduciary keeper" and does not enjoy the right to "exchange, sell, and put away the thing he hath to whom he will." The claim that the Hull controversy undermined Parliament's position as a custodian of property is brushed aside with the observation that "any man may sell his armes bought with his owne money, and so may the King sell such things as his owne purse hath purchased, but not what is bought by the common purse."[127]

A similar argument was put forward in the anonymous pamphlet *A New Plea for the Parliament* (1643) to challenge the view that Parliament had wronged the king "in taking away his proper Rights his Cinque-Ports, his Navy, his Magazine, bought with his owne money, which are his owne as properly as any mans Jewells or Plate is his own." The author's riposte is that "the King had nothing of this kind, but either it was committed to his trust by the Kingdome, or purchased by his moneys." If the former, then "it was for [the kingdom's] preservation, not for its destruction," something that is best promoted "by the Votes and Apprehensions of the representative Body of the Kingdome (the best Judges herein)."[128] If the goods in question were instead "bought by the Kings proper moneys," they might be acquired with the intention of either benefiting or harming the kingdom. If the king had the latter intention, as the author implies he did in the case of Hull, then once again "the representative Kingdome, that knowes no Law, but *salutem populi*, apprehending our misery ought to prevent it."[129] Even if it could be claimed that Charles I "owned" his munitions store in the way that a freeholder owned his property, Parliament was still justified in appropriating these in the name of the common good. Although the point being made here is that, irrespective of how they had been acquired, goods such as arsenals were of public concern in a way that subjects' private property was not, there are clear echoes of the arguments put forward by the supporters of ship money in 1637.[130]

Ideas of necessity and *salus populi* also feature prominently in John Marsh's *An Argument Or, Debate In Law* (1642). According to Marsh, Parliament's alleged expropriation of the king's possessions was not only consistent with its claims to be protecting subjects' property but may even have been required by it. Marsh begins by stating his commitment to the idea laid down in Magna Carta that "no free-man shall be taken and imprisoned, or be disseised of his Free-hold or liberties, but by lawfull judgement of his Peers, or by the Law of the land."[131] He then argues that, "if the Law be such, that the King by such grants, which are against Law, and the weal publick, cannot take away my free-hold or livelihood from me," then "it will follow, that if the King, either by action, or omission, go about to endanger the weal publick, and endeavour the destruction of it … those who are intrusted with the common good, (as the Parliament at this time is) may by all meanes possible, indeavour the preservation of it."[132] Since the king's property itself posed a threat to that of his subjects, defending the latter meant taking away the former.

Turning later in the pamphlet to consider the Hull controversy, Marsh insists that Parliament's actions involved "no devesting of the pretended property of the King." If Marsh's attempt simultaneously to claim that Parliament did not "devest" the king of his property and that this property was in any case "pretended" seems tautologous, his argument becomes even more problematic when he apparently admits both that the king's property title is valid and that Parliament has expropriated him. The point he now wishes to make is that, while it is true that "this priviledge of the King is at this time taken from him," this is fully justified, for "it were better that the King should loose his priviledge, then that the kingdom should perish."[133] Whatever his line of reasoning, the gist is clear enough: Parliament's actions in Hull were justified and did not contradict the Parliamentarians' opposition to the king's arbitrary interference with property rights.

FROM POPULAR SOVEREIGNTY TO PARLIAMENTARY ABSOLUTISM

Whereas Marsh's appropriation of Royalist appeals to *salus populi* were confined to the king's property, the anonymous author of *A Just Complaint* (1643) went further still, claiming that all property rights were subordinate to the demands of public necessity. According to this pamphlet, "for our lives and fortunes to be at the publike service, when necessity and the good of the Common-wealth shall require them, its owne generall and paramount interest will justifie the divesting of any particular or private property." This is because property rights are not absolute but "were dispenced unto us upon that condition, that we should labour to maintain the whole before any part."[134] Whereas Parliament's supporters had initially based their case on the inviolability of the subject's property, they were now insisting on its contingency.

The author maintains, however, that his argument is consistent with Parliament's earlier pronouncements, and in particular the Petition of Right:

> *What is become of our Petition of Right?* Why if you understand, it is even where, and in the same plight that it was, no way lessened or abrogated by those Ordinances: 'Tis true, that doth confirme and establish the right and property of the Subject, and secure every individuals interest from any unjust and illegal usurpation, but this doth not divest the paramount property of the publique: If any one shall refuse (like this disobedient sonne to the Common-wealth) to part with his interest, when the necessity of the publique calls for it; he doth unjustly withhold and keep back the generall Paramount property of the Common-wealth.[135]

The subject's private property must always be balanced against the public property of the "commonwealth," a term that seems to denote here not merely a political structure but also a public economic sphere, a common wealth.[136] Taking their queue from Parker's *Observations*, the Parliamentarian pamphleteers moved well beyond the ancient constitutionalist arguments that had characterized the debates of the 1610s and 1620s. Private property continues to protect the subject's liberties from "unjust and illegal usurpations," but the prior property right enjoyed by the corporate body of the people forms the bedrock of its sovereignty.

A similar line of argument is put forward in *The Subject of Supremacie* (1643). The anonymous author begins by mounting a defence of subjects' property on the familiar grounds that "where there is *propriety* or *Mastership*, he that takes ought from the owner without his consent, makes him his Vassall."[137] But he then comes to consider, and ultimately concede, the charge that, when the two Houses seek to legislate without the consent of the king, as they did in the case of the Militia Ordinance, they are exercising an arbitrary power. This being so, the question Parliament's opponents would immediately ask is: "What shall become of the Subjects property, if the King may not prevent the Houses of an Ordinance to take all?" The author's answer involves accepting the premise while denying the implicit conclusion. It may well be that such a power is "arbitrary," but subjects need have "no feare of the *Parliament*," for "no man will rob himselfe, and the two Houses represent the whole Realme, which the King out of them cannot doe."[138] Parliament's representative nature is thus invoked to legitimate acts that, when carried out by the king, are condemned in the harshest of terms.

In *A Political Catechism*, published anonymously in May 1643,[139] radical arguments such as these sit alongside more traditional defences of subjects' property rights. The author continues to argue that "no Moneys may be Levyed, neither for Peace nor War, no not under Pretence of *Publick Necessity*, (as Shipmoney and Monopolies were) without the House of Commons first propound and grant it."[140] In justifying this standard common law argument, the author clearly goes beyond it, claiming that the Commons is "solely entrusted with the first Propositions concerning the Levies of moneys."[141] The Lower House is presented as a kind of executive council, entrusted with the specific task of protecting subjects' liberties and properties: "If the House of Commons be an *Excellent Conserver of Libertie*," the author insists, "it must needs have some Power in some Cases to Levie Money even without the Kings consent; or else it will be utterly unpossible to conserve Liberty at all."[142] While paying lip service to the older preoccupation with defending the subject's property, *A Political Catechism* fully embraces the more radical view that Parliament is a legitimate arbitrary power that can tax the people at will.

However, it was Parker, whose *Observations* had introduced the language of popular sovereignty into Parliamentarian thought, who made the case for parliamentary absolutism most emphatically. Defending Parliament's actions at Hull in *The Contra-Replicant* (1643), Parker initially argues in favour of the inviolability of property. He distinguishes between "matters of a private nature," in which "Princes are absolute," and "publike affaires, where the publike safety or liberty is touched":

> In their own pallaces Princes may dispose of Offices, but in the State
> if they make Patents prejudiciall to their revenues, to their preroga-
> tives, or to the peoples interest; the Judges shall pronounce them de-
> ceived in their grants, and make the deeds void and null in Law:
> Princes cannot alien any parcells of their Crownes, *Hull* may not bee
> transferred to the King of *Denmark*, nor *Portsmouth* to *France*, nor
> *Falmouth* to *Spaine*, for Kings have no sole propriety in such things,

and the same reason is in the superintending Offices of Royalty itselfe; they are not transferable at pleasure.[143]

The king's property rights in his private possessions are thus left intact, but his property in public goods is subordinated to the demands of the public. In this way Parker is able to legitimate Parliament's seizure of the arsenal at Hull, while resisting the implication that this placed all private property at risk.

Later, however, Parker does away with such distinctions altogether: "The House of Commons without the other States hath had an arbitrary power at all times, to dispose of the treasure of the Kingdome; and where they give away one subsidy, they may give 20 and where they give 50000*l* at one subsidy they may give fifty times so much, and all this whether war or peace be."[144] Parliament, Parker continues, has the power to do anything, even "subject the whole Kingdom for ever to the same arbitrary rule as *France* grones under," for "to have then an arbitrary power placed in the Peers and Comm. is naturall and expedient at all times, but the very use of this arbitrary power, according to reason of State, and warlick policy in times of generall dangers and distresse is absolutely necessary and inevitable."[145]

In making these assertions, it is clear that Parker was being deliberately provocative. Nevertheless, such claims were grounded in his view that Parliament was the physical embodiment of the fully sovereign, self-owning corporate body of the people. This was a view that, as we saw, was central to his argument in the *Observations*, and that he repeated in his most philosophically ambitious work, *Jus Populi* (1644). Not only was this idea more difficult to square with the facts in 1644 than in 1642, now that Parliament was waging a war against a significant proportion of the population, but the terms in which Parker expressed it were even more striking. Responding to the objection raised by his critics that "*if the peoples power be not totally involved* [i.e., transferred to the king in the original grant of sovereignty], *then they remain still, as well superior to the Parliament as to the King*," Parker argues that "tis not rightly supposed that the people and the Parliament are severall in this case: for the Parliament is indeed nothing else, but the very people it self artificially congregated, or reduced by an orderly election, and representation, into such a Senate, or proportionable body."[146] It may be the case, Parker admits, that "Parliament differs many wayes from the rude bulk of the universality," but "in honour, in majestie, in commission, it ought not at all to be divided, or accounted different as to any legall purpose."[147]

Having boldly reasserted the controversial claim put forward in the *Observations*, Parker then goes on to launch a virulent attack on the arbitrary measures of the king and his followers. The charge that Parliament's actions constitute a no less arbitrary interference with property rights is one that Parker conveniently ignores. He excoriates the "State-Theologues," who "instead of giving the subjects a just and compleat propriety in the King," "doe now buzze into the Kings eares" the nefarious doctrine that "the subject and all that he possesses" are at "the meer discretion of the King."[148] These are people who have learned from Machiavelli to treat subjects not "*as Gods inheritance, or as the efficient, and finall causes of Empire, but as wretches created for servility, as mutinous vassills, whose safety, liberty, and prosperity is by all meanes to be opposed, and abhorred, as that which of all things in the world is most irreconcileably adverse to Monarchy.*"[149] Sallust's critique of the Roman emperors' "luxury and covetousnesse *publice egestatem, privatim opulentiam* [public poverty, private opulence]"[150] is held up for imitation as a "rare *arcanum imperii*," and embodied in the pseudo-Machiavellian precept "*make the Court rich, and keep the countrey poor.*"[151]

Parker then expands this attack on the Royalists into a broader critique of despotic power. He does so in the context of an intriguing Aristotelian conjectural history that considers the various forms of power arising prior to the establishment of government in order to show that none of these could serve as the basis for the prerogative powers being claimed by the king. The first three kinds of power Parker discusses – marital, parental, and fraternal – are all characterized as "orders" rather than forms of "jurisdiction" and so are not the source of monarchical authority. Moreover, all of these powers involve some form of coordination, rather than domination by an individual: marital because, men and women being made of one flesh, women share in the power and are not subordinate to it; parental because "in the family the power of the Mother does participate with the power of the Father, and by its mixture and co-ordination cannot but be some qualification to its rigour"; and fraternal because, even if we accept that upon the death of the father power descends to the eldest son – and "much might be said" against this – that power itself is "conditionate" and "must in the same manner be applied to the power of the Brother."[151]

We then turn to a form of power that is characterized by the domination of a single individual: this is the power "of Masters or Lords, which from the Greek we terme *Despoticall*, from the Latine, *Herile*."[153] However, like its predecessors, this power does not constitute a form of "Jurisidiction" since it "proposeth no ends of Justice in it selfe."[154] This non-political, arbitrary power is, Parker implies, what Charles's prerogative amounts to, the upshot being that, if the Royalists were to have their way, the English people would be reduced to slavery.

Parker then describes slavery at great length, in terms familiar from the ship money controversy:

> A *slave* (according to *Aristotle*) *is he, who is so wholly his Lords, as that he hath no propertie remaining in himselfe: he only lives, or hath a being to his Lord; but is as dead, nay nothing to himself. Whatsoever may be acquired by him, whatsoever may accrue any other way to him, it rests immediately in his Lord: and his person, his life, all that Nature hath endowed him withall, is so his Lords, that at discretion he may be beaten, tortured, killed, or libidinously used, &c.* His very Lord is not called his, as he is called his Lords: for he is his Lords absolute possession, as a horse, or any reall or personall chattell is.[155]

Although Parker is willing to accept that Aristotle may be right to believe "some men so servile by nature, and so nearly approaching to bruit beasts, that they cannot governe themselves, nor live but by the soules of other men," he insists that we may "yet wholly reject Dominicall power notwithstanding."[156] This is because such a power "has no eye at all upon the good or conservation of the slave, or at least, none but secundary; the very definition of it leaves the slave utterly disinherited of himself, and subject to his masters sole ends."[157] However unfit certain individuals might be for self-government, this could not legitimate an institution designed merely to exploit them, turning them into a form of property to be used for the convenience of another.

The harmful consequences of despotic power, Parker claims, are felt not only by the individual enslaved by it but more broadly throughout society:

> Servile Government does not onely shew it self injurious and violent in devesting the propriety of those which are subjected to it, but also the more publike and sublime propriety; which the Common-wealth,

the Society of Mankinde, nay God himself has in the parties enslaved.
If the lord may destroy his slave at pleasure, then he may destroy that,
which in part is belonging to another: then the condition of a slave is
worse than of a beast, or any inanimate Cattels; and this is most unnaturall, and publikely detrimentall.[158]

The reason for this is that despotic power undermines not only the freedom
of the individual subject to it but the sovereignty of the people as a whole.
Arbitrary government, in other words, "rob[s] slaves of that naturall interest
which they have in themselves, and States of their publike Interests which
they have both above lords and slaves."[159] It is against this expropriation of
both individuals and the state, Parker implies, that Parliament has taken up
arms against the king.

In spite of the rhetorical and philosophical heights which the Parliamentarians' leading pamphleteer reached, the shift in Parliamentarian thought
over the course of 1642–44 reveals the conceptual challenges posed by
Parliament's transition from being a representative body entrusted with
supplying the people's consent to being an executive council laying a claim
to the power to dispose at will of all the material goods of the kingdom.
Parker's theory of popular sovereignty was put forward at a time when most
pamphleteers were content to excoriate Charles I for undermining the
ancient constitution and skirt around the question of the legitimacy of
Parliament. It appeared to provide a theoretical framework for attacking
the king's violation of private property, while defending Parliament's apparently no less arbitrary courses of action. Yet it relied on an account of
Parliament as "vertually the whole kingdome it selfe" that seemed increasingly difficult to square with the facts, as opposition to its policies mounted.

One group in particular, which emerged from the radical congregations
in London and became an influential force within the rank and file of the
New Model Army from 1647, began to voice its hostility towards the Parliamentarians' conflation of Parliament with the people. This group was
the Levellers, who fully embraced the Parliamentarians' opposition to
Charles I's arbitrary power – in spite of briefly flirting with the possibility
of forming an alliance with him – but eventually turned its arguments
against Parliament.

In *Innocency and Truth Justified* (1646) the leading Leveller, John Lilburne, noted approvingly the "principle ... notably discussed by the Author
of the printed observations upon some of his Majesties late answers and

expresses" that "power is but secondary and derivitive in Princes," but added sardonically: "And say I in counsells likewise."[160] In the following chapter we shall see how the Levellers took over the Parliamentarians' ideas of popular sovereignty but did so in a way that denied Parliament the privileged role granted to it by its supporters.

2

"Selfe Propriety" in Leveller Political Thought

It is often claimed that the Levellers were little more than a motley group of disaffected individuals who briefly entered into a loose alliance to pursue certain shared interests.[1] They were certainly driven by a number of different preoccupations and ideals – freedom of conscience for the Protestant sectaries, reform of the legal system, abolition of monopolies – that do not easily fit together into a single theoretical framework. Nevertheless, it is possible to identify a political principle that features prominently in many of the Levellers' more speculative writings, which underpins their central commitment to extending the franchise and redrawing electoral boundaries. This was the view that political power originated in the people and that government could only derive its legitimacy through the express consent of those subject to it.

The main source for this way of thinking about political power was the Parliamentarian literature discussed in the previous chapter, in which the Levellers were deeply versed.[2] The figure who appears to have made the greatest impression on the Levellers was Henry Parker. In *Regall Tyranny Discovered* (1647) the Leveller leader John Lilburne quotes Parker's account of popular sovereignty almost verbatim:

> Power is originally inherent in the People, and it is nothing else but that might and vigour, which such and such a Society of men contains in it self, and when by such and such a Law of common consent and agreement, it is derived into such and such hands, God confirms the Law: And so man is the free and voluntary author, the Law is the instrument, and God is the establisher of both (as the observator in the first page of the first part of his most excellent observations, doth observe).[3]

As we shall see, this commitment to popular sovereignty led the Levellers to embrace some of the Parliamentarians' arguments, particularly their attack on the king's arbitrary interference with his subjects' property. But from the outset the Levellers were anxious to resist Parker's conflation of popular sovereignty with parliamentary absolutism. To claim that power originated in the people, they insisted, was not a justification for the exercise of arbitrary power by Parliament, however loudly Parliamentarians declared themselves to be the people's representatives.

There was nothing particularly original in this argument per se; indeed, much the same point had been made several years previously in one of the earliest of the Royalists' responses to Parker's *Observations*: the *Animadversions upon Those Notes Which the Late Observator hath published*, issued in July 1642. Responding to the view that "the Community … is to be lookt at in Parliament," the anonymous author asks: "Well, But good Sir, may not the people withdraw the power of representation, which they granted to the Parliament; was their grant so absolute, and so irrevocable, that they dispossest themselves wholly of taking or exercising that power, their owne proper persons?"[4] By divorcing the people from their representatives and emphasizing the contingent nature of the consent granted to Parliament, the *Animadversions* puts forward a line of attack that has much in common with that of the Levellers. Whatever power Parliament may enjoy by virtue of its representative nature, this did not entitle it to act arbitrarily, as Parker had claimed. A difference always remained between representatives and represented.

THE CONCEPT OF "SELFE PROPRIETY"

In rebutting the Parliamentarians' absolutist arguments, the Levellers were not content simply to restate the views of their enemy's enemy, but developed a novel concept that would long outlive the immediate controversies out of which it was born. This was the idea that every individual was, by nature, the true proprietor of himself and therefore that any encroachment upon his sphere, whether by a king or a supposedly representative institution, was illegitimate.

The concept of self-ownership was first put forward by Richard Overton, the most original and sophisticated of the Leveller theorists, in his pamphlet *An Arrow against All Tyrants and Tyranny* (1646):

> To every Individuall in nature, is given an individuall property by
> nature, not to be invaded or usurped by any; for every one as he is
> himselfe, so he hath a selfe propriety, else he could not be himselfe,
> and on this no second may presume to deprive any of, without man-
> ifest violation and affront to the very principles of nature, and of the
> Rules of equity and justice between man and man; mine and thine
> cannot be, except this be.[5]

In making this argument, Overton was taking up and reworking Parker's
idea that the corporate body of the people owns itself and cannot therefore
become the property of the king. As we saw in the previous chapter, Parker
had claimed that it would be "unnaturall" for a people to "give away its
owne proprietie in it selfe absolutely, and to subject it selfe to a condition
of servilitie below men."[6] The upshot of this idea was that even the Roman
people under the rule of the emperors could not be taken to have "grant[ed]
away their owne original right, and power in themselves, by granting a fiduciary use and administration of that right," for "the Emperour is not
proprietary of his subjects, or hath any interest at all in them to his own
use meerely."[7]

Parker's conclusion was that "the people could conferre no more on the
Emperour, then what it had in it selfe; and no man will say, that the people
had any power to destroy it selfe: and what end could the people have (if
that Law might bee said to bee the peoples act) in inslaving themselves, or
giving away the propriety of themselves?"[8] It is true that Parker occasionally
spoke of an *individual* as a potential owner of himself, for example in his
Aristotelian account of the slave as one who is "*so wholly his Lords, as that
he hath no propertie remaining in himselfe*."[9] But generally his idea of self-
ownership was constructed around the corporate body of the people, which
for him could be taken to be represented by Parliament, irrespective of
whether individuals had actually authorized this institution to speak in
their name.

By contrast, Overton's account of self-ownership is wholly focused on
the individual. It describes the sphere surrounding every person as something that protects him from invasion, as much by fellow subjects as by rulers. Overton establishes a link between an individual's ownership of himself
and external goods by arguing that the one is a precondition for the other.
It must be admitted that it is not entirely clear what the basis is for Overton's
view that there can be no private property without self-ownership. Indeed,

the precise nature of the connection between the two remained under-theorized until John Locke put forward his more fully fleshed out theory of self-ownership. Nevertheless, it is clear that Overton wished to use the self-ownership thesis to resist the absolutist arguments of Parker, including with respect to Parliament's right to deprive subjects of their private property. As Overton puts it in *An Arrow against All Tyrants*, "I may be but an Individuall, enjoy *my selfe* and my selfe propriety, and may write my selfe no more then my selfe, or presume any further; if I doe, I am an encroacher & an invader upon an other mans Right, to which I have no *Right*."[10]

For C.B. Macpherson, this emphasis on the individual served as incontrovertible evidence that the Levellers were not the radical egalitarians they had been previously taken to be but exponents of a theory of possessive individualism designed to legitimate the emergence of a possessive market society.[11] In particular, the claim that the individual has a property in himself is taken to mean that he has the right to alienate this property or, rather, to sell his labour in the market, including under the inevitably exploitative conditions that arise where unlimited capitalist accumulation is permitted. Yet Overton has nothing to say here about the alienability of labour or unlimited capitalist accumulation. Indeed, he expressly places limits on what individuals are entitled to do with their property in themselves. Self-ownership is described as pertaining to man's natural condition, having been – as Overton puts it – "implanted" into all men by God for the purpose of furthering the law of nature. Because no individual possesses the power to harm himself, he cannot entrust to others the power to do so: "He that gives more, sins against his owne flesh; and he that takes more, is a Theife and Robber to his kind."[12]

The individualism that characterizes Overton's theory is intended rather to respond to Parker's view that Parliament qua representative of the people has the right to interfere at will with an individual's person and property. By making the subject of self-ownership the individual rather than the corporate entity of the people, Overton is able to challenge Parker's claim that Parliament is entitled to act in the name of a self-owning body within which individuals and their property rights have become subsumed. All legitimate power, Overton claims, derives from the natural right that self-owning individuals possess over themselves. Therefore, "no more may be communicated then stands for the better being, weale, or safety thereof: and this is mans prerogative and no further, so much and no more may be given or received thereof."[13] By deriving political authority from individual self-ownership, Overton is able to argue that any power that is not exercised for the benefit of the individuals subject to it is illegitimate, whether in the hands of the king or Parliament.

Overton's approach is thus to redirect against Parliament the very arguments that the Parliamentarians had deployed to challenge the power of the king. Having atomized the people into its constituent parts, Overton argues that the power wielded by Parliament was constituted by the conditional grants made by each individual, much as Parliament had viewed the king's power as deriving from the people as a whole. We can see this in *An Arrow against All Tyrants*, where Overton argues that every man is by nature "a King, Priest and Prophet in his owne naturall circuite and compasse, whereof no second may partake, but by deputation, commission, and free consent from him, whose naturall right and freedome it is."[14] Addressing Henry Marten, the radical member of Parliament and Leveller sympathizer, Overton writes:

> The free people of this Nation, for their better being, discipline, government, propriety and safety, have each of them communicated so much unto you (their *Chosen Ones*) of their naturall rights and powers, that you might thereby become their absolute Commissioners, and lawfull Deputies, but no more; and that by contraction of those their severall Individuall Communications confer'd upon, and united in you, you alone might become their own naturall proper, soveraign power, therewith singly and only impowred for their severall weales, safeties and freedomes, and no otherwise.[15]

Overton is clear that it is individuals, not the body of the people, who have entrusted Parliament with their innate power. Although he refers here to "the free people," he is careful to specify that "each of them" has given his consent through "severall Individuall Communications" and that they have done this "for their severall weales, safeties and freedoms" rather than – as the Parliamentarians saw it – for the "common good."

Just as Parker had argued that it would have been contrary to nature for a free people to sell itself into bondage, so Overton claims that no individual would hand over to Parliament the kind of power that it had shown itself to be willing to deploy, not least in the persecution that he had himself experienced:

> For as by nature, no man may abuse, beat, torment, or afflict him-selfe; so by nature, no man may give that power to another, seeing he may not doe it himselfe, for no more can be communicated from the generall then is included in the particulars, whereof the generall is compounded.[16]

Because Parliament's power is composed of the self-owning individuals who voluntarily and conditionally submit to it, its power is limited by the inviolability of their natural property in themselves.

In *An Appeale From the degenerate Representative Body the Commons of England assembled at Westminster* (1647) Overton expands on this position, arguing that, if Parliament abuses the power granted to it by individuals, it can be reclaimed: "While the *Betrusted* are *dischargers* of their *trust*, it re-maineth in their hands, but no sooner the *Betrusted* betray and forfeit their *Trust*, but (as all things else in dissolution) it returneth from whence it came, even to the hands of the *Trusters*."[17] This, Overton continues, quoting himself, is because "all just *humaine powers* are but betrusted, conferr'd and conveyed by joint and common consent, *for to every individuall in nature, is given an individuall propriety by nature, not to be invaded or usurped by any*."[18] These "severall innate properties" constitute the source of Parlia-ment's power, being entrusted by each individual "to their *Elected Deputies* for their better Being, Discipline, Government, Property, and Safety."[19] The Parliamentarians had argued that an abuse of power on the part of the king justified anything that Parliament chose to do in response, even when this involved riding roughshod over individuals' property rights. For Overton, any attempt by Parliament to go beyond its trust and invade individuals' property in themselves would likewise be illegitimate and would entitle them to take their innate power back into their own hands.

Nowhere is Overton's strategy of turning Parker's theory against Parlia-ment clearer than in *An Appeale*. Quoting from the Book of Declarations, Overton notes that the Parliamentarians had repeatedly argued that "*the King is for the Kingdome, not the Kingdome for the King, and that the King-dome is no more his owne, then the People are his owne: If he had a propriety in this Kingdome, what would become of the Subjects propriety in their Lands throughout the Kingdome, or of their Liberties?"* In the same way, Overton continues, "the Commonality of England" may use this argument against "their Parliament-Members," who are "made for the people, not the people for them" and "no more then the people are the Kings, no more are the people the Parliaments; having no such propriety in the people, as the people have in their goods to doe with them as they list."[20] Just as in Parker's theory the king is the people's creature, lacking all property, so too, Overton claims, is Parliament.

Given this subversive appropriation of the Parliamentarian theory of popular sovereignty, it is unsurprising that Parker was deeply hostile to the Levellers, as can be seen in his *A Letter of Due Censure and Redargution* (1650). Written on behalf of the Commonwealth, the work is largely an ad hominem attack on Lilburne, designed to convict him in the court of public opinion, following his acquittal for high treason the previous year. When Parker did engage with the Levellers' ideas, he was particularly anxious to rebut their prioritizing of the individual over the collectivity: "You must give us leave to prefer the being of *England*, before the well-being of any Englishman: nay the well-being of *England*, before the being of any Englishman whatsoever."[21] Parker's hostility to Lilburne and his followers was perhaps motivated in part by his recognition that it was his own theory that provided the premise for their more radical conclusions.

It should be stressed, however, that the Levellers' radical appropriation of Parker's theory did not necessarily commit them to oppose Parliament outright. Indeed, in many cases they followed the pamphleteers discussed in the previous chapter in looking to Parliament to defend the people from the king, as can be seen, for example, in Lilburne's *Regall Tyranny Discovered*. Describing Parliament, in words that echo Overton's, as "the States representative of all the individuals of the State universall of *England*,"[22] rather than as a virtual representation of the corporate body of the people, Lilburne is nevertheless close to the Parliamentarians in his discussion of the relationship between Parliament and the king:

> Though the *King* be the Supream Officer, which is all, and the most he is; yet he is not the supream Power: for the absolute Supream Power is the People in generall, made up of every individuall, and the legall and formall supream Power is only their Commissioners, their collec-

tive or representative Body, chosen by them, and assembled in Parliament, to whom the *King* is and ought to give an account both of his Office and Actions; yea, and to receive rules, directions, and limitations from them, and by them.[23]

Lilburne follows Parker in deploying the principle of popular sovereignty to present Parliament as the supreme authority in England, the king being merely entrusted with his power by the people. It is true that a note of caution can be detected in the way he stresses that "the People in generall" is constituted by "every individuall," but broadly speaking Lilburne is willing to embrace Parker's argument.

The scepticism that can be detected in *Regall Tyranny Discovered* became more pronounced in late October 1647, when the Levellers penned the first *Agreement of the People*. This document was issued at the height of the Levellers' powers, when they harboured hopes of being able to use their influence within the victorious New Model Army to shape the post-Civil War settlement and still regarded Parliament as a viable medium for achieving their goals. Although the authors accepted that Parliament was the supreme institutional body in the kingdom,[24] they stressed that "the power of this, and all future Representatives of this Nation, is inferiour only to theirs who chuse them."[25] The reminder that behind Parliament lay the self-owning and hence "sovereign" individuals whom it represents, and that therefore Parliament could not simply be taken to be wielding this power on their behalf, immediately indicates that the *Agreement* is a Leveller and not a Parliamentarian document. This in turn yields a theory of representation different from Parker's and based on Overton's more individualist premise: not that Parliament "is" the people but that each individual appoints a deputy to represent his views.[26] Moreover, the power of Parliament extends only to "whatsoever is not expressly, or implyedly reserved by the represented to themselves."[27] As well as seeking to moderate Parker's absolutist arguments by rethinking the relationship between the people and Parliament, the *Agreement* carves out a space for sovereign individuals to carry out political activities directly, without Parliament's mediation.

FREEDOM AND PRIVATE PROPERTY

The question we must next consider is the role that self-ownership played in the Levellers' discussion of private property. Alan Cromartie has presented Overton's use of the language of self-ownership as evidence of the triumph of common law, given its tendency to regard any kind of right as a property right.[28] But it seems to me that Overton was trying to do something more specific: to ground a defence of private property in the property that individuals have in themselves. As Overton put it in his original formulation of the theory of self-ownership, "mine and thine cannot be, except this [selfe propriety] be."[29] By associating individual freedom with self-ownership, and presenting the latter as the foundation of private property, Overton offered a new way of framing the connection between property and liberty. Yet this connection remains somewhat indeterminate since it is never spelled out clearly in the Leveller writings why interference with private property necessarily undermines property in the self. The Levellers appear to regard incursions into private property as calling into question the very principle of property and, as such, also property in the self, but this idea is taken as given rather than being argued for in any great detail.

There is no doubt that the Levellers were as anxious as the Parliamentarians to condemn the king's attempt to undermine his subjects' property rights. In *Regall Tyranny Discovered* Lilburne takes up the Parliamentarian argument, first put forward in the context of the Hull controversy, that the king does not have the same title to England's towns and forts as his subjects do to their lands or goods, "the Towns being no more the Kings own, then the Kingdome is his own: And his Kingdome is no more his own, then his people are his own."[30] To allow the king to lay any claim to his subjects' material goods, Lilburne suggests, is to call into question their ownership of themselves, thus constituting "the root of all the Subjects misery, and of the invading of their just Right and Liberties."[31] Echoing the language of the Parliamentarian pamphleteers, Lilburne insists that kings are instead "only intrusted with their Kingdomes, and with their Towns, and with their People, and with the publike Treasure of the Common-wealth," and even those material goods that seem to belong to the king in a more direct sense, for instance the crown jewels, are "not the Kings proper Goods, but are only intrusted to him for the use and ornament thereof."[32] This last claim takes Lilburne's argument in a new direction since it raises the question of who owns such goods. To deny the king a property in his subjects' lands is to affirm the subjects' ownership of them; objects such as the crown jewels, however, do not appear to belong to anyone other than the king, and therefore denying the king's claim to them might imply that they are in some sense publicly owned, a property of the state, or part of "the publike Treasure of the Common-wealth."

The primary purpose of Lilburne's pamphlet is not to promote this public economic space but, rather, to create a private sphere surrounding each individual to protect him from the tyranny of the king. Defending this private space was a task that, at this stage in his career, Lilburne was willing to entrust to Parliament, whose members were "bound in duty to those that trust them, to see that the king dispose aright of his trust," or in other words to ensure that the king manages his trust "in such wayes, and by such Councels as the Law doth direct, and only for the publike good, and not to his private advantages, nor to the prejudice of any mans particular Interests, much lesse of the Publike."[33] There is thus, according to Lilburne, a reciprocal relationship between the political and economic spheres: England's existing institutions can guarantee the subject's property rights, and the subject – by virtue of his property ownership – is in turn able to exercise his will independently in the political sphere, thereby securing his freedom.

Another work that mounts a defence of subjects' property rights is *Vox Plebis*, published anonymously in 1646.[34] The concept of the "*liber Homo, or free Man*" is understood to involve, among other things, "*that no man shall be disseised, dispossessed,* (sequestered) *or put out of his Free-hold*: that is, lands or lively-hood, liberties, or free Customes; but by the Law of the Land."[35] The most striking feature of *Vox Plebis* is its extensive appropriation of Machiavelli's *Discorsi sopra la prima deca di Tito Livio*, seen for example in the idea that "all the Lawes that are made in favour of liberty, spring first from the disagreement of the people with their Governours."[36] Nevertheless, when it comes to the question of property, the author is highly critical of Machiavelli's view that rulers should "*maintain the publick, wealthy, and the particular poore,*" which he dismisses as "that common Maxime of all oppressing States."[37] This policy, the author claims, would reduce subjects to a condition of slavery, and "where a *State* holds their subjects under the condition of slaves, the conquest thereof is easie, and soon assured."[38] The author's concern is not so much with the specific act of interference by which a state would deprive subjects of their property but with the condition of dependence that would result from subjects' economic reliance on their rulers.

However, the author appears to accept that the state ought to retain some degree of power over the economic standing of individual subjects. In spite of his criticism of Machiavelli, he shares with him a concern with the threat posed by excessively wealthy individuals. In order to guard against this danger, the author suggests that the state should avoid heaping massive rewards on individuals since, "by making a few rich, you undoe multitudes, and lose the hearts of many, that by clemency may be gained."[39] Those who have been enriched at the expense of the rest "will think of nothing more then to preserve their ill-gotten treasure."[40] It may not be the state's business to keep its citizens poor, but the author was sufficiently worried about the consequences of their becoming excessively wealthy to insist that the state should not actively help them. Nevertheless, *Vox Plebis*'s resoundingly Machiavellian conclusion is that "it never turnes to a States advantage; to gaine the peoples hatred: the way to avoid it, is to lay no hands on the Subjects estates."[41] While the author's extensive appropriation of Machiavelli has no precedents in the Leveller literature, the point he wishes to make is the familiar one that the ruler, whether king or magistrate, ought not to interfere with an individual's property.

In *The Putney Projects* (1647) John Wildman considers several "enslaving principles," the chief of which, and the very *"foundation of tyranny,"* is: *"That all power and authority in this nation, is fundamentally seated in the Kings* WILL.*"*[42] This serves as the overarching principle, grouping together the others into a coherent whole. The fourth enslaving principle, and the one that concerns us here, is: *"That the estates, liberties, and lives of the whole Nation, are his* RIGHT *and* PROPERTY, *and at his absolute* WILL *and pleasure for the disposing whereof he neither* OUGHT *nor can be* REQUIRED *to render the least* ACCOUNT.*"*[43] Referring to the controversy surrounding the arsenal at Hull and echoing the Parliamentarian position, Wildman argues that the danger of the fourth enslaving principle is that, if the king "hath such a property in all the Townes of England, he hath the same property in all the people that he hath in their houses." The result would be that "he claimes the disposall of their persons by his personall commands, in the same manner, wherein a man commands the use of his money."[44] By asserting a right to his subjects' private property, the king is in effect turning his subjects into his own property, depriving them of their ownership of themselves and hence of their freedom.

Although in the *Putney Projects* Wildman focuses his attack on the king, the figure of Oliver Cromwell is never far beneath the surface. Everything that he says about the king may be taken as an implied critique of, or warning to, Cromwell. Towards the end of the work, Wildman spells out these implications, addressing Cromwell directly: "O my once much honoured *Cromwell*, can that breast of yours, which was the *quondam* royall pallace of principles of freedome, and justice can that breast, harbour such a monster of wickednesse, as this regall principle?"[45] As Cromwell was becoming increasingly powerful, the English people appeared to be losing sight of the grievances that had led them to oppose Charles I's arbitrary rule:

> Is it forgotten what a flood gate of Mischief was opened, by the Judges opinion in the case of Ship-money, which only bordered upon this position, of the Kings property in the whole nation? had not that opinion of the Judgment fear, such influence upon the Pulpit, that the peoples property was decryed, and the King fostered, in that destructive principle. THAT ALL IS HIS; and thence it was whispered in Councell, *that he is no Monarch who is bounded by any Law*.[46]

Wildman's fear is that Cromwell will prove himself no different from Charles I, trampling over individuals' property rights and thereby undermining their self-ownership.

The Levellers' concern with protecting private property manifested itself not only in their attacks on Charles I and the quasi-regal figure of Cromwell but also in their attacks on Parliament. There were numerous reasons for the Levellers' increasingly hostile attitude towards Parliament, among them issues of religious toleration, soldiers' pay, and the persecution experienced by the Leveller leaders at the hands of the parliamentary authorities. But among the most prominent complaints was that Parliament was arbitrarily interfering with individuals' property rights through levies such as the excise and was thus guilty of carrying out the very policies it had claimed to be standing against when it took up arms against the king.[47]

Initially the Levellers directed their attack specifically at the House of Lords. In part this was due to the Lords' prominent role in Lilburne's legal tribulations, and it is indeed in Lilburne's works that the most vituperative condemnation of the Lords is to be found.[48] In *Regall Tyranny Discovered* Lilburne accuses the peers of being "meer usurpers and inchroachers," who "were never intrusted by the people" but, instead, "sit by the Kings prerogative, which is meer bable, and shaddow, and in truth, in substance is nothing at all, there being no Law-making-power in himselfe, but meerly, and onely at the most, a Law-executing-power."[49] If the Lords are no more than stooges of the king, merely refracting the arbitrary power he claimed for himself, the same arguments that had been levelled at the king apply also to them. Lilburne describes "the *Lordly Prerogative* honour it self that they enjoy from the King (which was never given them by *common consent*, as all right, and just honour, and power, ought to be)" as nothing less than a "boon and gratuity, given them by the *King*, for the helping him to inslave and envassalise the People."[50] In addition to granting the title of "*Dukes, Earles,* and *Barons*" to those who helped him to enslave the people, the king "gave them by the Law of his own will, the estate of the *Inhabitants* the right owners thereof, to maintain the Grandeur of their *Tyranny, and Prerogative Peerage.*"[51] To allow the Lords this power, making "all the *Freemen* of England … answerable to their wills," would be to "make them as great slaves as the *Pesants* in *France* are (who enjoy propriety neither in life, liberty, nor estate) if they did not make us absolute vassals as the poore *Turks* are to the *Grand Seigneour*, whose lives, and estates he takes away from the greatest of them, when he pleaseth."[52] For Lilburne, it is thus clear that challenging the royal prerogative while leaving the Lords' power unchecked would do little to rescue the English people from their misery.

That the Levellers were particularly vehement in their criticisms of the House of Lords is not to say that the House of Commons was exempt, still less that it was viewed as the people's saviour, as Rachel Foxley has suggested.[53] In particular, when it came to criticizing measures such as the excise – a levy proposed by John Pym and supported by other leading figures in the House of Commons – it was Parliament as a whole that was attacked. In *Englands Birth-Right Justified* (1645) Lilburne argues that Parliament should act in accordance with written laws, for "take away the declared, unrepealed Law, and then where is *Meum & Tuum*, and Libertie, and Propertie?"[54] Noting that the supporters of Parliament "will say, the Law declared, binds the People, but is no rule for Parliament sitting, who are not to walke by a knowne Law," Lilburne replies: "*It cannot be imagined that ever the People would be so sottish, as to give such a Power to those whom they choose for their Servants*; for this were to give them a Power to provide for their woe, but not for their weal, which is contrary to their own foregoing Maxime."[55] Echoing Parker's claim that it would be "unnaturall" for a people to "subject it selfe to a condition of servilitie below men,"[56] Lilburne makes it clear that it would be no less contrary to freedom to grant arbitrary power to Parliament than to the king.

Later in *Englands Birth-Right* Lilburne expands these comments into a more general attack on Parliament. Maintaining that there was never "so desperate a wound given to the Lawes, Liberties and properties, as the predetermined judgement of Ship-mony,"[57] Lilburne highlights the injustice of the excise by drawing a contrast with traditional forms of taxation:

> When this Kingdom was in any way or possibility of subsistance, the auntient custome was, that Taxations should be raised by way of Subsidie, which is the most just, equitable, and reasonable way of all, for it sets every tub on his owne bottome, it layes the burthen upon the strong shoulders of the rich, who onely are able to beare it, but spareth and freeth the weake shoulders of the poore, because they are scarcely able to subsist, pay rent, and maintain their families.[58]

Lilburne's objection to the excise is not simply that it is levied without the consent of the people and is therefore arbitrary but that it "layes the burden heavily upon the poore, and men of middle quality or condition, without all discretion, and scarcely maketh the rich touch it with one of their fingers: yea, many of them are more and more advanced in their prosperous estate, through the great ruines, distractions, and miseries of the Kingdome."[59] It is thus condemned as a regressive measure that is unduly detrimental to the welfare of the poor and increases economic inequality.

In *The Legall Fundamentall Liberties of the People of England Revived, Asserted, and Vindicated* (1649) Lilburne, writing as an "Arbitrary and Aristocratical prisoner in the Tower of London," turns the relationship between liberty and property on its head. He recalls how Parliament had opposed the king's incursions into his subjects' property and reminds Parliamentarians of their own assertion that "it were a very great crime in us, if we had or should do any thing whereby the title and interest of all the Subjects to their lands were destroyed."[60] But, Lilburne claims, this is precisely what Parliament has achieved by incarcerating him and thereby depriving him of the liberty of his person. Parliament may claim that the measures it has adopted for raising revenues "shall not at all be imployed about any other occasion, then to the purposes aforesaid, which among others, are princi- pally for destroying Tyranny, maintaining of Liberty and Propriety."[61] How- ever, Lilburne argues:

> Propriety cannot be maintained, if Liberty be destroyed; for the Lib- erty of my Person is more neerer to me then my Propriety, or goods; and he that contrary to Law and Justice, robs or deprives me of the Liberty of my Person, the nighest to me, may much more by the some [*sic*] reason, rob and deprive me at his will and pleasure of my goods and estate, the further of from me, and so Propriety is overthrowne and destroyed.[62]

Lilburne is not using the language of self-ownership in this passage, distin- guishing between "propriety" in goods and "liberty" in the person. However, he moves seamlessly between the two, showing how the rights that one has in one's goods depend on the secure enjoyment of rights in one's person, most notably the right not to be imprisoned without cause or due process. Rather than defending rights to private property by appealing to the lan- guage of liberty, Lilburne defends the liberty of the person by invoking the language of property.

However, there is no doubt that the Levellers were anxious about Parlia- ment's increasingly cavalier attitude towards subjects' property rights in and of itself, particularly as Parliament's victory in the Civil War began to look increasingly assured. *A New Engagement* (1648) laments the fact that "the Parliament hath made no other use of those many signal opportunities put into their hands, then to continue their sitting at *Westminster,* and di- viding the publike treasure among themselves," and urges the Parliamen- tarian leadership to abolish the "Excise and all other Taxes."[63] Similarly, the authors of *A Declaration of the Wel-Affected In the County of Buckingham- shire* (1649) accuse Parliament, together with the New Model Army, of being "as Arbitrary as those that were before them, in maintaining all the foresaid oppressions upon us, with new vexations, as *Excise, Taxes, Freequarter, &c.* suffering their Committees to domineer over us."[64]

Such was the Levellers' opposition to the excise that the second and third *Agreements of the People* included a clause expressly banning Parliament from raising taxes at will. Whereas it had been central to the Parliamentarians' argument that the power of taxation resided in Parliament, the second *Agreement* stipulated:

> It shall not be in their Power, to continue Excize longer then twenty days after the beginning of the next *Representative*, nor to raise moneys by any other way, except by an equal rate, proportionally to mens real or personal Estates; wherein all persons not worth above thirty pound, shall be exempted from bearing any part of publike Charge, except to the poor, and other accustomary Charge of the place where they dwell.[65]

What was important for the Levellers was not only that taxes should be raised with the people's consent but that they should satisfy certain criteria. This was partly to prevent Parliament from exploiting its allegedly representative nature to claim for itself the right to charge the people at will, but more specifically to offer some protection to those most vulnerable in society. This concern for the poor points to a different motive for opposing Parliament's levies than merely that of defending private property – one that could, indeed, be antithetical to it. Although the Leveller writers we have thus far been concerned with generally sought to downplay the egalitarian suggestions to which passages such as these point, other more radical figures would, as we shall see, embrace them wholeheartedly.

PROPERTY AND THE PUTNEY DEBATES

If it is true that the Levellers were committed to defending private property, we must wonder why they were so widely accused of wishing to abolish it. The very name "Leveller," a term of abuse that began to be widely applied to the group from late 1647, served to associate them with egalitarian and redistributive measures. As Marchamont Nedham tells us in an editorial for the Royalist newsbook *Mercurius Pragmaticus*, it was Charles I who first branded the Agitators (the elected representatives of the New Model Army rank and file) "by the name of Levellers; in a most apt Title for such despicable and desperate Knot to be known by, that indeavor to cast downe and level the inclosures of Nobility, Gentry and Propriety, to make us all even: so that every Jack shall vie with a Gentleman and every Gentleman be made a Jack."[66] Accusations such as these featured prominently in works of anti-Leveller propaganda, such as Thomas Edwards's *Gangraena* (1646), Walter Frost's *A Declaration* (1648), and John Price's *Walwins Wiles* (1649).

We might be tempted to dismiss these charges as part of a smear campaign, but even slander must be based on an element of truth if it is to have any force. While the leading figures in the Leveller movement were anxious to rebut any accusations of economic levelling, there were those on the fringes who certainly provided ammunition to their enemies. It was during the Putney Debates, a series of discussions that took place in October and November 1647 between members of the New Model Army and the Levellers concerning the postwar settlement, that the divisions within the Levellers over the issue of property first became apparent. The debates brought together Grandees such as Cromwell and his son-in-law Henry Ireton, officers with Leveller sympathies such as Colonel Thomas Rainsborough, Agitators such as Edward Sexby, and the civilian Levellers Maximilian Petty and John Wildman.[67] The occasion for the debates was provided by the Agitators' publication in October 1647 of *The Case of the Army Truly Stated*, which put forward an alternative settlement to that of *The Heads of Proposals*, which had formed the basis of the negotiations with the king during the summer. But immediately before the debates commenced a new document was issued, the Levellers' *Agreement of the People*, and it is to this that attention soon turned.

The debate that has received most attention in the secondary literature is the one that took place on the second day of proceedings between the Grandees and the Levellers regarding the clause in the *Agreement* proposing an extended franchise. Historians have pored over this discussion in an effort to establish whether or not the Levellers were in favour of full manhood suffrage,[68] but they have been less attentive to a secondary debate, one that took place among the Levellers and their sympathizers, regarding the question of property. This arose in the Levellers' attempt to come up with an effective response to Ireton's charge that extending the franchise as the

Levellers proposed would result in the abolition of private property. Ireton had rejected the Levellers' view that all men subject to a government ought to have a say in choosing their rulers, insisting that only he who "hath an interest, hath a permanent interest there, upon which he may live, and live a freeman without dependence" ought to be given the vote.[69] To extend the vote to those without an interest in the kingdom, or in other words without landed property – a group outnumbering the currently enfranchised five to one, according to Ireton's calculations – would ensure the election of the propertyless to Parliament, who would then set about abolishing the institution of private property itself.

Moreover, since the Levellers were appealing to a natural birthright of all men to choose the government they lived under, Ireton believed that "by the same right of nature ... he hath the [same] freedom to anything that any one doth account himself to have any propriety in."[70] Property, Ireton believed, was established by convention and, as such, was threatened by the attempt to re-establish society on the basis of natural right. The only way to preserve it was to adhere to the principle, which Ireton regarded as "the most fundamental part of [the] civil constitution," that only those with landed property ought to have the franchise.[71]

J.D. Bass has suggested that Ireton's equation of manhood suffrage with the abolition of private property was nothing more than a rhetorical coup, designed to undermine the Levellers' otherwise strong case for extending the franchise.[72] Yet the response that Ireton's remarks elicited from his Leveller interlocutors suggests that Ireton was not entirely wide of the mark. They began by confidently rejecting Ireton's accusation and reaffirming their commitment to private property. This case was put forward initially by Thomas Rainsborough, who insisted that the issue of whether there was "property or no property" was crucial to the Levellers and warned that "if we do not all take care" property may soon cease to exist.[73] Maximilian Petty agreed with Rainsborough, pointing out that the reason "naturally free" men agreed to establish government was precisely because it was "the only means to preserve all property" and that it would therefore be absurd to suggest that extending the franchise would result in its abolition.[74]

However, as it became increasingly clear over the course of the debate that Ireton was not going to allow himself to be outmanoeuvred, the Levellers realized that they needed to change tack. It is at this point that a fissure began to open up between the Levellers at Putney and, in particular, between Rainsborough and Petty. It has already been observed by Christopher Thompson that a change took place in Petty's position over the course of the debates.[75] This involved giving in to Ireton's demand for a limited franchise, but to do so on the Levellers' terms: "I conceive the reason why we would exclude apprentices, or servants, or those that take alms, is because they depend upon the will of other men and should be afraid to displease [them]. For servants and apprentices, they are included in their masters, and so for those that receive alms from door to door."[76] It may be nonsense to suggest that the *Agreement*'s demands threatened private property, but Petty accepted that those who were economically dependent on others – servants, apprentices, and alms recipients – were ipso facto incapable of exercising a political will and should therefore be deprived of the vote.[77]

What has gone unnoticed is that Rainsborough's position also shifted. He remained committed throughout to the view he had put forward at the outset of the debate that "the poorest he that is in England hath a life to live, as the greatest he" and that therefore "every man that is to live under a government ought first by his own consent to put himself under that government."[78] However, faced with the repeated charge that this would result in the abolition of property, Rainsborough gradually moved to the view that this might be a price worth paying. He questioned "how this comes to be a property in some men, and not in others," condemning the positive law guaranteeing existing property rights as "the most tyrannical law under heaven."[79] Rainsborough's radical conclusion was that "it is impossible to have liberty but all property must be taken away"; if the vote is restricted to the propertied classes, "I would fain know what the soldier hath fought for all this while? He hath fought to enslave himself, to give power to men of riches, men of estates, to make him a perpetual slave."[80] While it was certainly not Rainsborough's initial intention at Putney to advocate the abolition of private property, his conclusion when confronted with the argument that those lacking property are unfit for political participation was that such a measure would certainly be preferable to denying the poor the vote.

THE LEVELLERS AND ECONOMIC LEVELLING

The Putney Debates revealed that there were figures associated with the Leveller movement who were prepared to countenance the possibility of overturning the established system of property. The idea that all individuals owned themselves and should therefore not be expected to submit to a government to which they had not given their consent, while devised by Overton to ground the individual's right to private property, could also have more radical, egalitarian implications. It is unlikely that the arguments put forward at Putney were directly taken up in subsequent Leveller thinking since William Clarke's transcriptions of the debates, uncovered in the library of Worcester College, Oxford, only in 1890, were not then in the public domain. Nevertheless, it appears to be the case that, in the months and years that followed, the two positions ossified, with the Leveller leaders becoming increasingly vocal in expressing their commitment to private property and denying the charge that they were secretly intent on abolishing it, while a number of figures on the margins of the movement echoed Rainsborough in arguing that freedom lay not in securing property but in doing away with it.

The prominence that Leveller voices had gained within the New Model Army from late 1647 transformed the Levellers from a fringe movement of the radical London congregations into a major political force that seemed poised to play a significant role in the postwar settlement.[81] The increasing conflict between Independents and Presbyterians, particularly after the outbreak of the second civil war, led the Independents to turn to the Levellers for support. In November 1648, at the Nags Head Tavern meeting, the Levellers seemed to have convinced the Independents not to put the king on trial but instead to reorganize the English polity according to a written constitution ratified by the English people, which they promptly provided in the form of the second *Agreement of the People*. In the end the Independents went back on their word and, after Pride's Purge of December 1648, the Levellers abandoned all hope of being able to frame the settlement on their terms. They sought first to gain the support of the Rump with the third *Agreement* and, when this too failed, resorted to attacking the new regime from the sidelines, before being definitively silenced by Cromwell's forces in 1650.

It was during this brief moment in the spotlight that the term "Leveller" began to be hurled at Lilburne and his associates, leading to some of the Levellers' most explicit anti-levelling pronouncements. In a *Whip for the present House of Lords* (1648) Lilburne declared, somewhat hyperbolically, that the Levellers have been "the truest and constantest asserters of liberty and propriety (*which are quite opposite to communitie and Levelling*) that have been in the whole land."[82] Whereas the first *Agreement* had remained vague on the question of property, the second and third included a clause stipulating that, in the words of the second, "no *Representative* shall in any wise render up, or give, or take away any the foundations of Common Right, liberty or safety contained in this *Agreement*, nor shall levell mens estates, destroy propriety, or make all things common."[83] The second and third *Agreements*, unlike the first, also placed restrictions on the franchise, specifying that the vote should be given only to "Natives or Denizons of *England*, such as have subscribed this Agreement; not persons receiving Alms, but such as are assessed ordinarily towards the relief of the poor; not servants to, or receiving wages from any particular person."[84]

Even after the Leveller movement had been marginalized, its leaders, writing from the Tower, continued to deny that they were in favour of "an equalling of mens estates, and taking away the proper right and Title that every man has to what is his own." This, the authors insisted, was something that they had "formerly declared against" – in the Petition of September 1648 – and they continued to maintain that "an inducing of the same is most injurious, unless there did precede an universall assent thereunto from all and every one of the People."[85] The qualifying clause here may point to a certain ambiguity in the Levellers' rejection of economic levelling: if the people's consent could be secured (for instance in the form of an *Agreement of the People*), then levelling might in theory be a good thing.[86] However, as if to dispel such doubts, the authors bring this discussion of property to a close by insisting that "we never had it in our thoughts to Level mens estates, it being the utmost of our aime that the Commonwealth be reduced to such a passe that every man may with as much security as may be enjoy his propriety."[87]

However, to claim with Macpherson that the Levellers were wholeheartedly and consistently committed to a defence of private property would be misleading. One demand frequently found in Leveller literature is for the abolition of base tenures.[88] While this is entirely consistent with the Levellers' support for independent property holding, the methods they advocate reveal a degree of flexibility. *A New Engagement* proposes overturning the system of landholding, so that "the Ancient and almost antiquated badge of slavery, *viz.* all base Tenures by Copies, Oaths of Fealty, Homage, Fines, at the will of the Lord, &c. (being the Conquerors marks upon the people) may be taken away."[89] Tenants would be encouraged to purchase their land by setting a favourable rate, but where somebody is unable or unwilling to acquire the freehold there would be a pre-established period of time after which "all Services, Fines, Customes, &c. shall be changed into, and become a certain Rent."[90] In this way "persons disaffected to the Freedom and welfare of the Nation, may not have that advantage upon the people, to draw them into a War against themselves upon any occasion, by vertue of an awe upon them in such dependent tenures."[91]

Another demand repeatedly made by mainstream Levellers was to open up the enclosures. In *An Appeale* Overton requests that "all grounds which anciently lay in Common for the poore, and are now impropriate, inclosed, and fenced in; may forthwith (in whose hands soever they are) be cast out, and laid open againe to the free and common use, and benefit of the poore."[92] Likewise, the Petition of September 1648 urges Parliament to open up "all late Inclosures of Fens, and other Commons, or have enclosed them onely or chiefly to the benefit of the poor."[93] Although this Petition includes a clause against "abolishing propriety, levelling mens Estats, or making all things common,"[94] it subscribes to the view that the government ought to intervene in order to improve the lot of the poorest in society. One clause exhorts MPs "that you would have considered the many thousands that are ruined by perpetual imprisonment for debt, and provided to their enlargement," while another goes further still, stipulating that "you would have ordered some effectual course to keep people from begging and beggery, in so fruitful a Nation as through Gods blessing this is."[95] Demands such as these may not have constituted a call for the abolition of private property, but it is easy to see how they could have been so construed in the context of Civil War polemic by those looking to tarnish the reputation of their opponents.

Perhaps the most telling sign that the Leveller leaders were not as opposed to economic levelling as they claimed is Lilburne's proposal in 1653 for an agrarian law. The purpose of this measure was:

[To] provide for all the old and lame people in *England*, that are past their work, and for all Orphans and Children that have no estate nor parents, that so in a very short time there shall not be a Beggar in *England*, nor any idle person that hath hands or eyes, by meanes of all which, the whole Nation shall really and truly in its *Militia*, be ten times stronger, formidabler and powerfuller then now it is.[96]

It is unclear whether Lilburne had changed his mind by 1653 on the question of levelling or was expressing views he had held all along but had concealed while he still harboured hopes of being able to influence the settlement. What is certain is that in this pamphlet Lilburne argued in favour of the re-distribution of wealth in order to provide for the poorest in society. He did not advocate the wholesale abolition of private property – nor can such a call be found in any of the writings of the mainstream Levellers – but he recognized the need to restrict its accumulation in a way that sits uneasily with earlier defences of property rights.

Even with these provisos in mind, there is no doubt that the leading figures in the Leveller movement were generally concerned with defending existing property rights. However, there were also more radical figures associated with the Levellers, who, as Christopher Hill puts it, "raised the property issue in ways the [mainstream Levellers] found embarrassing."[97] Many of the most radical works to emerge from the extreme wing of the Leveller movement appeared precisely when its leaders were putting forward their most moderate face in an attempt to forge an alliance with the Parliamentarian leaders, suggesting a growing rift within the movement at this crucial juncture.

Light Shining in Buckinghamshire and its sequel *More Light Shining in Buckingham-shire*, both published in March 1649, draw a connection not between property and liberty but between property and tyranny.[98] Both works begin with the premise that, as the later pamphlet puts it, "all men by Gods donation are all alike free by birth, and to have alike priviledg by vertue of his grant."[99] Therefore, as the earlier one insists, "no man was to Lord or command over his own kinde: neither to enclose the creatures to his own use, to the impoverishing of his neighbours."[100] There was nothing particularly radical in the view that man's most primitive condition was characterized by the absence of property: it was a staple of the natural law tradition and was espoused by Hobbes. Where these pamphlets differed was in their claim that man's natural condition of social and economic equality was normative also for the postlapsarian world.

Contemporary society is condemned in the harshest of terms in these tracts, which describe how "man following his own sensuality, became a devourer of the creatures, and an incloser, not content that another should enjoy the same priviledge as himself, but incloseth all from his Brother; so that all the Land, Trees, Beasts, Fish, Fowle, &c. are inclosed into a few mercinary hands; and all the rest deprived and made their slaves."[101] The institution of monarchy is inextricably linked with this process since those looking to expropriate their neighbours at first had to use "murther and cruely" and "they had alwayes a Commander in chiefe, which was the most blindest and desperatests wretch, and he was their chiefe and head, as *Nimerod*, and he became their King."[102] A reciprocal relationship is thus established between monarchy and private property. If monarchy was initially set up by those seeking to acquire property, it then becomes the chief source of private property: "Observe the rich possessors, incroachers, inclosers, see your holdings, your Pattents, and Charters, and Licence is from the King, and all tenures and holding of lands is from your King."[103]

In seeking a solution to the ills of contemporary society, these pamphlets present the abolition of monarchy as part of a wider process to rid England of social hierarchy, economic inequality, and the tyranny that these engender. *Light Shining in Buckinghamshire* refers approvingly to the Levellers' "principles to free all alike out of slavery," adding that "the removall of the Kingly power will be a main forwardnesse: and indeed the Kingly power is the being of Tyranny; for if no King, no Lord, no Patent, &c."[104] But a more pessimistic note is sounded in *More Light Shining in Buckingham-shire*, which regards the *Agreement of the People* as "too low and too shallow to free us at all: for it doth not throw down all those *Arbitrary Courts, Powers and Patents*."[105] The problem lies with the "petty Tyrants and Kings," who were given their power under the monarchy and who had willingly enslaved themselves to the king so that "the people may be slaves to them, and they to tyrannize."[106] The "Emperial King" may have been removed, but so long as there was private property the people would remain enslaved.

The Buckinghamshire pamphlets are short on detail regarding how to rid England of the vestiges of monarchy. However, in discussing the redistributive measures practised by the "Israelites Common-wealth," *Light Shining in Buckinghamshire* offers a fleeting vision of the egalitarian society that could be established in England, with distinct echoes of Sir Thomas More's *Utopia*.[107] Noting that "in Israel, if a man were poor, then a publike maintenance and stock was to be provided to raise him again," the author suggests that "so would all Bishops-lands, Forrest-lands, and Crown-lands do in our Land, which the apostate Parliament give one to another, and to maintain the needlesse thing called a King."[108] The governing principle among the ancient Israelites was that, "if all work alike," so too should all "eat alike, have alike, and enjoy alike priviledges and freedoms."[109] Those unable to work would also be provided for since "every seven years the whole Land was for the poor, the fatherless, widows and strangers, and at every crop a portion allowed them."[110] This, the author implies, is the kind of society that the Levellers are seeking to establish: he urges the "poor people" to mark "what the Levellers would do for you" and chides them for being "so mad as to cry up a King."[111] Only by abolishing the monarchy and the dysfunctional system of property associated with it, the author provocatively suggests, can a true commonwealth be established, "and he that did not like this, is not fit to live in a Common-wealth."[112]

A work that shares a great deal with the Buckinghamshire pamphlets is *Tyranipocrit, Discovered*, published anonymously in August 1649.[113] This is a longer piece that offers a sustained attack on the institution of private property and a proposal for an alternative society also inspired by More's *Utopia*. The author's starting point is that "God commanded al men to labour in tilling the earth, but now they that do till the earth, are made slaves to them that are too proud to do it."[114] This attack on the nobility is then combined with a Morean critique of a criminal justice system that punishes the poor disproportionately for crimes that the iniquities of the nobility have compelled them to commit: "If any poore artlesse theeves doe steale the goods from them, which they have stolen from the poore before … the poore theeves shall hang by their necks till they bee dead."[115] It is a society that, in short, revolves around the "hanging of poore, and maintaining of rich theeves."[116]

The cause of this problem lies in the fact that England's rulers "doe not care to cause an equallity of goods and lands, that so young, strong and able persons might labour, and old, weake, and impotent persons might rest."

Furthermore, the author continues, "they take no care to educate all mens children alike, and to give them like meanes to live on, that in so doing they might breake the gall of murmuration, that so all mankinde might live in concord, and labour for their livings one so well as another, according as God, nature, and reason would have them: they doe not labour to subject tyranny to reason, but they would subject reason to tyranny."[117] The benefits of economic equality are presented here in Platonic terms: it is necessary for bringing about social order and harmony, and hence for the triumph of reason over tyranny, both within the city and the soul. The enemies of this harmonious state – tyrants and their wealthiest subjects – are described as using "their wealth and power, not to build up, but to pull downe the Common-wealth."[118]

The task of defending the commonwealth from such enemies falls upon the "magistrates," presumably the rulers of the post-1649 regime. Addressing them in the second person, the author argues that, if they "make and main-taine an equallity of goods and lands, as God and nature would have, as justice and reason doth crave, then the gall of murmuration would bee broken, and then mankinde might live in love and concord as brethren should doe."[119] It is therefore the magistrates' duty "equally to divide and share such goods, as God hath given them a power to dispose of" by taking away "the superfluous riches from the rich, and divid[ing] them amongst the poore." This is to be achieved by placing a limit on the annual value of an individual's estate, which becomes progressively more stringent until "thou hast made them all alike rich."[120] Even once this has been accom-plished, "that is not enough," for the magistrate must make an annual as-sessment of "every mans estate, to see if they have not made their goods uneven, and if they have, then thou must make it even againe."[121]

Like More – and unlike other Christian humanist social reformers, such as Thomas Starkey and Juan Luis Vives, who sought to improve the lot of those worst off in society through poor relief – *Tyranipocrit, Discovered* looks for a solution to England's social ills in structural reforms designed to level estates. Acknowledging the difficulty of implementing his scheme, the author tells the magistrates:

> If you think it to be a hard matter, to make and maintain such a just equality, that none might exceed another in worldly wealth, as indeed

it is, yet do your best to do it, and if you cannot make all the poor rich, yet may you make the rich poorer, for your sinne is not so much in that some are too poor, as it is in that some are too rich, for if all men were rich, or all men poor, then all were wel.[122]

Unlike the mainstream Levellers, then, the author of *Tyranipocrit* fully embraces the idea of economic levelling, making this concept the lynchpin of his moral and political thought.

FREEDOM WITHOUT PROPERTY

It was out of this extreme fringe of the Leveller movement that perhaps the most radical voice of the Civil War period emerged. The group that called itself the True Levellers – and was instead labelled the "Diggers" by its detractors – never became a national force comparable to the Levellers, but the communities it established on St George's Hill, on Little Heath in Cobham, and in a number of other areas constituted a serious cause for concern for local landlords.[123] If during the Putney Debates Rainsborough had, when pressed, come to the uneasy conclusion that private property might be incompatible with the Levellers' demands for a political society based on popular consent, this idea became the centrepiece of the Diggers' political thought and practice. In a number of pamphlets written between 1648 and 1652, the Digger leader Gerrard Winstanley abandoned the Leveller conception of freedom as self-ownership and, with it, the view that this required the protection of private property.[124] Liberty was not a predicate of the individual but of the community, and it could only be achieved through the wholesale abolition of private property.[125]

Winstanley came to this conclusion only gradually. His early works treat freedom as an internal condition, something that man attains by throwing off the manacles of sin.[126] In *The Mysterie of God* (1648) the "anoynting" in the flesh of Jesus Christ is described, in Lutheran terms, as the thing that "sets us at liberty from the bondage of sin and the Serpent."[127] Winstanley urges his readers to "be filled with joy and peace through believing, wait with an humble thankfull heart still upon God ... for his freedome is a freedome indeed, to a full satisfaction."[128] Freedom was, then, not something that men should actively seek in this world but, rather, something that they should find within themselves by waiting upon God.[129]

Winstanley never abandoned the millenarianism that characterized these early writings; indeed, in his later works he repeatedly claimed that the idea of taking direct action by digging the commons was revealed to him in a trance by God.[130] But, as England veered towards the radical settlement of 1648–49, a noticeable shift began to take place in Winstanley's mind, both regarding the causes of the people's enslavement and the means of obtaining their freedom.

In *The New Law of Righteousnes*,[131] published in January 1649, Winstanley draws a link between sin and servitude by punning on the name Adam ("A-dam"), who represents the sin that every man carries within himself. Echoing his earlier argument, he describes Adam as "lying, ruling and dwelling within man-kinde. And this is he within every man and woman, which makes whole man-kinde, being a prisoner to him, to wonder after the beast, which is no other but self, or upon every thing whereupon self is stamped."[132]

However, Winstanley now describes another sense in which Adam enslaves the people:

> The first Adam is the wisdome and power of flesh broke out and sate down in the chair of rule and dominion, in one part of man-kind over another. And this is the beginner of particular interest, buying and selling the earth from one particular hand to another, saying, This is mine, upholding this particular propriety by a law of government of his own making, and thereby restraining other fellow creatures from seeking nourishment from their mother earth.[133]

The institution of property thus becomes the centre of gravity around which the other elements of Winstanley's thought revolve – original sin, lordly power, and particular interest – and the principal cause of men's enslavement. "There cannot be a universal libertie," he maintains, "til this universal communitie be established."[134]

In *A Declaration to the Powers of England* (1649) Winstanley and his co-authors, including William Everard, argue that men destroy one another "only to uphold civill propriety of Honor, Dominion and Riches one over another, which is the curse the Creation groans under, waiting for deliverance."[135] Whereas the earth was created by God as "a common Treasury for all to live comfortably upon," it has become "through mans unrighteous actions one over another, to be a place, wherein one torments another."[136]

With the institution of private property identified as the fundamental problem afflicting England, the solution Winstanley now advocates and attempts to put into practice in his Digger communities is the establishment of a communal system of economic production and distribution. The act of digging becomes the act of liberating oneself, both from the external shackles of private property and from the sinful condition that accompanies it.[137] When "the earth becomes a common treasury as it was in the beginning and the King of Rightousnesse comes to rule in every ones heart," Winstanley announces, "then he kils the first *Adam*; for covetousnesse thereby is killed."[138] Although he continues to urge his readers to "wait upon the spirit Reason," he now also implores them to take direct, political action: to "leave off dominion and Lordship one over another"[139] and, more important still, to "leave of this buying and selling of Land, or of the fruits of the earth."[140]

Digging is in part a symbolic gesture, as David Loewenstein has suggested,[141] but it is also intended to have a very practical function: "This declares likewise to all Laborers, and to such as are called poor people, that they shall not dare to work for hire, for any Landlord, or for any that is lifted up above others; for by their labours they have lifted up Tyrants and Tyranny; and by denying to labour for hire, they shall pull them down again."[142] By creating a space for the labouring classes to live a communal and self-sufficient life, landlords will be deprived of the labour required to keep their unjust system in place, and private property will become untenable.

The works written when the Digger communities were in their infancy offer a generous, optimistic vision of a society transformed into a common treasury. As the Diggers put it in *A Declaration to the Powers of England*, their hope was:

> That we may work in righteousnesse, and lay the Foundation of making the Earth a common Treasury for all both Rich and Poor, That every one that is born in the Land, may be fed by the Earth his Mother that brought him forth, according to the Reason that rules in the Creation. Not inclosing any part into any particular hand, but all as one man, working together, and feeding together as Sons of one Father, members of one Family; not one Lording over another, but all looking upon each other, as equals in the Creation.[143]

There is the sense here of a return to a pure, Edenic state, whose freedom consists not only in the ability of the poor to make a living without having to depend on their masters but also in the abolition of social hierarchy. It is as if the landlords too, whatever they might lose in material terms, will gain in freedom by living "all as one man," by being members of a single family in which all are "equals in the Creation."

In Winstanley's later writings, however, this utopianism gives way to a more pessimistic attitude. Faced with opposition and violent harassment from local landlords, and realizing that the people were not quick to heed his call, Winstanley began to conceive of a society divided into two spheres: the gentry would keep their enclosed lands, while the commoners would inhabit the commons and wastelands, according to the example set by the Diggers.[144] "Let the rich work alone by themselves, and let the poor work together by themselves," Winstanley argues in *New Law of Righteousnes*, "the rich in their inclosures, saying, *This is mine*; The poor upon their Commons, saying *This is ours*, the earth and fruits are common."[145] Winstanley may have kept at the back of his mind the view that private property was ultimately the work of the Devil,[146] but he was willing to deploy the language of mine and thine (or at least of "ours") for his own purposes. He even went so far as to claim that "the common Land is the poor Peoples Propertie."[147]

In parallel with this tension in Winstanley's thought, there is also a noticeable ambivalence towards the regime established in the wake of the regicide in 1649. In some of his more optimistic moments, Winstanley seemed to embrace the revolutionary settlement of 1649 as paving the way for a truly free, propertyless society. In early 1650 he published the pamphlet *Englands Spirit Unfoulded*, urging Englishmen to pledge their allegiance to the new regime by taking the engagement oath.[148] In this work he claims: "Those two Acts or Lawes which this present State Government hath made, since it cast out Kingly power and House of Lords; declares plainly what this State Government aimes at, and that is, that all *English* men may have their freedom in and to the Land; and be freed from the slavery of the *Norman* Conquest."[149] These two acts, ostensibly taking away "the Tirany of conquests, which is Kingly and Lordly power," have a more radical "meaning," as Winstanley puts it: "That the Land of *England*, shall be a common Treasury to all *English* men without respect of persons."[150]

Although this positive appraisal of the settlement of 1649 is not unique to this pamphlet,[151] more often we find Winstanley lambasting the new regime for having betrayed the Good Old Cause.[152] "O thou powers of *England*," he complains in *A Declaration to the Powers of England*, "though thou hast promised to make this People a Free People, yet thou hast so handled the matter, through thy self-seeking humour, That thou hast wrapped us up more in bondage, and oppression lies heavier upon us."[153] The point is made even more forcefully at the end of *A Watch-Word to the City of London* (1649), where Winstanley addresses Francis Drake, the main opponent of his Digger colony on St George's Hill and a "Parliament man":

> Was not the beginning of the quarrel between King Charles and your House this, the King pleaded to uphold Prerogative, and you were against it, and yet must a Parliament man be the first to uphold Prerogative, who are but servants to the Nation for the peace and liberty of every one, not conquering Kings to make their wil a Law? did not you promise liberty to the whole Nation, in case the Cavalier party were cast out? And why now wil you seek liberty to your self and Gentry, with the deniall of just liberty and freedome to the common people, that have born the greatest burden?[154]

Nowhere is this ambivalence regarding the Commonwealth more apparent than in *The Law of Freedom in a Platform*, issued in February 1652, long after the Digger communities had been suppressed. Here Winstanley seeks to present the achievements of the new regime as merely the prelude to a fully fledged social and economic overturning. Dedicating this work to Cromwell, he calls on the leaders of the Commonwealth to bring the republican revolution to its necessary conclusion by abolishing private property. Having defeated the Royalists, Cromwell and his associates have two options. They can either "set the Land free to the oppressed Commoners, who assisted you, and payd the Army their wages" or they can "onely remove the Conquerors Power out of the Kings hand into other mens, maintaining the old Laws still."[155] This being so, Winstanley pleads with Cromwell to be true to his promise to the common people "to have the possession given them of that Freedom in the Land," for until this is done they "lie yet under Kingly power."[156] The implication is clear: either Cromwell abolishes private property and fulfills the ambitions of those who supported him in his struggles against the Stuart monarchy or he has erected a Commonwealth in name only.

What is fascinating about *The Law of Freedom* is the way in which it en-
gages with the republican theories that had by 1652 become widely diffused
in England.[157] It does so in particular by responding to the claim made on
behalf of the Commonwealth that it alone is a "free-state." The concept of
freedom is foregrounded at the start of the work, where Winstanley argues:
"The great searching of heart in these days, is to finde out where true Freedome lies, that the Commonwealth of *England* might be established in
Peace." A variety of answers to this question are considered, from the view
that freedom "lies in the free use of Trading, and to have all Pattents, Li-
censes, and Restraints removed," to the claim that "it is true *Freedom*, that
the elder Brother shall be Landlord of the Earth, and younger Brother a
Servant." These are "Freedoms" of sorts, but "they lead to Bondage, and
are not the true *Foundation-Freedom* which settles a Commonwealth in
Peace." For Winstanley, only one kind of freedom would achieve this end:
"*The Commonwealths Freedom*," he believed, "*lies in the free Enjoyment of
the Earth.*"[158]

Winstanley's purpose was to oppose the republicans' confident celebration of the Commonwealth as a "free-state." No less than these writers did
Winstanley espouse the view that "there is a twofold Government, a Kingly
Government, and a Commonwealths Government."[159] However, the Parliamentarians had merely succeeded in removing "the person" of monarchy,
not "Kingly Law and Power" itself.[160] The choice facing England's new rulers
was clear: either they retained private property and with it the vestiges of
monarchical power, or they set up a true commonwealth, which "governs
the Earth without buying and selling."[161] There was, Winstanley believed,
"no middle path between these two; for a man must either be a free and
true Commonwealths man, or a Monarchical tyrannical Royalist."[162]

Even as late as 1652, Winstanley retained the hope – in words echoed by
James Harrington – that he would see "our Commonwealths Government
to be built upon his own Foundation."[163] That Winstanley should have been
critical of the republicans is unsurprising since, as we shall see in the next
chapter, they were heavily influenced by the more moderate Parliamentarian and Leveller writers to whom he was initially responding and, in particular, by their ideas of popular sovereignty and self-ownership.

3

The Commonwealth
and "Common Wealth"

It is frequently argued that the ideas put forward by the Parliamentarian opposition in the 1640s did not contribute to the decision to execute the king and still less informed the republican ideology to which the new regime appealed in its quest for legitimacy. Since the 1970s, revisionist historians have stressed that the regicide was carried out by a small minority of radicals who were able briefly to impose their will on a nation paralyzed by the traumas of civil war. It was certainly not the intention of those who took up arms against the king's forces in 1642 to overturn the ancient constitution, the very thing they were fighting to preserve. To understand why the English abolished the monarchy in 1649, it is argued, one need look not to the realm of ideas but instead to the various contingent factors that had left the Parliamentarians with few other options: Charles's intransigence after losing the first civil war; the divisions between the New Model Army and Parliament and, within Parliament, between Presbyterians and Independents; the lack of a viable pretender to the throne.[1] The republican ideology that emerged in the wake of the regicide can therefore be understood only as a post hoc justification of one of history's most dramatic unintended consequences, a "sudden creation," as Blair Worden has described it, without any roots in the opposition ideology of the 1640s.[2]

My aim in what follows is to challenge this view by arguing that the Interregnum republicans drew extensively on both the Parliamentarian pamphleteers and the Levellers, putting forward a defence of the regicide and of the regime established in its wake grounded in the theory of popular sovereignty. Worden is right to believe that the republicans were repudiating the ideal of the ancient constitution,[3] but in doing so they were not rejecting the whole intellectual world of the 1640s but appropriating the more radical

Parliamentarian and Leveller strands, which had themselves emerged in opposition to the prevailing language of the ancient constitution. In particular,
they adopted Parker's theory of popular sovereignty, deploying what had
been a language of opposition to legitimate – and implicitly also critique –
the new regime. Self-ownership was largely conceived of in the corporate
terms of the Parliamentarian pamphleteers, although the Levellers' individualist understanding of it may also be detected. Where the Levellers'
presence is unmistakably felt is in the republicans' commitment to the view
that a regime may only derive its legitimacy from popular sovereignty to
the extent that it obtains the people's consent on a regular basis. Although
the idea of popular sovereignty developed by the authors discussed in the
previous two chapters did not entail a commitment to republicanism in the
strict sense, it was successfully appropriated after the regicide by those who
wished to make the case for the new regime in republican terms.

This chapter focuses on two of the leading propagandists of the Interregnum: John Milton and Marchamont Nedham. It highlights their intellectual affinity to the Parliamentarians and Levellers by claiming that they
sought to present the new regime as an organic outgrowth of the political
struggles of the 1640s. The view that Charles I's extra-parliamentary taxation, by undermining the property rights of subjects, constituted an affront
to their liberty was transformed into a general attack on hereditary forms
of government: in laying claim to an inherited political office, it was
argued, kings were in effect asserting a property right over their realm and
its inhabitants.

Within this framework, the idea of self-ownership acquired particular
prominence, serving as an argument against all monarchical regimes. The
post-1649 republic was celebrated as a government founded on the principle
that the people owned themselves and that they were therefore also the true
proprietors of all the goods in the land. No longer anxious to defend individual subjects' property rights from the arbitrary power of the king, Milton
and Nedham believed that the Commonwealth should be the ultimate
bearer of property rights, a "common wealth" that could be economically
self-sufficient and that did not have to depend on any individual or group
to provide for its economic needs. This would not, however, entail an assault
on individuals' property rights; on the contrary, the English people would
prosper as a result of the unique ability of republican regimes to generate
wealth and thereby expand.

This line of argument intersected with a contrasting impulse that derived not from the debates of the 1640s but from the classical republican tradition, in which both Milton and Nedham were well versed.[4] This was the anxiety about the potentially corrupting effects of "luxury." Property may have been integral to liberty, but it did not follow that the more property a people held the freer it was. On the contrary, the possibility that property, particularly when disproportionately concentrated, could undermine freedom was one that greatly concerned both Milton and Nedham.

Steven Pincus has attempted to draw a neat division between the two writers on this issue, arguing that, whereas Milton was a "classical" republican who looked back to the agrarian world of antiquity and feared the corrupting effect of riches, Nedham regarded commerce as the best way of promoting the wealth and hence the success of the republic.[5] Pincus is right to highlight the discrepancies between these two strands of thought, but it is far from clear that Milton espoused the one and Nedham the other. Both writers found themselves torn between the two standpoints, on the one hand wishing to emphasize the capacity of a dynamic political system to generate prosperity and on the other hand worrying about the threat posed by excessive wealth. The fact that Milton may have placed greater weight on the dangers of luxury and Nedham on the benefits of prosperity is less interesting than the observation that they were both engaged with the problem of how to ensure that a republic in which freedom was defined by property ownership did not become enslaved by its own wealth.

ANTI-REPUBLICAN DEFENCES AND REPUBLICAN CRITIQUES OF THE COMMONWEALTH

The authors with whom this chapter is principally concerned were propagandists for the successive regimes that governed England after the regicide of 30 January 1649. Their purpose, ostensibly at least, was to win over a sceptical public by presenting these governments as embodying the principles that had been put forward to oppose the absolutism of the Stuart monarchy in the 1640s. However, in focusing on Milton and Nedham, I am only telling one story about the political thought of the Interregnum. In spite of the new regime's clampdown on dissenters, there were some who remained mortally opposed to republican government, calling for a return to the old

Stuart monarchy or, as in the case of Michael Hawke, urging Oliver Cromwell to make himself king.[6]

Moreover, not all of the republic's supporters were republicans. George
Lawson offered his cautious support to the new regime but only because
he saw it as the best hope for the re-establishment of the ancient constitution and the avoidance of yet another civil war.[7] There was also a group
of so-called de facto theorists, among them Anthony Ascham and Francis
Rous, who argued that the Commonwealth deserved the people's support
not because of any inherent advantages in republican forms of government
but simply because it had emerged victorious in the Civil War.[8] This line
of argument was invoked by the new regime in its quest for legitimacy,
featuring prominently, as we shall see, in Nedham's first work on behalf of
the Commonwealth.

Thomas Hobbes's *Leviathan* (1651), which maintained that the new regime was worthy of the people's obedience because of its capacity to offer
protection, may also be seen as offering a de facto theory of sorts.[9] With respect to ideas of property, Hobbes's argument in *Leviathan* remained largely
unchanged from *The Elements of Law* and *De cive*. Hobbes continued to
argue that "where there is no Common-wealth, there is no Propriety."[10] Perhaps responding to the Leveller idea of self-ownership, Hobbes stressed that
the "Right to every thing" that characterizes the state of nature stretches
"even to one anothers body."[11] It therefore remained Hobbes's conviction
that property, including one's property in oneself, is established by the sovereign, who has the right to distribute it as he pleases, retaining at all times
the power to dispossess the people and take property back into his own
hands. The upshot was that "the Propriety which a subject hath in his lands,
consisteth in a right to exclude all other subjects from the use of them; and
not to exclude their Soveraign, be it an Assembly, or a Monarch."[12] Hobbes
had warned in the early 1640s that the failure to recognize this principle
and the belief that subjects' property titles were absolute were among the
principal causes of the dissolution of commonwealths. Writing after what
he regarded as the collapse of civil society during the Civil War, he no doubt
felt vindicated, arguing that "if the Right of the Soveraign also be excluded
[from subjects' property], he cannot performe the office they [the people]
have put him into; which is, to defend them both from forraign enemies,
and from the injuries of one another; and consequently there is no longer
a Common-wealth."[13]

One of the most significant innovations in *Leviathan* is the theory of personation and representation put forward in chapter 16.[14] Hobbes begins by defining "person" as one "*whose words or actions are considered, either as his own, or as representing the words or actions of another man, or of any other thing to whom they are attributed, whether Truly or by Fiction.*"[15] Those whose words or actions are considered as their own Hobbes terms "natural persons," while those whose words or actions are considered as representing those of another are described as "artificial persons" or representatives.[16]

With this idea of representation Hobbes offers an ingenious response to the Parliamentarian claim that the people, as the bearers of sovereignty, are the proprietors of everything in the kingdom, including the king's power. Hobbes agrees that sovereigns, as artificial persons, fall into the category of those whose actions are "*Owned* by those whom they represent."[17] For the Parliamentarians, this claim served to empower the people – or Parliament – in standing up to the king: if the king was merely the trustee of the people's property, then they had every right to resist him when he acted contrary to the interest of the beneficiaries. Hobbes's tactic is not to deny the Parliamentarians' argument but to turn it to his advantage.[18] If it is true, as the Parliamentarians had claimed, that the king's actions are not his own but are to be regarded as those of another, then it would be absurd for the authors of those actions to oppose them. They would merely be opposing themselves and thus, as Hobbes puts it, fall into "contradiction." The dissolution of the English state in the 1640s, Hobbes believes, had been brought about by such a contradiction: it amounted to a breach of contract and was therefore unjust. Nevertheless, the Council of State is a legitimate power, a sovereign by acquisition whose actions are owned by the people and therefore cannot be justly resisted.

If there were theorists who supported the Commonwealth on non-republican grounds, others opposed it in specifically republican terms. For writers such as Edward Sexby, Titus Silus, and John Streater, the new regime was to be opposed not because it broke with the ancient constitution but because it did not depart from it enough. Streater is particularly interesting because of his subversive appropriation of Parliamentarian arguments.[19] The continuing relevance of the issues that had led Parliament to take up arms against the king is attested in *A Glympse of that Jewel, Judiciall, Just, Preserving Libertie* (1653), where Streater recalls how, when "the late King was at the height of his Supremacy, *Hambden* and *Chambers* brought their

Action against him at common Law, in the case of Ship-money; they knowing that the power to impose Laws and Taxes, consisted in the Consent of
the people represented in Parliament."[20] That Streater's purpose in drawing
attention to these earlier struggles is admonitory and not self-congratu-
latory is suggested by his claim in *A further Continuance of the Grand Politick Informer* (1653) that Cromwell and his men "have devoured all our
wealth and liberties."[21] Their plan, Streater alleges, is to burn all records so
as to abolish existing property titles, the effect of which will be that "all that
hold any Houses or Land by what little soever, when the Records of the Nation are burned, it shall be much at the descretion of the Judge to award
judgment either to the Plaintiffe or Defendant which so ever of them is
most a Saint *alies* [*sic*] an Hypocrite." The result of this and other policies
pursued by the Nominated Assembly, in power from July 1653, was that "he
that doth hold any thing must hold and enjoy it upon their terms, that he
must live and take the present Tyrants orders for better for worse."[22] The
struggles of the 1640s appear to have succeeded merely in replacing one arbitrary power with another.

After the establishment of the Protectorate in December 1653, arguments
such as these carried still greater force. In the editorials to *Observations Historical, Political, and Philosophical, upon Aristotle's first Book of Political Government*, a newsbook published between April and July 1654, Streater voiced
his concerns about England's apparent descent towards monarchy. Although the Instrument of Government stopped short of making the office
of Protector a hereditary one, the danger that this would ensue – as indeed
it did with the Humble Petition and Advice of 1657 – is one of Streater's
principal concerns. He argues that "the *Prince Hereditary* ruleth by a kind
of a Right; and being often mistaken reckoneth and accounteth a people
his vassals and slaves, sooner then he that is *elected*, which ruleth but by
consent, and standeth upon his good behaviour."[23] Having been imprisoned
at the hands of the Commonwealth for his previous newsbook, Streater was
reluctant to denounce Cromwell openly, but the implication of his comments is clear: irrespective of the actual policies carried out, a hereditary
ruler, simply by virtue of having inherited his office, takes away freedom.

No such caution was deployed by the anonymous authors of *Killing Noe
Murder* (1657), almost certainly Edward Sexby and Silus Titus, who explicitly
advocated tyrannicide to free England from Cromwell's despotism. Like

Streater, Sexby and Titus deployed the arguments first used against Charles I to attack Cromwell:

> If to decimate mens estates, and by his owne power to impose upon the people what Taxes he pleases: And to maintaine all this by force of Armes: If I say all this does make a Tyrant, his owne impudence cannot denie but he is as compleate a one as ever hath been since there have been Societies of Men.[24]

The English people, having fought for the principle that their property could not be arbitrarily taken away, were now being forced to submit to a new tyrant. But, the authors insist, "no English man can be ignorant, that it is his Birth-right to be master of his own Estate; and that none can command any part of it but by his own grant and consent, either made expressly by himself, or Virtually by a Parliament."[25] Believing that the main threat to Englishmen's liberty came not from a Parliament with absolutist pretensions – as the Levellers had done – but from a new quasi-monarch, Sexby and Titus turned to Parker's theory of popular sovereignty, echoing his language of virtual representation and bestowing their faith in Parliament.

MILTON'S ATTACK ON HEREDITARY MONARCHY

In contrast to all these writers, Milton was a firm supporter of both the Commonwealth and the Protectorate. He had stood on the sidelines during the Civil War, in spite of being moved – if his own claims are to be believed – by the "sad tidings of civil war in England" to cut short his travels on the Continent in the summer of 1639 and return home.[26] But with the execution of Charles I Milton saw an opportunity to make his mark on the political stage. In February 1649 – less than two weeks after the regicide – he published the first major defence of the new regime, *The Tenure of Kings and Magistrates*. Having been appointed as the Commonwealth's secretary for foreign tongues from March 1649, he was then commissioned to write a major vernacular piece, *Eikonoklastes* (1649), and two Latin defences, in 1651 and 1654, respectively, in an attempt to win over the largely hostile European republic of letters. A third Latin defence appeared in 1655, and in

1658 a second and much revised edition of the 1651 *Defensio*.[27] Finally, after issuing a number of shorter, occasional pieces in 1659, he published *The Readie and Easie Way to Establish a Free Commonwealth* (1660), a last blast of the republican trumpet amidst the impending return of the Stuart monarchy.[28] Having narrowly escaped with his life at the Restoration, Milton returned to the safer medium of poetry, completing and publishing his three great epics: *Paradise Lost* (1667), *Paradise Regained* (1671), and *Samson Agonistes* (1671).

Although Milton did not contribute personally to the paper war of the 1640s, there is no doubt that he was deeply affected by the turmoil of those years and influenced by the ideas to which it gave rise. In particular, he took to heart the view that a free people was one that could not be held to be the property of another. In an entry in his Commonplace Book from 1641–43 under the heading "Of Slaves," Milton argues that, to understand "what the law was concerning masters and slaves," one must turn to the *Corpus Iuris Civilis* and, more specifically, to the passage from the *Institutes* in which slavery is defined as the condition of being the property of somebody else, such that the master not only has "the power of life and death" over the slave but also "whatever a slave acquires belongs to the master."[29] What Milton found in the Roman law was precisely the line of argument then being deployed by Parliamentarians to oppose Charles's extra-parliamentary levies: if subjects are to be counted as free-men rather than slaves, they must be able to hold their property securely. Still a relatively obscure poet who was only then beginning his career as a public polemicist with a series of antiprelatical and pro-divorce tracts,[30] Milton was eagerly noting down ideas central to the Parliamentarian case, which he would draw on extensively in his republican writings.

The notion of the slave as the property of his master that Milton found in the *Institutes* lay at the heart of his republicanism. The regicide was, for Milton, not merely the overthrow of an oppressive and tyrannical ruler but the act by which the people asserted their self-ownership. Milton's opposition to hereditary rule was a central feature of his political thought throughout the Interregnum, and it can indeed be traced back to the early 1640s or even earlier.[31] In an entry from 1639–41 in the Commonplace Book under the title "King," Milton argues that, if the hereditary principle must be adhered to, the king should at least be led to believe that he has inherited his power "not on the basis of his coming of age, but on the basis of his deserts, and that he is to receive his father's authority, not as inherited spoils, but as the reward of worth."[32] Perhaps this was as much as Milton was willing to commit himself to in these uncertain years, even in a text not intended for publication, but we can already detect the hostility towards hereditary government that would become a staple of Milton's political thought.

Milton's critique of hereditary principles is most forcefully expressed in *The Tenure of Kings and Magistrates*, written largely during Charles's trial for treason. Milton's argument here is that any form of government in which power is treated as a kind of property to be passed down the generations is simply incompatible with freedom. If it were true, he claims, that "the King hath as good right to his Crown and dignitie, as any man to his inheritance," this would "make the Subject no better then the Kings slave, his chattell, or his possession that may be bought and sould."[33] How the king chooses to exercise his power is wholly irrelevant to the question of the subject's freedom; the simple fact of living under a hereditary ruler and so being the property of another is to be a slave. Monarchy – and not merely tyranny – is, for Milton, the scourge of a free people.[34]

If subjects living under a hereditary monarch are ipso facto the property of their king, this is as much as to say that monarchy is an illegitimate form of government. Milton makes this argument in *Pro Populo Anglicano Defensio* (1651), an impassioned and often vitriolic response to the French scholar Claude de Saumaise (Salmasius), whose *Defensio regia pro Carolo I* (1649) was the most celebrated attack on the new regime emanating from continental Europe.[35] Salmasius had offered two main arguments in support of his contention that the king had absolute *dominium* over his people, and Milton addresses both of these in turn in the *Defensio*. The first is the patriarchal argument that the absolute authority of kings derives from Adam's dominion over all his progeny. Milton dismisses this as a category error, accusing Salmasius of being "wholly in the dark in failing to distinguish the rights of a father from those of a king."[36] It is absurd, Milton claims, to regard the king as wielding patriarchal authority, for "our fathers begot us, but our kings did not, and it is we, rather, who created the king."[37]

The people are thus born free of any political authority, but the possibility remains that they might voluntarily sell themselves into bondage. This is the second of Salmasius's arguments challenged by Milton in the *Defensio*. Milton's objection is that, although we are our own masters vis-à-vis other human beings, we do not own ourselves to such a degree as to be able to

alienate our property in ourselves, for there is another being with a superior
property right in us. We are, Milton believes, "God's own," "his property
alone," and therefore we do not have the power to "deliver ourselves as slaves
to Caesar, that is to a man, a man who is unjust, unrighteous, and a tyrant."[38] John Locke, perhaps drawing on Milton, would use the argument
that men are "his Property, whose Workmanship they are" to proclaim the
institution of slavery to be illegitimate.[39] Milton draws a different conclusion, though one that Locke also embraces elsewhere in the *Two Treatises*:
those who submit themselves to a master such that "without their own consent they have become the [master's] inheritance ... certainly cannot be
considered citizens or free born or even free."[40] In fact, Milton believed, "we
must suppose that they are not members of any commonwealth; they are
instead to be counted as part of the property and possessions of their master
and his son and heir. For in respect to the owner's rights I see no difference
between them and slaves or cattle."[41] Milton's purpose is thus not specifically to reject the institution of slavery as a violation of natural law, as with
Locke; it is rather to denounce all hereditary forms of government as a kind
of slavery. The relationship between king and subject is equivalent to that
between master and slave, and is therefore not only illegitimate but, properly speaking, not a *political* relationship at all.

However, Milton was not content simply to reject the old form of government; rather, he sought to make a positive case for the benefits of republican rule. To this end, he took up Parker's theory of popular sovereignty,
which provided Milton with a language both to justify the regicide and to
celebrate the new regime.[42] Parker himself, who served the Commonwealth
as registrar of the prerogative office from July 1649, wrote several works in
support of the new regime, among them *The True Portraiture of the Kings
of England* (1650). But for Milton and other republicans of the Interregnum
it was Parker's pamphlets of the 1640s, and in particular the *Observations*,
that were of greatest interest.

Parker's *Observations* are brought to life most clearly in *The Originall
and End of Civill Power*, published in May 1649 under the pseudonym "Eutactus Philodemius."[43] The power wielded by rulers is, according to Philodemius, nothing other than "that *vigour* which every particular person hath
in himself."[44] It arises through the consent of the people to "conferre" their
power "into one or more persons, as best agrees with their own Temper,

and Constitutions of Policy," and it is, as Philodemius puts it, echoing the precise vocabulary of Parker, "meerly *fiduciary*, and not *inconditionate*."[45] The upshot is that "it is *unnaturall*, that any people should set up over themselves any one person, or collectaneous body of men to be *Lords Proprietaries* of their Rights and Interests, and to hold an *imperiall and Prerogative scourge* over their backs."[46]

In *The Tenure* Milton develops these lines of argument in a more radical direction. As the title of this work already suggests, the power of rulers is treated as a form of property. The "tenure" held by England's rulers is, Milton suggests, not a full property right but a right of usufruct that has been conditionally granted to them by the people, who remain the true proprietors of the commonwealth: "The power of Kings and Magistrates is nothing else, but what is only derivative, transferr'd and committed to them in trust from the People."[47] This idea is reminiscent of Parker's description of political power as a "trust" made by the people to the king.[48]

However, whereas Parker had argued that the power was "conditionate" and could be revoked *if abused*, Milton goes further. His view is that, if "the King or Magistrate hold his autoritie of the people," then the people retain the right at all times to "choose him or reject him, retaine him or depose him though no Tyrant, merely by the liberty and right of free born Men, to be govern'd as seems to them best."[49] Milton does not explain precisely how the people might go about deposing their rulers, but he appears to be siding with the Levellers, for whom government can only be legitimate if the people's consent is given on an ongoing basis through regular elections.[50] For Milton, it is not enough that there should be a nominally representative institution, Parliament, with the power to hold kings to account. Indeed, the word "Parliament" is conspicuous for its almost complete absence, at least in Milton's vernacular writings. Only if subjects have the power to appoint and depose their rulers can they be deemed free, for only then can they ensure that they are their own masters and not the property of another.

Why Milton should have offered such a radical argument in *The Tenure* is not immediately obvious. If his priority was to defend the legality of the trial taking place while he was writing, or of the sentence he hoped it would deliver, it appears to overshoot its target by a long way. The monarchomachs of the French Religious Wars – Milton's principal source – had been careful to restrict the right of resistance to "inferior magistrates," and even then only in cases of actual tyranny.[51] Given that Charles had been deposed by a group whose members could easily qualify as inferior magistrates – their claims to be acting on behalf of the people notwithstanding – and had been put on trial for treason, the standard resistance theory would appear to provide Milton with ample ammunition to make his case for the regicide.

Milton went so much further than his sources because he was not only seeking to justify the abolition of the old regime but also looking forward to the kind of society that could be established in its wake. More specifically, Milton hoped that such a society would embody the ideal of popular sovereignty. Milton describes the ancient Britons' practice of electing as kings those "whom they thought best" and deposing and executing them "when they apprehended cause" as "the most fundamental and ancient tenure that any King of *England* can produce or pretend to."[52] What Milton means by "tenure" is a right to hold office (from the Latin *tenere*), but he is also using the term in an economic sense: the king's title is merely a tenure, not an absolute property right, and one that he holds – in an inversion of the feudal hierarchy – of the people, the ultimate proprietors of the kingdom.

Those who claim to be a free people but do not possess the power to appoint and depose their rulers (to grant them their tenures) "may please thir fancy with a ridiculous and painted freedom, fit to coz'n babies; but are indeed under tyranny and servitude," for what they lack is "that power, which is the root and source of all liberty, to dispose and *oeconomize* in the Land which God hath giv'n them, as Maisters of Family in thir own house and free inheritance." Such a people, lacking this "natural and essential power of a free Nation," are, Milton concludes, "no better then slaves and vassals born, in the tenure and occupation of another inheriting Lord."[53] They are, in other words, not owners of themselves but the property of their masters. As such, they are slaves rather than free-men and, hence, not the subjects of any just political authority at all.

PRIVATE PROPERTY AND COMMON WEALTH

For Milton, a people's capacity to elect their rulers was necessary but not sufficient to prevent them from being reduced to a condition of slavery. If they were not to become the property of another, it was crucial that they should also be able to hold property in material goods securely. Numerous entries in the Commonplace Book from the period of the ship money controversy and associated paper war reveal that, although Milton was not an active participant in these debates, he took to heart the view that the king's attempt to seize his subjects' property without their consent was an affront to their liberty. In an entry from 1639–41, for example, he argues that "to say that the lives and goods of the subjects are in the hands of the K. and at his disposition" is "most tyrranous and unprincely."[54] In a similar vein, he approvingly cites the view of Philippe de Commynes, the French diplomat and writer, that "no king or prince hath due power to raise a penny on his subjects without thir consent."[55] The consequences of violating this principle – and the clearest indication of Milton's engagement with the crisis then raging – are summed up in his comment from 1639–41 that Harold Harefoot "by extracting ship money lost his subjects love."[56]

It was only after the regicide, however, that the full force of Milton's hostility towards Charles's extra-parliamentary levies became apparent. *Eikonoklastes* was commissioned by the Council of State as a reply to the hugely popular *Eikon Basilike* (1649), a supposed autobiography of Charles I that depicted the recently deceased king as a martyr to his people.[57] Responding to *Eikon Basilike*'s nostalgic treatment of Charles's reign, Milton recalls with bitterness how "the Pulpits resounded with no other Doctrine then that which gave all property to the King, and passive obedience to the Subject."[58] It was a doctrine that was all too well heeded by the king: "Who can number," Milton asks, "the extortions, the oppressions, the public robberies, and rapines, committed on the Subject both by Sea and Land, under various pretences?" The people's possessions were "tak'n from them" and "Piracy was become a project own'd and authoriz'd against the Subject."[59] Under the old monarchy, then, the people were incapable of holding property, lacking both ownership of themselves and of their goods.

In *The Readie and Easie Way*, first published in February 1660 and then expanded and reissued in April, these arguments are invoked as part of a last-ditch attempt to save the republic.[60] Milton contrasts the frugality of the republican magistrates – "perpetual servants and drudges to the publick at thir own cost and charges" – with the conspicuous consumption of kings.[61] The republic's rulers do not claim ownership of their people's goods; on the contrary, they are willing to sacrifice their own property in order to carry out their public duties. The king, by contrast, "must be ador'd like a Demigod, with a dissolute and haughtie court about him, of vast expence and luxurie, masks and revels, to the debauching of our prime gentry both male and female; nor at his own cost, but on the publick revenue."[62]

In addition to this general propensity of monarchs to live a life of luxury at the public's expense, if the Stuarts were restored, they would take special measures to "fortifie and arme themselves" against the people. They would ensure that the people are "so narrowly watch'd and kept so low, as that besides the loss of all thir blood, and treasure spent to no purpose, though they would never so fain and at the same rate, they never shall be able to regain what they now have purchased and may enjoy, or to free themselves from any yoke impos'd upon them."[63] In order to implement this vastly increased system of repression, additional funds would need to be raised, which would result in "a general confusion to men's estates, or a heavy imposition on all men's purses."[64] A return to monarchy would be a return to those very policies – impositions, forced loans, ship money – that had persuaded Englishmen to take up arms against their king in the first place.

Although the basic principle that the king ought not arbitrarily to interfere with subjects' property was shared by all of the Stuarts' opponents, it is clear that Milton was aligning himself specifically with the more radical position associated with Parker. As we noted in Chapter 1, the episode that prompted the shift in Parliamentarian ideology was the controversy surrounding the munitions store at Hull. In seizing the arsenal, which – it was claimed by the Royalists – had been bought with the king's own money and was therefore his property, Parliament had set a dangerous precedent that undermined property rights more generally and, as such, called into question its own claims to be the guardian of private property. It was in response to this charge that the Parliamentarians' argument began to shift: Parliament's role was not to secure individual property rights but to serve as the instrument through which a property-owning people could exercise its control over the material resources of the land.

Milton accordingly devotes significant space to the Hull episode in his works, most notably *Eikonoklastes*. It may be true, Milton concedes here, that the Hull arsenal had been bought by the king, but the money used to purchase it had been "most illegally extorted from his subjects of *England*, to use in a causeless and most unjust civil warr against his Subjects of *Scotland*."[65] Moreover, the town of Hull was "not his own, but the Kingdoms," and since the weapons held there had been bought with "public Mony," they did not belong to the king but were "public Armes."[66] Milton's conclusion is that Parliament was fully within its rights to place the magazine at Hull in "hands most fitt, and most responsible for such a trust," for "it were a folly beyond ridiculous to count our selves a free Nation, if the King not in Parlament, but in his own Person and against them, might appropriate to himself the strength of a whole Nation as his proper goods."[67]

In the *Defensio* Milton takes these arguments further and makes the case that the king not only lacked property in such public goods as his towns but was incapable of holding property at all. "Everything," Milton insists, "belonged to the Senate and people," and the king was "so far from having anything of his own that his very habitation belonged to them."[68] With this observation Milton is able to offer an additional challenge to Salmasius's view that the people could sell themselves into bondage and so become wholly subject to the dominion of an absolute monarch. To say this, Milton claims, would imply that the king could then sell his people to another, whereas in fact "it is well-known that a king cannot alienate even his crown property!" The absurd implication of Salmasius's argument is that the king, "who enjoys only the usufruct of the crown, as it is said, and of crown property by the grant of the people," would "be able to claim title to that people itself."[69] Milton's intention in denying the king the power to own property is to challenge his pretensions to have a property in his subjects: the people's ownership of the goods of the land is a mark of their ownership of themselves.

Milton's celebration of the English Commonwealth as a free-state rested on the absence within it of any figure claiming a property right over the people and their goods. In *Eikonoklastes* Milton defines a "Commonwealth"– in Aristotelian terms – as "a societie sufficient of it self, in all things conducible to well being and commodious life."[70] At least in this formulation, the ideal of commonwealth that Milton took the Commonwealth to embody was not that of a particular constitutional form, that is, of a constitution lacking a monarchical element; the commonwealth is, instead, conceived of as an autarkic economic community able to provide the material goods necessary for its members to lead comfortable and fulfilling lives. Such economic conditions must arise from within the society itself and must not in any way be supplied by a single individual since this would enable him to use his economic might to assert undue influence. If the commonwealth depends on "the gift and favour of a single person" for the "requisit things," "it cannot be thought sufficient of it self, and by consequence no Common-wealth, nor free; but a multitude of Vassalls in the Possession and domaine of one absolute Lord; and wholly obnoxious to his will."[71] A society can only be called a commonwealth to the extent that it is a common wealth. All its material resources must, in other words, be owned by itself; where instead citizens depend for their well-being on the will of an excessively powerful individual, they become themselves the property of their rulers. The result is that they no longer live in a political society at all but are instead a community of slaves.

MILTON'S CRITIQUE OF LUXURY

Although Milton regarded a people's capacity to supply its own material needs as integral to its liberty, he did not conclude that more wealth necessarily led to greater freedom. As David Armitage has emphasized, Milton was influenced by Sallustian and Machiavellian discussions of the corrupting effects of empire. According to this line of argument, the Romans' imperial conquests, by bringing in rich rewards and exposing the Roman people to the opulence of the East, had debased their spirit and so rendered them unfit for liberty. The decline of republics then appears to be an almost inevitable consequence of their success: while the freedom of republics is what enables their expansion, the resulting wealth and the corruption that accompanies it are among the greatest threats to their existence.[72]

Milton's preoccupation with the corrupting effects of luxury can be seen already in the early 1640s. In an entry from 1640–42 in his Commonplace Book he draws a contrast between the character of the Romans under the Republic and Empire. Whereas the former are described as "ripe for a more free government then monarchy," the latter are "growne unruly, and impotent with overmuch prosperity," thus becoming "slaves to thire owne ambition and luxurie."[73] It is unclear at this stage what bearing Milton regarded the example of the Romans' corruption as having for the English people. But during the Interregnum, as his early optimism began to give way to disillusionment, he began to apply the Sallustian and Machiavellian lessons of Roman imperial decline to his own country.

Milton was not, however, the backward-looking opponent of commerce and prosperity that Pincus has made him out to be.[74] Indeed, there is plenty of evidence to suggest that Milton regarded the tendency of republics to

promote wealth as one of their principal advantages over monarchies. This
is particularly pronounced in *The Readie and Easie Way*, where Milton
mocks those who cling to the unfounded belief that nothing but kingship
can restore trade, accusing them of overlooking "the frequent plagues and
pestilences that then wasted this citie." The reality is that "trade flourishes
no where more, then in the free Commonwealths of *Italie, Germanie* and
the Low Countreys."[75] If England, retaining its republican constitution, implemented his proposals, "ther can be no cause alleag'd why peace, justice,
plentiful trade and all prosperitie should not thereupon ensue throughout
the whole land."[76]

However, Milton could not make claims such as these without also warning about the dangers of excessive riches. In the same breath as he praises
the capacity of republics to generate prosperity, he worries about what
would happen "if trade be grown so craving and importunate through the
profuse living of tradesmen that nothing can support it, but the luxurious
expences of a nation upon trifles or superfluities."[77] Milton's concern is that
trade would not provide a means for a people to attain self-sufficiency but,
rather, would enable a class of merchants to become excessively powerful,
holding a whole nation hostage to its lust for extravagance. Even if the
people as a whole are able to resist the materialist impulses of the merchant
class, they would nevertheless feel compelled to buy into commercial society, for "if the people generally should betake themselves to frugalitie, it
might prove a dangerous matter, least tradesmen should mutinie for want
of trading."[78] Even as Milton seeks to extol the economic advantages of republican rule, he cannot help but comment on "those calamities which at-
tend always and unavoidably on luxurie" and, in particular, the "forein or
domestic slavery" that it breeds.[79]

Milton's anxiety regarding luxury appears to have increased with the
publication of the second edition of *The Readie and Easie Way* in April, after
the members of the Long Parliament excluded at Pride's Purge had been
reinstated (the Rump had been restored in May 1659). When Milton came
to revise the section on the "plentiful trade and all prosperitie" of republics,
he must have felt a sense of unease, for he inserted a passage that has no
counterpart in the first edition. Establishing a republic according to his
model, Milton believed,

> requires no perilous, no injurious alteration or circumscription of mens
> lands and proprieties; secure, that in this Commonwealth, temporal

and spiritual lords remov'd, no man or number of men can attain to
such wealth or vast possession, as will need the hedge of an Agrarian
law (never successful, but the cause of sedition, save only where it began
seasonably with first possession) to confine them from endangering our
public libertie.[80]

In the first edition Milton had been content simply to assert that his proposed republic would be a prosperous one. Now, however, he feels the need
to qualify this claim with the Machiavellian thought that the social composition of his society would protect it from the danger posed by overmighty individuals. As such, Milton is anxious to stress, his proposed
republic would have no need for the kind of redistributive measures that –
as we shall see in the following chapter – were a central feature of another
republican constitutional proposal, issued three years earlier.[81]

Milton's fear was not only that those with excessive riches might be in a
position to dominate others but also that they might themselves become
enslaved to their own greed. Political liberty was for Milton above all a
means to the end of "Christian liberty": the establishment of a republican
government that did not subject the people to arbitrary power and granted
them freedom of conscience would, Milton hoped, encourage the pursuit
of virtue and lead to a spiritual awakening. That republican rule could also
have the effect of promoting prosperity was at best of secondary importance. If – as Milton feared – riches might actually corrupt individuals in
such a way as to undermine their freedom, the tendency of republican regimes to generate wealth ought not to be celebrated as one of their inherent
advantages but treated as a threat that should be carefully guarded against.

As we have seen, in *The Readie and Easie Way* Milton attacked kings for
using public resources to indulge their lust for extravagance. One might expect Milton to argue that the consequence of such profligate spending would
be to reduce the people to a state of poverty. Yet he believed that kings, on
the contrary, have a stake in promoting the people's prosperity, their aim
being "to make the people, wealthy indeed perhaps and wel-fleec't for thir
own shearing, and for the supply of regal prodigalitie; but otherwise softest,
basest, vitiousest, servilest, easiest to be kept under; and not only in fleece,
but in minde also sheepishest."[82] Under a monarchy, in which the king holds
the right of arbitrary taxation, the people's property serves not to promote
their independence but to increase their value as a piece of property.

Perhaps Milton's greatest concern was that, at the same time as luxury corrupted the spirit of the English people and made them unfit for liberty, it rendered them incapable of even recognizing their miserable condition. Responding in the *Defensio* to Salmasius's charge that the regicides had "mutilated an island which under her kings had been happy and luxurious," Milton retorts that it was luxury itself that had "nearly ruined" the commonwealth, for it had made the English people "less conscious of its servitude."[83] The abundance of property that could be enjoyed by the people under monarchy served to mask the fact that they had relinquished the most fundamental property of all: their property in themselves.

At this stage Milton may have believed that the English people were capable of throwing off the bonds of self-deception that had kept them willingly enslaved to kings in the past. The tragic failure of England's republican experiment, however, confirmed his worst fears about the moral and intellectual inadequacy of the English, a pessimism that is nowhere more pronounced than in *Samson Agonistes*.[84] The theme of self-enslavement is introduced early in the poem in the Chorus's description of Samson's blindness as a "Prison within Prison" (l. 153), by which "Thou art become (O worst imprisonment!) / The Dungeon of thy self" (ll. 155–6). Samson – whose condition recalls that of the blind poet and failed redeemer of his people – represents the Good Old Cause, betrayed by its enemies. As he tells us later in the poem, the double bondage that he now faces was caused by the "foul effeminacy" (l. 410) of Dalila and the "servil mind" (l. 412) induced by his love.

This was the original cause of Samson's enslavement and, we might suggest, of the failure of the English Revolution:

These rags, this grinding, is not yet so base
As was my former servitude, ignoble,
Unmanly, ignominious, infamous,
True slavery, and that blindness worse then this,
That saw not how degenerately I serv'd. (ll. 415–19)

At the end of the poem Samson succeeds through his suffering in attaining the self-knowledge required to free himself from his internal and external prison, enabling him to carry out one last act of heroism. What remains unclear is whether the people, who in the past had been known to "love

Bondage more then Liberty; / Bondage with ease then strenuous liberty"
(ll. 270–1), will be able to follow Samson's example.

NEDHAM'S ATTACK ON LEVELLING

Milton was the propagandist who did most to enhance the status of the
Commonwealth among the European intelligentsia. But it was his friend,[85]
the infamous turncoat Marchamont Nedham, who emerged as the most
vociferous spokesman for the new regime at home.[86] Nedham's path to
becoming the Commonwealth's semi-official propagandist was far from
direct. After completing his BA at All Souls College, Oxford, in 1637 and
spending a brief period as an usher at Merchant Taylors' School and under-
clerk at Gray's Inn, he entered the political fray in 1643 as editor of the Parliamentarian newsbook *Mercurius Britanicus*. Its radical anti-Presbyterian
stance and its uncompromising hostility towards the king led to its suppression in 1646 and to Nedham's brief imprisonment. After a poorly
documented year that may have included some collaboration with the Levellers,[87] Nedham changed sides in 1647, launching and editing *Mercurius
Pragmaticus*. His Royalist loyalties remained firmly in place after Charles's
defeat in the second civil war, during the king's trial, and even after the
regicide. It was only in November 1649 that, after being imprisoned by
the new regime and narrowly escaping with his life, Nedham renounced
his Royalism, took the oath of engagement, and actively embraced the
cause of the Commonwealth.[88]

Nedham's first work for the new regime was *The Case of the Commonwealth, Truly Stated* (1650). Although it concludes with a chapter that an-
ticipates his subsequent writings, the central argument owes nothing at all
to ideas of popular sovereignty or to classical republicanism but is instead
rooted in the de facto theory prominent during the engagement controversy
then raging.[89] Nedham's claim is that the new regime merited the obedience
of the English people for no other reason than that, through the power of
the sword, it had established itself as the dominant force in the land; there
was nothing about its claim to be a "free-state" that made it worthy of any
particular respect. Indeed, Nedham dispassionately describes both the
emergence and the destruction of republics as a consequence of the power

of the sword: "What title have the Swiss, the Hollanders, Geneva, &c., to their liberty but the sword? On the other side what title have the Medicis to domineer over the free states of Florence and Sienna [*sic*] to the utter ruin of their liberties but only force."⁹⁰ All governments, Nedham insists, were established by military conquest, and it is the duty of subjects to submit to them for the simple, Hobbesian reason that "protection implies a return of obedience."⁹¹

Having established in Part I why the people ought to swear allegiance to the new regime, Nedham devotes most of Part II to lambasting its chief enemies: the Royalists, the Scots, the Presbyterians, and the Levellers. Drawing on the language of the Parliamentarians, Nedham accuses all four groups of posing a menace to the property of the English people. The Scots, it is claimed, "vie wealth with us in our own possessions, honors, and dignities," and the reward promised to their military leaders if they succeeded in defeating the forces of the Commonwealth was "large accessions of interest with other men's honors and possessions ... 'tis like a Scotch Covenanter's stomach will allow no distinction betwixt Presbyter and Independent but may digest the estate of an English Covenanter without so much as a scruple of regret or compassion."⁹² In this way, Nedham is able to draw a connection between the struggles of the Parliamentarians against the Royalists and those of the Commonwealth against its new enemies, presenting the latter as guilty of precisely those crimes that had led the people to take up arms against their king.

Nedham's most vicious diatribe is reserved for the Levellers, something that is particularly surprising given his likely association with the group in 1646–47. The focus of his attack is on the call made in the *Agreement of the People* for the extension of the franchise.⁹³ Nedham echoes the words of Henry Ireton at Putney, claiming that "'equality of right' in government at length introduceth a claim for 'equality of estates' and the making of such laws as the agrarian laws enacted by the popular boutefeus in Rome whereby it was made criminal for any man to grow richer than ordinary."⁹⁴ As Ireton had argued, there was an inevitable slide from political to economic equality. Whereas Ireton had claimed that the abolition of property would be an inadvertent consequence of the Levellers' political demands, Nedham – conflating Levellers with True Levellers – presented economic levelling as a central part of the Levellers' agenda:

From leveling they proceed to introduce an absolute community. And though neither the Athenian nor Roman levellers ever arrived to this high pitch of madness, yet we see there is a new faction started up out of ours known by the name of Diggers. Who, upon this ground that God is our common father, the earth our common mother, and that the original of propriety was men's pride and covetousness, have framed a new plea for a return of all men *ad tuguria*; that like the old Parthians, Scythian nomads, and other wild barbarians, we might renounce towns and cities, live at rovers, and enjoy all in common.[95]

In focusing on the Diggers, Nedham was no doubt using them as a stick with which to beat the Levellers. But his strategy may also point to a continuing sympathy for the Levellers: he is able to present himself as their opponent, while avoiding criticizing ideas that they actually espoused – ideas that, as we shall see, he would later appropriate as part of his republican theory.

The Levellers were already a spent force by 1650, and in subsequent writings Nedham no longer felt the need to distance himself from them. However, the charge of levelling was readily invoked to discredit the Commonwealth's more formidable enemies. His attack on the Royalists in the editorials of *Mercurius Politicus* rested in large part on the claim that "Kings, and all Standing Powers are indeed the *Levellers*."[96] What this amounted to was the charge of economic levelling:

If we take *Levelling* in the common usage and Application of the Terme in these daies, it is of an odious signification, as if it levell'd all men in point of Estates, made all things common to all, destroy'd *Propriety*, and introduced a community of enjoyments among men.[97]

The reason levelling is a natural feature of monarchy is, according to Nedham, that "it placeth every mans right under the will of another." The presence of an arbitrary, non-representative power in the person of the king in itself undermines principles of property, for "seating it self in an unlimited uncontrolable Prerogative over others, without their consent, [it] becomes the very bane of Propriety, and however disguised, or in what Form soever it appears, is indeed the very *Interest of Monarchy*." The consequence is that "under Monarchs we finde ever that the Subjects had nothing certain that they could call their own; neither lives, nor fortunes, nor wives, nor any thing else that the Monarch pleased to demand, because the poor people knew no remedy against the Levelling Will of an unbounded Soveraignty."[98]

Nedham acknowledges that, in kingdoms where "the Frame of Government hath been so well tempered, as that the best share of it hath been retained in the people's hands," some degree of property is possible, "and by how much the greater influence the People have had therein, so much the more sure and certain they have been, in the enjoyment of their Property."[99] But it seems an almost unavoidable reality of monarchy that kings should attempt to "worm the People out of their share in Government, by discontinuing of Parliaments," with the result that they are able to carry out their "Levelling designe, to the destroying of our Properties." The inescapable consequence of living under a monarchy is that the principle will prevail that "all was the Kings, and that we had nothing that we might call our own."[100]

POPULAR SOVEREIGNTY AND REPUBLICANISM

Nedham's editorials for *Mercurius Politicus* drew to an abrupt close in the summer of 1652. With the exception of the newsbook's weekly reports, Nedham did not break his silence until 1654, when he issued the anonymous tract *A True State of the Case of the Commonwealth of England, Scotland, and Ireland* in support of the newly established Protectorate. If the drying up of Nedham's propagandistic pen after August 1652 suggests a sense of disappointment with the Commonwealth, this appears to be confirmed by his comments in *A True State*.[101] The Rump, Nedham now claims, was dominated by men who "attempt and promote many things, the consequence whereof (however it might not be intended by the generality of them) would have been *A subverting the Fundamental Laws of the Land, the destruction of Propriety, and an utter extinguishing the Ministry of the Gospel*."[102] Whereas Parliament's role should be purely legislative, this "long-continued Parlament ... took upon them ordinarily to administer Laws and Justice, according to their own wills, and endeavoured to perpetuate the Office of Administration in their own hands, against the will of the People." Barebone's Parliament, established in July 1653, outdid even the Rump in its "dangerous attempts," not only undermining the rule of law but also bringing about "the utter subversion of Civill right and Propriety."[103] Disregarding his earlier celebration of the Commonwealth, Nedham now attacks it with the same arguments that he had previously deployed against its enemies.

However, in spite of this apparent volte-face, Nedham's priority in *A True State* continues to be to condemn monarchical forms of government. His ostensible purpose is to stress that the Protectorate did not amount to a restoration of kingship and to highlight the benefits of republican over monarchical rule, though the force of this critique is perhaps as much to warn Cromwell not to make himself king as it is to praise him for not being one. In making this point, Nedham now insists – apparently forgetting that he had turned against the Commonwealth – that the Protectorate is merely an updated version of the earlier regime: "Though the Commonwealth may now appear with a new face in the outward Form, yet it remains still the same in Substance, and is of a better complexion and constitution then heretofore."[104]

It is in order to substantiate this claim that Nedham turns to Parker and the theory of popular sovereignty. The tendency among historians to present Nedham as a "classical republican," and thus to stress the influence of the republican thought of classical antiquity and Renaissance Italy, has led them to pay insufficient attention to Nedham's intellectual affinity to his English predecessors and, in particular, Henry Parker. This is all the more surprising given that "the *Observator*" is one of the few contemporary authors cited by Nedham, and given that in the mid-1640s the two men had been political allies under the patronage of Lord Saye and Sele.[105]

Nedham's vindication of the Protectorate rests on the claim that, in spite of its superficial innovations, "the Foundation of this Government" remains firmly "in the People."[106] Nedham's argument, like Parker's, is premised on the dubious equivalence between Parliament and the people: even under the Protectorate, Nedham claims, it is "the people in Parlament" who wield absolute legislative power.[107] However, invoking popular sovereignty was even more problematic for Nedham than it had been for Parker, whose concern had been merely to make the case for the supremacy of Parliament within the English body politic in contrast to the manifestly less representative monarchical element. Nedham, by contrast, sought to use the concept to legitimate a whole political order, and one that, in the office of the Lord

Protector, included an element that at first glance appeared to have little to do with principles of popular sovereignty.

Yet, Nedham insists, the Protector ought to be distinguished categorically from the king of old, for he is "not a person claiming an hereditary Right of Sovereignty, or power over the Lives and Liberties of the Nation by birth, allowing the People neither Right nor Liberty, but what depends upon Royal grant and pleasure, according to the tenor of that Prerogative challenged heretofore by the Kings of *England*."[108] This is not because Cromwell is a more benign ruler than Charles I but because his authority derives from the sovereign power of the people: "The Government now is to be managed by a Person that is *elective*, and that Election must take its rise originally and virtually from the People."[109] The Protectorate thus obtains its legitimacy from its representative nature: not only is Parliament taken to be the people, acting in its legislative capacity, but its purported election of Cromwell as Lord Protector means that he too rules with the people's consent, "virtual" if not, as the Levellers had demanded, actual. Nedham is thus able to conclude that "all power both *Legislative* and *Executive*, doth flow from the Community."[110]

Whereas Parker had been content simply to assert that Parliament and the people were one and the same, Nedham recognizes that this line of argument requires defending. The vulnerability of Parker's argument had been exploited by the Levellers, and Nedham seems anxious to reply to their critiques.[111] One of the Levellers' main demands had been the redrawing of the electoral boundaries so that the composition of Parliament better reflected that of the nation at large. Nedham accordingly addresses the issue of the "Constitution of Parlaments," underscoring the Protectorate's fulfilment of radical demands in his insistence that "the Elections of persons to sit in Parlament, are distributed in all Counties, with much more equality and proportion than heretofore, according to what hath been often declared, and propounded by the Army."[112] Nedham also stresses that "full provision is made to prevent Frauds in Elections, and false Returns," another issue much discussed by the Levellers.[113]

It is, however, the vexed question of the franchise that most preoccupies Nedham in his attempt to substantiate the claim that Parliament is a true "re-presentation" of the people. The narrow property threshold had been one of the main bugbears of the Levellers, for whom a Parliament elected only by a propertied elite could not justly claim to represent the people. Nedham appears to accept this argument and, although he does not share the Levellers' desire for manhood suffrage, he does present the allegedly wider franchise of the Protectorate Parliament as crucial to its claims to stand for the people:

> Whereas the liberty of Electing is restrained only to such qualified persons in each County, whose Estates real or personal are valuable at the summ of 200*l*. and they declared capable to elect Members to serve in Parlament; let it be consider'd, that the liberty of that kind is drawn forth to a greater latitude, than in the daies of Kings, when this Priviledg was exceedingly curtailed, and communicated to those alone who were called *Free-holders*, as if they alone had been the men that ought to be free: But now we conceive it is circumscribed with such prudence and caution, that it fits neither too straight nor too loose, to the Body of our Nation.[114]

By claiming that the Protectorate is underpinned by a truly representative parliament, Nedham is able to present this regime as not only the realization of the ideal of popular sovereignty that had inspired the Parliamentarians' struggle against the king but also as fulfilling the Levellers' demands that a regime acting in the name of popular sovereignty must actually obtain the people's consent.

THE DANGERS OF LUXURY AND THE "EXCELLENCIE" OF FREE-STATES

Nedham is particularly anxious to stress the contrast between the Protectorate and monarchy with respect to property rights. The king, Nedham believes, is "a person claiming an hereditary Right of Soveraignty, or power over the Lives and Liberties of the Nation by birth, allowing the People neither Right nor Liberty, but what depends upon Royal grant and pleasure." The upshot is that, "if the Commonalty enjoyed any thing they might call their own, it was not so much to be esteemed as a matter of Right, as a Boon and effect of grace and favour."[115] Because the people are themselves treated as property by their kings, their goods are liable to be taken away arbitrarily.

This, Nedham warns, would be the miserable fate of the English people if the monarchy were restored. The debts amassed by the exiled Stuarts would have to be "discharged out of the purses of this exhausted Nation," as if there were no distinction between the royal family's personal finances and the public's. Moreover, the inevitably vindictive policies of a restored Stuart king would mean that "no mans life, no mans Estate can be secure,"[116] for his aim would be "the inthroning himself upon an Interest of meer will and power, against the common Interest of the People; by which means our Lives and Liberties, our Wives and Children, our Estates and Fortunes, would all be exposed as sacrifice to the boundles ambition and cruelty of a race of Tyrants."[117] The effect would be to "enervate the natural vigor and courage of the People, and exceedingly debase the honour of this free Nation."[118]

If monarchy stood squarely for arbitrary interference with property, it is less clear what the republic stood for. Like Milton, Nedham on the one hand wished to present the new regime as one that would secure private property and promote wealth, but on the other hand he feared the consequences of excessive riches. Whereas Milton, viewing the commonwealth as a vehicle for the promotion of liberty and virtue in the individual, tended to emphasize the dangers of luxury, Nedham was more preoccupied with the Machiavellian question of how the state as a whole could attain *grandezza*.[119] The capacity of republican forms of government to generate wealth could therefore be detached from the question of the moral well-being of the individual; prosperity could instead be celebrated because of its role in promoting glory.

In 1656 Nedham collected the editorials published in *Mercurius Politicus* between September 1651 and August 1652 and republished them, in a revised form, as *The Excellencie of a Free-State* ("excellencie" perhaps standing in for the untranslatable Machiavellian concept of *grandezza*).[120] Nedham had no difficulty in this work explaining which economic measures republican regimes would *not* implement: they could be sure not to interfere with property arbitrarily in the way that monarchies did. In discussing the various possible objections to republican rule, the first that Nedham addresses – and the one that he is evidently most anxious to rebut – is the charge that it would lead to the levelling of estates and so to interference with property. Nedham's response is that "this way of Free-State, or Government by the People in their successive Assemblies, is so far from introducing a community, that it is the onely preservative of Propriety in every particular."[121]

As Nedham suggests in the epistle to the reader, this is because "most of the Nobility and Gentry of this Nation have fair Estates of their own, free, without any dependence upon the Crown; and they would be as unwilling to render up their Estates and Posterities in the paw of the Lion, as the Commoners themselves."[122] It is therefore also likely to be a stable regime, which the better off as well as the poorest would be willing to embrace: a far cry from the kind of mercantile state dominated by elite tradesmen that Milton had warned against.

However, Nedham also points to the importance of preventing excessive inequalities of wealth, drawing on the Machiavellian idea that overmighty individuals pose a danger to the state.[123] It is, Nedham argues, "ever the care of Free-Commonwealths, for the most part, to preserve not an Equality, (which were irrational and odious) but an Equability of Condition among all Members."[124] The result is that there will not be the opportunity for individuals to "aspire beyond Reason" and to become "such petty Tyrants, as would usurp and claim a Prerogative, Power, and Greatness above others, by Birth and Inheritance."[125] It would, in other words, be impossible for anyone to claim any kind of hereditary property over the people in the way that kings did.

This argument gives way, in the editorial from *Mercurius Politicus* in which it is originally put forward, to a rare tribute to Venice. Echoing Machiavelli's *Discorsi sopra la prima deca di Tito Livio*, Nedham argues that Venice has managed to retain its freedom for so many years by imposing strict limits on the wealth of its senators "*that none of them grow over rich,*" adding that "*one of her prime Principles of State is, to keep any man, though he have deserved never so well by good success or Service, from being too great or popular.*"[126] Perhaps sensing the tension of this apparent praise for levelling principles with his earlier remarks, in *The Excellencie* the reference to Venice's measures for capping the wealth of its senators is dropped. Nedham is still concerned with preventing individuals from becoming overmighty, repeating his view that "one prime Principle of State" is to stop anybody from becoming "too great or popular," but he no longer suggests that the way to do this is to place limits on the accumulation of property.

Another intriguing modification, which may point to Nedham's subversive intentions in *The Excellencie*, is the explanation for why it is necessary to prevent individual citizens from becoming too powerful. In his editorial for *Mercurius Politicus* Nedham had explained that Venice had limited its senators' wealth because it regarded it to be "a notable means (as indeed it hath been) in securing her self from the Rapes of usurpation."[127] In *The Excellencie* this passage is subtly though tellingly altered. Nedham now writes: "It is a notable means (and so esteemed *by all Free-States*) to keep and preserve a *Commonwealth* from the Rapes of Usurpation."[128] The inference that Nedham appears to be inviting his readers to draw is that the transition from Commonwealth to Protectorate amounted to a usurpation caused by the failure to prevent a certain unnamed individual from becoming "too great or popular."

In *The Case of the Commonwealth* Nedham discussed, as an additional reason for avoiding excesses of wealth, the Sallustian view that the rich posed a threat not only to the freedom of their fellow citizens but also to themselves since they risked becoming enslaved by their own addiction to wealth.[129] He explained that the reason men brought up under a monarchy would rather opt for a life of slavery than become free-men was: "*A generall corruption and depravation of Manners,* by luxurious courses, when a Nation is even swallowed up with Riot and Luxury, so that being slaves to their own lusts, they become the more easily enslaved to the lust of another."[130] Echoing Milton's idea of a "double tyrannie, of Custom from without, and blind affections within,"[131] Nedham's argument was that man's inner corruption through luxury enfeebled the spirit, making him vulnerable to domination. Luxury thus provided the ideal precondition for the establishment of monarchy.

In *The Excellencie* Nedham argues, echoing this language, that "in Free-States the People are less Luxurious, than Kings or Grandees use to be." This is because:

> Where Luxury takes place, there is a natural tendency to Tyranny, as there is from the Cause to the Effect: for, you know the Nature of Luxury lies altogether in Excess. It is a Universal Depravation of Manners, without Reason, without Moderation; it is the Canine appetite of a corrupt Will and Phant'sie, which nothing can satisfie ... That Form of Government must needs be the most excellent, and the Peoples Liberty most secured, where Governours are least exposed to the baits and snares of Luxury.[132]

Nedham draws on numerous examples to show that the transition from monarchical and oligarchic to popular government yields a parallel shift from luxury to a more frugal ethic among the ruling classes. As ever, the paradigmatic case is that of Rome, "where we finde it in the dayes of *Tarquin*, dissolved into Debauchery." Although "upon the change of Government, their manners were somewhat mended," the Senate, by establishing a standing power, "first let in Luxury, then Tyranny."[133] It was only after these "Grandees" were deposed – a thinly veiled reference to Cromwell's dissolution of the Rump – that "Liberty, and Sobriety began to breath again." Nedham's conclusion is that, "since the Grandee or Kingly Powers, are ever more luxurious, than the popular are, or can be: and since Luxury ever brings on Tyranny, as the onely bane of Liberty; certainly the Rights and Priviledges of the People, placed and provided for, in a due and orderly succession of their Supreme Assemblies, must needs remain more secure in their own Hands, than in any others whatsoever."[134] There is thus throughout Nedham's writings a strand of thought that undermines Pincus's depiction of him as an unambiguous proponent of an emerging commercial society. For all Nedham's insistence that the republican regimes championed by him were guardians of private property, he could not conceal his unease about the potential dangers of luxury.

In the end, however, Nedham came to the conclusion that a state geared towards economic expansion, which offered its citizens incentives to exert themselves, was more likely to achieve greatness than one that sought to control the distribution of property in the interests of preventing corruption. Within Nedham's Machiavellian framework, prosperity is both an end in itself – a constituent feature of what makes the state great – and one of the most effective means of promoting the military expansion upon which he believed true greatness to depend. As he informs his readers in the Introduction to *The Excellencie*, republics are "the most commodious and profitable way of Government, conducing every way to the enlarging a people in Wealth and Dominion."[135] In monarchies the people have no interest in exerting themselves since the fruits of their labour automatically become the king's. By contrast, Nedham claims, "under this Government, the People are ever indued with a more magnanimous, active, and noble temper of Spirit, than under the Grandeur of any standing power whatsoever." This is because of "that apprehension which every particular Man hath of his own immediate share in the publick Interest, as well as of that security which he possesses in the enjoyment of his private Fortune, free from the reach of any Arbitrary Power."[136] The fact that citizens of a republic are able to enjoy their property without fearing that it could be taken away at the whim of their rulers is lauded not because of its benefits for the individual but because it makes it possible for the state to acquire "Wealth and Dominion."

Crucially, Nedham's point is not that all citizens necessarily prosper under republics but that they have the impression of sharing in the gains made by the state as a whole, provided these are allocated according to merit. Even those who do not actually benefit from the successes of the republic feel no resentment:

> If the Commonwealth conquer, thrive in Dominion, Wealth or Honour, he reckons all done for himself; if he sees Distributions of Honour, high Offices, or great Rewards, to Valiant, Vertuous, or Learned Persons, he esteems them as his own, as long as he hath a door left open to succeed in the same Dignities and Enjoyments, if he can attain unto the same measure of Desert.[137]

Insofar as Nedham is interested in the effects of prosperity on the individual, this is purely instrumental: by giving their citizens the opportunity to succeed, republics promote the virtue that is necessary for the state to achieve greatness. Citizens will "aspire unto great Actions, when the Reward depends not upon the Will and Pleasure of particular Persons, as it doth under all standing Powers; but is conferred upon Men (without any consideration of Birth or Fortune) according to merit, as it ever is, and ought to be in Free-States, that are rightly constituted."[138]

For both Milton and Nedham, monarchical forms of government were to be rejected on the grounds that they implied a property relationship between rulers and ruled, a relationship that was, according to Milton, by definition non-political. By freeing themselves of their masters and affirming their ownership of themselves, the people established a society in which they were themselves the ultimate proprietors of everything. The "common wealth" advanced the freedom of its members through being a self-sufficient community in which no individual could use his wealth to create structures of dependence.

However, Milton's and Nedham's desire to present the English republic as embodying the ideals that had motivated the Parliamentarians to take up arms against the king made them unwilling to entertain the possibility that the government might need to carry out a degree of "levelling" if it was to prevent the return of would-be masters. This meant that both authors found themselves on the one hand celebrating the republic's capacity to promote private property and on the other hand worrying about the risks that this entailed. Neither could satisfactorily resolve this tension.

Instead, as I shall argue in the next chapter, the task fell to James Harrington, who in 1656 produced the most sophisticated and influential republican tract of the seventeenth century. By reversing the relationship between popular ownership of property and republican rule, Harrington abandoned the language of self-ownership that had underpinned Milton's and Nedham's argument, and took the radical step of wholeheartedly embracing the redistribution of property.

4

James Harrington's
Equal Commonwealth

James Harrington emerged in the 1650s as the leading English republican of the Interregnum, radically reshaping the way in which the relationship between property and freedom was understood. However, of the scant knowledge we have of his life prior to the publication of his magnum opus, *The Commonwealth of Oceana* (1656), there is little that presages his subsequent ideological commitments. The eldest son of Sir Scapcote Harrington, James belonged to the minor branch of an ancient and formerly influential family that had included numerous office-holders and royal favourites.[1] After a period of study at Trinity College, Oxford, and at the Inns of Court, he embarked on a grand tour of Europe in 1631, an experience that seems to have left a greater mark on his intellectual development than his formal education. He probably returned to England in the mid-1630s, though almost nothing is known of his activities there until the end of the first civil war. What is certain, however, is that in May 1647 he became a gentleman groom of the royal bedchamber, attending upon Charles I during his captivity at Holmby House, Carisbrooke Castle, and Hurst Castle. After playing a significant role in the ultimately fruitless negotiations at Newport, Harrington was dismissed from his position by Parliament, probably for pressing the king's case too hard.[2] He was allegedly present on the scaffold during Charles's execution, an event that evidently caused him much distress.[3]

Harrington then retired to his estate in Lincolnshire, before re-emerging on the political scene with the publication of *Oceana*. Offering first a general statement of his political theory and then a detailed constitutional proposal for England, Harrington aspired to produce not merely a vindication of the English republic but, more ambitiously, a plan for the establishment of a state that attained both liberty and "immortality." He spent the subsequent five years defending and propagating his ideas in the hope of seeing them realized in England, both in a spate of occasional and somewhat terser tracts – among them *The Prerogative of Popular Government* (1657), *The Art of Lawgiving* (1659), and *A System of Politics* (composed between 1659 and 1661, though left unpublished at Harrington's death) – and, in the crucial months between the collapse of the Protectorate and the Restoration, at the Rota Club, a debating society set up by him. In spite of the best efforts of his vocal supporters in Parliament, Harrington was unable to prevent the return of the Stuarts, and therefore the failure of his political project. After being imprisoned in 1661 on suspicion of involvement in a conspiracy, he suffered a likely nervous breakdown and spent his remaining fifteen years in obscurity, falling silent on political matters.[4]

In the five years between the publication of *Oceana* and his arrest, Harrington made a groundbreaking intervention in the debate about freedom and property. His contribution was to reformulate the connection between the two so as to make the case not for an absolute defence of existing property rights – as had most of his predecessors – but for the view that property should be in the hands of the people. As we learn from the Horatian epigraph on the title page of *Oceana*, greed and the excessive accumulation of wealth are a central preoccupation of Harrington's work: "Tantalus a labris sitiens fugientia captat / Flumina: quid rides? Mutato nomine, de te / Fabula narratur" ("Tantalus, thirsty soul, catches at the streams that fly from his lips – Why laugh? Change but the name, and the tale is told of you").[5] The self-destructive greed displayed by Tantalus exemplifies the moral hazards of luxury, which Horace struggles against by urging his readers to "set bounds to the quest of wealth, and as you increase your means let your fear of poverty lessen, and when you have won your heart's desire, begin to bring your toil to an end."[6] The Horatian epigraph, as Eric Nelson has argued, serves to highlight Harrington's anxiety about the corrupting effects of immoderate wealth.[7] Harrington's aim, as advertised on the title page, was to alert his readers to the nature of the threat they faced and thereby to save them from suffering the same fate as Tantalus.

Still more can be gleaned about the central concern of *Oceana* by foregrounding the quotations from and commentary on Francis Bacon's essay "Of the True Greatness of Kingdoms and Estates," which are inserted in a brief section prior to the Preliminaries. What becomes clear from this passage is that the danger represented by Tantalus is not so much that of wealth in itself but of its unequal distribution. Quoting from Bacon's essay, Harrington writes:

> Let states that aim at greatness (saith Verulamius) take heed how their nobility and gentlemen do multiply too fast, for that maketh the common subject grow to be a peasant and base swain, driven out of heart and in effect but a gentleman's labourer. Even as you may see in coppice woods, if you leave the staddles too thick, you shall never have clean underwood, but shrubs and bushes; so in countries, if the gentlemen be too many, the commons will be base.[8]

Harrington's concern is that the wealthy, unlike Tantalus, will be able to sip all the water they need and grow so vigorously that the multitudes beneath them are unable to thrive.

As Harrington explains, Bacon "harps much upon a string which he hath not perfectly tuned, and that is the balance of dominion or property."[9] It is this doctrine that explains why an overmighty nobility poses such a threat to England's civic life and that underpins Harrington's view that a degree of economic equality is necessary for the attainment of liberty. Bacon, like Machiavelli before him, narrowly missed this discovery, Harrington claims, but he did recognize the important consequences of Henry VII's policies to reduce the power of the nobility, praising "the profound and admirable device of Panurgus [Henry VII] King of Oceana, in making farms and houses of husbandry of a standard; that is, maintained with such proportion of land unto them as may breed a subject to live in convenient plenty and no servile condition, and to keep the plough in the hands of the owners and not mere hirelings."[10] Commenting on this passage, Harrington adds: "The tillage, bringing up a good soldiery, bringeth up a good commonwealth, which the author in the praise of Panurgus did not mind, nor Panurgus in deserving that praise; for where the owner of the plough comes to have the sword too, he will use it in defence of his own, whence it hath happened that the people of Oceana, in proportion to their property, have been always free."[11]

Harrington thus establishes from the outset the crucial connection between freedom and property ownership. Anxious as he was about the consequences of material inequality, and no doubt aware of the difficulties faced by Milton and Nedham, Harrington develops an entirely different argument that jettisons the concept of self-ownership in favour of the view that freedom is only possible in an "equal" commonwealth. The consequence is that Harrington is able to present redistributive economic measures as not merely consistent with his concept of liberty but integral to it.

LIBERTY AND ORDERS

Harrington's most sustained discussion of freedom in *Oceana* is to be found in the passage from the Preliminaries dealing with the "goods of the mind." This Platonic discussion concerns the relationship between reason and passion in the human soul and in the government of the city.[12] Harrington begins by examining the nature of the soul, which he describes as "mistress of two potent rivals, the one reason, the other passion, that are in continual suit."[13] At stake in this conflict is liberty: "Whatever was passion in the contemplation of a man, being brought forth by his will into action, is vice and the bondage of sin; so whatever was reason in the contemplation of a man, being brought forth by his will into action, is virtue and the freedom of soul."[14] Following Plato's *Timaeus*, Harrington then draws a parallel between the soul of the natural body and the government of the body politic. Maintaining that "government is no other than the soul of a nation or city," he argues that, "if the liberty of a man consist in the empire of his reason, the absence whereof would betray him unto the bondage of his passions; then the liberty of a commonwealth consisteth in the empire of her laws, the absence whereof would betray her unto the lusts of tyrants."[15]

The connection established here between rationality, virtue, and freedom seems to point to a positive theory of liberty. However, as the discussion develops, it becomes clear that Harrington does not conceive of freedom in terms of man's self-realization through the attainment of reason. There is, indeed, a subversive element to Harrington's analysis that challenges the Platonic understanding of reason and passion to which it appears to be subscribing. Reason, it turns out, is nothing other than interest.[16] This, Harrington believes, can be divided into three categories: private reason ("the interest of a private man"), reason of state ("the interest ... of the ruler or rulers"), and the reason of the entire population ("the interest of mankind").[17] When he speaks of reason prevailing over the passions, what he is really referring to is the triumph of the interest of mankind, which he also refers to as "right reason," over the interest of the private individual or of the ruling classes. This, Harrington makes clear in *The Prerogative of Popular Government*, is not simply the sum total of the private interests of individuals but something qualitatively different:

> All civil laws acknowledge that there is a common interest in mankind … Upon this acknowledgement of mankind, a man that steals is put to death, which certainly is none of his private interest; nor is a man put to death for any other man's private interest; therefore there is a common interest of mankind distinct from the parts taken severally.[18]

However, Harrington has no faith in the capacity of individuals to lay aside their private interests for the common good since "a man doth not look upon reason as it is right or wrong in itself, but as it makes for him or against him."[19] The solution lies instead in engineering the soul of the city in such a way as to divert the private interests of individuals towards right reason.[20] The maxim of government by laws and not men is meaningless, Harrington acknowledges, since "they that make the laws in commonwealths are but men."[21] But Harrington is confident that, through the complex mechanism described in *Oceana*, citizens will be compelled to enact laws that reflect the interest of mankind and not of private individuals.

In describing the freedom of man and the city as consisting in the triumph of reason over passion, Harrington's purpose is not merely to draw a parallel between the two but to argue that they are inextricably linked. Harrington appears to be following Plato here, for whom living in a free political community is indispensable for attaining the self-realization in which freedom is thought to consist. But Harrington's argument does not turn on the view that living in a free-state results in a psychological or moral alteration in the individual. If the freedom of the state consists in the empire of laws and not men, the freedom of the individual consists simply in living in such a state. Although the individual will not necessarily become more rational as a result, his self-interest will be channelled by the orders of the state to promote the interest of mankind. The consequence will be that no individual will be able to impose his private interest on the community and all citizens will live in a condition of independence.

The main body of *Oceana* is concerned with describing in painstaking detail how such a mechanism could be established and how it would operate.

So momentous is the task of setting it up that it requires the exceptional wisdom of a quasi-divine legislator such as Lord Archon; lesser mortals like Oliver Cromwell could, it would seem, only achieve it with much guidance from a sage such as Harrington. Yet the principle behind it, Harrington explains in the Preliminaries, is simple enough for even the most primitive of political minds to grasp:

> That such orders may be established as may, nay must, give the upper hand in all cases unto common right or interest, notwithstanding the nearness of that which sticks unto every man in private, and this in a way of equal certainty and facility, is known even unto girls, being no other than those that are of common practice with them in divers cases. For example, two of them have a cake yet undivided, which was given between them. That each of them therefore may have that which is due, "Divide," says one unto the other, "and I will choose; or let me divide, and you shall choose." If this be but once agreed upon, it is enough; for the divident dividing unequally loses, in regard that the other takes the better half; wherefore she divides equally, and so both have right.[22]

Mere self-interest on the part of both girls will result in an equitable distribution of the cake, without the need for an appeal to any higher moral values. Thus, when Matthew Wren, an otherwise astute critic of Harrington, objects that the two girls would act in the common interest only by virtue of being subject to a power that would enforce the equal division of the cake, it is clear that he has entirely missed the point. No coercion of the will would be necessary at all, for so long as the correct orders are in place, the two girls, acting as they inevitably would out of self-interest, could not help but divide the cake equally.[23]

The same idea is expressed perhaps even more memorably in Harrington's description of a pageant that he claims in *A Discourse upon this saying* (1659) to have witnessed during Shrovetide festivities in Rome:

> I saw one which represented a kitchen, with all the proper utensils in use and action. The cooks were all cats and kitlings, set in such frames, so tied and so ordered, that the poor creatures could make no motion to get loose, but the same caused one to turn the spit, another to baste

the meat, a third to skim the pot and a fourth to make green sauce. If the frame of your commonwealth be not such as causeth everyone to perform his certain function as necessarily as this did the cat to make green sauce, it is not right.[24]

What is particularly revealing about this comical scene is not only the sense of determinism – the cats' movements are physically constrained such that it is impossible for them to perform any activity other than to prepare a roast – but that what causes the cats to act at all is their instinctive desire to break free from the bizarre contraption in which they are ensnared. It is precisely because the cats, just like the girls, are assumed to be motivated by self-interest that, provided their movements are channelled in the correct way by the orders, they will end up acting according to right reason.

When converted into the language of constitutional theory, the actions of dividing and choosing are redescribed as "debating" and "resolving." In order to ensure that the state looks to the interest of the whole of mankind (in other words, to "right reason"), Harrington maintains that there should be a division within the legislative process between debating bills and deciding whether or not to enact them into law. Those debating, without being expected to relinquish their private interest, would be compelled by the institutional mechanism within which they operate to propose laws to which the other party, no less self-interestedly, could be expected to consent. The consequence would be that, as with the girls dividing the cake, the interest of the whole would be promoted, even as individuals pursued their private interest.

However, there is a crucial difference between the two cases that Harrington does not spell out sufficiently clearly in *Oceana*.[25] Whereas in the analogy of the cake the presumed equality between the two girls made it irrelevant who cut and who chose, at the political level the very existence of two distinct groups is predicated on the view that humans are fundamentally unequal. In any society, Harrington believes, there is a natural division among men, with a small group being distinguished from the rest of the population by virtue of their noticeably superior wisdom:

Let us take any number of men, as twenty, and forthwith make a commonwealth. Twenty men, if they be not all idiots – perhaps if they be – can never come together, but there will be such a difference in them that about a third will be wiser, or at least less foolish, than all the rest. These upon acquaintance, though it be but small, will be discovered and (as stags that have the largest heads) lead the herd; for while the six, discoursing and arguing one with another, show the eminence of their parts, the fourteen discover things that they never thought on, or are cleared in divers truths which had formerly perplexed them.[26]

Harrington does then to an extent subscribe to the Platonic view that, for reason to prevail in the state, the masses must be led by the wisdom of a natural aristocracy. He does not, however, succumb to the naïve view that a higher intellectual faculty entails a more altruistic temperament. A people ruling without the assistance of the aristocracy cannot be "wise," Harrington claims in *Aphorisms Political* (1659), but an aristocracy ruling without the people cannot be "honest."[27]

It is for this reason that Harrington institutes a division between debating and resolving, a point that Wren entirely fails to grasp, much as he had misunderstood the force of Harrington's analogy of the girls cutting a cake: "What security can Mr. *Harrington* give us, that the six in their consultations shall not aim rather at their own advantage then that of the fourteen, and so make use of the eminence of their parts to circumvent the rest?"[28] The answer is, of course, precisely none. Far from requiring the aristocracy to relinquish their private interest, Harrington's system depends entirely on their acting self-interestedly, much as the contraption for turning cats into chefs was built on the assumption that they would attempt to break free from it. As Harrington puts it in *The Rota* (1660), "two assemblies thus constituted must necessarily amount unto the understanding and the will, unto the wisdom and the interest of the whole nation; and a commonwealth, where the wisdom of the nation proposeth and the interest of the people resolveth, can never fail in whatever shall be farther necessary for the right constituting of itself."[29] The good orders that Harrington proposes would enable his commonwealth to harness the wisdom of the wisest citizens without thereby causing their interest to prevail over that of the people as a whole. This would create a self-perpetuating system in which good orders breed further good orders, ensuring the triumph of right reason over passion, the empire of laws over men, and freedom over slavery.

The minutiae of this mechanism, discussed at great length in the main body of *Oceana*, can be summarized as follows. The debate would be carried out by a senate, consisting of three hundred "knights" (citizens worth at least £100 per annum) elected by the whole body of citizens, with a third of seats being up for election each year.[30] Motions would be put forward by magistrates within the senate and an orderly process of debate would ensue according to a rigid, hierarchical system.[31] The bills would then be proposed to the popular assembly, known as the "prerogative tribe," a representative body of 1,050 citizens, three-sevenths of them from the same elite also eligible to sit in the senate, four-sevenths elected from those citizens earning less than £100 per annum.[32] This assembly would be expressly forbidden to debate the bill in question or make any amendments to it: its sole function would be to vote whether or not to enact it into law.[33]

Harrington stresses the importance of the size of the prerogative tribe, questioning "whether there can be any safe representative of the people, not constituted of such a number and by such rules as must take in the interest of the whole people."[34] He attacks the Levellers' proposal to establish a representative assembly of four hundred, "this being the first example of a commonwealth wherein it was conceived that five hundred thousand men or more might be represented by four hundred." For Harrington, such an assembly could only bring about an oligarchic form of government since "the representation of the people in one man causeth monarchy, and in a few causeth oligarchy; the many can be no otherwise represented in a state of liberty than by so many, and so qualified, as may within the compass of that number and nature embrace the interest of the whole people."[35]

A crucial feature of Harrington's mechanism is the "rotation," which, by preventing anybody from holding the same office successively for more than one term, guarantees a constant renewal of office-holders, promoting wider participation in government and preventing corruption. To complete the picture and present his constitution as conforming to the classical ideal of the mixed constitution, Harrington adds a monarchical element: "The commonwealth consisteth of the senate proposing, the people resolving, and the magistracy executing, whereby partaking of the aristocracy as in the senate, of the democracy as in the people, and of monarchy as in the magistracy, it is complete."[36]

By ensuring a strict division between the functions of debating and resolving, Harrington's constitution checks the undue influence of any individual or group, thus ensuring that the interest of the whole is promoted. Wren's objection that "Government is not in the Law, but in the person whose Will gives a being to that law" therefore rings hollow.[37] It is certainly the case that laws cannot arise independently of men, but Harrington's point is that, provided the correct orders are in place, the will of every individual will be channelled in such a way as to come together to advance the interest of mankind. There is no division between the law and the wills of men, but "whatsoever upon debate of the senate is proposed unto the people, and resolved by them, is enacted *auctoritate patrum et jussu populi*, by the authority of the fathers and the power of the people, which concurring make a law."[38] The achievement of such a constitutional mechanism, as Harrington puts it in *The Prerogative of Popular Government*, would be the triumph of reason in the soul of the city: "In the frame of such a government as can go upon no other than the public interest, consisteth that whole philosophy of the soul which concerneth policy ... The main of this philosophy consisteth in deposing passion and advancing reason unto the throne of empire."[39]

THE DOCTRINE OF THE BALANCE

As we saw at the start of this chapter, Harrington shared Nedham's and Milton's concern with the problem of luxury and its corrosive effects on liberty. However, unlike Milton and Nedham, he was prepared to countenance using state power to restrict individual holdings. Indeed, such levelling measures were at the heart of his proposed political order and were justified by his claiming not only that they were compatible with liberty but also that they were indispensable to it.

Making this claim required abandoning the language of self-ownership and proposing an alternative way of thinking about the relationship between property and liberty. Harrington's solution is contained in the "doctrine of the balance," which he regarded as his most significant theoretical innovation. In its most epigrammatic form, this theory held that "such (except it be in a city that hath little or no land, and whose revenue is in trade) as is the proportion or balance of dominion or property in land, such is the nature of the empire."[40] In other words, forms of government (the "superstructure") are, or ought to be, rooted in the distribution of landed wealth (the "foundation"). Only when certain conditions are met in the balance can the particular constitutional form of the "commonwealth" be established and so liberty be attained.

Harrington develops this argument through an ingenious reworking of the classical typology of constitutional forms. Monarchy arises when "one man be sole landlord of a territory, or overbalance the people, for example, three parts in four"; aristocracy comes about when "the few or a nobility, or a nobility with the clergy, be landlords"; and "if the whole people be landlords ... the empire (without the imposition of force) is a commonwealth."[41] Although Harrington generally seems to distinguish between the aristocracy and the people in qualitative terms – as noted above, he thought that in any population there would be a minority distinctly wiser than the rest – he does occasionally make a crudely numerical division. In *The Art of Lawgiving*, for instance, he suggests that, where the balance is in the hands of between one and three hundred citizens, a monarchical constitution arises; where the figure is between three hundred and five thousand, there is an aristocracy; and where the balance is in five thousand citizens or more, there would be the basis for a commonwealth.[42] Why Harrington settles on these figures is not altogether clear. Given that the population of England stood at around 4.5 million, his claim that dividing England's landed property between five thousand citizens would constitute a "popular" balance seems particularly problematic. Harrington occasionally hints at the existence of a subclass of propertyless servants,[43] but nowhere does he indicate whether their exclusion from property ownership renders them unfree and, if so, what implications this has for the freedom of the rest of society.[44]

Aristotle, the most influential exponent of the classical theory and the authority Harrington is evidently following here,[45] had offered a similarly schematic account of the constitutional forms in Books 2 and 3 of the *Politics*, before complicating the picture in Book 4 by arguing that, in practice, even the best constitution will involve some kind of mixture.[46] Harrington likewise recognizes that the reality is more complicated than his threefold typology would suggest, indicating that all constitutions must involve an interplay of some kind between the group possessing the balance and the rest of society. We have already noted that Harrington incorporates an aristocratic and, to a lesser extent, monarchical element in his ideal constitution. He is clear that the role played by the few does not depend on their sharing in the balance, for he distinguishes sharply between a nobility that holds an "over-balance in dominion or property unto the whole people," which is "incompatible with popular government," and a nobility holding an "under-balance," which is "not only safe, but necessary unto the natural mixture of a well-ordered commonwealth."[47]

The other constitutional forms also require the collaboration of elements of society not participating in the balance. The "Gothic" polities established in the wake of the fall of the Roman Empire are variously described as aristocratic constitutions with a monarchical element to keep the competition among the nobles in check and as monarchies in which the king rules with the assistance of the nobility.[48] But even if constitutions are never entirely pure, Harrington is anxious to avoid the suggestion that sovereignty is shared between the different elements. Instead, he argues in *A System of Politics*, for a constitution to be viable, it will have to ensure that the balance is located entirely in one of the three elements, whose undivided sovereign power consists in its complete control of the function of resolving.[49] Whatever the constitutional superstructure of Oceana, the people hold the balance and therefore the result is entirely in their hands: "If the result be wholly and only in the people, the people are in liberty, or the form of the government is democracy."[50]

As we have seen, Harrington defined individual freedom as the condition of living in a "rational" commonwealth governed by the laws and not the arbitrary dictates of men. Now Harrington adds that, in order for such a commonwealth to be established, property must be in the hands of the people, however narrow that category turns out to be. This argument differs radically from Milton's and Nedham's: whereas they had been concerned with the protection of existing property rights, claiming that any infringement of them amounted to a violation of the possessor's self-ownership, Harrington's point was that property ought to be distributed in such a way as to ensure that a popular government could be established. In short, for Harrington freedom required that the people should have property.

In seeking to explain the precise nature of the relationship between landownership and sovereignty, Harrington offers two distinct, though not mutually exclusive, answers. The first, which has generally been given greater weight, concerns the link between property and military power. This is an argument that Harrington develops in *Oceana* by engaging with his great nemesis and teacher, Thomas Hobbes.[51] Although Harrington agrees with Hobbes that the law without the power of the sword is "but paper," he adds that "he might have thought of this sword that without an hand it is but cold iron." The army that holds the sword "is a beast that hath a great belly and must be fed; wherefore this will come unto what pastures you have, and what pastures you have will come unto the balance of property, without which the public sword is but a name or mere spitfrog."[52] As Harrington puts it in *The Art of Lawgiving*, "wherever the balance of a government be, there naturally is the militia of the same; and against him or them where the militia is naturally, there can be no negative voice."[53] Property, according to this line of argument, determines political power only in an indirect sense: it enables one to control the power of the sword, which in turn engenders obedience.

Perhaps the clearest statement of this position is to be found in *A System of Politics*, where Harrington reformulates his account of the three constitutional forms in such a way as to highlight the connection between land-ownership and military power.[54] The monarchical constitution, or as he now describes it "the sword of an absolute monarchy," comes about when a single individual holds at least two-thirds of the land and "divides it into military farms at will and without rent, upon condition of service at their own charge in arms whenever he commands them." Likewise, "the sword of a regulated monarchy" arises when the few "being lords of the whole or of two parts in three of the whole territory, let their lands by good penny-worths to tenants at will, or by their leases bound at their commands by whom they live to serve in arms upon pay." Finally, the commonwealth is described as a society of armed citizens, whose possession of the land enables them to bear arms independently in defence of their liberty: "If a people, where there neither is lord nor lords of the whole, nor of two parts in three of the whole territory, for the common defence of their liberty and of their livelihood, take their turns upon the guard or in arms, it is the sword of democracy."[55]

The relationship between property, arms-bearing, and political power has been given particular prominence in J.G.A. Pocock's celebrated interpretation of Harrington as "England's premier civic humanist and Machiavellian."[56] According to this account, developed in a number of seminal works from the 1950s to the 1970s,[57] Harrington was seeking to draw a connection between the English ideal of the independent country gentleman, and the classical and Machiavellian ideal of the citizen-in-arms.[58] Having property is merely a vehicle for the independent ownership of arms, and it is the Machiavellian argument about the central role of arms-bearing in citizenship that grounds Harrington's doctrine of the balance.[59] According to Pocock, therefore, economic relationships between men are of scant importance for understanding Harrington's political theory. Pocock claims that Harrington "considers the man solely in his capacity of soldier, and never comes near to asking how the relations which he enters into as producer and consumer will determine his action as a citizen."[60] Harrington, Pocock believes, "is interested in property only in so far as it subjects or liberates men's capacity to be arms-bearers and citizens," a situation that arises only when there is a popular balance.[61]

Harrington's second way of approaching the relationship between landownership and sovereignty, which is largely neglected by Pocock, is grounded in the claim that the nature of the balance determines whether one is economically dependent or independent.[62] As Harrington puts it in *Oceana*, "as much as he who wanteth bread is his servant that will feed him, if a man thus feed an whole people, they are under his empire."[63] There is, according to this approach, a direct relationship between economic and political power: having the means to provide others with the necessities of life creates a situation of dependence, and it is in this way that political hierarchies are established. On the other hand, where the balance is in the people, all citizens are economically independent and so able to rule themselves.

Whatever the basis of the connection between property ownership and political power, Harrington recognizes that it might come undone, that a "contradiction" might arise between the foundation and superstructure. Harrington once again develops this argument by reworking the classical theory of constitutional forms, and in particular the notion that each of the three "pure" forms has a corresponding corrupt version, in which the private interest of the ruling classes prevails over the common good. For Harrington the distinction between the pure and corrupt forms turns not on moral questions such as these but on whether the government is constructed on sound economic foundations. Where the government is properly settled on the land, it can be classified as pure; where, through the use of force, an individual or group is able to acquire power without being the true landlord of the nation, the government is "not natural but violent."[64] This argument is expressed most synthetically in *The Art of Lawgiving*:

> The art of lawgiving is of two kinds: the one (as I may say) untrue,
> the other true. The untrue consisteth in the reduction of the balance
> unto arbitrary superstructures, which requireth violence, as being
> contrary unto nature. The other in the erecting necessary superstruc-
> tures, that is such as are conformable unto the balance or foundation;
> which, being purely natural, requireth that all interposition of force
> be removed.[65]

The question this immediately raises is what generates the force needed to
establish a corrupt government. As we have seen, the reason holding the
balance yields political power is largely to do with the fact that it enables
one to control the military. However, this being so, it is unclear how anyone
or any group not holding the balance could amass so much force as to be
able to overwhelm the possessor of the balance.[66]

Perhaps what Harrington has in mind is the idea that a weaker military
force could prevail through its superior determination, organization, or fortune,[67] but that he is unconvinced by this account is suggested by the way
he reformulates the distinction between pure and corrupt forms in the
last published statement of his political theory, *A System of Politics*. Government can be divided into "national" (where a state is governed "independently, or within itself") and "provincial" (where it is governed "dependently,
or by some foreign prince or state").[68] In both cases, it is force that causes
the people to submit to government; the difference is that when government
is national the force is "natural," whereas when government is provincial it
is "unnatural." What Harrington means by natural force is "riches," that is
to say, it is the force exerted by an army that is properly settled on the land.[69]
He does not specify what he means by unnatural force, but the implication
is clear enough: it is force exerted by the arms of a foreign power, presumably controlled by those wielding the balance in that state.[70] Harrington's
argument, much tighter than in its previous incarnation, is that the distinction between pure and corrupt forms of government is the distinction between national and provincial administration – an argument that had a
particular resonance in 1660, given the role played by France in the return
of the Stuart monarchy.

However it comes about, Harrington is clear that "corruption" can only
refer to the condition that arises when those wielding political power are

not in possession of the balance. Therefore, to say that a people is too "co-rrupt" for a commonwealth cannot be a description of their moral qualities but must simply be another way of saying that they do not hold the balance. Machiavelli's claim that a "corrupt [people] is not capable of a common-wealth" turns out, according to Harrington, to mean simply that they are no longer in possession of the balance, for "corruption in this sense signi-fieth no more than that the corruption of one government (as in natural bodies) is the generation of another; wherefore, if the balance alter from monarchy, the corruption of the people in this case is that which maketh them capable of a commonwealth."[71]

Given Harrington's ambition to establish a constitution capable of promoting the common good out of self-interest, his attempt to deny the importance of virtue should come as no surprise. He is aware that "the corruption which he [Machiavelli] meaneth is in manners,"[72] but he insists that virtue has no independent role to play in politics, in no way affecting the viability of a given constitutional form. In considering whether it will be possible for a republic to flourish in England, and so for the people to enjoy their freedom, one need look no further than the distribution of land. Harrington does not deny the existence of such a thing as the cor-ruption of manners, but claims that "this also is from the balance":

> For the balance, swaying from monarchical into popular, abateth the luxury of the nobility and, enriching the people, bringeth the govern-ment from a more private unto a more public interest, which, coming nearer, as hath been shown, unto justice and right reason, the people upon a like alteration is so far from such corruption of manners as should render them incapable of a commonwealth, that of necessity they must thereby contract such reformation of manners as will bear no other kind of government.[73]

In determining whether or not a people is capable of popular government, the only relevant issue is the balance; the moral character of individual cit-izens, so important to other English republicans such as Milton, is irrel-evant. In this way, Harrington establishes a connection between freedom and property based not on the protection of existing property rights but on ensuring that property resides in the people.

THE EQUAL COMMONWEALTH

In spite of the eulogizing tone Harrington adopts when discussing the popular balance, the point he wishes to stress above all else is its ineluctability. In the Second Part of the Preliminaries of *Oceana*, he assumes the tone of the dispassionate economic historian, merely describing the shifts in patterns of landownership that have produced the popular balance. The story Harrington tells is first European in scope and then more narrowly focused on England. He describes how "ancient prudence" – the idealized political culture of classical antiquity, characterized by a popular balance and republican government – gradually collapsed internally, making way for "modern prudence," which has dominated European politics (with the exception of Venice) ever since. Although modern prudence was ultimately introduced with the barbarian invasions, Harrington is clear that these could only have come about as a result of Rome's internal decline and in particular "the sink of luxury" let in "through a negligence committed in their agrarian laws," by which the Romans "forfeited the inestimable treasure of liberty for themselves and posterity."[74] With modern prudence came a new division of property, the "Gothic balance," a highly unstable system of landownership characterized by fierce competition among the aristocrats who possess the balance and between them, the king, and people.[75]

The ancient constitution is treated by Harrington, in a deliberately subversive move, as the paradigmatic example of modern prudence: "This government, being indeed the masterpiece of modern prudence, hath been cried up to the skies as the only invention whereby at once to maintain the sovereignty of a prince and the liberty of the people; whereas indeed it hath been no other than a wrestling match" between king, aristocracy, and people.[76] Modern prudence was thus destined to collapse as a result of its inherent tensions, but Harrington dates the beginning of its end to the reign of Henry VII (or "Panurgus") and his land reforms. Drawing extensively on Bacon's *History of the Raigne of King Henry the Seventh*, Harrington describes how this king, having acquired the crown more by the nobles' favour than by right, sought to reduce his dependence on the nobility by passing reforms to undermine their power. In so doing, and in particular by stipulating that all farmhouses above a certain size be granted enough land to free the middle classes from dependence on the nobility, Henry VII ended up inadvertently empowering the people, who "living not in a servile or in-digent fashion, were much unlinked from dependence upon their lords and, living in a free and plentiful manner, became a more excellent infantry, but such an one upon which the lords had so little power, that from henceforth they may be computed to have been disarmed."[77]

This process continued under Henry VIII ("Coraunus"), whose dissolu-tion of the monasteries resulted in a further transfer of land into the hands of the people. The consequence was that by the time of Elizabeth I ("Queen Parthenia") modern prudence was no longer supported by the Gothic bal-ance but persisted only as a result of "the perpetual love tricks that passed between her and her people into a kind of romance."[78] It was only a matter of time before this spell would be broken and the people would seek to ac-quire political power commensurate with their economic standing, resolv-ing the contradiction between the foundation and superstructure. The impression given by this historical narrative is that the emergence of the popular balance was simply the consequence of the inherent instability of the Gothic balance, that the Civil War took place because of the internal collapse of the ancient constitution, and that Harrington's purpose was simply to devise a constitution compatible with the popular balance that had, by chance, been established in England.

However, there is no doubt that Harrington viewed the popular balance as more than a mere accident of history: it was, as we have seen, the only means by which a state capable of promoting liberty could be set up. The upshot is that, in order to advance freedom, the government ought not to refrain from interfering with property, as most of his predecessors had argued, but actively promote its distribution in the hands of the people. In contrast to Milton and Nedham, Harrington wholeheartedly embraced lev-elling, placing the "agrarian" at the centre of his constitutional proposal.

The agrarian is designed to prevent anyone from amassing an estate worth more than £2,000. Harrington settles on this apparently arbitrary figure on the grounds that, having estimated the "dry rent" of all the lands in England at £10 million, it would ensure that property could not come into fewer than five thousand hands.[79] This, in turn, would guarantee that the balance would remain with the people, for, as Harrington argues in *The Art of Lawgiving*, "the balance in a thousand hands might affect the gov-ernment with an hankering after monarchy; in two thousand hands it might

usurp it, so as did the Roman nobility, and thereby cause feud between the
senate and the people," whereas when the land is in five thousand hands
the commonwealth is safe.[80] The popular balance may be the foundation
of Harrington's state, but maintaining it seems to require interventions carried out at the level of the superstructure. Only with this institution in place
can the "equal commonwealth" be established: "One as is equal both in the
balance or foundation and in the superstructures, that is to say in her agrarian law and in her rotation."[81]

It is clear that the ideological commitment lying behind this proposal
is not a puritanical suspicion of wealth per se. Indeed, the effect of the
agrarian will not be to limit material prosperity but, on the contrary, to
stimulate growth:

> The land through which the river Nilus wanders in one stream is
> barren, but where he parts into seven, he multiplies his fertile shores
> by distributing, yet keeping and improving, such a propriety and nu-
> trition as is a prudent agrarian unto a well ordered commonwealth
> Nor ... is a political body rendered any fitter for industry, by having
> one gouty and another withered leg, than a natural. It tendeth not
> unto the improvement of merchandise that there be some who have
> no need of their trading, and others that are not able to follow it.[82]

Arguments such as these undermine Steven Pincus's attempt to place Harrington alongside Milton in the category of the backward-looking "classical" republicans who opposed the nascent commercial society championed
by more progressive theorists such as Nedham.[83] A commonwealth so constituted that its wealth is spread throughout the population in a healthy
proportion is ideally placed to make further economic gains – something
that will not undermine its liberty, provided such gains are also distributed
evenly. In *The Art of Lawgiving*, after stipulating the combined value of national and provincial property that the people of England and her provinces
would be allowed to hold, Harrington argues: "Should the commonwealth
increase in provinces, the estates at this rate, both of her citizens and pro-
vincials, would be more and greater than ever were those of the ancient nobility of these nations, and without any the least hazard unto liberty."[84] The
purpose of the agrarian is, then, to enable England to maintain the popular

balance on which its liberty depends, while at the same time allowing its people to prosper.

It is not only the republicans discussed in the previous chapter who were opposed to redistributive measures but, as Nelson argues, all classical republicans prior to Harrington, influenced as they were by Cicero's attack on Rome's agrarian laws.[85] Harrington was evidently aware of the controversial nature of his position, observing that "agrarian laws of all others have ever been the greatest bugbears, and so in the institution were these; at which time it was ridiculous to see how strange a fear appeared in everybody of that which, being good for all, could hurt nobody."[86] It is for this reason that Harrington designs the law in such a way as to make it as unobtrusive as possible. Rather than sanctioning the heavy-handed confiscation of estates, the agrarian would seek to achieve redistribution within families through tweaking the inheritance laws. Anyone with an estate worth more than £5,000 and with more than one son would be forced either to divide the lands equally between his sons, if doing so would leave each with more than £2,000, or to divide the lands so that none received more than £2,000.

It is perhaps also for this reason that Harrington is so anxious to stress the conservative intentions behind the agrarian, insisting that its effect would be to maintain stability and preserve the status quo.[87] All constitutions, he claims, require an agrarian law if they are to avoid the kind of turmoil recently brought about in England by the contradiction in its balance, for "without an agrarian, government, whether monarchical, aristocratical or popular, hath no long lease."[88] In *The Art of Lawgiving*, Harrington expands on this point, describing how, in the absence of an agrarian law, both monarchical and republican constitutions will inevitably collapse, albeit for different reasons:

> As monarchy by pomp and luxury reduceth her nobility through debt into poverty, and at length unto such a level with the people upon which no throne ever stood or can stand; such was the case of this nation under her latter princes. And a commonwealth, by her natural ways of frugality, of fattening and cockering up of the people, is apt to bring estates unto such excess in some hands, as, eating out the rest, boweth the neck of a free state or city unto the yoke, and exposeth her unto the goad of a lord and master.[89]

Simply left to their own devices, all constitutions will tend towards corruption as a result of their internal dynamics: monarchies by impoverishing the nobility and so bringing about a transfer of property to the people, republics by allowing some citizens to enrich themselves to such an extent that the balance shifts into their hands. The purpose of the agrarian is simply to arrest these natural cycles and promote stability; it is only because the balance happens to be in the hands of the people that Harrington's law is framed as it is.

By presenting the agrarian in these terms, Harrington may have been trying to reach out to those who regarded any infringement of property as a violation of freedom. If this was his intention, however, he was overly optimistic. Of all the issues to which Matthew Wren objects in his *Considerations on Mr. Harrington's Commonwealth of Oceana* (1657), the agrarian is undoubtedly the one he opposes with the greatest vigour. Not allowing himself to be tricked into believing that Harrington's inheritance laws are anything less than a full-scale attempt to redistribute property, Wren's first charge relates to a point already discussed: that the popular balance is at the same time supposed to be the foundation of Harrington's state and the consequence of policies pursued by it. This, Wren believes, makes the agrarian "Unjust," for "if it be truly asserted that Government is founded on Propriety (*Page* 4.) then Propriety subsists in Nature before Government, and Government is to be fitted to Propriety, not Propriety to Government."[90] It would therefore be "against the first and purest Notions of justice to bring in a Government not only differing from but directly destructive of the settled propriety of *Oceana*, in which it is confest (*Page* 101.) to be 300 persons whose Estates exceed the Standard of 2000*l. per annum*."[91] The attempt to influence the balance, Wren contends, flies in the face of the principle that lies at the heart of Harrington's political theory: that political power ought to follow property. It therefore amounts to an injustice according to the criteria established by Harrington himself.

In *The Prerogative of Popular Government*, a point-by-point response to Wren's *Considerations*, Harrington seeks to brush this objection aside by claiming that he has simply been misunderstood: "Whereas in natural and domestic vicissitude, I assert that empire is to follow the legal state of property, he imposeth as if I had asserted empire must follow the natural state of property."[92] This response is, however, somewhat inadequate, for if property is established by law, it is difficult to see how it could be the foundation of government.[93] Moreover, it appears to be in tension with Harrington's account of the origins of government in *The Art of Lawgiving*. While Harrington appears to accept the Aristotelian view that political society emerges out of earlier forms of association, he rejects the claim that the earliest form of government – the family – was necessarily monarchical. Harrington does not deny that some families – those that arise when one man has sufficient property to support a wife and children – might be monarchical in nature. But it is equally possible, if a group of individuals each with broadly similar holdings decide to dwell together, for a "popular family" to be established.[94] Harrington does not specify how property is originally individuated, but what is crucial is that it evidently predates any form of civil association.[95]

Harrington may have dismissed Wren's first objection too readily, but the same cannot be said of his response to Wren's second objection: that the agrarian would not be fixed at £2,000 but would be constantly lowered. Wren's argument was that the people, having the vote and possessing arms, would seek to deprive the wealthiest of their holdings, "and cannot terminate in any thing but Levelling, or at least Reducing the Rate of Estates to that passe, that the keeping it from going any lower shall be the Concern of a greater Number of Men then they make up who have an Interest in the further debasing of it."[96] Passing an agrarian law would then be but the first step towards the outright levelling of estates, making Harrington guilty of advocating – whether inadvertently or otherwise – a policy that only the most radical of writers had been previously willing to contemplate.

Harrington's response is that the people would never seek to limit estates to less than £2,000 because to do so would be against their interest. The people "are not levellers, nor know they why, and yet it is because to be levellers were to destroy themselves."[97] The reason is that levelling would undermine "industry," the people's most significant source of revenue. It would do so first by increasing the risk of civil war, "of all other the greatest obstruction to industry," and second by reducing holdings to such an extent as to make them incapable of supporting labour:

> The land of Oceana, as hath been demonstrated, being levelled or divided equally among the fathers of the families only, cometh not to above ten pounds a year unto each of them, whereas every footman costeth his master twenty pounds a year; and there is not a cottager having a cow upon the common, but with his own labour, at one shil-

ling a day, gets twenty pounds a year; which, the land being levelled, were impossible, because there would be nobody able to set a labourer on work, or to keep a servant; wherefore neither would nor could the people by counsel go about any such business.[98]

The consequence of levelling would be that profits from the land would be less than the cost of labour. Even those previously without property would lose out since their freeholds would yield less than the wages they would otherwise have been able to earn.[99] Harrington is therefore able to claim that "by levelling, they who use the word seem to understand: when a people rising invades the lands and estates of the richer sort, and divides them equally among themselves; as for example – nowhere in the world; this being that, both in the way and in the end, which I have already demonstrated to be impossible."[100] Since the agrarian would be in place from the outset, Harrington is even able to reassure his readers, somewhat misleadingly, that "property is that which is every man's own by the law of the land, and of this there is nothing stirred, but all entirely left as it was found, by the agrarian of Oceana."[101]

Not allowing himself to be discouraged by counter-arguments such as Wren's, Harrington remained steadfast in his commitment to the agrarian, continuing to advocate it even after the Restoration, albeit in cautious terms. In *A System of Politics* he argued:

> Equality or parity has been represented as an odious thing, and made to imply the levelling of men's estates; but if a nobility, how inequal soever in their estates or titles, yet, to come to the truth of aristocracy, must as to their votes or participation in the government be *pares regni*, that is to say peers or in parity among themselves; as well likewise the people, to attain to the truth of democracy, may be peers or in parity among themselves, and yet not as to their estates be obliged to levelling.[102]

Perhaps even more clearly than in *The Prerogative of Popular Government*, Harrington distinguishes here between equality of political power, which his agrarian would promote by preventing anyone from amassing enough property to subvert the commonwealth, and absolute economic parity. Yet essentially Harrington's position on the agrarian is much as it had been prior to the Restoration, suggesting that, his protestations to the contrary notwithstanding, his aim was not merely to preserve the status quo but actively to promote a popular balance.

We can only speculate how Harrington interpreted the Restoration and, in particular, whether he viewed it as invalidating his analysis of English history or indeed the doctrine of the balance itself. But it seems highly unlikely that he would have reacted to it in the detached manner of the economic historian he claimed to be. His continuing call for an agrarian law suggests that he felt vindicated in the view he had expressed in *Oceana* that "the nation where you cannot establish an equal agrarian is incapable of her liberty."[103]

THE IMMORTAL COMMONWEALTH
AND INDIVIDUAL FREEDOM

The argument I have been putting forward is that Harrington is able to advocate redistributive policies, and to use the language of liberty to support them, precisely because he does not make property a constituent feature of his definition of freedom. Whereas his predecessors had, through the notion of self-ownership, built property into their concept of liberty, Harrington argues that to be free is simply to live in a particular kind of state. The connection between property and liberty is thus one step removed and is based on the fact that such a state can only be established if certain economic conditions are met.

This account has taken it for granted that Harrington was a theorist of liberty – that he offered a detailed and sophisticated discussion of the concept and that he regarded liberty as a value that ought to be actively promoted. There is reason, however, to question this assumption. It must be recognized that Harrington's theory was also motivated by other ambitions, most notably that of achieving stability and promoting expansion. In *Oceana* Harrington goes so far as to argue that a well-constituted commonwealth will not only be long-lasting but actually "immortal." Much as buildings "stand the firmer and the longer for their own weight, nor ever swerve through any other internal cause than that their materials are corruptible," states are preserved by the weight of their own history. But since the materials of a state are its people, and since "the people can never die nor, as a political body, are subject to any other corruption than that which deriveth from their government," there is no reason to suppose that an equal commonwealth could not be permanent. The moral degeneration of its individual members would pose no danger: "As man, seeing the world is perfect, can never commit any such sin as can render it imperfect or bring it unto a natural dissolution, so the citizen, where the commonwealth is perfect, can never commit any such crime as can render it imperfect or bring it unto a natural dissolution."[104]

It is, however, possible that even a commonwealth so constituted as to be impervious to internal or "natural" collapse might come to be overthrown by external conquest. The only way to guard against this scenario, Harrington argues, is to construct a state that is geared not only towards internal stability but also towards external expansion, for "if your liberty be not a root that grows, it will be a branch that withers."[105] It is for this reason that Harrington dismisses the Machiavellian distinction between expansionist but unstable states such as Rome and stable but militarily weak ones such as Venice. Nothing is lost from the point of view of stability in pursuing an expansionist foreign policy; indeed, the very orders that Harrington views as necessary for achieving the one have the additional effect of promoting the other.[106] Taking up Machiavelli's view that no state could ever achieve military glory by relying on mercenaries or auxiliaries, Harrington argues that, just as a commonwealth of citizen-soldiers guarding their liberty is conducive to internal peace, so too is it uniquely suited for increase.[107]

In support of this position, Harrington claims that "the true cause whence England hath been an overmatch in arms for France lay in the communication or distribution of property unto the lower sort."[108] Observing that "some will have men, some will have money to be the nerve of war," Harrington argues that "a well-ordered commonwealth doth these things [military conquests] not by money, but by such orders as make of her citizens the nerve of her wars."[109] The most important factor in determining a state's capacity for military success is neither the size of its pockets nor the ability of its soldiers but the quality of its orders. Only by ensuring that wealth is sufficiently spread to produce a people capable of bearing arms independently can one hope to achieve military glory, for "victory is more especially entailed upon courage, and courage upon liberty, which groweth not without a root planted in the policy or foundation of the government."[110] The result of such expansion will be not only to secure freedom

at home – and in the process also maintain stability – but also to fulfill the
"duty" to spread it abroad, thereby "put[ting] the world into a better condition than it was before."[111]

For a number of commentators, the ideal of the immortal commonwealth suggests not merely that Harrington had other preoccupations besides promoting liberty but that he was actually an opponent of it. J.C. Davis
claims that *Oceana*, which he characterizes as a utopian text, ought to be
distinguished from works of classical republicanism on the grounds that,
whereas the latter promote self-government and individual freedom, the
former advocates a world of "subjects constrained, as far as possible, to act
out a predetermined pattern of morality over which they have no control
and which they may not change."[112] The ideal of the immortal commonwealth, Davis argues, is in tension with the republican ideal of the *vivere ci-
vile*, for it is "a dead society, a human machine, programmed forever for the
repetitious performance of the same functions; the epitome of the totali-
tarian state."[113]

A similar, though more interesting, case is put forward by Jonathan
Scott, for whom *Oceana* is a deliberate subversion of classical republicanism that draws on the Hobbesian ontology of matter in perpetual motion
to oppose the republican ideals of autonomy, virtue, and political participation – or, in other words, of liberty. Harrington presents his readers with
a "republican Trojan horse,"[114] advocating a republican constitutional
form whose aim – no less than that of Hobbes's Leviathan – is to constrain
motion in a way similar to that of the contraption devised to compel cats
to prepare a roast. Harrington's ideal commonwealth is, Scott contends, a
world of peace, of billiard balls moving in a controlled manner along predetermined paths, but it is "a world without liberty, and without meaningful political activity."[115]

It is certainly the case that Harrington's constitution takes away liberty
in the Hobbesian sense – although this is not Scott's argument – and possibly also in the republican sense, if we take this to mean, as Scott does, the
attainment of autonomy and virtue through active political participation.
However, as we have seen, Harrington conceives of liberty in a way that
does not require the self-realization of the individual; for him, liberty is the
condition of living in a commonwealth, which in turn depends on there
being a popular balance of property. Harrington was not therefore an opponent of liberty but an advocate of a version of liberty that did not require

any particular moral qualities in the individual. Harrington is explicit on this point: "The spirit of the people is no wise to be trusted with their liberty, but by stated laws or orders; so the trust is not in the spirit of the people, but in the frame of those orders, which, as they are tight or leaky, are the ship out of which the people, being once embarked, cannot stir, and without which they can have no motion."[116] If Harrington's constitutional structure appears to undermine the autonomy of the individual, that is precisely because he conceives of the individual and his private interest as a danger to liberty and therefore as needing to be constrained by the laws.

However, Harrington's scepticism about the role played by individuals in advancing liberty raises the question of how committed he was to advancing individual liberty. At first glance, Harrington appears to regard the freedom of the state as an end in itself, treating individuals as entirely irrelevant to the success of his system: "As man is sinful, but yet the world is perfect," he argues in *Oceana*, "so may the citizen be sinful and yet the commonwealth be perfect."[117] It is true that, in opposing the maxim "give us good men and they will make us good laws" and proposing instead "give us good orders, and they will make us good men,"[118] Harrington seems to be suggesting that the orders might effect a moral change in men, but this is unlikely to mean anything more substantial than that they will become good *for the state*, or that their private interests will be guided by the orders towards the common good.

However, Harrington argues explicitly that his system will promote the freedom of individual citizens. Responding to Hobbes's claim that the writers of classical antiquity and their modern followers describe not "the liberty of particular men, but the liberty of the commonwealth," Harrington argues that "he might as well have said that the estates of particular men in a commonwealth are not the riches of particular men, but the riches of the commonwealth; for equality of estates causeth equality of power, and equality of power is the liberty not only of the commonwealth, but of every man."[119] The distinction between the liberty of the state and the individual is, Harrington believes, fundamentally misconceived: placing property in the hands of the people gives rise to an equal commonwealth, and in this way the freedom of the state and of its individual members will be secured.

There is, moreover, an alternative dimension to Harrington's discussion of freedom that gives far greater prominence to the individual. According to this way of setting up the argument, the popular balance would promote individual freedom not only by making an equal commonwealth possible but also because there is something intrinsically liberating about being a property holder. As we noted in our discussion of the balance, the reason landownership yields political power is in part that it enables one to control the military and in part that it results in a relationship of dependence between those with property and those without. The upshot is that in a commonwealth the people, by virtue of possessing the balance, will be independent of the will of anybody else and, as such, free. As Harrington argues in *The Art of Lawgiving*, "the first personal division of a people is into freemen and servants. Freemen are such as have wherewithal to live of themselves; and servants, such as have not."[120] Framing his argument in terms of the neo-Roman dichotomy between free-men and slaves, Harrington defines being free in terms of having the means of supporting oneself without having to depend on the assistance of another.

In *A System of Politics* Harrington extends this way of thinking about freedom to the political sphere. Repeating the view that "the man that cannot live upon his own must be a servant; but he that can live upon his own may be a freeman," he argues that "where a people cannot live upon their own, the government is either monarchy or aristocracy; where a people can live upon their own, the government may be a democracy."[121] There is, however, a crucial difference between a free individual and a free people. Whereas an individual who has the material means to live independently "may yet, to spare his own and live upon another, be a servant," such a course of action is simply not available to a whole population of freeholders: "A people that can live upon their own cannot spare their own and live upon another, but (except they be no servants, that is, except they come to be a democracy) they must waste their own by maintaining their masters, or by having others live upon them." Therefore, Harrington argues, no doubt with a nod in the direction of the recent restoration of the Stuarts: "Where a people that can live upon their own imagine that they can be governed by others, and not lived upon by such governors, it is not the genius of the people; it is the mistake of the people."[122] Harrington's commonwealth may thus be described as a free-state not because – as he argues elsewhere – it is a "rational" political community governed by the laws but because it is a society of independent property holders. The wide distribution of property is not a means to achieving the kind of political order in which freedom is thought to lie but is in itself the locus of liberty.

A similar view of freedom may be found in Harrington's reply in *Oceana* to Hobbes's famous assault on the republican concept of liberty. Mocking the people of Lucca for writing the word *Libertas* on the turrets of their city, Hobbes had declared that the Lucchesi were in fact no more free than the Turks, for "whether a commonwealth be monarchical or popular, the freedom is the same."[123] Harrington's response is that, while it may be true that there is the same degree of freedom "from the laws" in Constantinople as in Lucca, the difference in the degree of freedom "by the laws" in the two cities could not be greater. This is because, "whereas the greatest bashaw is a tenant, as well of his head as of his estate, at the will of his lord, the meanest Lucchese that hath land is a freeholder of both, and not to be controlled but by the law."[124] What makes the Lucchesi free is that, as the owners of the land on which they live, they are equipped with the material means to enjoy an independent existence.[125] By contrast, the Turks, lacking all property rights, are a nation dependent on the grand vizier and, as such, are no better than slaves. The issue at stake is once again not the kind of state that a popular balance makes possible but the role of property ownership in protecting one from becoming subject to the arbitrary control of another.

This alternative way of conceptualizing the relationship between freedom and property is perhaps most extensively developed in *The Prerogative of Popular Government*. Wren had objected in his *Considerations* that neither the goods of the mind nor of fortune truly constituted a "principle of government," insisting instead that these things are "at best but fair endowments of persons fit to be intrusted with a Government already settled or resolved on."[126] One man's wisdom, courage, or riches do not in themselves establish his rule over another, for "there must be something before all these in the Nature of Government, without which it will be as unjust to define Sovereignty and subjection, as it would be to oblige Mr. *Harrington* to give his cloaths or money to the next man he meets wiser or richer then himself."[127]

Harrington's reply is that, "if the people have clothes and money of their own, these must either rise (for the bulk) out of property in land, or at the least out of cultivation of the land or the revenue of industry." The critical question for Harrington is whether these goods are held dependently or independently. If the former, "they must give such part of their clothes and money, to preserve that dependence out of which the rest ariseth, to him or them upon whom they depend, as he or they shall think fit or, parting with nothing unto this end, must lose all; that is, if they be tenants, they must pay their rent or be turned out."[128] The people whose possessions are all held at the mercy of their landlord would have no power to resist his arbitrary commands but would be obliged to pay him whatever sums he demanded.

The question is not simply whether one has possessions or not but whether one is able to enjoy them securely:

> So if they have clothes and money dependently, the balance of land is in the landlord or landlords of the people; but if they have clothes and money independently, then the balance of land must of necessity be in the people themselves, in which case they neither would, if there were any such, nor can, because there be none such, give their money or clothes to such as are wiser, or richer, or stronger than themselves. So it is not a man's clothes and money, or riches, that obligeth him to acknowledge the title of his obedience unto him that is wiser or richer, but a man's no clothes nor money, or his poverty.[129]

Harrington's response to Wren is that it is not excessive wealth but excessive poverty that results in relationships of domination. So long as an individual has property and is therefore able to survive without having to rely on anybody else, there is no reason for him to become awed into submission by the other's greater riches. But where he lacks property altogether, he will find that he is wholly subject to the other's will. It is for this reason that, according to this way of setting up the argument, a people can only be free if they have property.

Although Harrington is running two different arguments about the relationship between property and freedom, they are not in tension but in fact complementary: in both cases, Harrington's claim is that there can only be freedom when property is in the hands of the people. According to the first and dominant approach, a people is free only if it is ruled by a government that is constituted in such a way as to prevent the private interest of any individual or group from undermining the common good. This can, in turn, arise only if property is in the hands of the people. The second argument is that to have property is in itself to be materially independent and therefore to be able to go about one's business without fearing that the very means of keeping body and soul together will be arbitrarily taken away.

What both ways of formulating the argument eschew is the language of self-ownership, which the theorists discussed in the previous chapters had developed as a way of defending the existing property rights of English freeholders against interference by their rulers. This enables Harrington to resolve the tension that was apparent in his predecessors' work, most notably in that of Milton, between on the one hand worrying about the dangers of excessive inequalities of wealth and on the other hand categorically rejecting any interference with existing private property on the grounds that it constituted an affront to liberty. Harrington's innovation was one that would have a lasting impact, eclipsing the notion of self-ownership for a quarter of a century.

REPUBLICAN LIBERTY IN THE RESTORATION CRISIS

This chapter focuses on two authors who demonstrate in different ways how the connection between property and liberty could be made without having recourse to the problematic and outmoded vocabulary of self-ownership. Henry Neville, an associate of Harrington's in the 1650s, appropriated the Harringtonian doctrine of the balance, adapting it to the new realities of the Restoration. Algernon Sidney returned to a mode of argument constructed around the individual and his ownership of property rather than – as in the Harringtonian model – the structure of property ownership in society as a whole. As has been often noted, Sidney's political thought had much in common with the republicanism of Milton and Nedham.[1] However, by presenting the capacity to own property as a *consequence* of freedom, rather than as constitutive of it, Sidney was also able largely to eschew the language of self-ownership.

THE REVIVAL OF THE ANCIENT CONSTITUTION

After the political and intellectual experiments of the previous twenty years, Restoration political thought, much as political practice, was concerned with turning back the clock, reviving the pre-Interregnum intellectual traditions on which the Stuarts' claim to rule had rested. Works by Matthew Hale, the earl of Clarendon, and others emphasized the divine right of kings, the role of the royal prerogative in maintaining stability, and the danger of republican ideas.[2] In the 1660s Thomas Hobbes composed *Behemoth* (published posthumously in 1681 but appearing in an unauthorized edition in 1679), a history of the Civil War whose purpose was to teach the English what had brought about the dissolution of their polity in the 1640s–

50s, thereby helping them avoid a similar calamity in future. Among the principal causes of the Civil War, according to Hobbes, was the presence of "an exceeding great number of men of the better sort" steeped from their school days in "the bookes written by famous men of the ancient Graecian and Roman Commonwealths concerning their Policy and great actions, in which the popular government was extolled by the glorious name of Liberty, and Monarchy disgraced by the name of Tyranny." This education, Hobbes contends, led the "democraticall gentlemen" to fall "in love with their formes of government," and "out of these men were chosen the greatest part of the House of Commons, or if they were not the greatest part, yet by advantage of their eloquence were always able to sway the rest."[3] It is also interesting to note in this connection Hobbes's staunch opposition to the Whigs' call to exclude the duke of York from the succession, as expressed in his 1679 reply to William Cavendish, the fourth earl of Devonshire. His argument is that, although a king has every right to disinherit his heir, he cannot be forced to do this, for "then the people is a Multitude of lawlesse men relapsed into a condition of warr of every man against every man. Which by making a King they intended to avoid."[4]

Whatever role classical republicanism had played in the Civil War, it had been all but snuffed out by the time Hobbes was writing.[5] The Licensing Act of 1662 rendered it unlawful to say things that considerations of prudence had already made virtually unsayable. The range of topics listed by the licensor Roger L'Estrange for proscription included: "All Printed Papers pressing *the Murther of the late King*" and "All Treatises Denying *His Majesties Title* to the *Crown of England*," as well as more specific theoretical propositions such as "*Coordination*, The *Sovereignty* of the *Two Houses*, or of the *House* of *Commons*."[6] Among the works that L'Estrange thought fit for suppression were Parker's *Observations* and *Jus Populi*, Nedham's *Mercurius Politicus* and *A True State of the Case of the Commonwealth*, and Milton's *The Tenure of Kings and Magistrates*. With Harrington probably suffering a nervous breakdown following his imprisonment at the hands of the new regime in 1661 and never recovering sufficiently to put his political pen to paper again, with Milton narrowly avoiding execution and retreating to poetry,[7] and with Nedham once again changing sides to embrace the cause of England's new political masters, the times were far from propitious for the ideas of property and freedom that had emerged during the political struggles of the 1640s–50s.

It was only in the late 1670s and early 1680s, when a growing number of Englishmen began to feel that the backlash had gone too far, that the ideas of the Civil War began to resurface. The catalyst here was the anxiety about the succession of the openly Catholic duke of York, which gave those in Parliament and beyond who wished to speak out against the increasingly reactionary Restoration monarchy a platform from which to do so. The connection between popery and arbitrary power was made repeatedly in the parliamentary debates of these years.[8] Ralph Montagu, addressing the House of Commons in 1680, expressed his belief that "a Bill for banishment of all the considerable Papists out of England, may be very necessary: and if at the same time that we endeavour to secure ourselves against popery, we do not also do something to prevent arbitrary power, it will be to little purpose; for the one will be sure to have a hand to bring in the other."[9] Inevitably, concerns about arbitrary power also brought into play the issue of property, as can be seen in Colonel John Birch's view that "till laws are made to begin in the next king's time, that, whoever he is, he may not be able to destroy the Protestant Religion, nor our Property, we can never be safe."[10] With still greater alarm, it was argued in the Parliament of 1680 that, if Catholicism were allowed to triumph in England, "they will burn us, and damn us. For our estates, they will take our lands, and put monks and friars upon them."[11]

The close relationship between anti-popery and political concerns is also evident in the pamphlet literature. The fear that a Catholic king would introduce arbitrary power can be seen in Elkanah Settle's *The Character of a Popish Successour*, a pamphlet written immediately before the third Exclusion Parliament of March 1681 and probably commissioned by the earl of Shaftesbury: "How is an arbitrary absolute popish tyrant any longer a lawful successor to a Protestant established and bounded government, when lawfully succeeding to this limited monarchy, he afterwards violently, unlawfully, and tyrannically overruns the due bounds of power, dissolves the whole royal constitution?"[12] Or, in the rather more succinct formulation by David Clarkson, "as soon as the Papacy is admitted, all Title and Property is lost and extinct among us."[13]

Perhaps the most interesting discussion of the implications for property of the Catholic succession can be found in Andrew Marvell's revealingly entitled 1677 tract *An Account of the Growth of Popery and Arbitrary Government in England*. Claiming that "the alteration of Religion would necessarily introduce a change of Property," Marvell argues that, if a Catholic king were allowed to ascend to the throne, there would be "no considerable Estate in England but must have a piece torn out of it upon the Title of Piety, and the rest subject to be wholly forfeited upon the account of *Heresy*":

> Another *Chimny mony* of the old *Peter pence* must again be payed, as tribute to the Pope, beside that which is established on his Majesty: and the People, instead of those moderate Tithes that are with too much difficulty payed to their Protestant Pastors, will be exposed to all the exactions of the Court of Rome, and a thousand artifices by which in former times they were used to draine away the wealth of ours more then any other Nation. So that in conclusion, there is no Englishman that hath a Soul, a Body, or an Estate to save, that Loves either God, his King, or his Country, but is by all those Tenures bound, to the best of his Power and Knowledge, to maintain the established *Protestant Religion*.[14]

For Marvell, who appears to have known something about the Treaty of Dover then being negotiated, the spectre of popery was inextricably connected with anxieties about arbitrary taxation such as those that had featured prominently in the anti-Stuart pamphlets of the 1640s. Already lamenting the levies being raised by Charles II, Marvell presents the Catholic Church as an additional court, whose aim is to suck out as much wealth from England as it can.

As Tim Harris among others has argued, the debates of the 1670s and 1680s were to a large extent framed in the language of the ancient constitution, which had been marginalized by the more radical lines of argument that had emerged over the course of the 1640s and 1650s.[15] In addition to the republication of such ancient constitutionalist works as Philip Hunton's *Treatise of Monarchy*, countless original tracts drawing on the language of the ancient constitution were penned, many of them dealing with issues of property. Sir Philip Warwick, in a tract of 1694 with the quintessentially ancient constitutionalist subtitle *True Weights and Measures Between Sovereignty and Liberty*, speaks of "the raising of money or taxes" as "one of those particulars, wherein our Monarch is limited, for he cannot raise money upon the Subject, but by his Commons, and with the consent of the Lords, or by concurrence of them both."[16] Likewise, Marvell maintained that "no money is to be levied but by the common consent. No man is for life, limb, goods, or liberty at the Soveraigns discretion: but we have the same Right (modestly understood) in our Propriety that the Prince hath in his Regality."[17]

Arguments such as these were not the preserve of the Whigs but were also voiced by their opponents, albeit with different polemical intentions. John Nalson, an Anglican minister who dedicated one of his works to the duke of York, remarked that "the Property of the *English* Subjects" is "so great and absolute" that "the extraordinary occasions of the publick cannot by Law be supplied out of their Estates, without their consent and concurrence by their Representatives in the House of Commons."[18] Even the absolutist Nathaniel Johnston, who complained that "all being now so jealous of any breach made upon their Property, that Princes are looked upon as Tyrannical and Arbitrary, that shall, for the necessary support of the Government, lay any imposition upon the People, without their consents," could celebrate the protection offered to property by the ancient constitution.[19] Explicitly rejecting Hobbes's view that "the Sovereign should be so absolute and so arbitrary, that he should upon Exigents of State, or at his own pleasure, have the disposal of every Subjects fortune," Johnston assured his readers that "we have our Properties so well secured and provided for, by the gracious Grants of our Sovereigns in *Magna Charta*, the Petition of Right, and other Acts" that all the subjects need to worry about is to "endeavour to defend, in our several capacities, the Royal Prerogatives of Kings; which as much appertain to them, and in a more transcendent way, than our Properties are ascertained unto us."[20] Whigs and Tories could thus agree that the purpose of property was to prevent the king from exceeding the power that he could legitimately exercise within the framework of the ancient constitution and thus to defend the subject's liberty. The difference between the two sides is that, whereas the Whigs made this point to proclaim the illegality of measures such as the hearth tax and warn the king against further interferences with his subjects' property, the Tories did so to urge obedience to a king who was merely seeking to uphold the ancient constitution.

Property was then widely treated in this period – much as it had been prior to the 1640s – as a component of the ancient constitution, whose purpose it was to maintain a proper equilibrium between king and subject. Yet the revival of the ancient constitution in Whig political thought did not preclude the emergence of more radical lines of thought – whether through rejection or subversive appropriation of the ancient constitution. Whereas Sidney's espousal of the neo-Roman concept of liberty was a reaction to the new prominence of the ancient constitution, Neville made extensive use of it, presenting it as an ideal that could only be salvaged by being refashioned along Harringtonian lines.

NEVILLE AND THE DOCTRINE OF THE BALANCE

Henry Neville, who had been an active figure in the politics of the Commonwealth, though somewhat marginalized during the Protectorate, had largely withdrawn from public life when he published his most significant work of political theory, *Plato Redivivus* (1681). After the Restoration he retired to his native Berkshire, but memories of his involvement in the Rota Club during the last days of the republic led to his arrest in October 1663 and imprisonment in the Tower. After being freed the following year, he went into self-imposed exile in Italy, where he remained until 1667 or 1668. He then returned to England, publishing several books, including an English translation of Machiavelli's works in 1675, but largely managing to avoid courting controversy.

Like his hero Machiavelli, Neville had never embraced the life of *otium*, and with the Exclusion Crisis he saw an opportunity to play his part in the political debates then raging by attempting to revive the Harringtonian ideas that he had espoused from the 1650s. Written in 1679–80 and published to coincide with the sitting of the Oxford Parliament in 1681, *Plato Redivivus* is a dialogue in three parts between an English Gentleman, a Noble Venetian, and a Doctor, who probably serves as Neville's mouthpiece. The Gentleman is asked by the visiting Venetian to explain how it has come about that England, which has long been esteemed as "one of the most considerable people in the world," is "now of so small regard," and is plagued by "the disunion of the people and the governors; the discontentment of the gentry, and turbulency of the commonalty."[21] This provides the occasion for a lively disquisition into the nature of political power, the causes of England's decline, and possible remedies.

So indebted is *Plato Redivivus* to Harrington's work that John Starkey, Neville's publisher, commented in his prefatory epistle on his fear that "a

considerable part of this treatise being a repetition of a great many principles and positions out of *Oceana*, the author would be discredited for borrowing from another and the sale of the book hindered" (68).[22] Such
borrowings may have been in part acts of self-plagiarism, if Hobbes's view
– as recounted by John Aubrey – that "Henry Neville had a finger in that
pie [*Oceana*]" is correct.[23] Yet there are also significant points of departure
from Harrington, not least of which is the disquisition into the origins of
property with which *Plato Redivivus* begins.[24]

Neville's discussion of property begins with a Hobbesian account of a
pre-political condition in which "every man by the first law of nature
(which is common to us and brutes) had, like beasts in a pasture, right to
everything; and there being no property, each individual, if he were the
stronger, might seize whatever any other had possessed himself of before,
which made a state of perpetual war" (85). It is to escape this condition that
"every man consented to be debarred of that universal right to all things;
and confine himself to a quiet and secure enjoyment of such a part, as
should be allotted him." Out of this division of goods arose "ownership, or
property," and it was in order to preserve this that it became "necessary to
consent to laws, and a government; to put them in execution" (85). Property
is, then, something that is artificial rather than natural or divinely instituted, and established through universal consent rather than by force or
first occupancy.

As well as being chronologically prior to government, property is logically prior to it. Drawing extensively on Harrington's doctrine of the
balance, Neville argues that property is the basis for political power. Constitutional forms are, or ought to be, determined by the distribution of
property, so that monarchy arises when an individual holds all the property
in the land, aristocracy when it is possessed by the few, and democracy when
it is in the hands of the many. Like Harrington, Neville believes that each
of these forms has a corrupt counterpart, which comes about not when rulers act in their private interest but when they rule without holding the balance of property (88–92). Politics is thus, for Neville as for Harrington, a
science that consists in preserving the stability of a state by maintaining a
correct relationship between the distribution of property and political
power. "There is," Neville believed, "no maxim more infallible and holding
in any science, than this in politics; that empire is founded in property.

Force or fraud may alter a government; but it is property that must found and eternize it" (87). This insight lies at the heart of *Plato Redivivus* and, Neville believes, holds the key to resolving the instability afflicting England.

Although, as we shall see, Neville's willingness to accept the Restoration causes him to part ways with Harrington, his republican sympathies are put in evidence early on in the work, where the English Gentleman discusses the merits of the three forms of government found in classical antiquity. Neville's use of the dialogue form is of crucial importance here since it enables him to put into the mouth of his interlocutors words that may otherwise have been too dangerous to express. The fact that the Gentleman is ostensibly discussing only classical forms of government also gives the impression of detachment, adding a further layer of protection for the author from possible recriminations. Nevertheless, we can be fairly confident that Neville shared the Gentleman's Harringtonian analysis and believed its lessons to apply also to his own time.

Monarchy is the first form of government discussed by the Gentleman. Even in its pure form, he claims, it is by definition "absolutely despotical" since it is "altogether unlimited by any laws, or any assemblies of nobility or people" (88). It is therefore meaningless to speak, as Aristotle does, of tyranny as the corruption of monarchy: "Arbitrary government cannot be called tyranny, where the whole property is in the prince, (as we reasonably suppose it to have been in those monarchies); no more than it is tyranny for you to govern your own house and estate as you please" (89). Arbitrary power is simply a fact of life when the balance is held by an individual since subjects lack the economic basis for an independent existence.

It may be, Neville points out, that those living under monarchy enjoy personal estate "in the largest portion," but this does not equate to property, for "the prince may when he pleases take away their goods by his tenants and vassals" (89–90). It is simply impossible, Neville concludes, for property to be held securely under a monarch:

> The whole possession of the country, and the whole power lies in the hands and breast of one man; he can make laws, break and repeal them when he pleases, or dispense with them in the meantime when he thinks fit; interpose in all judicatories, in behalf of his favourites; take away any particular man's personal estate, and his life too, without

the formality of a criminal process, or trial; send a dagger, or a halter
to his chief ministers, and command them to make themselves away;
and in fine, do all that his will, or his interest, suggests to him (90).

To possess the balance is to possess untrammelled arbitrary power, including the suspending and dispensing prerogatives alluded to here that were
being successfully claimed by the restored Stuarts. Monarchical rule, in
which this power is by definition held by a single person and exercised over
a whole population, is therefore incompatible with popular freedom.

Neville has little to say about aristocracy, commenting simply that this
is the constitutional form "where the better sort, (that is, the eminent and
rich men,) have the chief administration of the government" and that
"wherever there was an aristocracy, there the property, or very much of the
overbalance of it, was in the hands of the *Aristoi* or governors" (91). Democracy, "where the chief part of the sovereign power, and the exercise of
it, resides in the people," is clearly Neville's preferred form of government.
He describes how it is "much more powerful than aristocracy; because the
latter cannot arm the people, for fear they should seize upon the government" (92). In making this point, Neville is – like Harrington before him –
drawing on "the divine Machiavel," as he refers to him here, who believed
that a state can only be free, and hence capable of *grandezza*, if its people
are armed. Whereas for Machiavelli an armed and politically engaged citizenry bred healthy instability, Neville shared Harrington's ambition of creating a state that was not only expansionist but also immortal. To achieve
this, Neville envisaged a constitutional mechanism to engineer an orderly
interaction between the senate and people that would replace Machiavelli's
tumults. Characterizing this by the motto "at the command of the people,
by the authority of the senate," Neville's democratic constitution is identical
with Harrington's fictional Commonwealth of Oceana: "It does consist of
three fundamental orders; the senate proposing, the people resolving, and
the magistrates executing" (92).

If this more abstract part of Neville's work restates Harrington's theory
virtually unchanged, when Neville turns to the situation in England he
adapts the theory to take into consideration the developments that had
taken place since the Restoration. Harrington had written in support of the
English republic – albeit against its increasingly monarchical tendencies –

which he had both presented as the inevitable outcome of centuries of English history and praised for being the only kind of state in which the people could attain freedom. The Restoration was therefore a very awkward event from a Harringtonian perspective, and it may go some way towards explaining why Harrington's intellectual output dried up after 1660. Not only would Neville, who helped care for Harrington during his illness, have to navigate a world that was hostile to republics and deeply fearful of a return to the chaos of the 1640s–50s, but the fact that the monarchy had returned also posed difficulties of a more theoretical kind for proponents of Harrington's account of English history. Neville's problem was that of repackaging Harrington's theory for a world that was at first glance deeply unsympathetic to it.

NEVILLE AND THE RESTORATION MONARCHY

In spite of Neville's evident preference for the "democratic" constitution, he seemed reconciled to the Restoration; he explicitly disowned any desire for a return to republican rule, let alone to the violence that had preceded it.[25] He praised Charles II as "a gracious and good" prince, who had never "attempted to do, any the least act of arbitrary power, in any public concern," and even commended the duke of York as "a most glorious and honourable prince." That Neville had espoused republican views in the Interregnum did not necessarily make him an opponent of the current regime: "Even those (so many of them as have their understandings yet entire) which were of the anti-royal party in our late troubles," Neville assures his readers, "have all of them the greatest horror imaginable to think of doing any thing, that may bring this poor country into those dangers and uncertainties, which then did threaten our ruin" (80). Fully fledged republicanism, Neville recognized, was simply not an option in the Restoration.

Instead, Neville seeks to refashion monarchy in such a way as to make it more palatable to those with republican sympathies. To this end, he distinguishes between two kinds of monarchy: absolute and mixed or limited. Whereas all the monarchies of classical antiquity were absolute, the only absolute monarchy still in existence, according to Neville, is that of the Turks. Here alone does the prince own all the property in the realm, for

the conquered lands that were distributed to the soldiers were not hereditary and hence did not bestow property rights, as in the "Gothic" monarchies of Europe, but were "merely at will" (108).[26] The result was that
the timariots "enjoyed their shares whilst they remained the Sultan's soldiers, and no longer; being turned out both of his service, and of their ti-
mars, when he pleases" (108–9). This absolute monarchy shares with all
the ancient monarchies discussed earlier the distinction of being an entirely
arbitrary form of government, in which subjects have nothing with which
to protect themselves from the will of the king. When all property is in
the hands of an individual, arbitrariness is the natural state of affairs and
not merely a consequence of tyranny.

Neville's point in offering this account is, of course, to provide a contrast
with limited monarchy. Yet he seems curiously reluctant to condemn absolute monarchy; indeed, at one point he appears to present it as a legitimate,
in some cases even desirable, form of government. Going back to his
Harringtonian discussion of the pure and corrupt constitutional forms, he
argues that the Turkish monarchy has the significant merit of being founded
on an appropriate balance. As a result, the absolute power wielded by the
Ottoman emperor cannot be described as tyrannical, "unless you will call it
oppression for the grand seignior to feed all his people out of the product
of his own lands":

> Though they serve him for it, yet that does not alter the case; for if
> you set poor men to work and pay them for it, are you a tyrant? Or
> rather, are not you a good commonwealths-man, by helping those to
> live who have no other way of doing it but by their labour? (137)

With this striking claim, Neville appears to be challenging the central republican contention that the mere possession of arbitrary power, however
benignly deployed, in itself removes freedom. He also wilfully reverses a
commonplace association, seen for example in *Oceana*, between Turkish
rule and despotism, providing a disorienting, counter-intuitive argument.[27]

The polemical intention behind this provocative remark is, however,
not to propose that England become an absolute monarchy such as the
Ottoman Empire but to highlight the still greater flaws of the French monarchy, which Charles II was not only dependent on but increasingly seeking

to emulate. The absolutism to which the French king pretends has, by contrast with that of the Turkish emperor, no grounding in the balance, which
is popular:

> The king of France knowing that his people have, and ought to have
> property; and that he has no right to their possessions; yet takes what
> he pleases from them, without their consent, and contrary to law: so
> that when he sets them on work he pays them what he pleases, and
> that he levies out of their own estates. (137)

The consequence is that "the people are perpetually complaining, and the
king in perpetual anxiety; always in fear of his subjects, and seeking new
ways to secure himself" (137). Absolute monarchy might have some benefits
when resting on proper foundations, but the attempt to build it over a popular balance, such as existed in France and still more so in England, had no
chance of succeeding.

By contrast, mixed or limited monarchy is presented by Neville as an
ideal form of government that had once made England a great nation but
had become internally corrupted to the point of being unsustainable. As
Pocock has noted, Neville is attempting to reconcile two traditions of
thought that were on the face of it mutually exclusive: the common law
discourse of the ancient constitution and Harringtonian republicanism.[28]
In part this is achieved by blurring Harrington's distinction between the
ancient or "Gothic" constitution and the ideal Oceanic commonwealth constituted by a people debating, a senate resolving, and a magistrate executing.
Ancient constitutionalist claims about how "the people by the fundamental
laws, (that is, by the constitution of the government of England) have entire
freedom in their lives, properties, and their persons" sit alongside a Harringtonian account of the interplay between the senate and people in the
legislative process (130). The nobility's role in Neville's ancient constitution
is not to engage in a "wrestling match" with the king, as Harrington would
have it, but to carry out the function of debate, much as in the democracies
of classical antiquity:

> Our government imitates the best and most perfect commonwealths
> that ever were: where the senate assisted in the making of laws; and

by their wisdom and dexterity, polished, filed, and made ready things
for the more populous assemblies; and sometimes by their gravity and
moderation, reduced the people to a calmer state; and by their authority and credit stemmed the tide, and made the waters quiet, giving
the people time to come to themselves. (130)

Harrington had condemned the Gothic constitution as an inherently unstable form of government whose final overthrow during the Civil War
had paved the way for the return of ancient prudence, making possible
the establishment of an immortal commonwealth. For Neville, by contrast, the ancient constitution provided a model for precisely such a commonwealth.

Yet Neville is aware of the controversial nature of this account, and he
uses the dialogue form to question whether granting the king the extensive
prerogative powers entrusted to him by the ancient constitution is truly
compatible with the freedom of his subjects. The first issue debated is that
of the king's power to call Parliaments, which the Gentleman lists as one of
the vital prerogatives of the Crown. This alarms the Doctor (and, we may
conjecture, Neville as well), who tells the Gentleman that "you have made
us a very absolute prince," and wonders: "If the king have all this power,
what do our liberties or rights signify?" (121). The Gentleman seems unper-
turbed by this reply, pointing out that the king's right to choose when to
call a Parliament does not entitle him to rule indefinitely without one (122–
3). He appeals to the "common law; which is of as much value (if nor more)
than any statute, and of which all our good acts of parliament, and Magna
Charta itself, is but declaratory." The Gentleman insists, moreover, that
"though the king is entrusted with the formal part of summoning and pro-
nouncing the dissolution of parliaments, which is done by his writ; yet the
laws (which oblige him as well as us) have determined how and when he
shall do it" (124). There is, he concludes, simply no reason to fear the king's
prerogative, for "though we do allow such powers in the king; yet since they
are given him for edification and not destruction, and cannot be abused
without great danger to his ministers, and even to himself: we may hope
that they can never be abused but in a broken government" (126).

Having heard this response to the Doctor's concerns, the Venetian inter-
rogates the Gentleman on the most controversial of all the king's prerogative
powers:

I have heard much talk of the king's negative voice in parliaments; which in my opinion is as much as a power to frustrate, when he pleases, all the endeavours and labours of his people, and to prevent any good that might accrue to the kingdom by having the right to meet in parliament: for certainly, if we in Venice had placed any such prerogative in our duke, or in any of our magistracies, we could not call ourselves a free people. (128)

The Gentleman's response largely evades the issue, reiterating the ancient constitutionalist assurances about the capacity of the common law to guarantee that the king's prerogative powers would be exercised only for the common good. There is a hint of a less positive assessment of the negative voice when the Gentleman describes it as a power "to blast all without deliberating," in contrast to the two Houses' power of veto, which is but "a deliberative vote." But in the end the Gentleman restates his conviction that the institutions and traditions embodied in the ancient constitution ensure that even such an extensive arbitrary power would not undermine the subject's liberties, thereby entirely missing the republican point (129–30).

It is only when the Doctor probes the Gentleman on the Court of Chancery that the latter recognizes the need to move beyond the language of the ancient constitution and address the republican concerns being raised by his interlocutors. The Doctor, who proves himself even better schooled in republican theory than his Venetian patient, asks "whether you do not believe it a solecism in the politics to have such a court amongst a free people. What good will Magna Charta, the Petition of Right, or St Edward's laws do us to defend our property, if it must be entirely subjected to the arbitrary disposal of one man, whenever any impertinent or petulant person shall put in a bill against you?" (131). Drawing on Harrington's doctrine of the balance, the Gentleman responds by claiming that institutions such as the Court of Chancery are "but the superstructure" and therefore do not in themselves pose a danger. Rather than worrying about these, the Gentleman insists, "we must settle the foundation first. Everything else is as much out of order as this: trade is gone; suits are endless; and nothing amongst us harmonious. But all will come right when our government is mended; and never before, though our judges were all angels" (132). The problem with the English polity is not to do with the presence of institutions that permit the exercise of arbitrary power, or of unscrupulous individuals willing to make use of them to promote their own ends, but rather with the fact that the ancient constitution has been undermined by changes in the distribution of property. England's foundation no longer supports its superstructure, and its endemic instability cannot be resolved unless this issue is addressed.

The cause of this "corruption" is the transfer of land from the king and nobility to the people over the course of the fifteenth and sixteenth centuries. The Gentleman begins by arguing that "this harmonious government of England being founded as has been said upon property, it was impossible it should be shaken so long as property remained where it was placed" (132). Had the Anglo-Saxons established an agrarian law to prevent fluctuations in the distribution of property, the ancient constitution would have remained firmly in place, and the conflict of the previous half-century would have been averted. But without this mechanism, property moved away from the king and aristocracy and into the hands of the people, in a process virtually identical with the one described by Harrington in *Oceana*:

> The fortieth part of the lands which were at the beginning in the hands of the peers and church, is not there now: besides that not only all villainage is long since abolished, but the other tenures are so altered and qualified, that they signify nothing towards making the yeomanry depend upon the lords. The consequence is: that the natural part of our government, which is power, is by means of property in the hands of the people; whilst the artificial part, or parchment in which the form of government is written, remains the frame. (133–4)

To explain why a change in the distribution of property would undermine the viability of a constitution, Neville offers as an analogy the relationship between masters and servants. If you have an estate worth £5,000 or £6,000 per year, you might be able to keep forty servants. But if "at length by your neglect, and the industry and thrift of your domestics, you sell one thousand to your steward, another to your clerk of the kitchen, another to your bailiff, till all were gone: can you believe that these servants, when they had so good estates of their own, and you nothing left to give them, would continue to live with you, and to do their service as before?" (134). Property is a means to purchase dependence, and it is this alone that can support claims to sovereignty; to attempt to rule over men without the means to keep them in one's pay can only lead to instability.

English kings have, like the master in the Gentleman's example, "alienated their own inheritance." The result is that "the crown-lands, that is, the public patrimony, is come to make up the interest of the commons." In former times, when the king possessed the balance and "never asked aid of his subjects, but in time of war and invasion," he could rule in a wholly arbitrary fashion. By contrast, England's present ruler "must have a precarious revenue out of the peoples' purses; and be beholden to the parliament for his bread in time of peace" (135). Whereas the essence of a stable monarchy is that the people are dependent on the king, the situation in contemporary England, where the people possess the balance and supply the king with the material resources required for effective government, is precisely the reverse. So long as the people are the principal landowners, "this alone (though there were no other decay in government) is enough to make the king depend upon his people: which is no very good condition for a monarchy" (ibid.).[29]

THE ANCIENT CONSTITUTION IN A HARRINGTONIAN KEY

Writing during the Interregnum, Harrington believed that the Civil War had put an end to the Gothic polity, realigning the political superstructure with the foundation of property that had been forged over the course of the previous two centuries. It was therefore an epochal moment in English history that had at last made possible his ideal of the immortal commonwealth. Neville, by contrast, while recognizing that there had been a "bloody war, which in the close of it, changed the whole order and foundation of the polity of England," believed that this was but a temporary solution to a deeper problem whose effects were once again being felt: "The old government is alive again: yet it is very visible that its deadly wound is not healed; but that we are to this day tugging with the same difficulties, managing the same debates in parliament, and giving the same disgusts to the court and hopes to the country, which our ancestors did before the year 1640" (147). The Civil War, celebrated in Harrington's narrative as the first step towards a cure for England's malady, is now recast as its most visible symptom. Neville's hope was that, by offering his readers this account of the underlying causes of England's troubles, he might be able to create a viable superstructure without first having to experience the trauma of another civil war. The way to do this, he believed, was to attempt to salvage the ancient constitution.

Having focused in the Second Dialogue on the causes of England's instability, Neville turns in the Third to the question of "how all these troubles may be prevented for the future, by taking away the cause of them." The way to do this follows from the diagnosis of England's instability offered in the previous dialogue: "If you agree that our government is broken; and that it is broken, because it was founded upon property, and that foundation is now shaken: it will be obvious, that you must either bring property back to your old government, and give the king and lords their lands again; or else you must bring the government to the property, as it now stands" (152). The latter had been the purpose behind Harrington's project, not just because he had viewed property as the primary driver of history and hence not easily altered by human agency but also because of his clear preference for the popular balance. Neville also believed that it was futile to attempt to alter the balance of property, but the political solution he proposed was far less ambitious than Harrington's. The shift in property ownership did not require a fundamental overhaul of the political system and the establishment of "a commonwealth, or democracy": "Our house need not be pulled down, and a new one built; but may be very easily repaired, so that it may last many hundred years" (174). Whereas Harrington had sought to rebuild England's constitutional edifice in order to make it immortal, Neville proposes a few minor repairs to keep the rickety structure standing.

Nevertheless, Neville's solution comes across as radical when compared with the measures being contemplated by his Whig contemporaries. Neville is clear that those who believe that England's troubles could be resolved simply by excluding the duke of York from the succession have entirely missed the point. Doing so might, through "love-tricks between the prince and his people,"[30] allow for a temporary respite, but it does not constitute a permanent solution. Indeed, if the English embark upon this course, "we shall not only miss our cure; or have it deferred, till another government make it; but remain in the confusion we now suffer under; and besides that, shall be sure to feel, first or last, the calamity of a civil and foreign war" (171). What is instead required is a more fundamental change that will once and for all realign England's foundation with its superstructure.

To achieve this goal, Neville argues, there must be a significant transfer of power either to the king or to the people (172–3). We have already seen, in Neville's attack on the French monarchy, that simply placing greater power in a king lacking the balance would only make matters worse. Besides, as Neville now argues, there are certain fundamental differences between England and France that would make this impossible to achieve: "Our nation has no such poor and numerous gentry [as France], which draw better revenues from the king's purse, than they can from their own estates: all our country people consisting of rich nobility and gentry, of wealthy yeomen, and of poor younger brothers" (179). The result is that the king will never be able to use his wealth to buy an army with which to establish absolute power. If in an ideal world the group holding the balance would also hold the reins of power, Neville recognized that a range of more subtle considerations might come into play in determining whether or not it might be possible for a corrupt form to be established.

The French model was then neither desirable nor practicable. But the possibility remained of transferring property to the king so as to reverse the changes that had taken place since the start of the sixteenth century. Neville's relatively positive account of the Ottoman Empire might suggest that such a strategy would hold some appeal, but he now makes the republican claim that this solution would be incompatible with popular freedom: "The cause of all our distractions coming ... from the king's having a greater power already, than the condition of property at this present can admit without confusion and disorder, it is no like to mend matters for them to give him more; except they will deliver up to him at the same instant their possessions and right to their lands, and become naturally and politically his slaves" (175). A transfer of property from people to king might result in a legitimate form of government, but the people would then be economically dependent on their rulers and so bereft of political freedom.

Having dismissed the view that there should be a rebalancing in favour of the king, Neville finally offers his remedy, which consists in placing a power in the people commensurate with their economic standing. Whereas for Harrington this had involved the violent and complete destruction of the old order, Neville believes it can be achieved by tinkering around the edges. His solution is to create four councils to assist the king in the exercise of those prerogative powers that "now being in the crown do hinder the execution of our laws, and prevent by consequence our happiness and settlement" (185). These are the power of making war and peace, command of the armed forces, the right to nominate the officers of the kingdom, and control of the public purse – that is, the prerogative powers that had been most vociferously opposed by the Parliamentarians during the Civil War (186–7).[31] Citing the series of failed regimes that had emerged in the wake of the regicide, Neville insists that such constitutional change would have to be wrought with the king's consent, though he is confident that the king would have no choice but to agree (177–8).

The supposed transfer of power to the people in fact involves nothing more radical than giving power to a select group of councillors, who "should have no other instructions, but to dispose of all things and act in their several charges, for the interest and glory of England; and [who] shall be answerable to parliament, from time to time, for any malicious or advised misdemeanour" (187). It is highly questionable whether such a reform, which Neville describes as "rectifying an ancient monarchy" (195), is adequate to the task of resolving the fundamental problem facing England that Neville had previously outlined. What is clear is that Neville believed that the only way in which the Whigs would be able to save their cherished ideal of the ancient constitution was to approach the problem from a Harringtonian perspective, and that the only way of saving Harringtonian theory was to embrace the ancient constitution.

SIDNEY AND REPUBLICAN LIBERTY

In contrast to Neville, Algernon Sidney had no interest in defending either Harrington's theory or the ancient constitution.[32] Sidney had, like Neville, been active in the politics of the Civil War and Interregnum, having been elected to the Long Parliament in 1645 and having served on the Council of State from 1652. Also like Neville, Sidney largely withdrew from political life at the Restoration, spending most of his later years in exile, although he did become involved once again in radical politics after his return to England in 1677. In early 1683 he took part in the Rye House Plot, a botched plan to assassinate Charles II and the duke of York, for which he was tried and executed for treason.

It was during this crucial period of political engagement in 1680–83 that Sidney wrote the *Discourses concerning Government*, as the unfinished and somewhat disjointed work of republican theory would be entitled when it was posthumously published in 1698. The manuscript of this work was discovered by the authorities during Sidney's arrest in 1683 and used against him at his trial. Like John Locke's *Two Treatises of Government*, the *Discourses* was written as a response to Sir Robert Filmer's *Patriarcha*, first published in 1680 – some fifty years after its composition – and highly influential in Tory circles. Perhaps even more than *Plato Redivivus*, the *Discourses* reveals the continuing relevance of the republican literature of the Interregnum to the debates of the Exclusion Crisis. Sidney's discussion of the relationship between property and freedom in particular points to the marked influence of republicans such as Milton and Nedham, although as we shall see he diverges from them in avoiding the language of self-ownership.[33]

Sidney's account of freedom has been widely discussed in the secondary literature. However, the attempt to describe it using the familiar but anachronistic categories of negative and positive liberty has resulted in much confusion. In the first place, there is disagreement as to which of the two concepts of freedom Sidney's discussion falls into. Alan Houston believes that "in many respects Sidney's argument for individual freedom was a straightforward expression of the desire for 'negative liberty,' for an 'area within which a man can act unobstructed by others.'"[34] Paulette Carrive, by contrast, treats Sidney as wholeheartedly embracing a positive concept of liberty, although admittedly in her account this concept appears to have more to do with independence than self-mastery or self-realization.[35] If Sidney can be variously treated as a theorist of negative and positive liberty, one would be tempted to conclude that these categories ought simply to be discarded.

However, a number of scholars have instead proposed that Sidney's discussion of liberty includes elements of both. Blair Worden believes that Sidney was able to "forge a bond between the negative concept of liberty implicit in theories of natural rights and the more positive concept of liberty that is Machiavelli's."[36] Thomas West also regards Sidney as deploying both positive and negative liberty. Sidney's definition of freedom as "independency upon the will of another" is treated as though it were equivalent to "absence of external restraint," thus serving as the main textual basis for West's attempt to introduce Sidney into the canon of liberal thinkers. West's misinterpretation of this crucial passage is all the more surprising since, as we shall see, Sidney is explicit here in distinguishing between his account of freedom and the Hobbesian view that it consists merely in absence of interference.[37] Yet, alongside this supposedly negative account of freedom, West also detects a positive dimension: "Sidney alludes to a different understanding of liberty"

in which "liberty is acting in accordance with reason, not passion."[38] The precise relationship between these two aspects of Sidney's discussion of liberty
is unfortunately not spelled out.

The scholar who goes furthest in presenting Sidney as a theorist combining negative and positive freedom is Jonathan Scott.[39] Whereas West had
focused on the negative aspects of Sidney's discussion of freedom, Scott
dismisses the notion of freedom as "an 'independency from' the will of
others," which he too takes to be equivalent to non-interference, as "more
accessible to the modern mind" and hence apparently less worthy of being
discussed.[40] Scott is instead interested primarily in the supposedly positive
dimension to Sidney's conception of freedom. He describes this, in Rous-
seauian terms, as "the coercive side of liberty – that people must be made
free," claiming that "for Sidney the whole point of politics lay in the positive
potential of the state as a coercive moral instrument."[41] There is, however,
no textual evidence to support this claim. While it is true that Sidney regarded political society as necessary for lifting man out of a condition of
"fierce barbarity" and inculcating in him the virtues, nowhere does he indicate that this had anything to do with freedom.[42]

Attempts to present Sidney's theory of freedom as strictly negative or
positive, or as eccentrically combining the two, do not stand up to scrutiny.
For what Sidney presents in the *Discourses* is perhaps the clearest statement
of the neo-Roman theory to be found in seventeenth-century England.[43]
Although the *Discourses* is not a systematic treatise, having been composed
as a section-by-section response to Filmer's *Patriarcha* and left unfinished
at the author's death, the concept of liberty it espouses is coherent and consistent. Sidney is clear in distinguishing it from a Hobbesian understanding
of freedom as non-interference, insisting from the outset, in words that recall those of Locke, that "the liberty asserted is not a licentiousness of doing
what is pleasing to everyone against the command of God; but an exemp-
tion from all human laws, to which they [the people] have not given their
assent" (9).[44] Sidney's understanding of liberty is thus negative in the sense
that it is formulated in terms of an absence of something. This absence, however, is not of interference but of dependence; to be free, for Sidney, is not
to be able to go about one's business unimpeded but to be governed only
by laws to which one has consented.

In a section entitled "To depend upon the Will of a Man is Slavery," Sidney expands on this view:

> As liberty solely consists in an independency upon the will of another,
> and by the name of slave we understand a man, who can neither dis-
> pose of his person nor goods, but enjoys all at the will of his master;
> there is no such thing in nature as a slave, if those men or nations are
> not slaves, who have no other title to what they enjoy, than the grace
> of the prince, which he may revoke whensoever he pleaseth. (17)[45]

Sidney makes the crucial distinction between unimpeded action, which
even the slave may enjoy, and the possession of freedom, which consists in
not being subject to the will of another. He accepts that, as he puts it in the
title of section 10, "Such as enter into Society, must in some degree diminish
their Liberty," but his purpose in defining liberty in this way is to argue
against Hobbes that to submit to political authority is not necessarily to
renounce freedom altogether (30).[46] "It were a folly hereupon to say," Sidney
believes, "that the liberty for which we contend, is of no use to us, since we
cannot endure the solitude, barbarity, weakness, want, misery and dangers
that accompany it whilst we live alone, nor can enter into a society without
resigning it; for the choice of that society, and the liberty of framing it
according to our own wills, for our own good, is all we seek" (31). Sidney's
purpose in defining freedom as non-dependence is thus to explain why it
might be plausible to speak of certain types of political society as "free" and
others as not. The Hobbesian account of freedom as non-interference may
ultimately have eclipsed the neo-Roman theory, as Quentin Skinner has
argued.[47] But in the short term the stark simplicity of Hobbes's rival vision
helped Sidney, like Harrington before him, to articulate with greater clarity
what was distinctive about his way of thinking about freedom.

However, Sidney's principal target in the *Discourses* is not Hobbes but
Filmer, and it is accordingly the latter's discussion of freedom that receives
the most sustained treatment. Whereas Hobbes's pure negative theory of
freedom is at least accorded a certain degree of respect, Sidney pours scorn
on Filmer's claim that absolute regimes, if benign, could be conducive to –
rather than simply not undermining – liberty:

> Nothing can be more absurd than to say, that one man has an absolute
> power above law to govern according to his will, *for the people's good,*
> *and the preservation of their liberty*: For no liberty can subsist where
> there is such a power; and we have no other way of distinguishing

between free nations and such as are not so, than that the free are
governed by their own laws and magistrates according to their own
mind, and that the others either have willingly subjected themselves,
or are by force brought under the power of one or more men, to be
ruled according to his or their pleasure. The same distinction holds
in relation to particular persons. He is a free man who lives as best
pleases himself, under laws made by his own consent; and the name
of slave can belong to no man, unless to him who is either born in
the house of a master, bought, taken, subdued, or willingly gives his
ear to be nailed to the post, and subjects himself to the will of another. (440–1)[48]

The question whether an absolute ruler acts for the common good is irrelevant for Sidney: the mere presence of arbitrary power, irrespective of the
use to which it is put, is in itself incompatible with freedom. As Christopher
Hamel points out, Sidney is in this regard more radical than Locke, for
whom a degree of discretionary power in the hands of the king is conducive
to the public good.[49] While it is true that "the weight of chains, number of
stripes, hardness of labour, and other effects of a master's cruelty, may make
one servitude more miserable than another," such considerations have no
bearing on the question of the freedom of the slave: "He is a slave who
serves the best and gentlest man in the world, as well as he who serves the
worst; and he does serve him if he must obey his commands, and depends
upon his will" (441).

THE ROLE OF PROPERTY IN SIDNEY'S POLITICAL THOUGHT

It might be wondered what role ideas of property could play in this account
of liberty. If to live independently of the will of another is simply to consent
to the laws to which one is subject, property ownership would appear to
have little bearing on Sidney's understanding of freedom. Perhaps as a result, most commentators have neglected the theme of property in Sidney's
work[50] and would be likely to share Scott Nelson's view that "Sidney did
not have much to say about the role of property."[51] In fact, Sidney had a
great deal to say about it in the *Discourses*, and he was no less anxious than

his predecessors to use the neo-Roman theory to defend subjects' property rights. However, Sidney differed in that he did not present property holding as constitutive of freedom but as dependent on it. His position was that, if one was subject to an absolute ruler with the power to intervene at will in one's affairs, one's property would be liable to be taken away arbitrarily, which was as much as to say that one had no property at all. Sidney was thereby able to establish a connection between freedom and property that did not rely on the concept of self-ownership.

Sidney's interest in issues of property may have been heightened by the circumstances of his life. Born into one of the most prominent aristocratic families of his day, Sidney nevertheless spent much of the 1660s and 1670s as a relatively impoverished exile in the Low Countries and France. As several scholars have emphasized, he felt acutely the injustice of being a second son without a certain inheritance, condemned to a lifetime of dependence first upon his father, who was to die only six years before him, and then upon his elder brother.[52] He spent much of his later life quarrelling with his siblings over the terms of his father's will, desperately trying – and eventually managing – to eke out a stable existence for himself and prevent his father from, as he put it, making "his other children slaves, unto his eldest son."[53] This struggle, which after his father's death in 1677 he pursued through the very Court of Chancery against which Neville's Doctor had railed, first against his elder brother Philip and then against his younger brother Henry, is likely to have been in Sidney's mind as he came to write the *Discourses.*

Whatever the role of these biographical factors, the *Discourses* was not written to support Sidney's legal disputes with his siblings – though it would be used against him in another, more serious trial – but to mount a theoretical and polemical case against the absolutism of the restored Stuarts. Sidney's aim was to demonstrate why granting England's new rulers the arbitrary power they were seeking would result in the overthrow of property. If, according to Sidney, it was nonsensical to maintain that an absolute monarch could promote his subjects' freedom, it was equally absurd to claim that such a ruler could be a custodian of their property. Those such as Filmer who claimed that an absolutist king had the right to take his subjects' property at will had missed the point, for in such circumstances the king "has all in himself, and they have nothing that is not from him, and depending upon his will" (349).

This was, Sidney believed, precisely the predicament in which Englishmen found themselves after the judges in the ship money case had reached
the conclusion that "*in cases of necessity the king might provide it by his own
authority, and that he was judge of that necessity,*" for "if the sentence of those
perjur'd wretches had stood, the subjects of England by consequence would
have been found to have nothing to give" (349). Moreover, the English
people would not even have been able to claim that an injustice was being
committed against them since the king's monopoly would extend even to
principles of justice. Subjects would then lack the means to mount a moral
case for resisting him:

> If the lives and goods of subjects depend upon the will of the prince,
> and he in his profound wisdom preserve them only to be beneficial
> to himself, they can have no other right than what he gives, and with-
> out injustice may retain when he thinks fit: If there be no wrong, there
> can be no just revenge; and he that pretends to seek it, is not a free
> man vindicating his right, but a perverse slave rising up against his
> master. (284)

Sidney's point is that to be subject to the will of another is to be incapable
of having a property right, or even to be able to lay claim to that right. His
appeal is to resist the king's absolutist ambitions as the only way of defending property, rather than to defend property as a means of resisting the
king's absolutist ambitions.

This point is made even more forcefully later in the *Discourses*, where
Sidney argues that, just as no subject of an absolute monarch could possibly
be regarded as having an obligation to provide the king with revenues,
"neither king nor tyrant can be obliged to preserve the lands, goods and
liberties of their subjects if they have none" (402). The reason anyone subject to an arbitrary power would be bereft of property is:

> As liberty consists only in being subject to no man's will, and nothing
> denotes a slave but a dependence upon the will of another; if there be
> no other law in a kingdom than the will of a prince, there is no such
> thing as liberty. Property also is an appendage to liberty; and 'tis as
> impossible for a man to have a right to lands or goods, if he has no
> liberty, and enjoys his life only at the pleasure of another, as it is to

enjoy either when he is deprived of them. He therefore who says kings and tyrants are bound to preserve their subjects' lands, liberties, goods and lives, and yet lays for a foundation, that laws are no more than the significations of their pleasure, seeks to delude the world with words which signify nothing. (402–3)

Property rights are, for Sidney, contingent upon the possession of freedom. As Hamel has argued, this inverts the relationship between property and freedom that is to be found in Locke: whereas Locke treats property as the broad concept that encompasses liberty, for Sidney property rights arise as a result of liberty.[54] Those subject to arbitrary power might de facto be able to enjoy their land or goods, but they lack full property rights. Their estates would be granted to them at the discretion of their ruler and would be liable to be taken away arbitrarily. Just as Filmer's claim that liberty could be advanced by an absolute monarch acting for the common good is dismissed as nonsensical, so too is the view that such a ruler could secure property: both liberty and property are by definition taken away by the mere presence of arbitrary power.

Given this account of the relationship between property and liberty, it is unsurprising that Sidney should have been deeply concerned about the tendency of absolute monarchs to impoverish their subjects. While it might be theoretically possible for a regime that maintained all property in its own hands to allow its subjects to prosper, Sidney argues that it is in the interest of such a regime to keep its people poor. This point features prominently in the *Court Maxims*, a series of dialogues composed in the mid-1660s, though unpublished in the author's lifetime and unknown to scholars until their discovery by Blair Worden in the 1970s. In the Sixth Dialogue, Philalethes – the "moral, honest Courtier and lover of state truth" – explains to the "Commonwealthsman" Eunomius that "as long as the people continue strong, numerous, and rich, the king can never be happy." Eunomius's predictable objection is that rulers benefit from the prosperity of their subjects: "If rich, they will be content and quiet for fear of confiscations. But if poor and that by means of the governors, they will soon grow to furious resolutions, having little to lose."[55] Philalethes, however, believes that it is instead among a thriving population that dissension arises, for "generally all people grow proud when numerous and rich; they think themselves masters of all. The least injury puts them into a fury. But if poor,

weak, miserable, and few they will be humble and obedient. The present
sense of their wants hinders them from applying their thoughts beyond
anything but getting of bread, and their weakness keeps them quiet, abasing
their spirit."[56]

In putting these words into the mouth of a proponent of absolutist
monarchy, Sidney is making the neo-Roman point that independent property holding conduces to an independence of spirit. The republican
interlocutor, however, avoids spelling out this implication, seeking instead
to challenge the courtier on his own terms. He makes two arguments that
are especially troubling for Philalethes. The first is that, "the people being
impoverished, the king must grow poor too, having nothing but what he
has from them."[57] Philalethes accepts that such an objection could be significant, "for our principal business is to get money, and if the saving fails,
we are disappointed," but he insists that, on the contrary, "as the people's
power, number, and riches decrease, the king's power will increase." This is
because "when the people are low the king will be master of them and all
they have, and so far richer than if the people enjoyed the highest prosperity and plenty. If rich and powerful, it is impossible to keep them in awe;
the king must depend upon them, be at their discretion, have nothing but
what they will freely give him."[58] To allow the people to prosper would be
to promote their freedom to such a point as to invert the proper (according
to proponents of absolutism) relationship of dependence between the king
and his subject. The result is that the king would be rendered incapable of
imposing "illegal burdens" such as ship money, for a propertied citizenry
would include those such as John Hampden and Sir Arthur Heselrig, who
"will choose, as they did (with hazard and great expense, danger, and trou-
ble), to make a long suit against the king rather than pay each of them forty
shillings ship money."[59]

The second major objection that Philalethes faces is that the consequence
of so impoverishing the people would be to render the state incapable of defending itself from foreign conquest. Here Philalethes concedes the point.
One of the principal methods of "impoverishing and bringing the people
low" advocated by Philalethes is the destruction of trade, "for there is no
keeping a people low while that continues which increases their number,
riches, and strength."[60] But, as he points out, promoting trade has the consequence of stimulating population growth, which in turn spurs on further
trade.[61] The Hollanders, who have implemented precisely the kind of trade-

oriented foreign policy that Philalethes urges against, bear out this truth: "The greatest advantage to their state is the increase of people that they may have the more trade, and of trade that they may have the more people."[62] The upshot, as Philalethes himself argues, is that the state would be equipped with the necessary resources to achieve military glory. The Venetians "endeavour to increase trade and people, which succeeds so well as with those helps they have been able for twenty years to war with little loss against all the power of the Ottoman empire." By contrast, the duke of Florence, "following the maxims of a politic prince, has by destroying trade ruined many he suspected, forced others to change their habitation, and so weakened the spirited commonwealth's men of Florence that he reigns securely."[63] Philalethes thus appears to condemn himself even according to the absolutists' own logic, according to which one of the prime justifications of absolute power was security. Faced with the charge that, if England were reduced to the condition of Florence, it would be vulnerable to foreign conquest, Philalethes can only reply feebly that "the danger yet is far off" and "it is prudence to provide against the greatest and nearest danger, which is at home."[64]

Sidney's purpose in the *Court Maxims* was to show that even the most generous reading of the courtier's position reveals its inadequacy. In the *Discourses* Sidney was in a less charitable mood. His preoccupation was not only with the practical consequences of an impoverished population for the state but with the moral implications for individual citizens.[65] Contrasting the situation in Italy when it was "inhabited by nations governing themselves by their own will" with the present "thin, half-starv'd inhabitants of walls supported by ivy," Sidney makes the case for the dynamism generated by a prosperous citizenry. He points out, echoing his argument in the *Court Maxims*, that, while the Italians of old "had a propriety in their goods, they would not suffer the country to be invaded, since they knew they could have none if it were lost" (260). Sidney accepts that "this gave occasion to wars and tumults" but makes the Machiavellian point that it also "sharpened their courage, kept up a good discipline, and the nations that were most exercised by them, always increased in power and number" (260).[66]

Whereas in the *Court Maxims* Eunomius had criticized the policy of keeping the people poor on the grounds that it would make the state prone to foreign invasion, here Sidney emphasizes its consequences for the well-being of individuals. It may be true that the "fatherly care" of Italy's various monarchical rulers has established peace among the Italian states, but it has resulted in such depravity that "their sleep is only interrupted by hunger, the cries of their children, or the howling of wolves" (260), perhaps an ironic reference to Hobbes's view that the security offered by Leviathan is the sole remedy for the natural tendency of man to be *homini lupus*. Bustling cities have been replaced by "a few scatter'd silent cottages; and the fierceness of those nations is so temper'd, that every rascally collector of taxes extorts without fear from every man, that which should be the nourishment of his family" (260). The people are so impoverished, in other words, that they are not even able to make a stand to defend their property, in the way that men such as Hampden and Heselrig did in England. In such a situation, the only way of keeping the tax collector at bay is to make the people so destitute as to have nothing left to give.

However, in the *Discourses* Sidney is no less anxious to criticize an alternative strategy of absolute monarchs: that of enabling subjects to enjoy a degree of wealth merely in order to maximize their own power. As we have seen, Sidney believed that to be subject to the will of another is to be incapable of property. In the absence of independence, subjects' possessions are ultimately the property of their rulers; rather than grounding their freedom, they merely increase their value as a form of property. In making this argument, Sidney is challenging Filmer's view that the people stand to benefit from living under an absolute monarch, who will promote "*multitude of people and abundance of riches*," something that should be commended, even if it is carried out "*not out of affection to his people, yet out of natural love unto himself*" (267). Much as freedom cannot be advanced by arbitrary power, however benignly employed, nor can property be defended by it.

Absolute rulers "consider nations, as grazers do their herds and flocks, according to the profit that can be made of them: and if this be so, a people has no more security under a prince, than a herd or flock under their master" (267–8). Whereas rulers should act for the good of the people, "our author teaches us, that they only seek what they can make of our bodies and goods, and that they do not live and reign for us, but for themselves." The implication is that "they look upon us not as children, but as beasts, nor do us any good for our own sakes, or because it is their duty, but only that we may be useful to them, as oxen are put into plentiful pastures that they may be strong for labour, or fit for slaughter" (268). The important issue for Sidney in the end is not whether individuals are impoverished or allowed to prosper but whether they live independently of the arbitrary will of their rulers; if they do not, full property rights become impossible and individuals' economic condition is determined solely by their rulers' interest.

Nevertheless, Sidney does hint at a theme that, as we saw in chapter 3, was central to the republican literature of the 1650s: the danger of luxury.[67] Even when wealth is held independently – and hence does not serve merely to fatten its possessor for the abattoir – there is the risk that its corrupting influence will undermine freedom. Sidney draws a contrast between riches and virtue, claiming that states that promote virtue will see a decline in a concern with riches: "In well-govern'd states, where a value is put upon virtue, and no one honoured unless for such qualities as are beneficial to the publick," Sidney argues, "virtue itself becomes popular, as in Sparta, Rome, and other places, where riches (which with the vanity that follows them, and the honors men give to them, are the root of all evil) were either totally banished, or little regarded" (253). Whereas elsewhere Sidney describes poverty as an instrument of subjugation, here he speaks of it as "the mother and nurse" of virtue. But his worry is not so much that luxury will lead to a corruption of manners – as with Milton – but that it will corrupt the institutional mechanisms of the state: "When vanity, luxury and prodigality are in fashion, the desire of riches must necessarily increase in proportion to them" (255).

The danger, for Sidney, is that this will turn political power into a commodity to be bought and sold on the market. Power will then be "in the hands of base mercenary persons," who will "make as much profit of their place as they can," with the result that "not only matters of favour, but of justice too, will be exposed to sale; and no way will be open to honours or magistracies, but by paying largely for them." There will then be a vicious circle in which those who have used their wealth to purchase power will deploy their power to amass ever greater wealth, for "he that gets an office by these means, will not execute it *gratis*: he thinks he may sell what he has bought; and would not have entered by corrupt ways, if he had not intended to deal corruptly" (255).

This preoccupation with luxury suggests that Sidney might have looked favourably on the kinds of redistributive measures that had been advocated by Harrington. The fact that he avoided the language of self-ownership meant that supporting such policies would have been less problematic for him than it had been for Milton. Yet nowhere did Sidney make any pronouncements that suggest that he was any less committed to defending existing property rights than those theorists of the 1640s–50s who had invoked the concept of self-ownership. Rejecting this concept was not in itself evidence of a shift in attitude towards agrarian laws, and Harrington's support for them appears not to have made them any less controversial. Indeed, their association with his name may have made it even more dangerous to advocate them after the Restoration. But what Harrington appears to have succeeded in achieving, whether directly as in the case of Neville or indirectly as in the case of Sidney, is banishing the notion of self-ownership from discussions of freedom and property. As we shall see in the next chapter, however, this victory would prove to be short-lived.

6

Locke's *Two Treatises of*
Government and the Revival
of Self-Ownership

John Locke wrote the *Two Treatises of Government* not, as was once believed, as a vindication of the Glorious Revolution but to provide ideological ammunition to the Whigs during the Exclusion Crisis.[1] To that end, he put forward in the *Two Treatises* a radical argument according to which all legitimate power originated in the consent of the people, who reserved the right to overthrow their rulers when they acted in breach of their trust.

Locke came to radical politics somewhat late in life. Born in 1632 and educated at Westminster School and Christ Church, Oxford, he spent the first part of his adult life as a conservative, even reactionary, Oxford don. His correspondence from the later 1650s reveals a profound sense of disillusionment with the republican experiment then in progress, and he duly welcomed Charles II's return with a poem in a university collection, *Britannia Rediviva* (1660).[2] His early forays into political thought were deeply conservative works, written in support of the restored monarchy and Anglican Church, and emphasizing the duty of subjects to obey the commands of the sovereign, even where these were unjust.[3]

The turning point in Locke's life came in 1666 when a chance encounter with Sir Anthony Ashley Cooper, the future first earl of Shaftesbury, led to an intimate relationship that would eventually thrust Locke into the centre of Whig politics. Locke entered Cooper's household in London in 1667 as his personal physician, remaining there until the latter's fall from grace in 1675. Soon after his arrival in London, Locke wrote the *Essay on Toleration*, which moderated his earlier hardline position. He then spent several years in France, where he made substantial progress on his magnum opus, *An Essay concerning Human Understanding* (begun in 1671, largely completed by 1686 and published in 1689). Returning to England in 1679, Locke once

again became associated with Shaftesbury – as he had by then become –
and it was probably at Shaftesbury's prompting that he composed the *Two
Treatises* as a defence of the Whigs' struggle against the restored Stuarts.

We are given an insight into Locke's intentions in the *Two Treatises* by
his inclusion of an extract from Book IX of Livy's *History of Rome* on the
title page of the 1698 edition. In this passage Livy appeals to the gods to defend the weak from the pride of the mighty, who are "not content with
their own, or with that of others" and "are not to be placated unless we
yield to them our blood to drink and entrails to tear out."[4] This passage
should be read not only as a general attack on the greed of the powerful
and their exploitation of the weak but, more specifically, as an attempt by
Locke to align himself with the Roman republican tradition associated
with Livy. Moreover, it alerts us in a particularly graphic way to an idea
central to Locke's theory of property and his political thought more generally: self-ownership.[5] It describes how the powerful have their eye not
only on their subjects' goods but also on their bodies, treating them as a
kind of property and thus denying them a property in their own persons.
As we shall see, this concept, all but forgotten following Harrington's interventions in the 1650s, is at the very centre of Locke's political theory.

In appropriating this concept, Locke was tapping into the English debates
of the 1640s–50s and attempting to provide a solution to the theoretical
problems faced by his predecessors. Like them, Locke used self-ownership
to mount a defence of existing property rights by presenting any interference with them as an affront to one's ownership of oneself and therefore
of one's freedom. As we have seen, Locke's precursors often failed to spell
out why interference with one's property in external goods necessarily undermined one's property in oneself. Locke sought to explain the connection
between the two through a conjectural history in which private property
was presented as deriving from naturally free individuals' ownership of their
persons. His purpose in doing so was to place on a firmer theoretical foundation the claim made by an earlier generation of anti-absolutist thinkers
that a free political society is one whose citizens are property holders.

Locke's theory of property has received considerable attention in the secondary literature, particularly since the publication of James Tully's seminal
work *A Discourse on Property: John Locke and His Adversaries*. However,
no detailed study of Locke's theory of property has situated it within the
context of the English debates discussed in this book.[6] The context that is

generally thought to supply the questions Locke was addressing in chapter 5 of the *Two Treatises* is the natural law tradition and, in particular, Hugo Grotius's and Samuel Pufendorf's disquisitions into the origins of private property.[7] There is no doubt that Locke, whose library included works by both authors, was deeply influenced by them.[8] Part of his purpose in chapter 5 was to offer an explanation for the transition from communal to private property that was immune to Sir Robert Filmer's critique of Grotius and thus resisted the former's conclusion that the only plausible basis for a system of private property was God's donation of the earth to Adam and his heirs.[9]

However, Locke intervened in this debate not merely out of a narrow preoccupation with the philosophical or historical origins of private property but because of the broader implications of this issue for his political theory. Scholars have typically treated Locke's discussion of property in chapter 5 as a self-standing theory designed merely to justify the institution of property as it existed in Locke's own day. Yet the chapter occupies a pivotal place in the *Two Treatises*, serving as a bridge between Locke's discussion of the state of nature and civil society, and explaining the connection between the natural freedom that men relinquished in submitting to government and the political freedom that Locke believed they continued to enjoy in a justly constituted political society. As such, Locke moved beyond the concerns of the natural lawyers and engaged with the problem of the relationship between property and liberty that was a central preoccupation of the authors discussed in this book.

LOCKE AND REPUBLICAN LIBERTY

Locke's status as one of the most influential theorists of liberty in the anglophone tradition is almost universally accepted. Yet what exactly liberty meant for Locke is a question that continues to elicit scholarly controversy. The tendency to regard Locke as the intellectual father of liberalism has led many commentators to assume that what he meant by liberty is what subsequent liberals have meant by it – namely, the absence of interference. In his essay "Two Concepts of Liberty" Isaiah Berlin groups Locke with John Stuart Mill and Adam Smith as a theorist of negative freedom concerned with "reserving a large area for private life over which neither the state nor any other authority must be allowed to trespass."[10] Likewise, for John Marshall, "the primary expression of this liberty in the *Two Treatises* was the type of liberty now classically known as negative, the freedom to follow the promptings of one's own will and not to be forced by other men to follow their will."[11]

These attempts to present Locke as a pure negative theorist of freedom are problematic, as even Berlin recognized. One passage in particular has led several commentators to question this reading and even to suggest that Locke espoused a positive concept of freedom. This is the passage in which Locke contends that "*Law*, in its true Notion, is not so much the Limitation as *the direction of a free and intelligent Agent* to his proper Interest," and that it "ill deserves the Name of Confinement which hedges us in only from Bogs and Precipices. So that, however it may be mistaken, *the end of Law* is not to abolish or restrain, but *to preserve and enlarge Freedom*" (305–6). Freedom appears in this passage to be defined not as an absence of something but as a condition enhanced by the guiding spirit of the law. Moreover, because Locke is seeking to justify his view that children, born "ignorant and without the use of *Reason*," are not "presently *free*" (305), there appears to be a connection between rationality and freedom, a central feature of many positive theories of freedom. For Berlin, this passage shows that Locke, in spite of being at heart a theorist of negative freedom, could also think of freedom in positive terms as "self-mastery, the elimination of obstacles to my will, whatever these obstacles may be – the resistance of nature, of my ungoverned passions, of irrational institutions, of the opposing wills or behaviour of others."[12]

Whereas Berlin left unexplained the relationship between these two aspects of Locke's discussion of freedom, several other scholars have presented Locke as combining positive and negative freedom into a holistic theory. According to Peter Laslett:

> Locke's theory of freedom is not merely absence of restraint, it is positive. It is something which is enlarged by the creation of society and government, which is given substance by the existence of laws, the laws of the law courts. It can be negatively defined, therefore, as being under no other legislative power but that established by consent in the commonwealth, and positively as the progressive elimination of the arbitrary from political and social regulation.[13]

Nancy Hirschmann also regards Locke as offering a "dual theory of freedom" that, inflected by views about class and gender, combines elements of positive and negative liberty.[14] Other commentators have gone further still, presenting Locke as a theorist of positive freedom through and through. Tully, for example, believes that "Locke's positive concept of law enables him to develop a positive concept of liberty."[15]

A far simpler reading is possible if we are willing to do away with the anachronistic categories of positive and negative freedom, and recognize the republican character of Locke's discussion of liberty.[16] Locke's argument in the passage quoted above is not that freedom is self-realization according to a normative account of human nature that is promoted by law but, rather, that laws create the space for man "to dispose, and order, as he lists, his Person, Actions, Possessions, and his whole Property" (306), without the arbitrary interference of another. It is true that Locke regards rationality as a necessary condition for freedom – a point we shall return to – but this is nothing more than the basic intellectual ability necessary for attaining legal personality that all adults (except "lunatics," "idiots," and "madmen") possess.

Such an interpretation has been avoided not only by liberals wishing to appropriate Locke as one of their own but also by contemporary republican theorists.[17] Their ambition to offer republicanism as an alternative to liberalism has made them reluctant to identify the neo-Roman concept of liberty in a figure as central to the liberal tradition as Locke, who is confined to a footnote in Quentin Skinner's *Liberty before Liberalism*[18] and given scarcely greater prominence in Philip Pettit's *Republicanism: A Theory of Freedom and Government*.[19] Yet the reluctance of modern scholars to appreciate Locke's republicanism was not shared by his earlier readers. Writing in 1781, Josiah Tucker no doubt thought he was making an uncontroversial point when he listed Locke alongside Andrew Fletcher and Jean-Jacques Rousseau as one of "the most eminent Republican Writers."[20] Locke's influence on subsequent liberal theorists should not prevent us from recognizing that, although he was certainly not a republican in the strict sense, his political thought shared a great deal with, and emerged from the same intellectual traditions as, the writers discussed earlier in this book.

Locke defines freedom at the beginning of chapter 4 of the Second Treatise, whose title – "Of Slavery" – is itself indicative of his republican preoccupations:

The *Natural Liberty* of Man is to be free from any Superior Power on Earth, and not to be under the Will or Legislative Authority of Man, but to have only the Law of Nature for his Rule. The *Liberty of Man, in Society*, is to be under no other Legislative Power, but that established, by consent, in the Common-wealth, nor under the Dominion of any Will, or Restraint of any Law, but what the Legislative shall enact, according to the Trust put in it. (283)

Although Locke appears to be offering two definitions of liberty – one for the state of nature, the other for political society – they are in fact two sides of the same coin.[21] In both cases, freedom is understood in terms of not being subject to the "will" of another man. In the state of nature this includes any "Legislative Authority of Man," such a thing being by definition absent prior to the establishment of political society, although Locke does recognize the right of individuals to use force to punish transgressions against the law of nature (271–2). It is wrong to see even this kind of freedom as "negative" in the Hobbesian sense, for it consists not in the performance of actions without interference but in not being subject to arbitrary power. Certainly such a *"State of perfect Freedom"* gives men the right, as Locke puts it in an earlier chapter, "to order their Actions, and dispose of their Possessions, and Persons as they think fit," but what is crucial for Locke is that they should be able to do this "without asking leave, or depending upon the Will of any other Man" (269).

When we renounce the state of nature in order to set up political society, Locke accepts that with it we must give up this perfect freedom. Yet liberty is still possible, provided that political society is set up according to certain criteria. What he wishes to resist is the Hobbesian argument that, since freedom is simply absence of interference, to submit to political authority is always to lose one's freedom, or at least to lose one's freedom with respect to those actions that are prohibited or commanded by law. It is true that Locke has to offer a slightly different formulation of his concept of freedom in order to make it compatible with the obligations of political society, but the essential structure of the concept is the same since in both cases what is viewed as taking away freedom is arbitrary power.[22]

What Locke needs to explain, then, is why certain kinds of political authority undermine freedom whereas others do not, why the "restraint" of the law might in some cases result in relationships of dependence, while in others it "hedges us in only from Bogs and Precipices." Locke's answer, already indicated by the idea that political freedom consists in being subject only to those laws passed "according to the Trust" placed in the legislative authority, is at first glance the conventional neo-Roman one: *"Freedom of Men under Government,* is, to have a standing Rule to live by, common to every one of that Society, and made by the Legislative Power erected in it; A Liberty to follow my own Will in all things, where the Rule prescribes not; and not to be subject to the inconstant, uncertain, unknown, Arbitrary Will of another Man" (284). The crucial point for Locke is that the laws to which one is subject should not be the mere dictates of individuals but should be passed by a legislative authority "which the publick has chosen and appointed" (356). Insofar as the legislative assembly is treated as an expression of the will of society as a whole, Locke can define political freedom, no less than natural, as the condition of not being "subject to the arbitrary Will of another, but freely to follow his own" (306).[23]

However, this way of setting up the argument raises the question of what it means in practice to say that the legislative assembly was established with the consent of society. It does not mean, as it had done for the Levellers, that this body ought to be elected by every individual subject to its laws, for Locke is largely uninterested in the question of the franchise.[24] Indeed, Locke has little to say at all about the nature or composition of Parliament.[25] To consent to law, according to Locke, does not mean to elect one's representatives but – more abstractly – to consent to the original establishment of political society. As Locke recognizes, this way of setting up the argument is deeply problematic since none of Locke's contemporaries was alive when society was established, and hence they were evidently not in a position to give or withhold consent.

Locke turns to this problem in chapter 8 of the Second Treatise, where, after repeating his view that *"Every Man* being, as has been shewed, *naturally free,* and nothing being able to put him into subjection to any Earthly Power, but only his own Consent," he raises the question of "what shall be understood to be a *sufficient Declaration of* a Mans *Consent, to make him subject* to the Laws of any Government" (347). Locke's answer is that there are two ways in which one can give one's consent – express and tacit:

> No body doubts but an *express Consent,* of any Man, entring into any Society, makes him a perfect Member of that Society, a Subject of that

Government. The difficulty is, what ought to be look'd upon as a *tacit Consent*, and how far it binds, *i.e.* how far any one shall be looked on to have consented, and thereby submitted to any Government, where he has made no Expression of it at all. (347–8)

It is at this point in his argument that Locke introduces the issue of property: "Every Man, that hath any Possession, or Enjoyment, of any part of the Dominions of any Government, doth thereby give his *tacit Consent*, and is as far forth obliged to Obedience to the Laws of that Government, during the Enjoyment, as any one under it" (348). Property occupies a central position in Locke's thought because, as the means by which men are able to consent to society, it grounds his concept of political liberty.

Locke proceeds to suggest that property includes, in addition to estates, "a Lodging only for a Week," "travelling freely on the Highway," and even "the very being of any one within the Territories of that Government" (348). For Ellen Meiksins Wood, this shows that Locke's aim is to make consent the source of obligation without introducing the Leveller principle that even those lacking private property ought to be enfranchised since all that is required of them is to give their tacit consent by inhabiting a territory.[26] Yet if this were Locke's intention, it would seem strange to introduce this idea with the claim that consent is given by owning property, and indeed Locke only offers this expansive idea of consent on this occasion. Elsewhere he is explicit that simply living in a territory cannot be sufficient: "Submitting to the Laws of any Country, living quietly, and enjoying Priviledges and Protection under them, *makes not a Man a Member of that Society*: This is only a local Protection and Homage due to, and from all those, who, not being in a state of War, come within the Territories belonging to any Government, to all parts whereof the force of its Law extends" (349). If everybody living in a territory could be taken ipso facto to have consented, the distinction between arbitrary and non-arbitrary power would break down, and with it Locke's understanding of political liberty. We can therefore only make sense of Locke's notion of tacit consent if we take him to be referring to property in the narrower sense.

The reason holding property has this crucial function in Locke's theory is that "every Man, when he, at first, incorporates himself into any Commonwealth, he, by his uniting himself thereunto, annexed also, and submits to the Community those Possessions, which he has, or shall acquire, that do not already belong to any other Government" (348). Property is something that man acquires while still in the state of nature and that political society is set up to safeguard. As a result, property ownership is treated as the means by which subsequent generations share in the original act of establishing political society carried out by their ancestors, according to which naturally free, property-owning agents agreed to establish a political community and submit themselves and their property to its jurisdiction. The upshot is that to interfere with individuals' property is to take away their consent and thus to deprive them of liberty.

SELF-OWNERSHIP AND NATURAL LIBERTY

At the most basic level, Locke believed that property is not something that man has but something that he is. The state of nature is a *"State of Liberty"* in which man has an "uncontroleable Liberty, to dispose of his Person or Possessions" but not a *"State of Licence,"* for he lacks the "Liberty to destroy himself, or so much as any Creature in his Possession" (270–1). The reason the state of nature does not include the power gratuitously to destroy oneself is that "Men being all the Workmanship of one Omnipotent, and infinitely wise Maker; All the Servants of one Sovereign Master, sent into the World by his order and about his business, they are his Property, whose Workmanship they are" (271).[27] If, as Waldron contends, Locke's theological premises underpin his views about human equality,[28] they also ground his conception of natural liberty, these being the two fundamental characteristics of Locke's state of nature (269). For to argue that men are born the property of God is to claim that no man is born the property of another and that therefore "there cannot be supposed any such *Subordination* among us" (271) as Filmer had maintained when he argued that *"Men are born in subjection to their Parents,* and therefore cannot be free" (144).[29]

Accepting such a position and combining it with Filmer's view that the king, as the direct descendant of Adam, is the father of the entire human race would lead to the conclusion that there existed

a Divine unalterable Right of Sovereignty, whereby a Father or a Prince hath an Absolute, Arbitrary, Unlimited, and Unlimitable Power, over the Lives, Liberties, and Estates of his Children and Subjects; so

that he may take or alienate their Estates, sell, castrate, or use their
Persons as he pleases, they being all his Slaves, and he Lord or Proprietor of every Thing, and his unbounded Will their Law. (148)

In insisting that men are born the property of God, Locke is challenging
the view that any human being could by right of fatherhood, whether bio-
logical or in Filmer's extended sense, acquire a property right over another.
In other words, the right of fatherhood could not serve as the basis for the
institution of slavery or arbitrary power.

Locke also wishes to resist the view that God's donation of the earth to
Adam, as described in the Book of Genesis, constitutes a grant of sovereignty.
It is to this issue that Locke turns in chapter 4 of the First Treatise, where
he offers two further critiques of Filmer's position. The first is that, "whatever God gave by the words of this Grant, I *Gen*. 28. it was not to *Adam* in
particular, exclusive of all other Men: whatever *Dominion* he had thereby,
it was not a *Private Dominion*, but a Dominion in common with the rest of
Mankind" (161). Drawing on ideas of natural community in Grotius and
Pufendorf, Locke claims here that God's original grant of "dominion"
cannot be taken to bestow any particular rights on an individual or group
without also bestowing them on the community as a whole. It cannot therefore serve as the foundation of natural monarchy.

Second, Locke argues, even if it were true that the original grant was made
to Adam alone, that would not give him *political* power over men. Whereas
Filmer had conflated property with sovereignty by speaking of "dominion,"
an ambiguous term in which ideas of property and political power overlap,[30]
Locke is clear that that the two concepts must be kept apart:

> But yet, if after all, any one will needs have it so, that by this Donation
> of God, *Adam* was made sole Proprietor of the whole Earth, what will
> this be to his Soveraignty? And how will it appear, that *Property* in
> Land gives a Man Power over the Life of another? Or how will the Pos-
> session even of the whole Earth, give any one a Soveraign Arbitrary
> Authority over the Persons of Men? (169)[31]

The property that God grants mankind is a property over the material resources of the world, a property that is originally held in common; it is not
a property of one man over his fellow men and, as such, has nothing to do
with sovereignty.

The state of natural freedom is not quite the condition of complete liberty that characterizes Hobbes's state of nature. Being the property of God makes us perfectly free in relation to other men but imposes certain restrictions on us in relation to our Maker. Yet there is a second aspect of natural freedom that emphasizes not man's dependence on God but his self-ownership. We find this idea in chapter 5 of the Second Treatise, where Locke begins his account of the origin of private property with the assertion that "every Man has a *Property* in his own *Person*. This no Body has any Right to but himself" (287). Men are understood to be free from other men not because of a prior claim on the part of God but because they are themselves their own masters: there is a sphere over which they have ownership and with which nobody else can interfere.

This argument appears to raise a problem in Locke's theory, for if men are the property of God, how can they be themselves the proprietors of their persons? God and man seem to hold rival claims to property, something that some scholars have presented as an inconsistency in Locke's thought.[32] If, as David Armitage suggests, chapter 5 was written later than the rest of the *Two Treatises*, this might explain Locke's failure to spell out the relationship between these two apparently contrasting claims.[33] It is illustrative in this connection to turn to the *Essay concerning Human Understanding*. As Tully points out, there is a distinction between the object of which God is the proprietor ("we") and that in which we ourselves have a property (our "person").[34] This latter term, never properly delineated in the *Two Treatises*, is defined in the *Essay concerning Human Understanding* as "a Forensick Term appropriating Actions and their Merit; and so belongs only to intelligent Agents capable of a Law, and Happiness and Misery."[35] One's "person" is then not coterminous with one's whole being; it is instead that part of oneself that makes one capable of being held legally responsible for one's actions.[36] Reason plays a crucial role here since it is through possessing a rational faculty that men are able to become, or create, persons – entities connected to their bodies but morally distinct from them and subject to ownership by themselves rather than by God.[37] Locke is clear that those such as children and the insane, lacking full rationality, are not proprietors of their person and thus not capable of liberty.

There are, then, two dimensions to Locke's understanding of natural freedom. It is, first, the condition of being the property of God and therefore not of anyone else; and, second, of being the proprietor of one's person. The question we must next turn to is what compels men to renounce the condition of natural liberty and "joyn and unite into a Community" (331). Locke's argument does not rely, as does Hobbes's, on a bleak account of the state of nature as a state of war. The latter is an entirely distinct condition in Locke's theory and is dealt with in a separate chapter: occurring in civil society as well as in the state of nature, it arises when force is exercised by one man upon another unjustly, that is, not for the purpose of enforcing natural law (280). In theory at least, the state of nature could be peaceful and lawful, a far cry from Hobbes's *bellum omnium contra omnes*. In order to understand why men renounce the state of nature in order to establish political society, and why living in such a society is nevertheless compatible with freedom, we must consider Locke's account of the origins of private property.

FROM PROPERTY IN THE PERSON TO PRIVATE PROPERTY

Although the Lockean compact does not require the absolute submission to the sovereign demanded by Hobbes's theory, Locke's relatively positive depiction of the state of nature means that it is not immediately obvious, as it is in Hobbes, why men should want to give it up. Locke appears to resolve this problem when he stresses the great "Inconveniences" that exist in the state of nature, "where Men may be Judges in their own Case" (276).[38] The right that men have not only to determine for themselves whether their actions are consistent with natural law but also to judge whether others are in breach of it and to "punish the transgressors of that Law to such a Degree, as may hinder its Violation" (271) suggests that Locke's state of nature, if not necessarily a state of war, has the potential to descend into one. Men may not be fundamentally egotistical, as Hobbes believed, but Locke is sufficiently realistic to recognize that they could not be trusted to apply the law of nature with impartiality when their own interests were at stake.

However, these "inconveniences" are not intrinsic to man's natural condition; they arise, rather, as a result of two developments that take place in the state of nature. The first is the creation of private property, which Locke describes as deriving from the individual's ownership of his person; the second is the invention of money. It is, Locke believes, "by being Master of himself, and *Proprietor of his own Person*, and the Actions or *Labour* of it" that man has "in himself *the great Foundation of Property*" (298) in external goods. The capacity for labour appears to be inextricably linked in Locke's mind to personhood: it is a constitutive element of our person, perhaps even its defining feature, and as such it is something that we own. By labouring on a natural resource, we mix into it something of our own person and thereby acquire a property right in it. Whatever one "removes out of the State that Nature hath provided, and left it in, he hath mixed his *Labour* with, and joyned to it something that is his own, and thereby makes it his *Property*" (288).[39] This principle applies also, Locke claims, to "the *Earth it self*": "*As much Land* as a Man Tills, Plants, Improves, Cultivates, and can use the Product of, so much is his *Property*" (290).

This theory of appropriation offered an alternative to the view of natural law theorists such as Grotius and Pufendorf that private property was established through consent, an argument that – as Armitage has shown – Locke shared until as late as 1677–78.[40] Locke's reasons for rejecting this account in the *Two Treatises* are twofold. He was in the first place anxious to make as strong a case as possible for the original community of goods since this was one of the foundations of his critique of Filmerian patriarchalism. He agreed with Filmer's critique of Grotius's position, arguing that, "if such a consent as that was necessary, Man had starved, notwithstanding the Plenty God had given him" (288). In order to explain how a system of private property could emerge from the original community of goods, and thus resist Filmer's claim that the world was donated to Adam, he had to provide a theory that did not suffer the pitfalls of Grotius's argument. Second, he sought to offer an account of the origins of property that would enable him to explain, in a way that the theorists discussed in the previous chapters failed to do, precisely why arbitrary interference with private property necessarily undermined self-ownership and was hence incompatible with liberty.

Taken on its own, the claim that we acquire a property over something that we do not own simply by mixing into it something that we do is not terribly convincing. For Robert Nozick, its absurd implication is that, if we were to mix a can of tomato juice that we owned into the sea, we would acquire a property right in the sea rather than having wasted our juice.[41] Even leaving aside the problematic suggestion that a non-physical entity such as labour could be combined in any meaningful sense with a material good, the notion that we might acquire a property right in the whole of the mixture is, Nozick believes, patently nonsensical.

Several scholars, anxious to salvage Locke's theory of property, have been tempted to dismiss the "mixing" argument and instead focus on apparently separate lines of reasoning. One approach has been to regard the property right acquired by labouring on an object as deriving from the value added by this activity.[42] Locke seems to be thinking along these lines when he stresses that "the *Property of labour*" outweighs the "Community of Land" since it "*puts the difference of value* on every thing" (296).[43] He develops this point by contrasting the productivity of the land in America with that in England, claiming that "in the wild woods and uncultivated wast of America left to Nature, without any improvement, tillage or husbandry, a thousand acres will yield the needy and wretched inhabitants as many conveniences of life as ten acres of equally fertile land doe in Devonshire where they are well cultivated" (294).[44] According to this interpretation, the idea of mixing labour should not be given too much weight: it is at best a device for describing the way in which we add value to goods.

Another influential interpretation, put forward by Tully among others, is that labouring is a creative activity in which we are not so much mixing ourselves with an existing object as bringing into being a new one or, to be more precise, transforming a resource so that it becomes useful for the preservation of life. As such, we acquire a "maker's right" in this new object akin to the right that Locke regards God as having in his own creation.[45] Locke views labour as a duty that man owes to God, deriving from his wish that his creation should not perish uselessly.[46] Because labour is sanctioned – indeed *required* – by natural law, it is regarded as a pre-eminently rational activity.[47] The property right that one acquires in an object thus derives from the uniquely rational quality of labour and the way in which it alters the quality of an object by bringing it into conformity with God's plan for the world:

> God gave the World to Men in Common; but since he gave it them for their benefit, and the greatest Conveniences of Life they were capable to draw from it, it cannot be supposed he meant it should always remain in common and uncultivated. He gave it to the use of the Industrious and Rational, (and *Labour* was to be *his Title* to it;). (291)

The mere activity of labouring, if divorced from this rational pursuit – that is, if it is not carried out with the intention of preserving God's creation – would not be capable of generating property rights.

Any interpretation of Locke's theory of property must take these dimensions into account: simply mixing something one owns with something one does not would fail to create a property right if it lacked a basis in natural law, as in the case of Nozick's spilling of his tomato juice into the sea. But what this approach fails to explain is why labouring should necessarily entitle us to the ownership of the product of our own labour rather than to some other manifestation of divine favour – for example, a property right in the fruits of other people's labour. For Lawrence Becker, what is crucial is that natural resources are of no *use* until they are appropriated through labouring on them; one would therefore only invest such effort if one expected to reap the rewards. It would be an injustice for somebody to gain the benefits of another's labour, though Becker's conclusion is that this cannot create a specific right to the object in question but a more general right to a benefit as a reward for one's efforts.[48]

This conclusion seems, however, to fly in the face of Locke's basic purpose in chapter 5, namely, to explain how property rights are generated by labour. To square this circle, other scholars anxious to downplay the mixing argument have resorted to supplementing Locke's theory with arguments that have little if any textual basis. John A. Simmons, for instance, believes that the view that labour is commanded by natural law can be made to yield property rights in the goods created by our labour if we present Locke as reasoning along "rule-consequentialist" lines. By providing an incentive, the principle that one is entitled to the fruits of one's labour would bring about the most efficient system for the production of goods and thereby offer the best means of promoting the preservation of mankind. As such, natural law would not merely command individuals to work productively but also to appropriate the goods thereby created.[49]

A more straightforward solution is possible if we take seriously the mixing argument. Doing so would not necessarily mean discarding the value-adding or natural law argument: as Simmons has emphasized, Locke was a pluralistic thinker, often supporting his conclusions with distinct lines of reasoning.[50] The idea that the goods generated through labour are a product of – and hence in some sense contain – one's property in one's person not only explains why one acquires a property right in the goods one produces but helps us to understand why Locke attaches such importance to the private ownership of those specific goods. By mixing one's labour with an ethically inert natural resource, one transforms it into something redolent with

moral value: it becomes an expression of the natural freedom that one enjoys by virtue of being the proprietor of one's person.

Locke's state of nature is not merely peopled by natural beings seeking
self-preservation, as with Hobbes, but by property holders intent on securing their possessions. It is this desire that would ultimately compel men to
submit to government, but not before a second development had taken
place in the state of nature: the invention of money.[51] Before this moment,
the law of nature provided a constraint on the acquisition of property in
the form of the "spoliation" or, as Simmons prefers to call it, "non-waste"
proviso,[52] namely, that man ought to appropriate only those goods that he
can use before they spoil: "Whatever is beyond this, is more than his share,
and belongs to others" (290).[53] Even if by one's labour one were able to appropriate all the apples on a tree, it would be against the law of nature to
pick more than one could use and so deprive others of the opportunity to
take their share without any advantage to oneself. Such apples would simply
not have the moral property of goods produced by rational labour, that is,
labour for the purpose of promoting the law of nature. They would not advance the first law of nature, self-preservation, and would manifestly violate
the second, the preservation of mankind.

It is commonly thought that there is a second limitation to appropriation
in the state of nature, namely, the "sufficiency" proviso, according to which,
in appropriating natural resources, one must leave "enough, and as good"
for others. Jeremy Waldron has, however, convincingly argued that this is
not properly a limiting proviso at all but merely a condition that Locke regards as existing when the first appropriations in the state of nature were
made.[54] Moreover, Locke is clear in presenting this as a condition that arises
precisely because of the non-waste limitation. The locution "enough, and
as good" occurs immediately after Locke has laid out the spoliation proviso
and is introduced by the conjunction "since," as if it were explained by his
previous argument (291). So long as the non-waste proviso is maintained
and the condition of plenty persists, there would "be then little room for
Quarrels or Contentions" (290), and it would therefore be difficult to see
why men would willingly forsake the state of nature. However, there is a
definable moment in Locke's theory at which this condition no longer obtains. That moment is the invention of money.

So significant is this development that several commentators have divided Locke's theory into three stages, with the state of nature after the introduction of money occupying a middle position between the original

state of nature and civil society.[55] What money allows man to do is accumulate property without violating natural law, for it becomes possible to exchange perishable goods for a universally recognized, non-perishable unit of value.[56] It might be objected that even money could not be legitimately accumulated: although it would not perish, it would – at least beyond a certain point – cease to be "useful" in any meaningful sense. There may indeed be some truth in this, for Locke, who always discusses money in the most disparaging of terms, seems sceptical as to whether it can be said to be useful in the same way that perishable goods are: "The greatest part of *things really useful* to the Life of Man ... *are* generally things *of short duration*; such as, if they are not consumed by use, will decay and perish of themselves: Gold, Silver, and Diamonds, are things, that Fancy or Agreement hath put the Value on, more then real Use, and the necessary Support of Life" (299–300). But Locke does not wish to prescribe, as Aristotle had done, what the proper use of an object is.[57] In spite of the mocking tone he assumes when speaking of money as "*a little piece of yellow Metal*," he cannot deny that it has "altered the intrinsick value of things" (294). It may be risible for somebody to desire to exchange useful, perishable goods "for a piece of Metal, pleased with its colour" or "for a sparkling Pebble or a Diamond, and keep those by him all his Life," but in doing so he is not wasting the earth's resources and therefore "he invaded not the Right of others" (300).

The introduction of money into the state of nature thus gives men "the opportunity to continue and enlarge" (301) their possessions, at one stroke transforming the state of nature from a state of plenty into one of scarcity. Locke's confident assertion that "he that leaves as much as another can make use of, does as good as take nothing at all" (291) is no longer valid. The problem posed by this new state of nature is how to ensure that the law of nature, which commands the preservation of mankind as a whole, is not violated. The situation we have described could in theory result in the concentration of wealth into so few hands that virtually the whole population would be left to starve to death. Moreover, with the introduction of money, the state of nature is transformed from a world in which anybody can appropriate whatever goods his labour can produce and his body consume into a world in which one man's gain is another's loss. The result is an inevitable competition for scarce resources, with the potential for conflict that this creates. It is primarily as a solution to this problem that men agree to establish political society.

PRIVATE PROPERTY AND POLITICAL LIBERTY

"The great and *chief end*," Locke wrote, "of Mens uniting into Common-wealths, and putting themselves under Government, *is the Preservation of their Property*" (350–1). Political power is, for Locke, "*a Right* of making Laws with Penalties of Death, and consequently all less Penalties, for the Regulating and Preserving of Property" (268). Men thus agree to relinquish their quasi-political right to be themselves the arbiters of natural law,[58] with respect not only to their own actions but also to those of others. They do this through covenanting among themselves to form a community:

> Men being, as has been said, by Nature, all free, equal and independent, no one can be put out of this Estate, and subjected to the Political Power of another, without his own *Consent*. The only way whereby any one devests himself of his Natural Liberty, and *puts on the bonds of Civil Society* is by agreeing with other Men to joyn and unite into a Community, for their comfortable, safe, and peaceable living one amongst another, in a secure Enjoyment of their Properties, and a greater Security against any that are not of it. (330–1)

This differs markedly from Hobbes's original contract, in which individuals consent to grant their rights to an individual or assembly, authorizing him or it to act on their behalf. The Hobbesian contract includes no explicit agreement to form a political society, this being instead generated as a result of the sovereign's power to unify the disparate wills of individuals. By contrast, Locke's contract is an agreement to form a social bond and, moreover, to do so for a specific purpose, namely, to preserve peace and protect property. How this is to be achieved in practice and who is to be entrusted with the power given up by individuals in order to establish society are questions that Locke does not consider in any great detail: he is content to indicate that "when any number of men have so *consented to make one Community* or Government, they are thereby presently incorporated, and make *one Body Politick*, wherein the *Majority* have a Right to act and conclude the rest" (331).

Property is thus, for Locke, both chronologically and logically prior to political society. But, as we noted earlier, the individuation of private property would not in itself have led to the need for government had money not been invented, transforming the state of nature from one of plenty into one of scarcity. That political society is established to cope with the specific problems ushered in by the age of scarcity is clear from a crucial passage in chapter 5:

> Men, at first, for the most part, contented themselves with what un-assisted Nature offered to their Necessities: and though afterwards, in some parts of the World, (where the Increase of People and Stock, with the *Use of Money*) had made Land scarce, and so of some Value, the several *Communities* settled the Bounds of their distinct Territories, and by Laws within themselves, regulated the Properties of the private Men of their Society, and so, *by Compact* and Agreement, *settled the Property* which Labour and Industry began. (299)

The property that man's natural freedom enables him to appropriate comes under threat as a result of the natural developments that take place within the state of nature. It is "to avoid these Inconveniencies which disorder Mens Properties in the state of Nature" that "Men unite into Societies, that they may have the united strength of the whole Society to secure and defend their Properties, and may have *standing Rules* to bound it, by which every one may know what is his" (359).

In an influential and controversial interpretation of this aspect of Locke's theory of property, Tully has argued that the condition of scarcity renders existing property titles not only insecure but actually unjust. He begins by suggesting that the original community of goods described by Locke is not, as is commonly believed, a "negative" one, according to which the world belongs to nobody but is available for the appropriation of all.[59] It is instead, Tully contends, a "positive" community, where all men have an inclusive claim right to the land and its fruits.[60] The upshot is that property rights can only be legitimate insofar as they do not violate the so-called sufficiency proviso. With the introduction of money and the ensuing scarcity of goods, the law of nature is violated, property titles are invalidated, and communal ownership of goods is reinstated. The purpose of establishing political society is then not to secure existing property titles but to individuate property afresh on a conventional basis in a way that is compatible with the law of nature.[61]

The passages that Tully draws on in putting forward this thesis are, as Waldron has shown, problematic.[62] Although it is clear that the laws play a role in securing and regulating property rights, these rights are not created ex nihilo in civil society but, rather, are the rights that men establish in the state of nature. Not only does such an interpretation fit more easily with the language Locke uses – "determine," "settle," "regulate," rather than "create" or "establish" – but it is supported by the otherwise unintelligible claim made repeatedly in the *Two Treatises* that civil society is established in order to protect the property rights that men establish in the state of nature.

One of Tully's preoccupations in presenting Locke as a theorist of conventional property was to reject C.B. Macpherson's then prominent interpretation of Locke as a proponent of unlimited capitalist appropriation.[63] According to this approach, the three restrictions that Locke initially places on the acquisition of property – spoliation, sufficiency, and the limitations of one's own labour power – are all dispensed with over the course of his analysis, leading to the conclusion that the emerging capitalist class for whose benefit Locke is allegedly writing would be entitled to the boundless acquisition of property, including by exploiting other people's labour. Leaving aside the numerous anachronisms and inaccuracies in this reading,[64] what Macpherson fails to grasp is the underlying motivation behind Locke's theory of property. This is not to bolster the rights of existing property holders against the claims of the labouring classes or some kind of social-democratic political party acting on their behalf. Nor is it, as Richard Ashcraft argues, to win over the landed Whigs by reassuring them that the political revolution being promoted by Locke, Shaftesbury, and their associates would not imperil their property.[65] Rather, Locke's intention is to defend the English people from the absolutism of the restored Stuart monarchy, in particular its attempt to raise revenue without obtaining Parliament's consent,[66] and to justify the people's right of resistance.

As we saw in the first section of this chapter, the concept of freedom that underpinned this commitment was the republican one. What worried Locke about Charles II was precisely what had worried an earlier generation about Charles I: his attempt to rule his country arbitrarily. Given this preoccupation, it might therefore seem surprising that Locke was willing to place significant prerogative powers in the hands of the executive. In a chapter entitled "Of Prerogative," he argues:

Since a Rational Creature cannot be supposed when free, to put himself into Subjection to another, for his own harm: (Though where he

finds a good and wise Ruler, he may not perhaps think it either necessary, or useful to set precise Bounds to his Power in all things) *Prerogative* can be nothing, but the Peoples permitting their Rulers, to do
several things of their own free choice, where the Law was silent, and
sometimes too against the direct Letter of the Law, for the publick
good. (377)

This passage has been highlighted by Skinner, for whom Locke's support
of the prerogative is expressed "in vehemently anti-republican terms."[67]
Lena Halldenius has attempted to rescue the republican Locke by treating
arbitrary power not as *any* kind of discretionary power but as power "that
is unreasonable and coercive in the sense of being unchecked by the good
of the people," and by claiming that, for Locke, "you are under the arbitrary
power of another person when that person's will to do you moral harm, or
encroach upon your rights, is unchecked. That person's power to do you
good can, however, by definition not be arbitrary."[68] These are certainly the
terms in which Locke is willing to allow for some prerogative power to be
placed in the hands of the government. However, if we are willing to accept
Halldenius's reading, we must concede with Skinner that Locke is here de-
parting from the structure of the republican theory and, indeed, from the
definition of freedom as "to be under no other Legislative Power, but that
established, by consent, in the Common-wealth" that he had offered earlier
in the *Two Treatises*.

 If my account of Locke's theory of property is correct, we might be able
to explain why Locke can grant his rulers a degree of prerogative power
without betraying the republican tenet that arbitrary – that is, non-consensual – power is contrary to freedom. As we have seen, for Locke property has
its origins in our self-ownership or natural freedom and, through the act of
mixing our labour with natural resources, comes to contain something of
our natural liberty. Because of the significance property thereby acquires
and because political society is set up with the express purpose of safeguard-
ing it, holding property according to the terms laid down by the government
is the way in which we grant our (tacit) consent to it. So long as the government – even when possessing prerogative powers – acts in order to secure
its subjects' property, it can be said to be acting with their consent and therefore non-arbitrarily. As soon as it begins to interfere with their property,
however, that consent is ipso facto withdrawn, with the result that the government becomes by definition arbitrary and freedom is taken away.

When Locke argues that the "chief end" of submitting to government is the preservation of property, he is using the term "property" in an unconventionally broad sense. This is clear from the following passage, which immediately precedes this claim:

> If Man in the State of Nature be so free, as has been said; If he be absolute Lord of his own Person and Possessions, equal to the greatest, and subject to no Body, why will he part with his Freedom? Why will he give up this Empire, and subject himself to the Dominion and Controul of any other Power? To which 'tis obvious to Answer, that though in the state of Nature he hath such a right, yet the Enjoyment of it is very uncertain, and constantly exposed to the Invasion of others. For all being Kings as much as he, every Man his Equal, and the greater part no strict Observers of Equity and Justice, the enjoyment of the property he has in this state is very unsafe, very unsecure. This makes him willing to quit this Condition, which however free, is full of fears and continual dangers: And 'tis not without reason, that he seeks out, and is willing to joyn in Society with others who are already united, or have a mind to unite for the mutual *Preservation* of their Lives, Liberties and Estates, which I call by the general Name, *Property*. (350)

There is a sense, then, in which the creation of political society is understood by Locke in terms of a parting with one's freedom. But what one gains thereby is not, as with Hobbes, merely security but also the protection of an institution in which a vestige of the natural liberty being renounced is congealed.

Many commentators have been struck by the unusual definition of property in this passage, particularly given its appearance towards the end of the Second Treatise, long after the main discussion of property in chapter 5. Some have concluded that elsewhere, and particularly in chapter 5, Locke is using property in the narrower sense.[69] Although there are times when this appears to be true,[70] Locke himself insists late in the Second Treatise that "by *Property* I must be understood here, as in other places, to mean that Property which Men have in their Persons as well as Goods" (383). He seems in these passages almost to be taking for granted his broad understanding of property, as if merely repeating it for the purposes of clarity rather than introducing a new definition. What he is seeking to remind his readers of by defining property as "Lives, Liberties and Estates" is that private property is more than just the material goods that we happen to own (our estates) or even our right to such material goods: it also contains something of our lives and liberties, that is, our "person." "Property" thus understood is the conceptual tool by which Locke makes the transition from natural liberty, which by being mixed into a natural resource is constitutive of private property, to political liberty.

As we saw in the second section of this chapter, the idea of self-ownership is only one aspect of Locke's definition of natural liberty; the other is being the property of God and therefore of no terrestrial being. Just as self-ownership is carried over into political society, so too is this other aspect of natural liberty, furnishing an alternative way of conceptualizing political liberty. Since men are the property of God, Locke argues, they are neither born the property of another human being, nor can they sell themselves into bondage. The legislative power "is *not,* nor can possibly be absolutely *Arbitrary* over the Lives and Fortunes of the People ... For no Body can transfer to another more power than he has in himself; and no Body has an absolute Arbitrary Power over himself, or over any other, to destroy his own Life, or take away the Life or Property of another" (357). Although, as we shall see, our property in our persons gives us the right to sell our labour, under no circumstances would we be entitled to sell ourselves to another. The master-slave relationship could not be justified by claiming that it had been voluntarily entered into by both parties, "for a Man, not having the Power of his own Life, *cannot,* by Compact, or his own Consent, *enslave himself* to any one, nor put himself under the Absolute, Arbitrary Power of another, to take away his Life, when he pleases" (284).

Locke's emphasis on the tacit consent given through property ownership does not preclude him also relying on a more traditional republican argument that stresses the actual consent that men give to the government they live under. Although Locke is primarily concerned with the hypothetical consent given at the original founding of political society, he does occasionally present consent as something that might be expressly given in contemporary society, for instance through elections or through consenting to the laws one is subject to. In chapter 13 of the Second Treatise, for instance, Locke writes that "no Government can have a right to obedience from a people who have not freely consented to it: which they can never be supposed to do, till either they are put in a full state of Liberty to chuse their Government and Governors, or at least till they have such standing Laws, to which they have by themselves or their Representatives, given their free consent" (394). Even here, however, Locke adds that a necessary condition for a government to obtain the obedience of its people is that they should be "allowed their due property, which is so to be Proprietors of what they have, that no body can take away any part of it without their own consent, without which, Men under any Government are not in the state of Freemen, but are direct Slaves under the Force of War" (394). It would seem that governments, even when established through the explicit consent of their subjects, are bound by a duty not to interfere with existing property rights.

However, there is one case where Locke grants that governments do have a right to dispossess their subjects. Taxation, Locke believes, is a legitimate practice, for "Governments cannot be supported without great Charge, and 'tis fit every one who enjoys his share of the Protection, should pay out of his Estate his proportion for the maintenance of it" (362). Taxes, though, must be levied with the express consent of the people or their representatives, "for if any one shall claim a *Power to lay* and levy *Taxes* on the People, by his own Authority, and without such consent of the People, he thereby invades the *Fundamental Law of Property*, and subverts the end of Government. For what property have I in that which another may by right take, when he pleases to himself?" (362). The point Locke is making here is that the explicit consent given by the people to support their government overrides the concern with the tacit consent that would otherwise be taken away through the interference with their property. Where, by contrast, no express consent is given to a tax, Locke believes, subjects are deprived not only of the goods given over to the taxman but of all their property, including their lives and liberties.

The point that Locke wishes to emphasize here is that the mere possession of the power *arbitrarily* to take away the subject's goods is incompatible with the institution of property and therefore with liberty. He stresses that "*Men* therefore *in Society having Property*, they have such a right to the goods, which by the Law of the Community are theirs, that no Body hath a right to take their substance, or any part of it from them, without their own consent; without this, they have no *Property* at all. For I have truly no *Property* in that, which another can by right take from me, when he pleases, against my consent" (360–1). This being so, Locke concludes, "it is a mistake to think, that the Supream or *Legislative Power* of any Commonwealth, can do what it will, and dispose of the Estates of the Subject *arbitrarily*, or take any part of them at pleasure" (361).

Locke does not indicate what kind of constitutional system is needed to prevent this from happening and so to secure political liberty. However, what is clear is the kind of regime that Locke is seeking to oppose: absolute monarchy. There is, Locke argues, no risk of estates being disposed of arbitrarily where "the *Legislative* consists, wholly or in part, in Assemblies which are variable, whose Members upon the Dissolution of the Assembly, are Subjects under the common Laws of their Country, equally with the rest" (361). However, "where the *Legislative* is in one lasting Assembly always in being, or in one Man, as in Absolute Monarchies, there is danger still, that they will think themselves to have a distinct interest, from the rest of the Community; and so will be apt to increase their own Riches and Power, by taking, what they think fit, from the People." This is because "a Man's *Property* is not at all secure, though there be good and equitable Laws to set the bounds of it, between him and his Fellow Subjects, if he who commands those Subjects, have Power to take from any private Man, what part he pleases of his *Property*, and use and dispose of it as he thinks good" (361).

Moreover, such a government is, Locke believed, not only illegitimate but actually incompatible with political society: "*Absolute Monarchy*, which by some Men is counted the only Government in the World, is indeed *inconsistent with Civil Society*, and so can be no Form of Civil Government at all" (326).[71] The reason for this is that:

> Where-ever any two Men are, who have no standing Rule, and common Judge to Appeal to on Earth for the determination of Controversies of Right betwixt them, there they are still *in the state of Nature*, and under all the inconveniences of it, with only this woful difference to the Subject, or rather Slave of an Absolute Prince: That whereas, in the ordinary State of Nature, he has a liberty to judge of his Right, and according to the best of his Power, to maintain it; now whenever his Property is invaded by the Will and Order of his Monarch, he has not only no Appeal, as those in Society ought to have, but as if he were degraded from the common state of Rational Creatures, is denied a liberty to judge of, or to defend his Right, and so is exposed to all the

Misery and Inconvenience that a Man can fear from one, who being
in the unrestrained state of Nature, is yet corrupted with Flattery, and
armed with Power. (326–7)

The subject of an absolute monarch is still in the state of nature in the sense
that the government does not fulfill the function for which it was originally
set up, namely, to act as an independent arbiter of existing property rights.
Deprived of the property rights that ground his political freedom and lacking the natural freedom to follow the law of nature without the imposition
of any external rules, such a subject can have no redress from the arbitrary
commands of his ruler. He is, in other words, a slave.

In chapter 15 of the Second Treatise Locke expands on this point by contrasting political with paternal and despotic rule, in a manner that recalls
Henry Parker's argument in *Jus Populi*.[72] The difference between these forms
of power hinges on the status of property. Echoing his earlier remarks,
Locke defines political power as "that Power which every Man, having in
the state of Nature, has given up into the hands of the Society, and therein
to the Governours, whom the Society hath set over it self, with this express
or tacit Trust, That it shall be imployed for their good, and the preservation
of their Property" (381). This kind of power, Locke adds, is one that "can
have no other *end or measure,* when in the hands of the Magistrate, but to
preserve the Members of that Society in their Lives, Liberties, and Possessions; and so cannot be an Absolute, Arbitrary Power over their Lives and
Fortunes, which are as much as possible to be preserved" (382). Political
power is thus defined as power over property-holding subjects that extends
to their property but must be exercised with the intention of defending it.

This differs from paternal power, which Locke defines here as the temporary power of fathers to manage their children's affairs "for the Childrens
good, till they come to the use of Reason, or a state of Knowledge, wherein
they may be supposed capable to understand that Rule, whether it be the
Law of Nature, or the municipal Law of their Country they are to govern
themselves by" (381). Crucially, Locke argues, "the *Power of the Father doth
not reach* at all to the *Property* of the Child, which is only in his own disposing" (382). Since Locke later describes paternal power as including the power
"to manage their [children's] Property" (383), I take this to mean not that
children's property falls entirely outside the temporary jurisdiction of their
fathers but that fathers do not have the right permanently to alienate it be-

cause of the fundamental role it will come to play in their children's rational engagement with the political community once they reach adulthood.

Political power differs even more fundamentally from despotism. This is described as "an Absolute, Arbitrary Power one Man has over another, to take away his Life, whenever he pleases" (382). Those subject to despotic power are bereft of property rights not only over their possessions but also over themselves. Since nobody has this arbitrary power over his own life – this belonging to God – it is not something that one can pass over to another voluntarily; it is "*the effect only of Forfeiture*, which the Aggressor makes of his own Life, when he puts himself into the state of War with another" (382–3). Whereas political power arises when individuals voluntarily entrust "*Governours* for the Benefit of their Subjects, to secure them in the Possession and Use of their Properties" (383), despotic power consists in the power that lords exercise "for their own Benefit, over those who are stripp'd of all property" (384). Locke's conclusion is that "*Absolute Dominion*, however placed, is so far from being one kind of Civil Society, that it is as inconsistent with it, as Slavery is with Property" (384).

SHOULD LOCKE HAVE BEEN A LEVELLER?

Locke's theory of political freedom, I have argued, rests on the view that private property is established prior to political society and that this, arising out of the act of mixing one's labour into an unappropriated object, comes to embody the natural freedom that is renounced upon entering society. Holding property then serves as the means by which individuals consent to their government, which is entrusted with defending their property. This enables Locke to conclude that those subject to a government that fulfills the purpose for which it was set up live in a state of political freedom, defined as "a Liberty to follow my own Will in all things, where the Rule prescribes not; and not to be subject to the inconstant, uncertain, unknown, Arbitrary Will of another Man" (284). A strong connection is thus established between property, liberty, and self-ownership.

The question that this analysis raises – and which is not addressed head on – is whether Locke intended this argument to apply narrowly to the propertied classes or whether he had a more general preoccupation with the freedom of the people as a whole. For Ashcraft, Locke's emphasis on labour – as opposed to "appropriation" – as the origin of property makes him a far more radical thinker than has generally been recognized.[73] "The political message" of chapter 5, Ashcraft contends, is that

> artisans, small gentry, yeoman farmers, tradesmen, and merchants were all productive members of society and ought, therefore, to unite in the pursuit of their interests against an idle and wasteful landown-ing aristocracy in order to establish the kind of society in which all sections of the social structure could work together for the realization of the common good.[74]

This seems to me a misleading interpretation, for it fails to grasp Locke's central preoccupation with property ownership and its relationship to liberty. The significance of property is connected with its genesis in labour, but that is not to say that Locke was siding with the labouring classes of his own day against the landed aristocracy.

What, then, was Locke's view of the status of those who lacked property? Did he believe that their freedom depended on existing property holders being able to enjoy their property securely, or was he of the view that a free society was one in which all men held property? The tentative answer with which this chapter concludes is that, whereas Locke offered what Waldron has described as a theory of "special" rights to property, his discussion of the relationship between property and liberty committed him to the view that there was a "general" right of the kind Waldron associates with Hegel's justification for private property.[75] In other words, although the purpose of Locke's theory was to defend the rights of existing property holders on the grounds that arbitrary interference with their property took away their liberty, a truly free society according to Locke's own criteria was one in which all men were propertied citizens. At the same time as Locke sought to defend existing property rights, his theory actually required the redis-tribution of property.

Locke does not explicitly advocate economic levelling in the *Two Treatises*, but in the *Essay on Toleration* (1667) he recognizes that such a measure might be legitimate in some societies. In Sparta, Locke observed, "the mag-istrate, having a power of making rules of transferring properties from one man to another, may establish any [laws], so they be universal, equal and without violence, and suited to the interest and welfare of that society."[76]

Here Locke associates redistribution with the specific goals of Spartan society, namely, to produce able-bodied and warlike citizens, offering it as an example of how political considerations can at times override natural law. Nowhere does he suggest that a similar argument could apply to advancing freedom in the English polity. But Locke's failure to do so poses a serious problem for his theory.

Locke is clear in proclaiming his opposition to the institution of slavery, opening the first chapter of the *Two Treatises* by arguing that "Slavery is so vile and miserable an Estate of Man, and so directly opposite to the generous Temper and Courage of our Nation; that 'tis hardly to be conceived, that an *Englishman*, much less a *Gentleman*, should plead for't" (141). A society permitting slavery is, Locke believed, no longer a political society at all but a state of despotism in which all political bonds are dissolved:

> Whenever the *Legislators endeavor to take away, and destroy the Property of the People*, or to reduce them to Slavery under Arbitrary Power, they put themselves into a state of War with the People, who are thereupon absolved from any farther Obedience, and are left to the common Refuge, which God hath provided for all Men, against Force and Violence. (412)

The defining characteristic of slaves is that, "being Captives taken in a just War" and being "by the Right of Nature subjected to the Absolute Dominion and Arbitrary Power of their Masters," they are "not capable of any Property" (322–3).[77] By virtue of having alienated their natural freedom, or the property in their persons, slaves lack the capacity for property in external goods. It is for this reason that, according to Locke, slaves "cannot in that state be considered as any part of *Civil Society*; the chief end whereof is the preservation of Property" (323). This helps to explain Locke's view that, where governments interfere with their subjects' property and hence turn them into slaves, civil society breaks down altogether.

Locke's principal argument for treating slavery as an unjust institution is that he believed that men are the property of God and cannot therefore become the property of other men, even if they willingly consent to their bondage. Locke also offers a second argument in opposition to slavery, designed specifically to prevent those suffering from abject poverty from selling themselves to others. This is the right of the needy, sanctioned by the law of nature, to supply their wants from another's surplus goods. The up-shot of this right to charity is, according to Locke, that

> a Man can no more justly make use of another's necessity, to force him to become his Vassal, by with-holding that Relief, God requires him to afford to the wants of his Brother, than he that has more strength can seize upon a weaker, master him to his Obedience, and with a Dagger at his Throat offer him Death or Slavery. (170)

As Stephen Buckle points out, this argument is diametrically opposed to Pufendorf's view that necessity might in some cases – in particular where it is self-inflicted – justly lead to self-enslavement.[78] For Locke, there are simply no circumstances in which necessity can compel a free person to sell himself into bondage, for he can instead exercise his right to take whatever goods he needs to preserve his existence without thereby sacrificing his independence.[79]

Charity has been treated by some commentators, most notably Waldron, as a genuine limiting proviso on appropriation, carrying the same weight as the non-waste proviso.[80] Yet in the whole of the Second Treatise the word "charity" is used only once, and even then in an unrelated context (328). There is no reference to it at all in chapter 5 of the Second Treatise and no suggestion that Locke regards it as actually limiting the accumulative tendencies of men living in a money economy. As we have seen, there is nothing internal to the state of nature to prevent a state of scarcity from arising; the only possible solution to the uncertainty that it generates is to establish political society.

The problem for Locke's theory is that the consequence of scarcity is that not everyone will be able to hold property: there will be some people who, even if they have the *potential* to own property by virtue of having a property in their person, cannot realize that potential. This seems to be the predicament of the servant, who unlike the slave is so much a feature of Locke's society that he appears without so much as an apology. In order to explain the process of appropriation, Locke states that "the Turfs my Servant has cut ... become my *Property*, without the assignation or consent of any body" (289). The servant is one whose labour does not bestow any property upon him but rather upon his master. He may in theory be "capable" of property but, because of the circumstances in which political society was founded, he is born propertyless and so has to rely on the wages offered by others for his subsistence. By (reluctantly) legitimating scarcity in the state of nature and presenting it as the condition out of which political society emerged, Locke is in effect opening up his society to the very thing his theory is designed to oppose: the institution of slavery.[81]

I make this final observation neither to claim that Locke's theory was in its implications more "modern" than he could have anticipated nor to question its basic coherence. The figure of the servant does, however, seem to me to constitute a small but significant crux in Locke's attempt to make property holding the basis of political liberty. As we saw in chapter 3, the concept of self-ownership precluded even those like Milton who had major anxieties about luxury and economic inequality from contemplating the redistributive measures necessary to avoid these pitfalls. Locke did not take up the Sallustian strand of Milton's thought and nowhere expressed concerns about the corrupting effects of wealth, though he certainly made known his scorn for those who revered "*a little piece of yellow Metal*" (294).

Yet Locke's way of conceptualizing self-ownership might have made it more compatible with measures designed to prevent luxury than its original formulation by the Levellers and republicans in the 1640s–50s. For them, self-ownership connected freedom and property by grounding their claim that any arbitrary interference with the latter undermined the former. While Locke also appealed to self-ownership to make this argument, his view that property contained the natural liberty that one relinquished upon entering society, and that a state could only be free if its subjects had consented to it by holding property, suggests that the presence of those without property posed greater problems for him than he was willing to admit. If being free involved being a property holder, then self-ownership might require those with excesses of property to relinquish some in order to make it possible for the whole of society to own property and thus for nobody to be compelled to labour for the sake of somebody else. It is unlikely that Locke was deliberately addressing his predecessors' problem of reconciling the protection of existing property with the avoidance of luxury. However, it is interesting to consider whether these theorists might have thought differently about the relationship between property and liberty had they had access to Locke's concept of self-ownership.

CONCLUSION

This book was written with two main overlapping aims. The first is to enrich our understanding of the concept of liberty in seventeenth-century England by foregrounding the issue of property. It seeks to explain why property was given such a prominent position in the neo-Roman theory, and how the authors discussed attempted to articulate the connection between property ownership and freedom. The second is to recover and understand in its seventeenth-century context the concept of self-ownership. It traces the concept back to the debates of the 1640s, and in particular to the Levellers' individualist challenge to the Parliamentarians' theory of parliamentary sovereignty. It then considers the role played by ideas of self-ownership in the debates of the following decades, from the republican literature of the Interregnum to John Locke.

To emphasize that my principal preoccupation is historical is not, however, to disown any wish to contribute to contemporary debates. The project of uncovering the archaeological artefact that is the republican concept of liberty has always been bound up with presentist concerns, in particular a desire to challenge the dominance of liberalism in today's political culture. On the one hand, scholars of republicanism see themselves as proffering a largely forgotten tradition, entreating their readers to consider whether it may be worth taking up again.[1] On the other hand, they seek to question the standard narratives of Western political thought, in which liberalism and its intellectual forbears take centre stage, by emphasizing the role played by republican ideas – and the reaction to them – in shaping our heritage.[2] In proposing to reconsider the conventional account of republican liberty, my research will inevitably have some bearing on contemporary debates. Moreover, the concept of self-ownership is widely discussed by contemporary political theorists, in particular libertarians and their critics. My account of self-ownership may be of some relevance here, not least because of the tendency of many libertarians to invoke Locke in support of their cause. I should now like, by way of conclusion, to consider what I take to be the three principal insights that this book might offer to contemporary theorists.

The first concerns the vexed question of the relationship between republicanism and liberalism. Ever since republican liberty was put forward as an alternative to the pure negative concept, the charge has been made that all of its basic insights are captured just as well – indeed, it is often claimed, better – within the conventional framework.[3] In some cases, this has led liberals to attempt to incorporate aspects of the republican concept into their theories, thus depriving republicanism of its polemical edge. Richard Dagger, for example, has sought to save liberalism from its excessive preoccupation with subjective rights by infusing it with the "civically oriented concerns" of the republican tradition.[4] But more often liberals have dismissed the republican theory by simply denying that it has anything novel or coherent to say about the concept of liberty. Thus, Matthew Kramer argues, republicanism "does not provide an analysis of the concept of freedom that goes beyond the negative-liberty approach in any significant way"; "the modern exponents of negative liberty," he concludes, "can fare well in a confrontation – and reconciliation – with their civic-republican counterparts."[5] Or, as Larmore more tersely puts it, "Pettit himself imagines that he stands outside the liberal framework. In reality he does not."[6]

Criticisms such as these wilfully miss the point about republican liberty. They continue to assume that liberty must be a predicate of actions and that it can only be undermined as a result of some perceptible act of interference.[7] Insofar as the condition of domination can be said to take away freedom, they insist, this can only be by virtue of the reduction to the range of possible exercisable liberties. According to this analysis, a slave might be free to go about his business unimpeded, but only if he chooses not to carry out an act that would be bound to result in the master's coercive interference. His freedom would be reduced because there would be fewer possible courses of action to take, not because of any alleged relationship of dependence.[8] The insight that freedom is taken away by the presence of domination can, it is thus claimed, be easily accommodated within a standard conception of negative liberty.

It might in some cases be possible to redescribe the predicament of the slave in these terms, but to do so is to betray the spirit of the neo-Roman theory. For the essence of this argument is that freedom describes a particular *status*, that is, the status of those not subject to the arbitrary power of another person or group; the question of what it means for an *action* to be free is not one that the neo-Roman writers are especially interested in. As Quentin Skinner points out, freedom is already taken away by the simple fact of being subject to the will of another, irrespective of any choice-limiting acts that one may feel compelled to carry out.[9] The sense in which being in a condition of dependence takes away liberty is one that simply cannot be captured by the "triadic" structure of agent, constraint, and end that, since Gerald MacCallum's influential article, has been widely regarded by proponents of negative freedom as lying behind any coherent discussion of liberty.[10]

There are, then, two distinct concepts of liberty that characterize the republican and liberal traditions, and to attempt to coerce them into a single, monolithic theory is to do an injustice to both. Yet where the dichotomy between liberalism and republicanism is occasionally drawn too starkly is at the historical level. The pure negative theory associated with liberalism is typically traced back to Hobbes's account of liberty as the absence of external impediments to motion. To the extent that there were any precedents for this way of conceptualizing freedom, these are said to lie in the natural law tradition. Hobbes's theory of liberty, it is claimed, was subsequently taken up by Locke, who softened its most jagged edges before bequeathing it to eighteenth- and nineteenth-century utilitarians and liberals. Not only was this tradition entirely separate from the republican one, with its roots in Roman legal, moral, and political thought, but it was in its initial development self-consciously opposed to it.[11]

This genealogy of liberty offers an overly simplistic picture of the relationship between republicanism and liberalism. In making this argument, I should stress that I lay no claim to originality. Skinner himself has expressed doubts about the narrative he had traced in *Hobbes and Republican Liberty*, pointing out that the early Hobbes accepted the central insights of the republican theory and incorporated them into his own works, turning wholeheartedly against them only in *Leviathan*.[12] Going significantly further, Vickie Sullivan argues that the seventeenth century, far from being the moment when the distinction between a republican and proto-liberal discourse of freedom began to ossify, saw the emergence of a "synthesis" between the two.[13] Similarly, for Knud Haakonssen, "the opposition between liberalism and republicanism, while a source of inspiration for the recent revival of the latter, is more an invention of this revival than an ascertainable historical fact."[14] It is, he believes,

> impossible to see the division between a juristic-liberal and republican tradition as fundamental to post-Renaissance political thought. In Locke, Montesquieu, Rousseau, Price, most of the Scottish Enlightenment thinkers and the American founders – to take a wide selection – elements from both traditions go hand in hand. It is not between natural rights and republican citizenship that the fault lines lie.[15]

One of the upshots of structuring my narrative as I have done is to enable us to reconsider Locke's relationship to the republican tradition. Locke is widely regarded as one of the founding fathers of liberalism, and many of the most important works on the history of republicanism were written with the express purpose of challenging the alleged primacy of "Lockean liberalism." As such, they have merely reinforced the myth of Locke as the progenitor of liberalism, a myth that has only in recent years begun to be questioned, allowing Locke's connections to republicanism to come through.[16] My final chapter seeks to contribute to this revisionist reading of Locke by suggesting that some of the difficulties of this interpretation, flagged in particular by Skinner,[17] can be overcome if we focus on the connection between freedom and property in his theory. Locke emerges not as a "classical republican" in any straightforward sense – even the republicans of the Interregnum, I stress, were less "classical" than is often thought – but as the heir of a particular version of the neo-Roman theory of liberty that had played a central role in English debates over the course of the previous half-century.

The second implication of my book for contemporary debates that I would like to highlight relates to the concept of self-ownership. This concept is central to the libertarian tradition associated with Robert Nozick and left-libertarian critics such as Hillel Steiner, Philippe Van Parijs, and Michael Otsuka. Nozick begins his discussion of self-ownership in his highly influential work *Anarchy, State, and Utopia* by defining the concept of property as "the right to determine what shall be done with X."[18] Armed with this understanding of property, he then declares that it is easy enough to see how ideas of self-ownership might arise:

> This notion of property helps us to understand why earlier theorists spoke of people as having a property in themselves and their labor. They viewed each person as having a right to decide what would become of himself and what he would do, and as having a right to reap the benefits of what he did.[19]

Chief among the "earlier theorists" invoked by Nozick is undoubtedly Locke. Nozick's characterization of the Lockean concept of self-ownership is not entirely inaccurate. As we have seen, Locke and his predecessors did invoke self-ownership as part of a defence of individuals' property rights. However, as Nozick's theory is elaborated, it becomes apparent that his understanding of self-ownership diverges in important ways from the seventeenth-century concept that Nozick sees himself as appropriating.

Construed as the exclusive right to determine one's actions, self-ownership provides the theoretical foundation for the view that liberty consists simply in absence of coercive interference.[20] There is, Nozick believes, "a line (or hyper-plane) [which] circumscribes an area in moral space around an individual," such that any intrusion into this space would count as a violation of his self-ownership and therefore liberty.[21] Conversely, there can be no limits to what individuals are permitted to do with themselves, except insofar as their actions might result in an infringement of somebody else's property rights. This includes, as with any other type of property, the right of alienation or deliberate destruction – in other words, the right to sell oneself into bondage or to commit suicide.

The particular appeal for Nozick of the vocabulary of self-ownership to delineate this sphere is that it brings property to the fore since his purpose is to make a radical case for the inviolability of property rights and the injustice of any form of economic redistribution. In order to carry out their projects, Nozick argues, individuals must interact with the external world and appropriate resources. It is a fundamental component of their self-ownership that the products generated by their creative engagement with the world must accrue to them, for otherwise their capacities would be employed for the sake of others, which would undermine their property in themselves. The upshot of this argument, and the idea for which Nozick is perhaps most famous, is that "taxation of earning from labor is on a par with forced labor."[22] Taking away the fruits of individuals' labour contravenes their fundamental right of having complete control over the use of their body and talents and is thus no less a violation of the principle of self-ownership than the forcible appropriation of their labour by others.

Left-libertarians have attempted to rescue self-ownership from these inegalitarian implications, while remaining for the most part wedded to the concept of self-ownership as defined by Nozick.[23] Otsuka, for example, has sought to reconcile self-ownership and egalitarianism by pointing to a "hidden premise" that lies behind Nozick's conclusions. This is the premise that one's ownership rights are as full in respect of worldly resources as in respect of oneself.[24] Although Otsuka does have some quibbles about Nozick's account of self-ownership, he accepts that, if one were able to produce a good without making use of natural resources, one's rights over it would be virtually unlimited. Where instead worldly resources come into play, Otsuka believes that one's rights over the goods one produces are limited by Lockean principles of "justice in acquisition" (as he refers to the so-called sufficiency proviso), according to which the appropriation of previously unowned natural resources is just if and only if it "places nobody else at a disadvantage."[25] For Otsuka, this means that robust self-ownership requires not only the libertarian right itself but also having enough worldly resources so that one is not forced by necessity to work for another.[26] What this entails in practice is compensating those who are relatively untalented with enough capital resources to ensure that they are able, through voluntary exchanges, to attain the same level of welfare as their more talented counterparts.

For many non-libertarian theorists who might otherwise be drawn to self-ownership, the unpalatable consequences of Nozick's account are such that they feel they have no choice but to reject it. Attracta Ingram is clear that "we can hold the thesis that rights are properties only by being libertarians."[27] She accepts that it may be possible to construe self-ownership in non-libertarian terms by predicating it on something other than full liberal property rights and refers to Locke's "split ownership" (where one's property in one's person is subordinate to God's title) as a possible alternative.[28] But she ultimately dismisses any concept of "partial" self-ownership, concluding that "nothing less than full liberal self-ownership is adequate to the social role set for the doctrine," which is to guard against the involuntary submission to the authority of another.[29] Ingram's objection to the libertarian conception of self-ownership is that allowing self-owning individuals to appropriate all the material resources that they can will give rise to gross inequalities and a situation in which those with no or few holdings have nothing but their labour to sell. Having identified this fatal objection, Ingram abandons self-ownership in favour of the concept of "self-government" or "self-control."

G.A. Cohen, who initially embraced the concept of self-ownership as part of a Marxist critique of capitalist exploitation, ultimately reached the conclusion that it had to be relinquished to the libertarians.[30] The charge that the capitalist, by owning the means of production, is able to "steal" the surplus value generated by the labourer depends on the view that the rightful owner of one's labour is oneself. It depends, in other words, on the thesis of self-ownership. However, faced with Nozick's account of self-ownership, Cohen is forced to concede that "the welfare state does to tax-paying workers exactly what, in the Marxist complaint, capitalists do to workers: it forcibly extracts product from them."[31] Cohen does not accept that the capitalist's incursions into the wage-labourer's self-ownership rights are justified since he regards the contract between the two as a "sham." But he believes that Marxists cannot avoid the conclusion that "the welfare state makes the productive worker do by force of law what he does for the capitalist by force of circumstance."[32] Accepting that "libertarians lay siege to, and embarrass, Marxists in political philosophy," Cohen proposes to jettison the concept of self-ownership and find an alternative means of expressing his egalitarian anxieties about capitalist exploitation of workers.[33]

Feminist theorists such as Carole Pateman and Anne Phillips have also come to reject the concept of self-ownership, while often recognizing its inherent appeal.[34] Pateman acknowledges the attraction of self-ownership for feminists in light of the fact that the common law used to recognize wives as the property of their husbands and that, when Pateman was writing in the 1980s, it continued to recognize the right of husbands to their wives' bodies (marital rape was not yet a criminal offence in many jurisdictions, including England and Wales).[35] Yet Pateman argues that the concept should be rejected for two main reasons. First, its genesis in patriarchal social contract theories makes it a male-centred concept that serves to subordinate rather than to empower women. Traditional social contract theorists such as Locke, Pateman claims, viewed self-ownership as applying only to men; women entered civil society already subject to a "sexual contract" that turned them into the property of men. Second, Pateman argues, even if the patriarchal origins of self-ownership can be overcome, it is conceptually flawed because to treat an individual's right in himself as a property right is to allow him to decide how that property is to be used, which may include contracting out services for life in return for protection. This causes "the opposition between freedom and slavery to be dissolved," enabling "civil slavery" to become "nothing more than one example of a legitimate contract."[36]

Phillips's objection to self-ownership lies in the way the language of property, with its narrow focus on individual rights and its commodification of the body, precludes consideration of wider moral questions. Although Phillips accepts that different conceptions of property to Nozick's are possible, she concludes that "property claims make the individual property owners the centre of attention and establish their preferences and choices as the predominant concerns."[37] In spite of the progressive causes for which discourses of self-ownership have been deployed, Phillips concludes that the individualist quality of self-ownership makes it unsuitable for more mature reflections on the relationship between bodies, individual agency, and the social realm.

However, as I hope this book demonstrates, self-ownership need not, and in its original formulation did not, have the uninviting implications highlighted by these theorists. The concept of self-ownership was articulated in the seventeenth century not as part of a libertarian discourse about absolute property rights but as part of a republican complaint about arbitrary power. Arbitrary interferences with property were undoubtedly a major concern of the seventeenth-century writers discussed in this book, but Locke explicitly recognized the legitimacy of non-arbitrary taxation and several other theorists opposed the excessive accumulation of wealth. By understanding the intellectual history of the concept of self-ownership, contemporary theorists might be better placed to challenge Nozick's version of the concept.

The republican concept of self-ownership is a more capacious and inclusive concept than the libertarian one. Instead of a narrow preoccupation with the individual and his rights, it is concerned with political, economic, and social structures, and their potential to undermine liberty by instituting arbitrary forms of power. Self-ownership could plausibly be deployed as part of a critique of the power imbalances between the rich and poor without necessarily entailing a rejection of the redistributive measures designed to tackle them. It may also underpin calls for the democratization of the workplace, which Pateman regards as incompatible with the conventional libertarian or "contractarian" concept of self-ownership.[38] While it may not be able to sustain the Marxist critique that, in an exploitative labour contract, the labourer is a victim of "theft," it can provide a theoretical foundation for the charge that such an arrangement places the labourer under the arbitrary power of his employer and thus undermines his liberty.

Once the preoccupation with arbitrary power is brought to the fore, self-ownership also speaks more vocally to feminist concerns such as those raised by Pateman and Phillips. Far from legitimating civil slavery, a republican concept of self-ownership that forbids self-enslavement seems like a promising point of departure for a critique of the kinds of exploitative employment relationships discussed by Pateman. The objection to the potential for the vocabulary of property to contribute to the commodification of the body may persist, and there are no doubt other feminist issues, particularly to do with male-centric cultural norms, that it may be unable to address. But a concept that brings into focus the way in which social structures such as the workplace or marriage may engender relationships of dependence that are incompatible with liberty is surely one that warrants further examination by feminists.

The final, and to my mind the most important, contribution that I hope this book might make to contemporary debates is to encourage republicans to look afresh at the role of property in the particular theory of liberty that they are seeking to revive. For present-day republicans, the role of property in the neo-Roman tradition, to the extent that it is recognized at all, is a source of embarrassment. The view that property holding is constitutive of liberty seems to many to be an elitist proposition, a relic of a by-gone age when theorists could concern themselves exclusively with the fortunes of a small group of wealthy white males and assume that they were speaking for humanity as a whole. The role of property in the republican concept of liberty may be of interest to the antiquarian, but from the point of view of the contemporary political theorist it is best laid aside.

The charge of elitism is not entirely unjustified, though for at least some of the authors discussed in this book the connection between property and freedom served to promote egalitarian economic measures rather than to exclude those lacking property from the class of those worthy of being considered free. In the case of Locke, it could be argued that, although his theory is designed to defend existing property titles, it may in fact require the very redistributive measures that he was seeking to oppose.

Even ignoring these caveats, it is doubtful whether contemporary republicans are right to seek to brush property under the carpet. The liberal tradition to which they are in large part reacting claims to be neutral on the question of property. The concept of freedom that it espouses, it is argued, applies to all men and women irrespective of their economic status. The capitalist and wage-labourer or, to use a more twenty-first-century dichotomy, the CEO of a company and its lowest paid employee are equally free, provided that they are not interfered with in their economic enterprises by an overactive state. What the republican theory allows us to do, when we recognize the importance of property, is to question this central assumption of liberalism. With liberalism in retreat following the 2008 financial crisis and the rise of populists in the United States, Britain, and elsewhere, the need for alternative ideologies capable of nurturing tolerant, progressive, and multicultural societies while acknowledging the grievances of those who feel left behind is perhaps more pressing that it has ever been.

We can dismiss the privileged status of the property holder in the seventeenth-century version of the republican theory; we can even dismiss the category of the property holder as irrelevant to a world long transformed by the rise of commerce and industry. Yet we may nevertheless hold on to the basic insight that economic forms of dependence undermine freedom. Applying this insight to our present circumstances may not be straightforward, but a promising line of inquiry is whether economic inequality or absolute poverty may result in forms of dependence or domination that are incompatible with liberty. This idea sits uneasily with the negative concept of liberty and has been expressly rejected by many contemporary liberal theorists.[39] But it has also received scant attention in conventional republican discussions of liberty, focused as they are on political forms of domination. Pettit's version of republican liberty has been critiqued by Nancy Hirschmann on the grounds that its individualism precludes an understanding of the ways in which social structures and cultural norms – and the patriarchy in particular – reduce the freedom of certain groups, most notably women.[40] Once property is reinserted into the republican theory, it may be a more promising vantage point from which to view some of the feminist considerations raised by Hirschmann and others. More generally, it may enable republicanism to move beyond the occasionally stale debate about what constitutes arbitrary power in the political domain and address broader sources of domination in our society and economy.

As recent political developments have shown, the growing inequalities experienced by many societies have led those at the bottom of the income scale to feel disempowered and unfree, even if they are not being coercively interfered with by the state. Indeed, it is not the jackboot but the retreat of the welfare state and the securities it had offered, together with the loss of traditional manufacturing jobs, that has done the most to bring about this sense of alienation. The yearning to "take back control," inflamed though it has been by cynical and populist politicians for their own ends, is one that is capable of being understood and perhaps addressed through a republican lens.

It is not my intention in these closing remarks to make any normative claims about the kinds of economic policies that would promote or hinder freedom according to a republican model. My hope is simply that, by revealing the centrality of property to the neo-Roman concept of liberty in seventeenth-century England, I may have succeeded in encouraging contemporary republicans to reconsider a vital and unduly neglected aspect of their tradition and thereby to bring into sharper focus its continuing relevance to the issues we face today.

NOTES

INTRODUCTION

1 I use the terms interchangeably, following the usage of the authors I discuss. See Pitkin, "Are Freedom and Liberty Twins?," for a historically informed attempt to draw a conceptual distinction between them.

2 Most contemporary theorists, following Pettit, refer to the concept as "republican liberty," although Skinner continues to prefer to speak of "neo-Roman liberty," cautioning that many early modern writers who thought of liberty in these terms were not republicans in their political allegiances. See Skinner, "On Neo-Roman Liberty."

3 Skinner, *Hobbes and Republican Liberty*, argues that Hobbes's negative concept of liberty emerged as a reaction to the republican concept. On the relationship between Hobbes and humanist thought more generally, see Skinner, *From Humanism to Hobbes*.

4 I refer to "men" and use masculine pronouns throughout this study to reflect the male-centric worldview of the authors I discuss. I do not, however, consider the ideas that they express to be incapable of applying to women, and in the Conclusion I consider their possible relevance to feminist discourses.

5 See in particular Haakonssen, "Republicanism"; Honohan, *Civic Republicanism*; Pettit, *Republicanism*; Pettit, "Keeping Republican Freedom Simple"; Pettit, "Republican Freedom"; Pettit, *On the People's Terms*; Skinner, *Liberty before Liberalism*; Skinner, "Third Concept of Liberty"; Skinner, "Classical Liberty and the Coming of the English Civil War"; Skinner, "Freedom as the Absence of Arbitrary Power"; Skinner, *Hobbes and Republican Liberty*. Conceptual critiques include Kramer, "Liberty and Domination"; Larmore, "Critique of Philip Pettit's Republicanism"; Talisse, "Impunity and Domination"; Waldron, "Pettit's Molecule"; Wall, "Freedom, Interference and Domination." Critiques of a more historical kind include Sommerville, "English and Roman Liberty"; Worden, "Factory of the Revolution"; Worden, "Hobbes and the Halo of Power."

6   Pettit, *Theory of Freedom*, does, however, attempt to formulate a theory of free-
    dom that encapsulates both the notion of free persons, or "agency," and free ac-
    tions. The question of what makes an action or choice free is also a central
    concern of Pettit, *On the People's Terms*.

7   Pettit, *On the People's Terms*, 7–8; Skinner, *Liberty before Liberalism*, 41–4; Skinner,
    "Freedom as the Absence of Arbitrary Power," 85–6; Skinner, *From Humanism
    to Hobbes*, 141–2.

8   Pettit, *Republicanism*, 61; Skinner, *Liberty before Liberalism*, 91–6. However, in
    the forthcoming "On Neo-Roman Liberty" Skinner appears to abandon this sec-
    ond aspect of the neo-Roman theory to avoid giving the impression that free-
    dom is only taken away to the extent that individuals become aware of their
    status of subjection to arbitrary power.

9   Skinner, "Freedom as the Absence of Arbitrary Power," 97–8.

10 Skinner, "Third Concept of Liberty." This, at any rate, has been Skinner's view
    since *Liberty before Liberalism*; earlier formulations (e.g., Skinner, "Idea of Neg-
    ative Liberty") present it as a species of negative liberty that affords an important
    role to ideas of civic virtue and public service. Pettit is also clear in presenting
    republican liberty as distinct from both positive and negative freedom. See Pettit,
    Republicanism; Pettit, *Theory of Freedom*.

11 For a modern vindication of positive liberty, see Taylor, "What's Wrong with
    Negative Liberty."

12 Pettit, *Republicanism*, 8. Pocock, *Machiavellian Moment*, presents the concept of
    liberty in the Italian-Atlantic tradition as a positive, Aristotelian one. See Pocock,
    "Foundations and Moments," and Skinner, "Surveying *The Foundations*," for a
    debate between the two on this point.

13 See, for example, Pettit, *Republicanism*, 31; Skinner, "Freedom as the Absence of
    Arbitrary Power," 89–90.

14 This remains the most influential way of describing freedom in the republican
    register and has been recently restated in Pettit, *On the People's Terms*; Pettit, *Just
    Freedom*. See also Costa, "Neo-Republicanism"; Lovett, "Non-Domination";
    McCammon, "Domination"; Thompson, "Two Faces of Domination" (the latter,
    it should be stressed, proposes a rival theory of domination to Pettit's). Pettit,
    "Republican Freedom," 102, proposes an alternative formulation: "Liberty as the
    absence of alien or alienating control on the part of others." Skinner has, ho-
    wever, avoided the term "non-domination" on the historical grounds that it is
    not to be found in the early modern neo-Roman literature and on the concep-
    tual grounds that it fails to capture the concern with the possibility that liberty

may be taken away even where power is not exercised in a forceful way. In his
latest discussion of neo-Roman liberty Skinner also proposes abandoning his
earlier formulation of "living in dependence on others" since everyone lives in
dependence on the goodwill of others, but this doesn't necessarily entail a servile
relationship. See Skinner, "On Neo-Roman Liberty."

15   See Waldron, "Pettit's Molecule," for a critique of Pettit's failure to disentangle
the two arguments.

16   Pettit, *Republicanism*, e.g., 23, 36, 55.

17   Carter, "How Are Power and Unfreedom Related?," 64–5; Waldron, "Pettit's Molecule," 152. Pettit, "Republican Freedom," 117, insists that republican freedom is
not moralized since, for power to count as non-arbitrary, it must merely track
the subject's *avowed* interests rather than the interests as defined according to
some independent moral criterion. Thompson, "Two Faces of Domination," 58,
objects to this position, maintaining that the effect of domination is to make
people incapable of perceiving the domination inherent in the institutions and
norms under which they live and, thus, of knowing where their real interest (the
common good) lies.

18   Pettit, *Republicanism*, 124.

19   Ibid., e.g., 63.

20   Pettit claims that the shift from "arbitrary" to "uncontrolled" power is purely
terminological. See Pettit, *On the People's Terms*, 58.

21   Pettit, *Just Freedom*, xx.

22   Skinner, *Liberty before Liberalism*, 23–9.

23   Ibid., 60.

24   See in particular Skinner, "Freedom as the Absence of Arbitrary Power"; Skinner,
Hobbes and Republican Liberty; Skinner, "On the Liberty of the Ancients and the
Moderns."

25   Hoekstra and Skinner, "Liberties of the Ancients," 824–5.

26   Skinner, "Third Concept of Liberty"; Skinner, "Freedom as the Absence of Arbitrary Power"; Skinner, "On Neo-Roman Liberty." Skinner does, however, acknowledge that arbitrary power may also arise in such institutions as the family
and the workplace – a point that he stresses in particular in his forthcoming
chapter "On Neo-Roman Liberty."

27   Hoekstra and Skinner, "Liberties of the Ancients," 823–4; Skinner, "On Neo-
Roman Liberty." For the view that "freedom as independence" constitutes an alternative concept of freedom, lying somewhere between the republican and
liberal concepts, see List and Valentini, "Freedom as Independence."

28 Haakonssen, "Republicanism," 730.

29 Pettit, *Republicanism*, viii. See also Pettit, *On the People's Terms*, 9.

30 MacGilvray, *Invention of Market Freedom*, 29.

31 As Skinner, *From Humanism to Hobbes*, 144–7, points out, the Roman law category of the *liber homo* could in theory accommodate women as well as men, and it was possible for at least one of our authors to speak of "free men and women" (Goodwin, *Anti-Cavalierisme*, 4). That is not to say, of course, that the republican theory is not open to feminist critiques, such as that of Phillips, "Feminism and Republicanism."

32 However, the two terms do appear to move apart towards the end of the seventeenth century. In the third edition of the *Two Treatises of Government*, published in 1698, Locke amended many instances of "propriety" to "property" to specify that he was referring to property in the sense in which we now use the term.

33 See Sampson, "Property in Seventeenth-Century English Political Thought."

34 Pipes, *Property and Freedom*, xv, suggests that it is this broad understanding of property that "provides the philosophical link between ownership and freedom."

35 Tully, *Approach to Political Philosophy*, 77.

36 The point of departure for most modern discussions of property remains the eleven incidences of ownership set out in Honoré, "Ownership," 112–29.

37 Lilburne, *Whip for the present House of Lords*, 7. See below, 77.

38 [Wildman], *Putney Projects*, 20 (mispaginated as 18).

39 On the relationship between occupation and property, see Fitzmaurice, *Sovereignty, Property and Empire*.

40 I generally use the term "self-ownership," even though some of the authors I discuss – most notably Locke – speak of "property in the person." See Pateman, "Self-Ownership and Property in the Person," for an attempt to distinguish between the two conceptually.

41 Overton, *Arrow against All Tyrants*, 3. See below, 65.

42 See section IV below.

43 This idea was perhaps expressed most clearly the following century by Joseph Priestley in the context of the American Revolution: "By the same power, by which the people of England can compel them to pay *one penny*, they may compel them to pay the *last penny* they have. There will be nothing but arbitrary imposition on the one side, and humble petition on the other" (Priestley, "Present State of Liberty," 140).

44 Locke, *Two Treatises*, 287. See chapter 6, 199.

45 Overton, *Arrow against All Tyrants*, 4.

46 Locke, *Two Treatises*, 270–1.

47 See in particular Skinner, "On Neo-Roman Liberty."

48 *Digest*, 15.

49 Ibid. Skinner has recently highlighted the contrast between the two ways of thinking about freedom in the *Digest* and pointed out that they are put forward by different jurists. See Hoekstra and Skinner, "The Liberties of the Ancients," 823–4.

50 Aristotle, *Politics*, 15–16, 70.

51 *Digest*, 2.

52 Ibid., 1:15.

53 Ibid.

54 The idea of self-ownership as the precondition for slavery has, however, been discussed in contemporary political theory. See, for example, Ingram, *Political Theory of Rights*, 38.

55 *Digest*, 17.

56 This point is acknowledged by Skinner. See, for example, Skinner, *Liberty before Liberalism*, 40–1; Skinner, "On Neo-Roman Liberty."

57 However, Lee, *Popular Sovereignty*, 90–8, argues that, in its original Roman context, *dominium* was a private-law concept denoting property and would only start to blur with the concepts of *iurisdictio* and *imperio* in the works of medieval glossators and commentators such as Bartolus of Sassoferrato. On the relationship between *dominium* and *iurisdictio* in the Roman law tradition, see also Brett, *Liberty, Right and Nature*; Fasolt, *Limits of History*; Feenstra, "*Dominium* and *Ius in Re Aliena*"; Garnsey, *Thinking about Property*.

58 See Garnsey, *Thinking about Property*, 111–21. On the influence of Roman law on Locke's theory of property, see Fitzmaurice, *Sovereignty, Property and Empire*, 118–22.

59 Burgess, *Politics of the Ancient Constitution*; Cromartie, *Constitutionalist Revolution*; Pocock, *Ancient Constitution and the Feudal Law*; Sommerville, "English and Roman Liberty."

60 On the influence of *De legibus* on Stuart political thought, see Sechler and Greenberg, "There Is Scarce a Pamphlet that Doth Not Triumph in Bracton." I continue to refer to the author of *De Legibus* as Bracton, while noting that recent scholarship suggests that Bracton was in fact the editor of a text largely written by others. See, in particular, Brand, "Age of Bracton"; Brand, "Date and Authorship of *Bracton*." For a critique of this view, see Barton, "Authorship of *Bracton*."

61 Bracton, *Laws and Customs*, 1:29–30.

62 Ibid., 1:34.

63 Ibid., 1:30.

64 For example, Skinner, *Hobbes and Republican Liberty*, xi–xii. In his forthcoming book chapter "On Neo-Roman Liberty" he goes further still and presents common law texts such as Bracton's *De legibus* as indispensable sources of the neo-Roman tradition.

65 Skinner, "Classical Liberty, Renaissance Translation, and the English Civil War," 319.

66 Ibid., 310.

67 Ibid., 319.

68 Sommerville, "English and Roman Liberty," 204.

69 For Skinner's response to Sommerville's critique, see Skinner, *From Humanism to Hobbes*, 146–7. On the influence of Roman law on English common law, see also Skinner, "On Neo-Roman Liberty."

70 Bracton, *Laws and Customs*, 1:37.

71 Littleton, *Tenures*, 37.

72 Ibid.

CHAPTER ONE

1 Hill, *Puritanism and Revolution*; Stone, *Crisis of the Aristocracy*; Stone, *Causes of the English Revolution*.

2 Fletcher, *Outbreak of the English Civil War*; Kishlansky, *Monarchy Transformed*; Morrill, *Nature of the English Revolution*; Morrill, *Revolt in the Provinces*; Russell, *Origins of the English Civil War*; Russell, *Causes of the English Civil War*; Russell, *Unrevolutionary England*.

3 Burgess, *Politics of the Ancient Constitution*; Sommerville, "Ideology, Property and the Constitution"; Sommerville, *Royalists and Patriots*.

4 Wood, *Liberty and Property*, 224–31, by contrast, argues that the Parliamentarians remained committed to the mixed constitution, avoiding discussions of popular sovereignty for fear this would be invoked by the multitude.

5 Another non-consensual levy – imposed by the Church rather than the king – that gave rise to debates similar to those discussed in this chapter were tithes. See Brace, *Idea of Property*.

6 Peltonen, *Classical Humanism and Republicanism*, 220–8.

7 *Proceedings in Parliament 1610*, 189.

8 Ibid., 191.

9 Ibid., 191–2.

10 Ibid., 192.

11 *Proceedings in Parliament 1610*, 194–6.

12 *Commons Debates 1628*, 2:56.

13 Ibid., 2:57.

14 Ibid., 2:64.

15 Ibid., 2:66.

16 Ibid., 3:339.

17 See Burgess, *Politics of the Ancient Constitution*, 189–90, on the significance of the ship money case for subsequent debates.

18 See Skinner, *From Humanism to Hobbes*, 148.

19 Skinner, "Classical Liberty and the Coming of the English Civil War," distinguishes between two phases of Parliamentarian thought: the first, prompted by the king's extra-parliamentary levies, made the case for subjects' personal and property rights; the second, which Skinner dates from the controversies surrounding the Militia Ordinance, constituted a more thoroughgoing republican critique of the king's arbitrary power. See above, 18.

20 Another figure who resisted ship money and was initially intended to be the defendant in the test case was William Fiennes, Lord Saye and Sele, Henry Parker's uncle and patron. See Peacey, "Henry Parker and Parliamentary Propaganda," 49–76.

21 See Judson, *Crisis of the Constitution*, 270–1.

22 *Cobbett's Complete Collection*, cols. 903, 905. Hereafter all references to this work appear in brackets in the main text.

23 See Kahn, *Wayward Contracts*, 90–5, for a discussion of the issues of trust and contract in the ship money case.

24 Cromartie, *Constitutionalist Revolution*, 238–9, draws a contrast between the two defences: although both allow the king to interfere with his subjects' property in times of emergency, for St John this is sanctioned by positive law, whereas for Holborn it is sanctioned by the natural right of all men to yield to necessity.

25 Mendle, "Parliamentary Sovereignty," 108, regards Banks as putting forward a "loosely Bodinian" notion of royal sovereignty.

26 Mendle, *Henry Parker and the English Civil War*, 40.

27 Aristotle, *Politics*, 36. This aspect of Aristotle's theory of property is discussed in Frank, *Democracy of Distinction*, 54–9, 74–7. Aquinas, *Political Writings*, 205–20, offers the classic statement of the scholastic position.

28 For Cromartie, *Constitutionalist Revolution*, 236–9, the insistence that ship money did not provide a precedent for extra-parliamentary taxation is evidence of the constitutionalism of the Personal Rule. See also Judson, *Crisis of the Constitution*, 39–41.

29 *Proceedings in the Opening Session*, 482.

30 St John, *Speech or Declaration*, 1–2. Cromartie, *Constitutionalist Revolution*, 253n71, questions the authenticity of this text.

31 St John, *Speech or Declaration*, 2.

32 Ibid., 26.

33 On the explosion of print in the 1640s, see Achinstein, "Texts in Conflict"; Holstun, *Pamphlet Wars*; Peacey, "News, Pamphlets, and Public Opinion"; Raymond, *Pamphlets and Pamphleteering*; Smith, *Literature and Revolution*. McElligott, "Book Trade, Licensing, and Censorship," 135–42, points out, however, that the increase in publications in this period was also due to a proliferation of "steady sellers" such as textbooks for grammar schools and commentaries on the Bible.

34 See Mendle, "Ship Money Case." On the details of Parker's life, see Allen, *English Political Thought*, 426–35; Jordan, *Men of Substance*; Mendle, *Henry Parker and the English Civil War*; Peacey, "Henry Parker and Parliamentary Propaganda"; Zaller, "Henry Parker and the Regiment of True Government."

35 Peacey, "Henry Parker and Parliamentary Propaganda," presents Parker as a propagandist acting on behalf of moderate Parliamentarians such as Nathaniel Fiennes and the earl of Essex. This may be so, but it does not follow that Parker's political theory was any less radical or sophisticated, as Peacey claims.

36 [Parker], *Case of Shipmony*, 2.

37 Ibid., 3.

38 Ibid.

39 Ibid., 21.

40 Ibid., 22.

41 Ibid.

42 Ibid., 24.

43 Ibid., 40.

44 Hakewill, *Libertie of the Subject*, sig. A, 3ᵛ.

45 Ibid., 11, 12.

46 Ibid., 12–13.

47 Ibid., 24.

48 Ibid., 136–7.

49 Ibid., 137.

50 For the view that the common law discourse of the ancient constitution remained the dominant mode of thought in the 1640s, see Cromartie, *Constitutionalist Revolution*; Cromartie, "Parliamentary Sovereignty."

51 See Lee, *Popular Sovereignty*, 291–22; Mendle, *Dangerous Positions*; Mendle, "Royalist Origins of the Separation of Powers"; Sanderson, "*Answer to the Nineteen
   Propositions* Revisited"; Tuck, *Philosophy and Government*, 233; Weston and
   Greenberg, *Subjects and Sovereigns*. The latter work argues, in my view mis-
   takenly, that the *Answer* provides the material for a shift in Parliamentarian
   thinking towards what the authors describe as a "thoroughly novel principle of
   co-ordination in the legislative power" (3).

52 On Parker's theory of popular sovereignty, see Sabbadini, "Popular Sovereignty
   and Representation." See Cromartie, "Parliamentary Sovereignty," 144, for the
   contrasting view that "Parker's major intellectual achievement was not so much
   to abandon this existing mode of thought [the common law] as to offer a theo-
   risation of its most distinctive features."

53 [Parker], *Observations*, 1.

54 See Judson, "Henry Parker," 141.

55 Salmon, *French Religious Wars in English Political Thought*. This view is challenged in Mendle, "Parliamentary Sovereignty," 101.

56 [Parker], *Observations*, 5.

57 Ibid., 28. See Tuck, *Philosophy and Government*, 229–30; Cromartie, "Parliamentary Sovereignty," 158–9.

58 It is true that [Parker], *Observations*, 41, refers to the king as having some independent prerogative powers, but this point is left undeveloped and plainly con-
   tradicted by Parker's central thesis.

59 [Parker], *Observations*, 34. See Franklin, *John Locke and the Theory of Sovereignty*,
   26–7.

60 [Parker], *Observations*, 11.

61 Ibid., 13.

62 Ibid., 15.

63 Ibid., 4.

64 Ibid., 2.

65 Ibid., 5.

66 Ibid., 20.

67 See Tuck, *Philosophy and Government*, 242.

68 Ball, *Caveat for Subjects*, 6.

69 Ibid.

70 Ibid., 7.

71 On the date of composition, see Day, "Some Problems in the Authorship of Sir
    Robert Filmer's Works"; Laslett, "Introduction" to *Patriarcha*; Sommerville, "Au-
    thorship and Dating"; Tuck, "New Date for Filmer's *Patriarcha*"; Wallace, "Date
    of Sir Robert Filmer's *Patriarcha*." Although much of the work was probably
    complete by the time of the paper war, it is clear that Filmer is responding to
    the related controversies from the 1610s and 1620s discussed at the start of this
    chapter. Echoes of Filmer's argument are audible in Williams, *Jura Majestatis*;
    [Maxwell], *Sacro-sancta Regum Majestas*.

72 Filmer, *Patriarcha*, 19.

73 Ibid. In claiming that man is not born into community, Filmer quotes and then
    deliberately misinterprets Suárez, *Tractatus de legibus ac Deo legislatore*, 5:21–4.

74 Filmer, *Patriarcha*, 37.

75 Ibid., 31.

76 Ibid., 39.

77 Hobbes's position on property, unlike other aspects of his thought, is virtually
    identical in the two works, which can therefore be discussed together. I have gen-
    erally preferred to quote from the original English of the *Elements*, providing a
    reference to the equivalent passage from *De cive* where one exists. On Hobbes's
    discussion of property, see Lopata, "Property Theory in Hobbes"; Zarka, "Pro-
    priété chez Hobbes."

78 Hobbes, *On the Citizen*, 76; cf. Hobbes, *Elements of Law*, 109.

79 Hobbes, *Elements of Law*, 72; cf. Hobbes, *On the Citizen*, 28. See Tuck, *Natural
    Rights Theories*, 119–30, for the view that there is a shift between the *Elements*
    and *De cive* (and *Leviathan*) from a wider to a narrower understanding of natural
    right.

80 Hobbes, *Elements of Law*, 72; cf. Hobbes, *On the Citizen*, 29.

81 Hobbes, *Elements of Law*, 112; cf. Hobbes, *On the Citizen*, 29.

82 I use the masculine pronoun in order to avoid clumsiness, even though Hobbes
    is clear that the sovereign could also be a woman or an assembly.

83 Hobbes, *On the Citizen*, 85.

84 The two differ in that, whereas the servant consents to his position and is bound
    only by his obligation, the slave – not having consented and thus under no ob-
    ligation to his master – is at all times physically imprisoned or in chains. See
    Skinner, "On the Liberty of the Ancients and the Moderns," 132–3.

85 Hobbes, *Elements of Law*, 127; cf. Hobbes, *On the Citizen*, 102.

86 Hobbes, *Elements of Law*, 129; cf. Hobbes, *On the Citizen*, 104.

87 Hobbes, *Elements of Law*, 134. Hobbes, *On the Citizen*, 111, revises this argument significantly, introducing for the first time the notion of liberty as "the *absence of obstacles to motion.*" See Skinner, "Freedom as the Absence of Arbitrary Power," 82–123; Skinner, "On the Liberty of the Ancients and the Moderns," 142–6.

88 Hobbes, *Elements of Law*, 138; cf. Hobbes, *On the Citizen*, 116–17.

89 Hobbes, *Elements of Law*, 138; cf. Hobbes, *On the Citizen*, 117.

90 Hobbes, *On the Citizen*, 33. This formulation differs from that of Hobbes, *Elements of Law*, 75, where natural law is defined as those precepts "which declare unto us the ways of peace."

91 Hobbes, *Elements of Law*, 179; cf. Hobbes, *On the Citizen*, 143.

92 Hobbes, *Elements of Law*, 180; cf. Hobbes, *On the Citizen*, 150–1.

93 Hobbes, *Elements of Law*, 180; cf. Hobbes, *On the Citizen*, 150–2.

94 Hobbes, *Elements of Law*, 139. Hobbes, *On the Citizen*, 136, makes substantially the same point, albeit in a different section.

95 Hobbes, *Elements of Law*, 139–40.

96 Ibid., 140.

97 Ibid., 181–2. This passage is omitted from *De cive*, perhaps because Hobbes feared it might give the impression that such resistance was justified.

98 Hobbes, *Elements of Law*, 174; cf. Hobbes, *On the Citizen*, 136.

99 As Sommerville, "Ideology, Property and the Constitution," argues, this was the position of those who supported the king's right to tax without consent throughout the early seventeenth century. Sommerville, *Royalists and Patriots*, 152, claims that Hobbes was indeed "virtually the only absolutist to deny that subjects have rights of property against the crown."

100 On the "constitutional Royalists," see Smith, *Constitutional Royalism*; Wilcher, *Writing of Royalism*.

101 On the controversy surrounding the Militia Ordinance, see Mendle, "Parliamentary Sovereignty," 152–62. Tuck, *Philosophy and Government*, 225, argues that Parliament's initial constitutional stand against ship money gave way, with the controversy surrounding the militia, to "a wholly different mode of discourse."

102 *Miracle*, 18.

103 Bodleian Library, MS Rawlinson D. 398, fol. 250.

104 Ferne, *Resolving of Conscience*, 4, 20.

105 *Humble Petition*, 3.

106 [Digges], *Answer to a Printed Book*, 11–12. On Digges, see Smith, *Constitutional Royalism*, 223–36; Wilcher, *Writing of Royalism*, 202.

107 [Digges], *Answer to a Printed Book*, 12.

108 See Daly, "John Bramhall"; Sanderson, "Serpent-Salve"; Smith, *Constitutional Royalism*, 220–2.

109 [Bramhall], *Serpent Salve*, 84–5.

110 Ibid., 85.

111 Ibid., 171–2.

112 Ibid., 172.

113 *Briefe Discourse*, 1.

114 *Discourse or Dialogue*, 7–8.

115 *Plea for the Parliament*, 8; cf. *Cobbett's Parliamentary History*, vol. 2, col. 957.

116 For an account of Goodwin's political and religious thought, see Coffey, *John Goodwin and the Puritan Revolution*.

117 Goodwin, *Anti-Cavalierisme*, 2.

118 On the neo-Roman dimension to Goodwin's thought, see Skinner, "Freedom as the Absence of Arbitrary Power," 86.

119 Goodwin, *Anti-Cavalierisme*, 2–3.

120 Ibid., 16.

121 Bridge, *Wounded Conscience*, 25–6.

122 Bridge, *Truth of the Times*, 3. Bridge may be borrowing from Bramhall's distinction between dominion and possession in the *Sovereign Salve*, issued only a month or so earlier.

123 Bridge, *Truth of the Times*, 3.

124 Hunton, *Treatise of Monarchie*, 47. See Tuck, *Philosophy and Government*, 235; Weston and Greenberg, *Subjects and Sovereigns*, 58–61.

125 Hunton, *Treatise of Monarchie*, 47.

126 Sanderson, "Philip Hunton's 'Appeasement,'" 449; Peacey, "Henry Parker and Parliamentary Propaganda," 84.

127 *Maximes Unfolded*, 33.

128 *New Plea*, 8.

129 Ibid., 7–8.

130 Kahn, *Wayward Contracts*, 95–6, highlights the role of earlier Royalist ideas of necessity and reason of state in the Parliamentarian literature of the 1640s. See also Tuck, *Philosophy and Government*, 226–7; Mendle, "Parliamentary Sovereignty," 98.

131 Marsh, *Argument*, 8.

132 Ibid., 8–9.

133 Ibid., 29.

134 *Just Complaint*, 15.

135 Ibid., 16.

136 See Early Modern Research Group, "Commonwealth," for a genealogy of the term "commonwealth," including a discussion of its economic dimension.

137 *Subject of Supremacie*, 17.

138 Ibid., 30.

139 This is occasionally attributed to Parker (e.g., Peacey, "Henry Parker and Parliamentary Propaganda," 94), an attribution rejected in Mendle, *Henry Parker and the English Civil War*, 195.

140 *Political Catechism*, 8.

141 Ibid., 14.

142 Ibid., 8.

143 [Parker], *Contra-Replicant*, 14.

144 Ibid., 29–30.

145 Ibid., 30.

146 [Parker], *Jus Populi*, 18.

147 Ibid., 18–19.

148 Ibid., 21.

149 Ibid., 23.

150 Ibid.; cf. Sallust, *War with Catiline*, 104.

151 [Parker], *Jus Populi*, 23. Machiavelli's argument was in fact that *republics* (and not princes) ought to keep the *public* (and not the court) rich and their citizens poor. See Machiavelli, *Discourses*, 100.

152 [Parker], *Jus Populi*, 31, 32, 35.

153 Ibid., 36.

154 Ibid.

155 Ibid.

156 Ibid., 36–7.

157 Ibid., 37.

158 Ibid.

159 Ibid., 38.

160 Lilburne, *Innoncency and Truth Justified*, 57. On Parker's influence on the Levellers, see Mendle, *Henry Parker and the English Civil War*, 82–3.

CHAPTER TWO

1 According to Vernon and Baker, "What Was the First Agreement of the People?," the Levellers did not actually exist as an identifiable group until late 1647, and even then they were far from constituting a political party in any meaningful sense.

2 See Foxley, "Levellers," esp. 272–3; Levy, "Freedom, Property and the Levellers,"

121; Peacey, "John Lilburne and the Long Parliament," esp. 634; Sharp, "John Lilburne and the Long Parliament's Book of Declarations."

3 [Lilburne], *Regall Tyrannie discovered*, 40–1; cf. [Parker], *Observations*, 1–2.

4 *Animadversions upon Those Notes*, 12.

5 Overton, *Arrow against All Tyrants*, 3. See Cromartie, *Constitutionalist Revolution*, 271; Foxley, "Problems of Sovereignty in Leveller Writings," 645–6; Foxley, "Levellers," 281–2; Gleissner, "Levellers and Natural Law," 78; Wood, *Liberty and Property*, 237–8.

6 [Parker], *Observations*, 20. See above, 42.

7 [Parker], *Jus Populi*, 63 (mispaginated as 65).

8 Ibid., 66.

9 Ibid., 36.

10 Overton, *Arrow against All Tyrants*, 3.

11 Macpherson, *Political Theory of Possessive Individualism*, 139–42. One counter-argument to Macpherson's possessive individualist reading of the Levellers proposed by Hughes, "Gender and Politics," 171, which is undermined by the language used here by Overton, is that the Levellers do not present themselves as individual men but "very overtly as householders, as the heads of mutually supportive, clearly differentiated units of husbands, wives, servants and children."

12 Overton, *Arrow against All Tyrants*, 4.

13 Ibid.

14 Ibid.

15 Ibid.

16 Ibid.

17 Overton, *Appeale*, 6.

18 Ibid.

19 Ibid.

20 Ibid., sig. C, 2^r–C, 3^v (pagination interrupted).

21 [Parker], *Letter*, 20.

22 [Lilburne], *Regall Tyrannie discovered*, 33.

23 Ibid., 38–9.

24 It is generally thought that the *Agreement* was written by Lilburne, Overton, and other leading Levellers. This view is challenged in Vernon and Baker, "What Was the First Agreement of the People?"

25 *Agreement of the People*, 3. This is echoed in *Foundations of Freedom*, 10–11.

26 On the relationship between the Parliamentarians' and the Levellers' ideas of representation, see Sabbadini, "Popular Sovereignty and Representation."

27 *Agreement of the People*, 4.

28 Cromartie, *Constitutionalist Revolution*, 271.

29 Overton, *Arrow against All Tyrants*, 3.

30 [Lilburne], *Regall Tyrannie discovered*, 34. A similar argument is also made in Lilburne, *Innocency and Truth Justified*, 59.

31 [Lilburne], *Regall Tyrannie discovered*, 34.

32 Ibid.

33 Ibid., 37–8.

34 The question of authorship remains unresolved. It has been attributed to Wildman (Glover, "Putney Debates: Popular versus Elitist Republicanism"), Overton (Seaberg, "Norman Conquest and the Common Law," 798–99n1) and even Nedham (Worden, "Wit in a Roundhead," 320; Scott, *Commonwealth Principles*, 82–3).

35 *Vox Plebis*, 10.

36 Ibid., 3; cf. Machiavelli, *Discourses*, 29–31.

37 *Vox Plebis*, 63; cf. Machiavelli, *Discourses*, 100.

38 *Vox Plebis*, 63.

39 Ibid., 62.

40 Ibid.

41 Ibid., 64; cf. Machiavelli, *Prince*, 54–5, 58.

42 [Wildman], *Putney Projects*, 32.

43 Ibid., 20 (mispaginated as 18).

44 Ibid.

45 Ibid., 37.

46 Ibid.

47 On the Levellers' reaction to Parliament's Civil War taxation, see Morrill, *Nature of the English Revolution*, esp. 307, 321–8.

48 Orr, "Law, Liberty, and the English Civil War," esp. 155, argues that Lilburne's experience in custody led him to articulate a "negative," "Hobbesian" concept of liberty. The fact that Lilburne made extensive use of common law sources hardly supports Orr's contention, as he seems to believe, and his own account of Lilburne's understanding of freedom (161–2) serves in fact to highlight its republican character.

49 [Lilburne], *Regall Tyrannie discovered*, 43.

50 Ibid., 45.

51 Ibid.

52 Ibid., 65.

53 Foxley, "Problems of Sovereignty in Leveller Writings," esp. 643–4. Peacey, "John Lilburne and the Long Parliament," argues, more plausibly, that the Levellers – or at least Lilburne – were until early 1645 loyal to Parliament, then aligned themselves with the Independents and against the Presbyterians before turning against Parliament altogether by the summer of 1647.

54 Lilburne, *Englands Birth-Right Justified*, 3.

55 Ibid., 3–4.

56 [Parker], *Observations*, 20.

57 Lilburne, *Englands Birth-Right Justified*, 36.

58 Ibid., 45.

59 Ibid.

60 Lilburne, *Legall Fundamentall Liberties*, 6.

61 Ibid.

62 Ibid., 7.

63 *New Engagement.*

64 *Declaration of the Wel-Affected*, 5.

65 *Foundations of Freedom*, 13; cf. Lilburne et al., *Agreement of the Free People*, 6.

66 [Nedham], *Mercurius Pragmaticus*, no. 9.

67 For convenience, I refer to Leveller sympathizers within the New Model Army as Levellers.

68 See Baker, "Franchise Debate Revisited"; Davis, "Levellers and Democracy"; Hampsher-Monk, "Political Theory of the Levellers"; Macpherson, *Political Theory of Possessive Individualism*, 107–9; Skinner, *From Humanism to Hobbes*, 151–6; Thomas, "Levellers and the Franchise"; Thompson, "Maximilian Petty and the Putney Debate."

69 *Puritanism and Liberty*, 58. On Ireton's position, see Wood, *Liberty and Property*, 234–6.

70 *Puritanism and Liberty*, 58. Gleissner, "Levellers and Natural Law," 86, claims that the Levellers did not defend the right to vote by appealing to natural right.

71 *Puritanism and Liberty*, 58.

72 Bass, "Levellers," 429. Pocock, "Authority and Property," 58, also claims that the charge of economic levelling was "rather a stick to beat the Levellers with than a fear of anything specific."

73 *Puritanism and Liberty*, 55.

74 Ibid., 61–2.

75 Thompson, "Maximilian Petty and the Putney Debate," 68–9.

76 *Puritanism and Liberty*, 83.

77 See Macpherson, *Political Theory of Possessive Individualism*, and the critiques thereof in Hampsher-Monk, "Political Theory of the Levellers"; Thomas, "Levellers and the Franchise"; Thompson, "Maximilian Petty and the Putney Debate." See also Skinner, *From Humanism to Hobbes*, 151–4.

78 *Puritanism and Liberty*, 53. This echoes Lilburne, *Charters of London*, 4.

79 *Puritanism and Liberty*, 63, 61.

80 Ibid., 71.

81 On the Levellers' involvement in high politics in 1647–48, see Corns, *Uncloistered Virtue*, 130–5.

82 Lilburne, *Whip for the present House of Lords*, 2.

83 *Foundations of Freedom*, 12; cf. Lilburne et al., *Agreement of the Free People*, 7. This repeated a demand first made in *To the Right Honorable, the Commons of England*, 6. Other works denying the charge of communism include Lilburne, *Legall Fundamentall Liberties*, 75, where Lilburne attacks the Diggers.

84 *Foundations of Freedom*, 7. See also Lilburne et al., *Agreement of the Free People*, 3.

85 Lilburne et al., *Manifestation*, 4.

86 Hampsher-Monk, "Political Theory of the Levellers," 411, claims that in *A Manifestation* the Leveller leaders presented private property as conventional.

87 Lilburne et al., *Manifestation*, 5.

88 See Levy, "Freedom, Property and the Levellers," 120.

89 *New Engagement*. The demand is also made in *Foundations of Freedom*, 15.

90 *New Engagement*.

91 Ibid.

92 Overton, *Appeale*, 38.

93 *To the Right Honorable, the Commons*, 5.

94 Ibid., 6.

95 Ibid.

96 Lilburne, *Upright Mans Vindication*, 21–2. See Glover, "Classical Plebeians," 213.

97 Hill, *World Turned Upside Down*, 118.

98 See Hill, "Introduction," 28–31, on the possible connections between the authors of these works and the Diggers.

99   *More Light Shining in Buckingham-shire*, 3.

100 *Light Shining in Buckinghamshire*, 1–2.

101 Ibid., 2.

102 Ibid.

103 Ibid., 3–4.

104 Ibid., 5.

105 *More Light Shining in Buckingham-shire*, 16.

106 Ibid., 4, 7.

107 It is curious that Nelson, *Hebrew Commonwealth*, does not discuss the Bucking-
     hamshire tracts, given his contention that Hebraic thought was the main source
     for the promotion of agrarian laws in England. According to Nelson, the first
     English theorist to advocate agrarian laws was James Harrington.

108 *Light shining in Buckinghamshire*, 6.

109 Ibid., 7.

110 Ibid., 6.

111 Ibid.

112 Ibid., 7.

113 *Tyranipocrit, Discovered* has been attributed to Walwyn in Brailsford, *Levellers
     and the English Revolution*, 71n1; Lutaud, *Winstanley*, 183, 437; Lutaud, *Cromwell,
     les Niveleurs et la République*, 79–81. This attribution has been questioned in
     Morton, *World of the Ranters*, 196. Taft, "Appendix 1," 532–5, points out that the
     economic levelling it advocates is expressly rejected by Walwyn in other works
     published by him at around the same time.

114 *Tyranipocrit, Discovered*, 3. This critique of the idle nobility has echoes of More,
     Utopia, 16.

115 *Tyranipocrit, Discovered*, 18.

116 Ibid., 6.

117 Ibid., 20.

118 Ibid., 23.

119 Ibid., 33.

120 Ibid., 38.

121 Ibid.

122 Ibid., 53.

123 On the Digger communities, see Hill, "Introduction," 28–31; Davis, *Utopia and
     the Ideal Society*, 174. On the opposition to the Diggers, see Gurney, "Furious Di-
     vells?"

124 Brace, "Imagining the Boundaries," argues that Winstanley's rejection of private property was also a rejection of what she describes as the "bounded self." For an account of what is known about Winstanley's life, see Alsop, "Gerrard Winstanley"; Corns et al., "Introduction."

125 On the importance of the concept of liberty in Winstanley's thought, see Chernaik, "Civil Liberty in Milton, the Levellers and Winstanley."

126 On the religious dimension to Winstanley's thought and its possible sources, see Corns, *Uncloistered Virtue*, 150–9; Hill, "Religion of Gerrard Winstanley"; Loewenstein, "Gerrard Winstanley and the Diggers," 332–42; Smith, "Gerrard Winstanley," 51–5.

127 Winstanley, *Mysterie of God*, 273.

128 Ibid., 292.

129 Davis, *Utopia and the Ideal Society*, 178, emphasizes the passive nature of Winstanley's millenarianism.

130 See, for example, Winstanley, *New Law of Righteousnes*, 513–19; Winstanley, *Declaration to the Powers of England*, 14.

131 See Raymond, "In 1649, to St. George's Hill," 432–44, on the changes introduced in this work.

132 Winstanley, *New Law of Righteousnes*, 481.

133 Ibid.

134 Ibid.

135 Winstanley, *Declaration to the Powers of England*, 6.

136 Ibid. 6.

137 See Corns, *Uncloistered Virtue*, 168–9.

138 Winstanley, *New Law of Righteousnes*, 482.

139 Winstanley does not elaborate on this argument in any great detail. He occasionally seems to regard the abolition of private property as eliminating the need for government and its laws (e.g., Winstanley, *New Law of Righteousnes*, 507), but Winstanley, *Law of Freedom in a Platform*, 373, emphasizes the role of an established government with the power to put people to death for seeking to reintroduce private property. On this shift in Winstanley's thought, see Corns, *Uncloistered Virtue*, 172–4; Davis, "Gerrard Winstanley and the Restoration of True Magistracy"; Davis, *Utopia and the Ideal Society*; Hill, *World Turned Upside Down*, 41; Hill, "Religion of Gerrard Winstanley," 44–5.

140 Winstanley, *New Law of Righteousnes*, 523.

141 Loewenstein, "Gerrard Winstanley and the Diggers," 329.

142 Winstanley, *Declaration to the Powers of England*, 15–16.

143 Ibid., 10.

144 According to Davis, *Utopia and the Ideal Society*, 184–5, Winstanley never went beyond these demands and thus never actually advocated the wholesale abolition of private property.

145 Winstanley, *New Law of Righteousnes*, 519.

146 Winstanley, *Fire in the Bush*, 220.

147 Winstanley, *New-yeers Gift*, 114.

148 See Aylmer, "England's Spirit Unfoulded."

149 Winstanley, *Englands Spirit Unfoulded*, 162. The two acts that Winstanley refers to are those of 17 March 1649 abolishing the monarchy and 19 May 1649 declaring England to be a "Commonwealth and free State."

150 Winstanley, *Englands Spirit Unfoulded*, 162.

151 See, for example, Winstanley, *Law of Freedom in a Platform*, 243–8; Winstanley, *Humble Request*, 264.

152 Kennedy, *Diggers, Levellers, and Agrarian Capitalism*, 155–65, presents Winstanley as sharing the Levellers' sense of betrayal for the Parliamentarians' abandonment of the revolutionary cause that had, in his view, initially prompted them to take up arms against the king.

153 Winstanley, *Declaration to the Powers of England*, 8.

154 Winstanley, *Watch-Word to the City of London*, 100.

155 Winstanley, *Law of Freedom in a Platform*, 279.

156 Ibid., 280.

157 See Chernaik, "Civil Liberty in Milton, the Levellers and Winstanley," for a comparison between Milton and Winstanley.

158 Winstanley, *Law of Freedom in a Platform*, 294–5.

159 Ibid., 305.

160 Ibid., 280.

161 Ibid., 309.

162 Ibid., 290–1.

163 Ibid., 283.

CHAPTER THREE

1 Fletcher, *Outbreak of the English Civil War*; Kishlansky, *Monarchy Transformed*; Morrill, *Nature of the English Revolution*; Morrill, *Revolt in the Provinces*; Russell,

Origins of the English Civil War; Russell, *Causes of the English Civil War*; Russell, *Unrevolutionary England.*

2 Worden, "Marchamont Nedham and the Beginnings of English Republicanism," 49. See also Worden, *Rump Parliament*; Worden, "Classical Republicanism and the Puritan Revolution"; Worden, "English Republicanism"; Worden, "Republicanism, Regicide and Republic"; Pocock, *Machiavellian Moment*; Pocock and Schochet, "Interregnum and Restoration"; Corns, "Milton and the Characteristics of a Free Commonwealth." There have been some notable defections from this orthodoxy, among them Nuzzo, *Superiortà degli stati liberi*; Peltonen, *Classical Humanism and Republicanism*; Scott, *Commonwealth Principles*; Skinner, *Liberty before Liberalism*; Skinner, "Classical Liberty, Renaissance Translation, and the English Civil War"; Skinner, "History and Ideology in the English Revolution"; Smith, *Literature and Revolution*; Tuck, *Philosophy and Government.*

3 Worden, "Marchamont Nedham and the Beginnings of English Republicanism," 49–50.

4 As we saw in chapter 1, however, classical republicanism was not entirely absent from earlier debates. See in particular [Parker], *Jus Populi*, 23.

5 Pincus, "Neither Machiavellian Moment nor Possessive Individualism."

6 Hawke, *Right of Dominion*. On Civil War and Interregnum royalism, see Wilcher, *Writing of Royalism*; McElligott, "Propaganda and Censorship"; McElligott and Smith, *Royalists and Royalism.*

7 [Lawson], *Conscience Puzzled*; Lawson, *Political Sacra et Civilis*. See Franklin, *John Locke and the Theory of Sovereignty*, 53–86.

8 Ascham, *Confusions and Revolutions*; Nedham, *Case of the Commonwealth*; [Rous], *Lawfulness of obeying the Present Government*. See Burgess, "Usurpation, Obligation, and Obedience"; Judson, *From Tradition to Political Reality*; Kelsey, *Inventing a Republic*, 5-6; Skinner, "Conquest and Consent"; Skinner, "History and Ideology in the English Revolution"; Skinner, "Context of Hobbes's Theory of Political Obligation"; Wallace, "Engagement Controversy."

9 On Hobbes's relationship to the de facto theorists, see Skinner, "Conquest and Consent"; Skinner, "Context of Hobbes's Theory of Political Obligation."

10 Hobbes, *Leviathan*, 220.

11 Ibid., 198.

12 Ibid., 390.

13 Ibid., 504.

14 On Hobbes's theory of representation, see Brito Vieira, *Elements of Representa-*

tion; Pitkin, *Concept of Representation*; Runciman, *Pluralism and the Personality of the State*; Runciman, "What Kind of Person Is Hobbes's State?"; Skinner, "Hobbes on Persons, Authors and Representatives."

15 Hobbes, *Leviathan*, 244.

16 Ibid.

17 Ibid.

18 As Skinner, "Hobbes on Persons, Authors and Representatives," points out, Hobbes does, however, reject the Parliamentarians' idea that it is the corporate body of the people that entrusts its sovereign power to the king. For Hobbes, this entity does not exist in the state of nature; the sovereign instead receives his authority from "every one of that Multitude in particular," and the "Multitude of men, are made *One* Person, when they are by one man, or one Person, Represented" (Hobbes, *Leviathan*, 248).

19 On the relationship between Streater and the Levellers, see Smith, *Literature and Revolution*; Smith, "Popular Republicanism in the 1650s"; Raymond, "John Streater."

20 [Streater], *Glympse*, 2.

21 Streater, *Further Continuance*, 38. *The Grand Politic Informer* was a newsbook produced by Streater in mid-1653. *A further Continuance*, the fourth or fifth issue of the newsbook, is the only one to survive. See Raymond, "John Streater."

22 Streater, *Further Continuance*, 39.

23 [Streater], *Observations*, no. 2, 11.

24 [Sexby and Titus], *Killing Noe Murder*, 5–6. See Lutaud, *Des Révolutions d'Angleterre à la Révolution Française*.

25 [Sexby and Titus], *Killing Noe Murder*, 8.

26 Milton, *Second Defence*, 618–19. That is not to say, of course, that earlier prose works such as *Areopagitica* (1644) were not politically engaged.

27 See Dzelzainis, "Milton and the Protectorate in 1658."

28 On this stage of Milton's career, see Keeble, "General Introduction."

29 Milton, *Commonplace Book*, 410.

30 On the relaitonship between these works and Milton's later republican tracts, see Fallon, "Nascent Republican Theory," 311.

31 See Dzelzainis, "Republicanism"; Lovett, "Milton's Case for a Free Commonwealth"; Mueller, "Contextualizing Milton's Nascent Republicanism"; Sirluck, "Milton's Political Thought."

32 Milton, *Commonplace Book*, 433–4.

33 Milton, *Tenure*, 203.

34 For the view that Milton was fundamentally opposed to all forms of monarchy, see Norbrook, *Writing the English Republic*, 204; Skinner, "John Milton and the Politics of Slavery," 302–3; Wolfe, *Milton in the Puritan Revolution*, 223–4. Pincus, "Neither Machiavellian Moment nor Possessive Individualism," 710, argues that Milton, at least in the two Latin defences, was more narrowly opposed to tyranny. For the view that Milton did not take an anti-monarchical stance until *The Readie and Easie Way*, see Corns, "Milton and the Characteristics of a Free Commonwealth"; Knoppers, "Late Prose," 317; Worden, "Milton and Marchamont Nedham," 166. For a critique of Corns, see Dzelzainis, "Republicanism."

35 On the *Defensio* and its reception in England, see Sauer, "Milton's *Defences*," 446.

36 Milton, *Defence*, 326.

37 Ibid.

38 Ibid., 377. This argument can also be found in "Philodemius," *Originall and End of Civill Power*, 18–19.

39 Locke, *Two Treatises*, 271. See below, 197. Milton's *Defensio* appears in Locke's booklists from 1667 onwards, and Locke owned a copy of the 1689 edition of *The Tenure*. See Dzelzainis, "Introduction," xxv.

40 Milton, *Defence*, 472; cf. Locke, *Two Treatises*, 412.

41 Milton, *Defence*, 472.

42 On the relationship between Parker and Milton, see Keeble, "General Introduction." The view put forward in Fink, *Classical Republicans*, that Milton was a theorist of the mixed constitution seems to me entirely unfounded. See Dzelzainis, "Republicanism," 299, for a critique of this argument.

43 The attribution of this work to Anthony Ascham in Smith, *Literature and Revolution*, 180–2, has been generally accepted but seems to me problematic. It is difficult to imagine an author who regarded conquest as the source of political legitimacy simultaneously embracing popular sovereignty, or indeed styling himself as "Philodemius" ("lover of the people"). It seems more likely that this is a late work by Parker himself – who was not averse to self-plagiarism – or by one of his followers.

44 "Philodemius," *Originall and End of Civill Power*, 4; cf. [Parker], *Observations*, 1.

45 "Philodemius," *Originall and End of Civill Power*, 5, 13; cf. [Parker], *Observations*, 4.

46 "Philodemius," *Originall and End of Civill Power*, 14; cf. [Parker], *Observations*, 20.

47 Milton, *Tenure*, 202. On the idea of "trust" in Milton's thought, see Dzelzainis, "Introduction," xvii–xviii.

48 [Parker], *Observations*, 4. See Skinner, "John Milton and the Politics of Slavery," esp. 299, for the claim that Milton was drawing on Parker here.

49 Milton, *Tenure*, 204.

50 Although Milton never mentions the Levellers in his works, his silence here may be indicative of a degree of sympathy for them since his first assignment as secretary for foreign tongues had been to pen an attack on Lilburne's *The Second part of England's New Chains Discovered* (1649). On this point, see Norbrook, *Writing the English Republic*, 201–4; Loewenstein, "Milton's Prose and the Revolution," 95. On the relationship between Milton and the Levellers more generally, see also Hill, *Milton and the English Revolution*; Jenkins, "Shrugging off the Norman Yoke"; Keeble, "General Introduction"; Lewalski, *Life of John Milton*, 240; Wolfe, *Milton in the Puritan Revolution*. For a critique of the view that Milton was a Leveller sympathizer, see Dzelzainis, "History and Ideology."

51 This qualification is present even in the *Vindiciae, contra tyrannos*, the most radical of the monarchomach tracts. See Brutus, *Vindiciae, contra tyrannos*, 168. On the monarchomachs' influence on the writers of the English Civil War, see Salmon, *French Religious Wars in English Political Thought*. For the view that Milton was deliberately subverting Calvinist resistance theory, see Dzelzainis, "Milton's Politics," 78–9.

52 Milton, *Tenure*, 221.

53 Ibid., 236–7. See Fenton, "Hope, Land Ownership, and Milton's 'Paradise Within,'" 153, for a discussion of this passage that stresses the connection between economic power and individual liberty.

54 Milton, *Commonplace Book*, 446.

55 Ibid., 482.

56 Ibid., 480.

57 It was in fact written by the Royalist John Gauden, who was probably drawing on Charles's papers.

58 Milton, *Eikonoklastes*, 448.

59 Ibid., 435–6.

60 For Knoppers, "Milton's *The Readie and Easie Way*," the near inevitability of the Restoration suggests that Milton's intention was not to offer a constitutional proposal but to comment on the tragedy that was about to unfold.

61 Milton, *Readie and Easie Way*, 360; cf. [Streater], Observations, no. 2, 13.

62 Milton, *Readie and Easie Way*, 360.

63 Ibid., 378.

64 Ibid.

65 Milton, *Eikonoklastes*, 423.

66 Ibid., 428.

67 Ibid., 451.

68 Milton, *Defence*, 360. It is clear from Milton, *Defence*, 317, that he is using "senate" to refer to Parliament, something that is curious given that the unicameral Parliament then sitting was based on the former House of Commons (the Humble Petition and Advice of 1657 reinstated the "other House," much to the chagrin of the more committed republicans). By describing this institution as a senate and distinguishing it – in Roman vein – from the people, Milton may have been seeking to challenge the Parliamentarians' conflation between the two.

69 Milton, *Defence*, 461.

70 Milton, *Eikonoklastes*, 458. On the Aristotelianism of this passage, see Dzelzainis, "Milton's Classical Republicanism," 16. [Streater], *Observations*, no. 7, 50, also discusses the importance of self-sufficiency for the attainment of liberty.

71 Milton, *Eikonoklastes*, 458. See Fenton, "Hope, Land Ownership, and Milton's 'Paradise Within,'" on the connection between landownership and freedom, with particular reference to *Paradise Lost*.

72 Armitage, "Milton"; Armitage, "Empire and Liberty." See also Dzelzainis, "Milton's Classical Republicanism," 14, 22–3. Worden, "Marchamont Nedham and the Beginnings of English Republicanism," 57, stresses in particular the Machiavellian influence on this aspect of Milton's thought. For a critique of Armitage's interpretation, see Scott, *Commonwealth Principles*, 214–20.

73 Milton, *Commonplace Book*, 420.

74 Pincus, "Neither Machiavellian Moment nor Possessive Individualism," esp. 707, 710–14.

75 Milton, *Readie and Easie Way*, 385–6. On Milton's discussion of the economic benefits of republican rule in *The Readie and Easie Way*, see Hoxby, *Mammon's Music*, 77–90.

76 Milton, *Readie and Easie Way*, 374.

77 Ibid., 386.

78 Ibid.

79 Ibid., 387.

80 Milton, *Readie and Easie Way*, 2nd ed., 445–6.

81 On Milton's rejection of agrarian laws in *The Readie and Easie Way*, see Lewalski, *Life of John Milton*, 394.

82 Milton, *Readie and Easie Way*, 384.

83 Milton, *Defence*, 430.

84 While the possibility that this work may have been composed in the 1640s continues to elicit some scholarly controversy, it seems more likely, as Knoppers, "Headnote," xciii–xcvii, concludes, to have been written after 1660. See Worden, "Milton, *Samson Agonistes*, and the Restoration," for an interesting discussion of *Samson* that locates it firmly in the Restoration.

85 On the personal relationship between Milton and Nedham, see Worden, "Milton and Marchamont Nedham"; Worden, *Literature and Politics*. Lewalski, *Life of John Milton*, suggests that Milton may have had a hand in securing Nedham's release from Newgate Prison and his appointment as the new regime's semi-official propagandist.

86 As Raymond, "Marchamont Nedham," 387, argues, however, Nedham's work was also widely read on the Continent.

87 See Worden, "Marchamont Nedham and the Beginnings of English Republicanism," 66–7; Worden, "Milton, *Samson Agonistes*, and the Restoration," 320; Worden, *Literature and Politics*, 17–18; Scott, *Commonwealth Principles*, 82–4, 245–8.

88 The only book-length biography of Nedham remains Frank, *Cromwell's Press Agent*. On Nedham's various changes of allegiance, see also Peacey, "Henry Parker and Parliamentary Propaganda," 148–71; Raymond, "Marchamont Nedham"; Worden, "Marchamont Nedham and the Beginnings of English Republicanism"; Worden, "Milton and Marchamont Nedham"; Worden, "Milton, *Samson Agonistes*, and the Restoration"; Worden, *Literature and Politics*.

89 On Nedham's transition from the de facto theory to republicanism after the Battle of Worcester, see Worden, "Marchamont Nedham and the Beginnings of English Republicanism," 61–2; Worden, *Literature and Politics*, 24.

90 Nedham, *Case of the Commonwealth*, 22.

91 Ibid., 30.

92 Ibid., 82.

93 Cf. [Nedham], *True state*, 31, where he seems to be reaching out to his former friends by pointing out that the franchise under the Protectorate is wider than it had been previously.

94 Nedham, *Case of the Commonwealth*, 98. Attacking the Levellers by likening their proposals to the Gracchian agrarian reforms appears also to have been a trope of Royalist polemic. See, for example, Hawke, *Right of Dominion*, 77.

95   Nedham, *Case of the Commonwealth*, 109.

96   [Nedham], *Mercurius Politicus*, no. 92, 1462. This idea was echoed in [Streater], *Observations*, no. 11, 85.

97   [Nedham], *Mercurius Politicus*, no. 92, 1458.

98   Ibid., 1459 (mispaginated as 1456).

99   Ibid.

100   Ibid., 1459–60.

101   As Raymond, "Marchamont Nedham," 389–90, points out, Nedham was already calling for the establishment of a more stable government in the closing months of 1653.

102   [Nedham], *True state*, 13.

103   Ibid., 17.

104   Ibid., 28.

105   Ibid., 36. On Nedham's connection to Saye and Sele, see Peacey, "Henry Parker and Parliamentary Propaganda," 159–61.

106   [Nedham], *True state*, 28.

107   Ibid.

108   Ibid.

109   Ibid.

110   Ibid., 28–9.

111   On the connections between Nedham's and the Leveller's views about elections, see Worden, "Marchamont Nedham and the Beginnings of English Republicanism," 66.

112   [Nedham], *True state*, 31.

113   Ibid.

114   Ibid.

115   Ibid., 28.

116   Ibid., 49.

117   Ibid., 49–50.

118   Ibid., 50. These arguments are reworked in Nedham, *Interest will not Lie*, esp. 21.

119   On Nedham's Machiavellism, see Raab, *English Face of Machiavelli*, 159–64; Rahe, "Machiavelli in the English Revolution."

120   See Frank, *Cromwell's Press Agent*, on the textual variations between the editorials and *The Excellencie*. The mere fact of reissuing the material in a different context alters its meaning, with the result that, for Worden, "Marchamont Nedham and the Beginnings of English Republicanism," 77, *The Excellencie* constitutes "a daring and clever assault on the Protectorate."

121   Nedham, *Excellencie*, 84. See Scott, *Commonwealth Principles*, 156.

122 Nedham, *Excellencie*, sig. A, 3^r.

123 See Worden, "English Republicanism," 449. This further complicates the characterization of Nedham as a proponent of the commercial strand of republicanism in Pincus, "Neither Machiavellian Moment nor Possessive Individualism,"
given Pincus's claim that Machiavelli's economic ideas were largely rejected by
this group (708).

124 Nedham, *Excellencie*, 71.

125 Ibid., 72.

126 [Nedham], *Mercurius Politicus*, no. 88, 1396.

127 Ibid.

128 Nedham, *Excellencie*, 75 (emphasis added).

129 See Dzelzainis, "Milton's Classical Republicanism," 22–3.

130 Nedham, *Case of the Commonwealth*, 112. This is repeated verbatim in [Nedham],
Mercurius Politicus, no. 69, 1094. Cf. Sallust, *War with Catiline*, 4, 20–2, 104, 110.

131 Milton, *Tenure*, 190.

132 Nedham, *Excellencie*, 49.

133 Ibid., 52.

134 Ibid., 53.

135 Ibid., 19; cf. [Streater], *Observations*, no. 2, 10.

136 Nedham, *Excellencie*, 54.

137 Ibid.

138 Ibid., 55.

CHAPTER FOUR

1 On Harrington's family background, seeBlitzer, *Immortal Commonwealth*, 5–12;
Dickinson, *James Harrington's Republic*, 2; Höpfl, "James Harrington."

2 See Blitzer, *Immortal Commonwealth*, 21–6.

3 Pocock, "Historical Introduction," 5, even suggests that Harrington may have
been drawn to republicanism as a way of coping with his loss.

4 Harrington did, however, produce one final work, an unfinished essay in hylo-
zoic philosophy entitled *The Mechanics of Nature*.

5 Harrington, *Oceana*, 155; cf. Horace, *Satires*, 1.1:68–70.

6 Horace, *Satires*, 1.1:92–4.

7 Nelson, *Greek Tradition in Republican Thought*, 88.

8 Harrington, *Oceana*, 157; cf. Bacon, *Essayes*, 446.

9 Harrington, *Oceana*, 157.

10   Ibid., 158; cf. Bacon, *Essayes*, 447.

11   Harrington, *Oceana*, 158.

12   On Harrington's Platonism, see Blitzer, *Immortal Commonwealth*; Nelson, *Greek Tradition in Republican Thought*, esp. 115–21.

13   Harrington, *Oceana*, 169.

14   Ibid.

15   Ibid., 170. See Nelson, *Greek Tradition in Republican Thought*, 117–19.

16   See Blitzer, *Immortal Commonwealth*, 140–2; Cromartie, "Harringtonian Virtue," 933–95.

17   Harrington, *Oceana*, 171.

18   Harrington, *Prerogative of Popular Government*, 415. Blitzer, *Immortal Commonwealth*, 145, concludes that, in spite of such pronouncements, Harrington is really talking about the sum of private interests.

19   Harrington, *Oceana*, 172.

20   Nelson, *Greek Tradition in Republican Thought*, 109, suggests that this was an anti-Machiavellian argument, founded on a rejection of the Machiavellian view that Rome's success could be attributed to the tumults between the plebians and the nobility.

21   Harrington, *Oceana*, 171.

22   Ibid., 172. Scott, "Rapture of Motion," 153, interprets this passage too literally when he claims that, for Harrington, the business of governing was nothing more than "the division of material spoils."

23   [Wren], *Considerations*, 22–4.

24   Harrington, *Discourse*, 744.

25   He does, however, address this issue in *Prerogative of Popular Government*, 416.

26   Harrington, *Oceana*, 172–3.

27   Harrington, *Aphorisms Political*, 771–2.

28   [Wren], *Considerations*, 28.

29   Harrington, *Rota*, 810.

30   Harrington, *Oceana*, 241–8.

31   See Blitzer, *Immortal Commonwealth*, 40–1.

32   Harrington, *Oceana*, 267.

33   Ibid., 268–9.

34   Harrington, *Discourse*, 739.

35   Harrington, *Art of Lawgiving*, 657.

36   Harrington, *Oceana*, 174.

37   [Wren], *Considerations*, 8.

38 Harrington, *Oceana*, 174.

39 Harrington, *Prerogative of Popular Government*, 415.

40 Harrington, *Oceana*, 163. The only two states in which, according to Harrington, trade is of greater importance than land are Genoa and the United Provinces.

41 Harrington, *Oceana*, 163–4.

42 Harrington, *Art of Lawgiving*, 610. This undermines the claim put forward in Blitzer, *Immortal Commonwealth*, 122, that Harrington's division between king, nobility. and people is a purely qualitative one.

43 For example, Harrington, *Prerogative of Popular Government*, 430.

44 Macpherson, *Political Theory of Possessive Individualism*, 181, argues that the presence of this subclass of wage-earners, excluded from Harrington's commonwealth on the grounds that it lacks property, demonstrates the bourgeois nature of his thought.

45 On Harrington's Aristotelianism, see Cotton, *James Harrington's Political Thought*; Pocock, "Machiavelli, Harrington."

46 This is different from the Polybian mixed constitution, according to which the only way of avoiding the instability caused by *anacyclosis* is to create a constitution with elements of each of the three pure forms. Aristotle's argument is that the best possible state, the *politeia*, is a combination of two corrupt forms: oligarchy and democracy.

47 Harrington, *Oceana*, 259.

48 See, for example, Harrington, *Oceana*, 195–8.

49 Harrington, *System of Politics*, 842. Harrington does acknowledge at 835 that it is possible for the balance to be shared or "equal," but in that case civil war will be inevitable.

50 Harrington, *System of Politics*, 842. Note the change of vocabulary from "commonwealth" to "democracy," a term he uses consistently throughout *A System of Politics*.

51 Hobbes's influence on Harrington has been discussed in Fukuda, *Sovereignty and the Sword*; Rahe, *Republics Ancient and Modern*; Scott, "Rapture of Motion"; Sullivan, *Machiavelli, Hobbes*.

52 Harrington, *Oceana*, 165.

53 Harrington, *Art of Lawgiving*, 605.

54 Cotton, *James Harrington's Political Thought*, 22, goes so far as to argue that the three constitutions can be described in terms of three different military systems: mercenaries (monarchy), tenant soldiers (aristocracy), citizen militia (commonwealth).

55 Harrington, *System of Politics*, 847.

56 Pocock, "Historical Introduction," 15. It has also been discussed extensively in Blitzer, *Immortal Commonwealth*; Cotton, *James Harrington's Political Thought*; Cromartie, "Harringtonian Virtue."

57 See in particular Pocock, "Machiavelli, Harrington"; Pocock, *Machiavellian Moment*; Pocock, "Historical Introduction"; Pocock, *Ancient Constitution and the Feudal Law*.

58 Pocock, *Machiavellian Moment*. The point is also made in Worden, "James Harrington and *The Commonwealth of Oceana*," 92.

59 Pocock, "Machiavelli, Harrington," esp. 112, places greater emphasis on the Greek and particularly Aristotelian dimension to Harrington's thought than the Machiavellian.

60 Pocock, *Ancient Constitution and the Feudal Law*, 129.

61 Pocock, "Historical Introduction," 55.

62 This aspect of Harrington's thought is not altogether absent from Pocock's interpretation. See, for example, Pocock, "Machiavelli, Harrington," 111, 126–7. It is given greater prominence in Wood, *Liberty and Property*, 230–2.

63 Harrington, *Oceana*, 163. Blitzer, *Immortal Commonwealth*, 13, suggests that this view was informed by Harrington's experience of the disastrous economic conditions of rural England in the first half of the seventeenth century.

64 Harrington, *Oceana*, 164.

65 Harrington, *Art of Lawgiving*, 603.

66 Cotton, *James Harrington's Political Thought*, 36, presents this as an unresolved problem in Harrington's theory.

67 These possibilities are considered in Blitzer, *Immortal Commonwealth*, 119.

68 See Armitage, *Ideological Origins*.

69 Harrington, *System of Politics*, 834. For Blitzer, *Immortal Commonwealth*, 131, by contrast, Harrington held that all provincial government is a form of corruption rather than that all corrupt forms of government are provincial.

70 Blitzer, *Immortal Commonwealth*, 132, argues that, since Harrington recognizes that a state such as England can hold provincial empire over a far larger territory such as America, "when we come to provincial empire we are confronted with a basis of government which is totally unconnected with economics."

71 Harrington, *Oceana*, 202.

72 Ibid.

73 Ibid.

74 Ibid., 188.

75 Although Harrington, *Oceana*, 195, states clearly enough that the Gothic balance was aristocratic, elsewhere (e.g., Harrington, *Oceana*, 198) there is some ambiguity, occasionally giving the impression that it is better described as monarchical.

76 Harrington, *Oceana*, 196. On Harrington's attitude towards the ancient constitution, see Burgess, "Repacifying the Polity"; Pocock, *Ancient Constitution and the Feudal Law*.

77 Harrington, *Oceana*, 197.

78 Ibid., 198.

79 Ibid., 231. "Dry rent" is a right to rent in which the landlord does not have the power of collection by seizure of the tenant's goods, as in the case of rent under distress.

80 Harrington, *Art of Lawgiving*, 688.

81 Harrington, *Oceana*, 180. See Blitzer, *Immortal Commonwealth*, 106–7, 156–7; Davis, "Equality in an Unequal Commonwealth." Fukuda, *Sovereignty and the Sword*, 108–9, suggests that "equal commonwealth" refers exclusively to the equal access to office secured by the rotation and has nothing to do with economic equality. Macpherson, *Political Theory of Possessive Individualism*, 188, argues that it refers not to equality of wealth but to the equal opportunity for the generation of wealth.

82 Harrington, *Oceana*, 237–8. Cromartie, "Harringtonian Virtue," 999, draws a contrast between Harrington's favourable view of the growth of commerce and Machiavelli's belief that citizens should be kept poor.

83 Pincus, "Neither Machiavellian Moment nor Possessive Individualism." Rahe, *Republics Ancient and Modern*, 419–20, stresses that, in spite of Harrington's emphasis on land, he is not opposed to trade; his commonwealth for increase is as much about commercial as imperial expansion.

84 Harrington, *Art of Lawgiving*, 689.

85 Nelson, *Hebrew Commonwealth*, 57–8.

86 Harrington, *Oceana*, 231.

87 See Davis, "Equality in an Unequal Commonwealth," 230–1.

88 Harrington, *Oceana*, 164.

89 Harrington, *Art of Lawgiving*, 687.

90 [Wren], *Considerations*, 81–2.

91 Ibid., 82.

92 Harrington, *Prerogative of Popular Government*, 467.

93 As we shall see in the next chapter, Henry Neville would later come up with a more satisfactory reply.

94 Harrington, *Art of Lawgiving*, 602.

95 See Fukuda, *Sovereignty and the Sword*, 85, on the problematic nature of Harrington's discussion of the origins of property.

96 [Wren], *Considerations*, 85.

97 Harrington, *Prerogative of Popular Government*, 429.

98 Ibid., 430.

99 The implication here is that "the people" would include propertyless wage-labourers. See Pocock, "Historical Introduction," 58.

100 Harrington, *Prerogative of Popular Government*, 460. In spite of this language, Harrington avoids the charge of economic levelling in his most sustained attack on the Levellers (*Art of Lawgiving*, 656–60).

101 Harrington, *Prerogative of Popular Government*, 458.

102 Harrington, *System of Politics*, 840.

103 Harrington, *Oceana*, 331.

104 Ibid., 320.

105 Ibid., 324.

106 Armitage, *Ideological Origins*, presents *Oceana* as an attempt to break free from the Machiavellian view that the expansionism on which liberty depends is also a cause of internal instability that would ultimately bring about the demise of freedom.

107 Harrington, *Prerogative of Popular Government*, 444–5.

108 Harrington, *Art of Lawgiving*, 688. This passage is indebted to Bacon and includes a quotation from Bacon, *Essayes*, 410: "Money is like muck, not good except it be spread."

109 Harrington, *Art of Lawgiving*, 690.

110 Harrington, *Prerogative of Popular Government*, 456.

111 Harrington, *Oceana*, 328.

112 Davis, *Utopia and the Ideal Society*, 207.

113 Ibid., 239.

114 Scott, "Rapture of Motion," 151.

115 Ibid., 162.

116 Harrington, *Discourse*, 737–8.

117 Harrington, *Oceana*, 320.

118 Ibid., 205.

119 Ibid., 170; cf. Hobbes, *Leviathan*, 332.

120 Harrington, *Art of Lawgiving*, 665.

121 Harrington, *System of Politics*, 834.

122 Ibid., 835.

123   Harrington, *Oceana*, 170; cf. Hobbes, *Leviathan*, 332.

124   Harrington, *Oceana*, 170–1.

125   See Scott, *Commonwealth Principles*, 162–3.

126   [Wren], *Considerations*, 12.

127   Ibid., 12–13.

128   Harrington, *Prerogative of Popular Government*, 408.

129   Ibid.

CHAPTER FIVE

1   See, for example, Worden, "Republicanism and the Restoration," 153. Ashcraft, *Revolutionary Politics*, 223, however, claims that Sidney "incorporated much of Harrington's argument into his *Discourses*."

2   On Restoration political thought, see Champion, "Political Thinking between Restoration and Hanoverian Succession"; Harris, "Lives, Liberties and Estates"; Harris, *Restoration*; Houston, "Republicanism"; Pocock and Schochet, "Interregnum and Restoration"; Worden, "Republicanism and the Restoration."

3   Hobbes, *Behemoth*, 110. See Skinner, "Freedom as the Absence of Arbitrary Power," 140–2.

4   Hobbes, *Writings on Common Law*, 178.

5   Works displaying republican sympathies in the 1660s include "Misotyrannus," *Mene Tekel*; Bethel, *World's Mistake*; Sidney, *Court Maxims*.

6   L'Estrange, *Considerations and Proposals*, 8.

7   That is not to suggest, of course, that Milton's epic poems were devoid of political meaning, as we saw in chapter 3 in the case of *Samson Agonistes*. On the politics of *Paradise Lost*, see Radzinowicz, "Politics of *Paradise Lost*."

8   Scott, *Algernon Sidney and the Restoration Crisis*, is right to argue that popery and arbitrary government were intimately associated in the minds of the Whigs. However, as Pocock, "England's Cato," argues, it is unclear why Scott feels the need to claim that excluding the duke of York from the succession was therefore not a major preoccupation.

9   *Cobbett's Parliamentary History*, vol. 4, col. 1237.

10   Ibid., col. 1028.

11   *Debates of the House of Commons*, 400.

12   [Settle], *Character of a Popish Successour*, 20.

13   [Clarkson], *Case of Protestants*, 10.

14   Marvell, *Account*, 236–7.

15 Harris, *Restoration*.

16 Warwick, *Discourse of Government*, 44.

17 Marvell, *Account*, 225.

18 Nalson, *Common Interest*, 153.

19 Johnston, *Excellency Of Monarchical Government*, 30.

20 Ibid., 31–2, 33.

21 Neville, *Plato Redivivus*, 79. All subsequent references to *Plato Redivivus* will be inserted in brackets in the main text.

22 This anxiety is ultimately unjustified, Starkey indicates, not because of any particular originality in Neville but because Harringtonian principles are merely conclusions derived from the empirical study of historical change and so cannot be claimed exclusively by anyone.

23 Aubrey, *Brief Lives*, 1:293.

24 This passage may be intended to address a problem with Harrington's theory that [Wren], *Considerations*, 181–2, had picked up on – namely, that if property is the foundation of government, it must be natural and therefore ought not to be altered by measures such as agrarian laws. See Harrington, *Prerogative of Popular Government*, 467, for his somewhat unconvincing reply.

25 It is clear from the parliamentary debates of this period that there was widespread fear of a return to the turmoil of the 1640s–50s. See, for example, *Cobbett's Parliamentary History*, vol. 4, col. 980.

26 On the tradition of contrasting the security of Western European tenants with the precarious servility of Eastern tenants-at-will, see Pocock, *Ancient Constitution and the Feudal Law*.

27 However, [Jones and Sidney], *Just and Modest Vindication*, 19, also offer a relatively positive account of the Ottoman Empire, pointing out that, although the emperors "dispose Arbitrarily of the Lives and Estates of their Subjects," they nevertheless make sure to employ their revenues from the provinces only for "publick occasions" and never for themselves.

28 Pocock, *Machiavellian Moment*, 416–20. As Pocock, "Machiavelli, Harrington," argues, this approach was pioneered by the earl of Shaftesbury, the author of the *Letter from a Person of Quality*, and other so-called neo-Harringtonians. On Neville's ancient constitutionalism, see also Scott, *Commonwealth Principles*, 198.

29 Neville was perhaps thinking of the Commons' resolution of 3 July 1678: "That all Aids and Supplies to his majesty in parliament, are the sole Gift of the commons; and all Bills for the granting of any such Aids and Supplies ought to begin with the commons; the commons to direct, limit, and appoint, in such Bills, the

ends, purposes, considerations, conditions, limitations, and qualifications of those Grants" (*Cobbett's Parliamentary History*, vol. 4, col. 1005). See also [Jones and Sidney], *Just and Modest Vindication*, 20.

30 Echoing Harrington's reference to the "love tricks that passed between her [Queen Parthenia, i.e. Elizabeth I] and her people" (Harrington, *Oceana*, 198).

31 Cf. Neville, *Plato Redivivus*, 120, where Neville raises doubts about king's prerogative power with respect to foreign policy.

32 See Scott, *Commonwealth Principles*, 196–201; Matteucci, "Dal costituzionalismo al liberalismo," 22–3, for the view that Sidney was a theorist of the ancient constitution.

33 On the significance of the debates of the 1640s–50s for Sidney's work, see Scott, *Algernon Sidney and the English Republic*, 78–9, 106; Scott, *Algernon Sidney and the Restoration Crisis*, 4–8. For a critique, see Zook, *Radical Whigs and Conspiratorial Politics*, esp. xix–xx.

34 Houston, *Algernon Sidney and the Republican Heritage*, 117. Houston is quoting from Berlin, "Two Concepts of Liberty."

35 Carrive, *La pensée politique d'Algernon Sidney*, 93.

36 Worden, "Republicanism and the Restoration," 174.

37 West, "Foreword," xix. See also Scott, *Algernon Sidney and the Restoration Crisis*, 226. Carrive, *La pensée politique d'Algernon Sidney*, 92–3, by contrast, cites this same passage as evidence of Sidney's positive understanding of freedom.

38 West, "Foreword," xix.

39 Scott, *Commonwealth Principles*, 151–2, presents this tendency to combine negative and positive freedom as a feature of English republican thought more generally.

40 Scott, *Algernon Sidney and the Restoration Crisis*, 226. It is perhaps revealing of Scott's assumptions that he misquotes Sidney here: the locution Sidney uses is "independency upon," not "independency from."

41 Scott, *Algernon Sidney and the Restoration Crisis*, 226. For a critique of Scott's claim that Sidney offers a positive concept of liberty, see Hamel, *L'Esprit républicain*, 143–4.

42 Sidney, *Discourses concerning Government*, 83. Hereafter all references to this work appear in brackets in the main text.

43 See Hamel, *L'Esprit républicain*, for a convincing account of Sidney as a republican theorist.

44 Cf. Locke, *Two Treatises*, 270–1. Carrive, *La pensée politique d'Algernon Sidney*, 92, emphasizes the similarity between Locke's and Sidney's accounts of liberty.

Carswell, *Porcupine*, 185, goes so far as to suggest that the two men might have read one another's work.

45 In addition to the sources cited above, this passage is discussed in Nelson, *Discourses of Algernon Sidney*, 32; Skinner, *Liberty before Liberalism*, 71–2.

46 Hamel, *L'Esprit républicain*, 165, emphasizes the anti-Hobbesian dimension to Sidney's account of freedom.

47 Skinner, *Liberty before Liberalism*; Skinner, *Hobbes and Republican Liberty*.

48 On this passage, see Hamel, *L'Esprit républicain*, 163–4.

49 Hamel, *L'Esprit républicain*, 181–3. On Locke's views on prerogative power, see chapter 6 below, 208–9.

50 A notable exception is Worden, "Republicanism and the Restoration."

51 Nelson, *Discourses of Algernon Sidney*, 34. See also Nelson's comments at 59.

52 See Houston, *Algernon Sidney and the Republican Heritage*, 19; Scott, *Algernon Sidney and the English Republic*, 59–72; Scott, *Algernon Sidney and the Restoration Crisis*, 85–103; Worden, "Commonwealth Kidney of Algernon Sidney," 22–3.

53 British Library, MS Egerton 1049, fol. 7.

54 Hamel, *L'Esprit républicain*, 255–6. In Nelson, *Discourses of Algernon Sidney*, 35, the claim that property is an "appendage" to liberty is taken to mean that it is "subsumed in natural liberty" and therefore not a significant feature of Sidney's theory.

55 Sidney, *Court Maxims*, 71.

56 Ibid., 72.

57 Ibid., 75.

58 Ibid., 76.

59 Ibid.

60 Ibid., 73.

61 There are echoes here of Giovanni Botero's account of the mutually reinforcing connection between trade and population growth in *Delle cause della grandezza delle città* (1588), which became influential among "new humanists" such as Francis Bacon at the start of the seventeenth century.

62 Sidney, *Court Maxims*, 74.

63 Ibid.

64 Ibid., 78.

65 See Houston, *Algernon Sidney and the Republican Heritage*, 170.

66 On Sidney's Machiavellism, see Sullivan, "Muted and Manifest English Machiavellism."

67 Worden, "Commonwealth Kidney of Algernon Sidney," 18.

CHAPTER SIX

1 The case was first made in Laslett, "Introduction" to *Two Treatises* (originally published in 1960). On the dating of the *Two Treatises*, see also Dunn, *Locke*, 33–4; Goldie, "Introduction," xix–xxii.

2 Locke, *Correspondence*, 82–3, 136–7; Locke, *Verses on King Charles II's Restoration*.

3 Locke, *First Tract on Government*; Locke, *Second Tract on Government*. On the transition from Locke's early conservatism to his later radicalism, see Dunn, *Political Thought of John Locke*, 13–35; Laslett, "Introduction" to *Two Treatises*, 16–44; Tully, *Approach to Political Philosophy*, 46–52.

4 Locke, *Two Treatises*, 136. All subsequent references to the *Two Treatises* will be inserted in brackets in the main text.

5 Although for the sake of convenience I speak of self-ownership, Locke in fact believed that men owned not their selves but their "persons." On the significance of this distinction, see below, 199.

6 The seventeenth-century context for Locke's thought more generally has, however, been widely discussed, most notably in Wood, *John Locke and Agrarian Capitalism*; Ashcraft, *Revolutionary Politics*.

7 See Buckle, *Natural Law and the Theory of Property*; Fitzmaurice, *Sovereignty, Property and Empire*; Garnsey, *Thinking about Property*; Olivecrona, "Appropriation in the State of Nature"; Olivecrona, "Locke's Theory of Appropriation"; Olivecrona, "Term 'Property' in Locke's Two Treatises"; Tully, *Discourse on Property*.

8 Harrison and Laslett, *Library of John Locke*, 147, 215.

9 On Filmer's attack on Grotius, see Buckle, *Natural Law and the Theory of Property*, 162–3; Tully, *Approach to Political Philosophy*, 102–3.

10 Berlin, "Two Concepts of Liberty," 126.

11 Marshall, *John Locke*, 217. A similar view is put forward in Waldron, *Right to Private Property*, 181.

12 Berlin, "Two Concepts of Liberty," 146–7. Marshall, *John Locke*, 218, also treats this passage as evidence that Locke had a second, "positive" concept of liberty. A more convincing interpretation is to be found in Dawson, "Natural Religion," 126–7.

13 Laslett, "Introduction" to *Two Treatises*, 112. Simmons, *Lockean Theory of Rights*, 326–27, also argues that Locke's theory of liberty includes positive and negative elements.

14 Hirschmann, *Gender, Class, and Freedom*, 79–117.

15 Tully, *Discourse on Property*, 45. See also Goldie, "Introduction," xxv; Tully, *Approach to Political Philosophy*, 298. It is true that Tully, *Approach to Political Philosophy*, 301, describes Locke's account of civil liberty as "similar to republican or civic humanist theories," but these theories are described, in positive terms, as "participation in a self-governing commonwealth."

16 This argument has been convincingly put forward in Halldenius, "Locke and the Non-Arbitrary."

17 It is explicitly rejected in Bellamy, *Political Constitutionalism*, 147.

18 Skinner, *Liberty before Liberalism*, 55n177. Skinner, "On Trusting the Judgement of Our Rulers," explores Locke's relationship to republicanism, ultimately concluding that his failure to recognize the danger of discretionary power is "a serious weakness not merely of Locke's response to the democratical writers, but of the entire liberal tradition that has looked to Locke as its patron saint" (128).

19 The most detailed discussion of Locke – a brief paragraph – is Pettit, *Republicanism*, 40.

20 Tucker, *Treatise Concerning Civil Government*, 168.

21 By contrast, Pettit, *Republicanism*, 43, likens the idea of natural liberty to the negative concept and political liberty to the republican one.

22 Locke does not claim that all forms dependence take away freedom. Indeed, being the property of God and hence dependent on him is regarded as not merely compatible with but definitional of natural liberty. It is dependence on the will of another man, where this refers to the condition of being subject to a power to which one has not consented, that renders one unfree.

23 See Simmons, *Lockean Theory of Rights*, 327.

24 Dunn, *Locke*, 39; Waldron, *God, Locke, and Equality*, 119. See Knights, "John Locke and Post-Revolutionary Politics," for an attempt to establish Locke's position on this issue.

25 See Franklin, *John Locke and the Theory of Sovereignty*, 94.

26 Wood, *Liberty and Property*, 263–4.

27 There are echoes here of Milton. See above, 104. Locke may also have been drawing on Lawson, *Political Sacra et Civilis*, 1. On Lawson's influence on Locke, see Franklin, *John Locke and the Theory of Sovereignty*. On this passage, see Marshall, *John Locke*, 211; Ryan, *Property and Political Theory*, 15; Ryan, "Locke on Freedom," 34; Tully, *Discourse on Property*, 57–9.

28 See Waldron, *God, Locke, and Equality*.

29 Kramer, *John Locke and the Origins of Private Property*, 43–9, argues that it is a non sequitur to treat natural equality as entailing political equality, and political equality as entailing political freedom.

30 See Brett, *Liberty, Right and Nature*; Tuck, *Natural Rights Theories*.

31 For an account of Filmer's position, see Dunn, *Political Thought of John Locke*, 61–5; Tully, *Discourse on Property*, 56–60. As Tierney, "Dominion of Self and Natural Rights," 178–9, argues, elsewhere Locke can also be found playing on the polyvalence of "dominion."

32 Day, "Locke on Property"; Zuckert, *Natural Rights and the New Republicanism*, 240.

33 Armitage, "John Locke, Carolina and the *Two Treatises of Government*," 617.

34 Tully, *Discourse on Property*, 105. Waldron, *Right to Private Property*, 177–81, appears to accept this aspect of Tully's argument, in spite of his critique of much of the rest of it. For a critique of Tully, see Kramer, *John Locke and the Origins of Private Property*, 133–5; Ryan, "Locke on Freedom," 39; Tierney, "Dominion of Self and Natural Rights," 177.

35 Locke, *Essay concerning Human Understanding*, 346. On the concept of personhood in the *Essay*, and its role in Locke's understanding of liberty, see Kelly, *Propriety of Liberty*, 46–58.

36 Cherno, "Locke on Property," 51–2, by contrast, equates "person" with the body.

37 Locke may have been drawing on Cicero's discussion of *personae* in Book 1 of *De officiis*, where rationality – and the resulting capacity to find out one's duty – is one of the two components of personhood, alongside being embodied. See Cicero, *De officiis*, 108.

38 See Dunn, *Political Thought of John Locke*; Laslett, "Introduction" to *Two Treatises*, 99; McClure, *Judging Rights*, 157–9.

39 See Waldron, *Right to Private Property*, 181–98, for an account of this passage and of the exegetical controversies it has engendered.

40 Armitage, "John Locke, Carolina and the *Two Treatises of Government*," 617. On Grotius's and Pufendorf's accounts of the origins of property, see Buckle, *Natural Law and the Theory of Property*; Fressola, "Liberty and Property"; Tully, *Discourse on Property*.

41 Nozick, *Anarchy, State, and Utopia*, 175. Nozick's account of Locke's theory of property is discussed in Becker, *Property Rights*, 34; Drury, "Locke and Nozick on Property."

42 Buckle, *Natural Law and the Theory of Property*, 150–1; Cohen, *Self-Ownership*, 169–78; Day, "Locke on Property," 211; Milam, "Epistemological Basis of Locke's Idea of Property," 24. For a critique of this interpretation, see Olivecrona, "Locke's Theory of Appropriation," 231–3; Simmons, *Lockean Theory of Rights*, 249–51.

43 For Wood, Locke's concern with the productive value of labour derives from his reading of Baconian "agricultural improvers" such as Samuel Hartlib, Gabriel Plattes, and William Petty. See in particular Wood, *John Locke and Agrarian Capitalism*, 57–71.

44 An important context for Locke's discussion of property that is illuminated by passages such as these is his involvement with the American colonies. On the colonial dimension to Locke's ideas of property, see Armitage, "John Locke, Carolina and the *Two Treatises of Government*"; Armitage, "John Locke's International Thought"; Armitage, "John Locke: Theorist of Empire?"; Arneil, "Wild Indian's Venison"; Ince, *Colonial Capitalism and the Dilemmas of Liberalism*.

45 Tully, *Discourse on Property*, 120.

46 See Dawson, "Natural Religion," 119.

47 See Ashcraft, *Revolutionary Politics*, 262–4; Garnsey, *Thinking about Property*, 136.

48 Becker, *Property Rights*, 35–41.

49 Simmons, *Lockean Theory of Rights*, 243–9. For a critique of consequentialist interpretations of Locke's theory of property, see Kramer, *John Locke and the Origins of Private Property*, 189.

50 See Simmons, *Lockean Theory of Rights*.

51 For an overview of Locke's discussion of money, see Kelly, "General Introduction."

52 Simmons, *Lockean Theory of Rights*, 285–6.

53 Arneil, "Wild Indian's Venison," 68, suggests that Locke's preoccupation with spoliation was due to the widespread belief that taking more land than could be cultivated and allowing it to lie fallow was one of the chief causes of the decline of many of the American colonies.

54 Waldrón, "Enough and as Good," esp. 321–2; Waldron, *Right to Private Property*, 209–18. See also Arneson, "Lockean Self-Ownership," 45; Mautner, "Locke on Appropriation," 260. For the view that leaving "enough, and as good" is a genuine restriction in Locke's account of appropriation, see Baldwin, "Tully, Locke, and Land," 21; Becker, *Property Rights*, 42–3; Buckle, *Natural Law and the Theory of Property*; Drury, "Locke and Nozick on Property"; Kelly, "All Things Richly to Enjoy," 284; Olivecrona, "Appropriation in the State of Nature," 227–8; Ryan, *Property and Political Theory*, 17; Sreenivasan, *Limits of Lockean Rights in Property*, 48–9; Simmons, *Lockean Theory of Rights*, 283–4; Tully, *Discourse on Property*, 129–30; Wood, *John Locke and Agrarian Capitalism*, 55–6; Wood, *Liberty and Property*, 267.

55 Macpherson, *Political Theory of Possessive Individualism*, 211; Ryan, "Locke on

Freedom," 44–5; Sreenivasan, *Limits of Lockean Rights in Property*, 35; Tully, *Discourse on Property*, 145–54. See McClure, *Judging Rights*, 156–88, for a discussion of the moral character of money in Locke's political thought and in particular the way in which the creation of money affects individuals' capacity to understand the moral requirements of natural law. Ince, *Colonial Capitalism and the Dilemmas of Liberalism*, 46–7, highlights the significance of money as "a structurally necessary if conceptually ambiguous element that holds together the composite and contradictory edifice of Locke's theory of property, which attempts to formulate a universal defense of property rights against extralegal absolutist power in England, at the very same time it seeks to validate the expropriation of Native Americans by the extralegal imperial power of the English state."

56 Ince, *Colonial Capitalism and the Dilemmas of Liberalism*, 52, argues that money, by legitimating the enclosure of more land than is needed for one's immediate use, resolves the dilemma "between *letting waste* and *making waste*, or the loss of *potential value* and *actual value*."

57 See Tully, *Discourse on Property*, 147–8, for a discussion of this passage that stresses its Aristotelian quality.

58 Tully, *Approach to Political Philosophy*, 18, suggests that this actually amounts to a political power.

59 For example, Dunn, *Political Thought of John Locke*, 67. The conventional interpretation of Locke's original community as negative has recently been restated in Garnsey, *Thinking about Property*, 142–3.

60 Tully, *Approach to Political Philosophy*, 27. Simmons, *Lockean Theory of Rights*, 239–40, also believes Locke's original community to be positive.

61 Tully, *Discourse on Property*, 145–70. Tully, "Property, Self-Government and Consent," 129, revises his original thesis by suggesting that the sufficiency proviso was not violated with the introduction of money since the increase in opportunities to labour more than made up for the scarcity of land, and therefore original property titles were not rendered invalid prior to the establishment of civil society. Nevertheless, he continues to regard the laws as playing a strong role in determining property rights rather than merely securing and regulating the prepolitical property rights that men bring with themselves into society. For a critique of Tully's interpretation, see Baldwin, "Tully, Locke, and Land"; Buckle, *Natural Law and the Theory of Property*, 183–7; Cohen, *Self-Ownership*, 189–94; Simmons, *Lockean Theory of Rights*, 313; Waldron, "Locke, Tully and the Regulation of Property"; Waldron, *Right to Private Property*, esp. 140–56.

62 Waldron, "Locke, Tully and the Regulation of Property." See also Simmons, *Lockean Theory of Rights*, 212–13.

63 Macpherson, *Political Theory of Possessive Individualism*, 194–262.

64 These are dealt with effectively in Dunn, *Political Thought of John Locke*; Ryan, "Locke and the Dictatorship of the Bourgeoisie"; Tully, *Approach to Political Philosophy*, 73–94.

65 Ashcraft, *Revolutionary Politics*, esp. 246–50, 281. See also Waldron, *Right to Private Property*, 148.

66 See Dunn, *Political Thought of John Locke*, 216.

67 Skinner, "On Trusting the Judgement of Our Rulers," 125.

68 Halldenius, "Locke and the Non-Arbitrary," 267.

69 See, for example, Cherno, "Locke on Property," 52; Macpherson, *Political Theory of Possessive Individualism*, 248; Simmons, *Lockean Theory of Rights*, 222, 228. On Locke's "inconsistent" use of property, see McClure, *Judging Rights*, 16.

70 Locke is, for example, clearly using "property" in a narrower sense at 353 and 416.

71 Cf. Milton, *Defence*, 472.

72 See chapter 1 above, 59–61.

73 Ashcraft, *Revolutionary Politics*, esp. 272–81.

74 Ibid., 81.

75 Waldron, *Right to Private Property*, 4.

76 Locke, *Essay on Toleration*, 145.

77 See Laslett, "Introduction" to *Two Treatises*, 102–3.

78 Buckle, *Natural Law and the Theory of Property*, 118–24.

79 See Tully, *Discourse on Property*, 137.

80 Waldron, "Enough and as Good," 326–8; Waldron, "Locke, Tully and the Regulation of Property," 105–6; Waldron, *God, Locke, and Equality*, 177–84. On the role of charity in Locke's theory, see also Simmons, *Lockean Theory of Rights*, 327–37; Winfrey, "Charity versus Justice."

81 Pateman, *Sexual Contract*, 70–1, argues that the distinction set up by Locke between servitude and slavery breaks down because of the possibility that an individual, as the owner of his person, might choose to enter into a labour contract for life and thus become a "civil slave." See also Tully, *Discourse on Property*, 137; Waldron, *God, Locke, and Equality*, 177–9; Wood, *John Locke and Agrarian Capitalism*, 89–90.

CONCLUSION

1 See especially Pettit, *Republicanism*; Skinner, *Liberty before Liberalism*.

2 In particular, they have highlighted the contribution of republicanism to the American Revolution. See Baylyn, *Ideological Origins*; Pocock, *Machiavellian Moment*; Wood, *Creation of the American Republic*.

3 Larmore, "Critique of Philip Pettit's Republicanism"; Kramer, "Liberty and Domination"; Nelson, "Liberty"; Waldron, "Pettit's Molecule." Patterson, *Early Modern Liberalism*, dismisses the distinction between republicanism and liberalism by simply grouping all the authors she discusses, among them Milton and Sidney, under the banner of liberalism. See in particular her comments at 3.

4 Dagger, *Civic Virtues*, 4. See also Appleby, *Liberalism and Republicanism*.

5 Kramer, "Liberty and Domination," 56.

6 Larmore, "Critique of Philip Pettit's Republicanism," 239.

7 This is particularly apparent in Kramer, "Liberty and Domination," 50–6.

8 Carter, "How Are Power and Unfreedom Related?"; Kramer, "Liberty and Domination."

9 Skinner, "Freedom as the Absence of Arbitrary Power," 93–4.

10 MacCallum, "Negative and Positive Freedom." The core of MacCallum's argument is restated in Nelson, "Liberty."

11 Skinner, *Hobbes and Republican Liberty*.

12 Skinner, "On the Liberty of the Ancients and the Moderns."

13 Sullivan, *Machiavelli, Hobbes*. See also MacGilvray, *Invention of Market Freedom*, which dates the synthesis between the two traditions not to the seventeenth century but to the eighteenth.

14 Haakonssen, "Republicanism," 732.

15 Ibid., 731.

16 See in particular Halldenius, "Locke and the Non-Arbitrary."

17 Skinner, "On Trusting the Judgement of Our Rulers."

18 Nozick, *Anarchy, State, and Utopia*, 171.

19 Ibid.

20 See Arneson, "Lockean Self-Ownership," 36–7; Narveson, "Libertarianism vs. Marxism," 4–10.

21 Nozick, *Anarchy, State, and Utopia*, 57.

22 Ibid., 169.

23 A dissenting voice is Van Parijs, who argues that the right of self-preservation is inalienable and that self-ownership "must be defined in such a way that it does not allow people to sell themselves into slavery" (Van Parijs, *Real Freedom for All*, 235n4).

24 Otsuka, *Libertarianism without Inequality*, 20.

25 Ibid., 23.

26 Ibid., 32.

27 Ingram, *Political Theory of Rights*, 25.

28 Ibid., 34–8.

29 Ibid., 37.

30 Cohen, *Self-Ownership*.

31 Ibid., 151.

32 Ibid.

33 Ibid., 152.

34 For a more positive assessment of the possibilities of self-ownership discourses – albeit not the dominant "Lockean" version – for feminist theory, see Petchesky, "Body as Property"; Shanks, "Rhetoric of Self-Ownership."

35 Pateman, *Sexual Contract*, 14.

36 Ibid., 66.

37 Phillips, *Our Bodies, Whose Property?*, 143. See also Davies and Naffine, *Are Persons Property?*, 23.

38 Pateman, "Self-Ownership and Property in the Person," 51.

39 Benn, *Theory of Freedom*; Benn and Weinstein, "Being Free to Act and Being a Free Man"; Gray, *Liberalisms*; Miller, "Constraints on Freedom."

40 Hirschmann, *Subject of Liberty*, 26–9.

BIBLIOGRAPHY

MANUSCRIPT SOURCES

Bodleian Library, MS Rawlinson D. 398.
British Library, MS Egerton 1049. "The case of Algernone and Henry Sydney referred to Sir William Jones, as it stands in reason and common sense, which is true equity and the grounds of Lawe." [1680].

PRIMARY AND SECONDARY SOURCES

Achinstein, Sharon. "Texts in Conflict: The Press and the Civil War." In *The Cambridge Companion to Writing of the English Revolution*, ed. N.H. Keeble, 50–68. Cambridge: Cambridge University Press, 2001.
An Agreement of the People for A firme and present Peace, upon grounds of common-right and freedome. [London], 1647.
Allen, J.W. *English Political Thought, 1603–1644*. New York: Methuen, 1938.
Alsop, James D. "Gerrard Winstanley: What Do We Know of His Life?" In *Winstanley and the Diggers, 1649–1999*, ed. Andrew Bradstock, 19–36. London: Frank Cass, 2000.
Animadversions upon Those Notes Which the late Observator hath published upon the seven Doctrines and Positions. London, 1642.
Appleby, Joyce. *Liberalism and Republicanism in the Historical Imagination*. Cambridge, MA: Harvard University Press, 1992.
Aquinas, Thomas. *Political Writings*. Ed. R.W. Dyson. Cambridge: Cambridge University Press, 2002.
Aristotle. *The Politics and the Constitution of Athens*. Ed. Stephen Everson. Cambridge: Cambridge University Press, 1996.

Armitage, David. "Empire and Liberty: A Republican Dilemma." In *Republicanism: A Shared European Heritage*, ed. Martin van Gelderen and Quentin Skinner, 2 vols., 2:29–46. Cambridge: Cambridge University Press, 2002.

– *The Ideological Origins of the British Empire*. Cambridge: Cambridge University Press, 2000.

– "John Locke, Carolina and the *Two Treatises of Government*." In *Foundations of Modern International Thought*, 90–113. Cambridge: Cambridge University Press, 2013.

– "John Locke's International Thought." In *Foundations of Modern International Thought*, 75–89. Cambridge: Cambridge University Press, 2013.

– "John Locke: Theorist of Empire?" In *Foundations of Modern International Thought*, 114–31. Cambridge: Cambridge University Press, 2013.

– "John Milton: Poet against Empire." In *Milton and Republicanism*, ed. David Armitage, Armand Himy, and Quentin Skinner, 206–25. Cambridge: Cambridge University Press, 1995.

Arneil, Barbara. "The Wild Indian's Venison: Locke's Theory of Property and English Colonialism in America." *Political Studies* 44 (1996): 60–74.

Arneson, Richard J. "Lockean Self-Ownership: Towards a Demolition." *Political Studies* 39 (1991): 36–54.

Ascham, Anthony. *Of the Confusions and Revolutions of Governments*. London, 1649.

Ashcraft, Richard. *Revolutionary Politics and Locke's Two Treatises of Government*. Princeton, NJ: Princeton University Press, 1986.

Aubrey, John. *Brief Lives*. Ed. Andrew Clark, 2 vols. Oxford: Clarendon Press, 1898.

Aylmer, G.E. "'England's Spirit Unfoulded, or an Encouragement to Take the Engagement': A Newly Discovered Pamphlet by Gerrard Winstanley." *Past and Present* 40 (1968): 3–15.

Bacon, Francis. "The Essayes or Counsels, Civill and Morall." In *The Works of Francis Bacon*, ed. James Spedding, Robert Leslie Ellis, and Douglas Denon Heath, 9 vols., 6:365–518. London: Longman, 1861.

Baker, Philip. "The Franchise Debate Revisited: The Levellers and the Army." In *The Nature of the English Revolution Revisited*, ed. Stephen Taylor and Grant Tapsell, 103–22. Woodbridge: Boydell Press, 2013.

Baldwin, Thomas. "Tully, Locke, and Land." *Locke Newsletter* 13 (1982): 21–33.

Ball, William. *A Caveat for Subjects, Moderating the Observator*. London, 1642.

Barton, J.L. "The Authorship of *Bracton*: Again." *Journal of Legal History* 30 (2009): 117–74.

Bass, J.D. "'Levellers': The Economic Reduction of Political Equality in the Putney Debates, 1647." *Quarterly Journal of Speech* 77 (1991): 427–45.

Baylyn, Bernard. *The Ideological Origins of the American Revolution.* Cambridge, MA: Harvard University Press, 1967.

Becker, Lawrence. *Property Rights: Philosophic Foundations.* London: Routledge and Kegan Paul, 1977.

Benn, Stanley I. *A Theory of Freedom.* Cambridge: Cambridge University Press, 1988.

Benn, Stanley I., and W.L. Weinstein. "Being Free to Act and Being a Free Man." *Mind* 80 (1971): 194–211.

Bellamy, Richard. *Political Constitutionalism: A Republican Defence of the Constitutionality of Democracy.* Cambridge: Cambridge University Press, 2007.

Berlin, Isaiah. "Two Concepts of Liberty." In *Four Essays on Liberty.* Oxford: Oxford University Press, 1969.

Bethel, Slingsby. *The World's Mistake in Oliver Cromwell.* London, 1668.

Blitzer, Charles. *An Immortal Commonwealth: The Political Thought of James Harrington.* New Haven, CT: Yale University Press, 1960.

Brace, Laura. *The Idea of Property in Seventeenth-Century England.* Manchester: Manchester University Press, 1998.

– "Imagining the Boundaries of a Sovereign Self." In *Reclaiming Sovereignty*, ed. Laura Brace and John Hoffman, 137–54. London: Pinter, 1997.

Bracton, Henry de. *On the Laws and Customs of England.* Trans. and ed. Samuel E. Thorne, 4 vols. Cambridge, MA: Harvard University Press, 1977.

Brailsford, Henry Noel. *The Levellers and the English Revolution.* Ed. Christopher Hill. London: Cresset Press, 1961.

[Bramhall, John]. *The Serpent Salve, or, a Remedie For the Biting of an Aspe.* N.p., 1643.

Brand, Paul. "The Age of Bracton." *Proceedings of the British Academy* 89 (1996): 65–89.

– "The Date and Authorship of *Bracton*: A Response." *Journal of Legal History* 31 (2010): 2017–44.

Brett, Annabel. *Liberty, Right and Nature: Individual Rights in Later Scholastic Thought.* Cambridge: Cambridge University Press, 1997.

Bridge, William. *The Truth of the Times Vindicated.* London, 1643.

– *The Wounded Conscience Cured, the Weak One strengthened, and the doubting satisfied.* London, 1643.

A Briefe Discourse upon Tyrants and Tyranny. [London], 1642.

Brito Vieira, Mónica. *The Elements of Representation in Hobbes: Aesthetics, Theatre, Law, and Theology in the Construction of Hobbes's Theory of the State.* Leiden: Brill, 2009.

"Brutus, Stephanus Junius." *Vindiciae, contra tyrannos*. Trans. and ed. George Garnett. Cambridge: Cambridge University Press, 1994.

Buckle, Stephen. *Natural Law and the Theory of Property: Grotius to Hume*. Oxford: Clarendon Press, 1991.

Burgess, Glenn. *The Politics of the Ancient Constitution: An Introduction to English Political Thought, 1603-1642*. London: Macmillan, 1992.

– "Usurpation, Obligation, and Obedience in the Thought of the Engagement Controversy." *Historical Journal* 29 (1986): 515–36.

– "Repacifying the Polity: The Responses of Hobbes and Harrington to the 'Crisis of the Common Law.'" In *Soldiers, Writers and Statesmen of the English Revolution*, ed. Ian Gentles, John Morrill, and Blair Worden, 202–28. Cambridge: Cambridge University Press, 1998.

Carrive, Paulette. *La pensée politique d'Algernon Sidney: La querelle de l'Absolutisme*. Paris: Méridiens Klincksieck, 1989.

Carswell, John. *The Porcupine: The Life of Algernon Sidney*. London: Murray, 1989.

Carter, Ian. "How Are Power and Unfreedom Related?" In *Republicanism and Political Theory*, ed. Cécile Laborde and John Maynor, 58–82. Oxford: Blackwell, 2008.

The Case of the Army Truly Stated. London, 1647.

Champion, Justin. "Political Thinking between Restoration and Hanoverian Succession." In *A Companion to Stuart Britain*, ed. Barry Coward, 474–91. Oxford: Blackwell, 2005.

Cherno, Melvin. "Locke on Property: A Reappraisal." *Ethics* 68 (1957): 51–5.

Chernaik, Warren. "Civil Liberty in Milton, the Levellers and Winstanley." In *Winstanley and the Diggers, 1649–1999*, ed. Andrew Bradstock, 101–20. London: Frank Cass, 2000.

Cicero. *De officiis*. Trans. and ed. Walter Miller. London: William Heinemann, 1913.

[Clarkson, David]. *The Case of Protestants in England under a Popish Prince, If any shall happen to Wear the Imperial Crown*. London, 1681.

Cobbett's Complete Collection of State Trials and Proceedings for High Treason and Other Crimes and Misdemeanors. Ed. William Cobbett, 33 vols., vol. 3. London: Longman, 1809.

Cobbett's Parliamentary History of England. From the Norman Conquest, in 1066, to the Year 1803. Ed. William Cobbett, 36 vols. London: Hansard, 1806–12.

Coffey, John. *John Goodwin and the Puritan Revolution: Religion and Intellectual Change in Seventeenth-Century England*. Woodbridge: Boydell Press, 2006.

Cohen, G.A. *Self-Ownership, Freedom, and Equality*. Cambridge: Cambridge University Press, 1995.

Commons Debates 1628. Ed. Robert C. Johnson and Maija Jansson Cole, 6 vols., vol. 2. New Haven, CT: Yale University Press, 1977.

Commons Debates 1628. Ed. Robert C. Johnson, Mary Frear Keeler, Maija Jansson Cole, and William B. Bidwell, 6 vols., vol. 3. New Haven, CT: Yale University Press, 1977.

Corns, Thomas N. "Milton and the Characteristics of a Free Commonwealth." In *Milton and Republicanism*, ed. David Armitage, Armand Himy, and Quentin Skinner, 25–42. Cambridge: Cambridge University Press, 1995.

– *Uncloistered Virtue: English Political Literature, 1640–1660*. Oxford: Clarendon Press, 1992.

Corns, Thomas C., Ann Hughes, and David Loewenstein. "Introduction." In *The Complete Works of Gerrard Winstanley*, ed. Thomas N. Corns, Ann Hughes, and David Loewenstein, 2 vols., 1:1–94. Oxford: Oxford University Press, 2009.

Costa, M. Victoria. "Neo-Republicanism, Freedom as Non-Domination, and Citizen Virtue." *Politics, Philosophy and Economics* 8 (2009): 401–19.

Cotton, James. *James Harrington's Political Thought and Its Context*. New York: Garland, 1991.

Cromartie, Alan. *The Constitutionalist Revolution: An Essay on the History of England, 1450–1642*. Cambridge: Cambridge University Press, 2006.

– "Harringtonian Virtue: Harrington, Machiavelli, and the Method of the *Moment*." *Historical Journal* 41 (1988): 987–1009.

– "Parliamentary Sovereignty, Popular Sovereignty, and Henry Parker's Adjudicative Standpoint." In *Popular Sovereignty in Historical Perspective*, ed. Quentin Skinner and Richard Bourke, 142–63. Cambridge: Cambridge University Press, 2016.

Dagger, Richard. *Civic Virtues: Rights, Citizenship, and Republican Liberalism*. Oxford: Oxford University Press, 1997.

Daly, James. "John Bramhall and the Theoretical Problems of Royalist Moderation." *Journal of British Studies* 11 (1971): 26–44.

Davies, Margaret, and Ngaire Naffine. *Are Persons Property?* Burlington, VT: Ashgate, 2001.

Davis, J.C. "Equality in an Unequal Commonwealth: James Harrington's Republicanism and the Meaning of Equality." In *Soldiers, Writers and Statesmen of the English Revolution*, ed. Ian Gentles, John Morrill, and Blair Worden, 229–42. Cambridge: Cambridge University Press, 1998.

– "Gerrard Winstanley and the Restoration of True Magistracy." *Past and Present* 70 (1976): 76–93.

– "The Levellers and Democracy." *Past and Present* 40 (1968): 174–80.

– *Utopia and the Ideal Society: A Study of English Utopian Writing, 1516–1700*. Cambridge: Cambridge University Press, 1981.

Dawson, Hannah. "Natural Religion: Pufendorf and Locke on the Edge of Freedom and Reason." In *Freedom and the Construction of Europe*, ed. Quentin Skinner and Martin van Gelderen, 2 vols., 1:115–33. Cambridge: Cambridge University Press, 2013.

Day, J.P. "Locke on Property." *Philosophical Quarterly* 16 (1966): 207–20.

– "Some Problems in the Authorship of Sir Robert Filmer's Works." *English Historical Review* 98 (1983): 737–62.

Debates of the House of Commons, from the year 1667 to the year 1694. Ed. Antichell Greym, 10 vols., vol. 7. London: D. Henry and R. Cave, 1763.

A Declaration of the Wel-Affected In the County of Buckinghamshire. [London], 1649.

Dickinson, W. Calvin. *James Harrington's Republic*, Washington, DC: University Press of America, 1983.

The Digest of Justinian. Trans. Alan Watson, ed. Theodor Mommsen and Paul Krueger, 4 vols., vol. 1. Philadelphia: University of Pennsylvania Press, 1985.

[Digges, Dudley]. *An Answer to a Printed Book, Intituled, Observations upon Some of His Majesties Late Answers and Expresses.* Oxford, 1642.

A Discourse or Dialogue between the two now Potent Enemies. London, 1641.

Drury, S.B. "Locke and Nozick on Property." *Political Studies* 30 (1982): 28–41.

Dunn, John. *Locke: A Very Short Introduction.* Oxford: Oxford University Press, 2003.

– *The Political Thought of John Locke: An Historical Account of the Argument of the Two Treatises of Government.* Cambridge: Cambridge University Press, 1969.

Dzelzainis, Martin. "History and Ideology: Milton, the Levellers, and the Council of State in 1649." *Huntington Library Quarterly* 68 (2005): 269–87.

– "Introduction." In John Milton, *Political Writings*, ed. Martin Dzelzainis, ix–xxv. Cambridge: Cambridge University Press, 1991.

– "Milton's Classical Republicanism." In *Milton and Republicanism*, ed. David Armitage, Armand Himy, and Quentin Skinner, 3–24. Cambridge: Cambridge University Press, 1995.

– "Milton's Politics." In *The Cambridge Companion to John Milton*, 2nd ed., ed. Dennis Danielson, 70–83. Cambridge: Cambridge University Press, 1999.

– "Milton and the Protectorate in 1658." In *Milton and Republicanism*, ed. David Armitage, Armand Himy, and Quentin Skinner, 181–205. Cambridge: Cambridge University Press, 1995.

– "Republicanism." In *A Companion to Milton*, ed. Thomas Corns, 294–308. Oxford: Blackwell, 2001.

Early Modern Research Group. "Commonwealth: The Social, Cultural, and Conceptual Contexts of an Early Modern Keyword." *Historical Journal* 54 (2011): 659–87.

Fallon, Stephen M. "Nascent Republican Theory in Milton's Regicide Prose." In *The Oxford Handbook of Literature and the English Revolution*, ed. Laura Lunger Knoppers, 309–26. Oxford: Oxford University Press, 2012.

Fasolt, Constantin. *The Limits of History.* Chicago: University of Chicago Press, 2004.

Feenstra, Robert. "*Dominium* and *Ius in Re Aliena*: The Origins of a Civil Law Distinction." In *New Perspectives in the Roman Law of Property: Essays for Barry Nicholas*, ed. Peter Birks. Oxford: Clarendon Press, 1989.

Fenton, Mary C. "Hope, Land Ownership, and Milton's 'Paradise Within.'" *Studies in English Literature, 1500–1900* 43 (2003): 151–80.

Ferne, Henry. *The Resolving of Conscience.* York, 1642.

Filmer, Robert. "*Patriarcha*. The *Naturall* Power of Kinges Defended against the Unnatural Liberty of the People." In *Patriarcha and Other Writings*, ed. Johann P. Sommerville, 1–68. Cambridge: Cambridge University Press, 1991.

Fink, Zera S. *The Classical Republicans: An Essay in the Recovery of a Pattern of Thought in Seventeenth-Century England.* Evanston, IL: Northwestern University Press, 1945.

Fitzmaurice, Andrew. *Sovereignty, Property and Empire, 1500–2000.* Cambridge: Cambridge University Press, 2014.

Fletcher, Anthony. *The Outbreak of the English Civil War.* London: Edward Arnold, 1981.

Foundations of Freedom; or an Agreement of the People. [London], 1648.

Foxley, Rachel. "The Levellers: John Lilburne, Richard Overton, and William Walwyn." In *The Oxford Handbook of Literature and the English Revolution*, ed. Laura Lunger Knoppers, 272–86. Oxford: Oxford University Press, 2012.

– "Problems of Sovereignty in Leveller Writings." *History of Political Thought* 28 (2007): 642–60.

Frank, Jill. *A Democracy of Distinction: Aristotle and the Work of Politics.* Chicago: University of Chicago Press, 2005.

Frank, Joseph. *Cromwell's Press Agent: A Critical Biography of Marchamont Nedham, 1620–78.* Washington, DC: University Press of America, 1982.

Franklin, Julian H. *John Locke and the Theory of Sovereignty: Mixed Monarchy and the Right of Resistance in the Political Thought of the English Revolution.* Cambridge: Cambridge University Press, 1978.

Fressola, Anthony. "Liberty and Property: Reflections on the Right of Appropriation in the State of Nature." *American Philosophical Quarterly* 18 (1981): 315–22.

Fukuda, Arihiro. *Sovereignty and the Sword: Harrington, Hobbes, and Mixed Government in the English Civil Wars.* Oxford: Clarendon Press, 1997.

Garnsey, Peter. *Thinking about Property: From Antiquity to the Age of Revolution.* Cambridge: Cambridge University Press, 2007.

Gleissner, Richard A. "The Levellers and Natural Law: The Putney Debates of 1647." *Journal of British Studies* 20 (1980): 74–89.

Glover, Samuel Dennis. "The Classical Plebeians: Radical Republicanism and the Origins of Leveller Thought." PhD diss., University of Cambridge, 1994.

– "The Putney Debates: Popular versus Elitist Republicanism." *Past and Present* 164 (1999): 47–80.

Goldie, Mark. "Introduction." In John Locke, *Two Treatises of Government*, ed. Mark Goldie, xv–xliii. London: Everyman, 1993.

Goodwin, John. *Anti-Cavalierisme.* London, 1642.

Gray, John. *Liberalisms: Essays in Political Philosophy.* New York: Routledge, 1989.

Gurney, John. "'Furious Divells?' The Diggers and Their Opponents." In *Winstanley and the Diggers, 1649–1999*, ed. Andrew Bradstock, 73–86. London: Frank Cass, 2000.

Haakonssen, Knud. "Republicanism." In *A Companion to Contemporary Political Philosophy*, 2nd ed., ed. Robert E Goodin, Philip Pettit, and Thomas Pogge, 2 vols., 2:729–35. Oxford: Blackwell, 2007.

Hakewill, William. *The Libertie of the Subject: Against the Pretended Power of impositions.* London, 1641.

Halldenius, Lena. "Locke and the Non-Arbitrary." *European Journal of Political Theory* 2 (2003): 261–79.

Hamel, Christopher. *L'Esprit républicain: Droits naturels et vertu civique chez Algernon Sidney.* Paris: Classiques Garnier, 2011.

Hampsher-Monk, Iain. "The Political Theory of the Levellers: Putney, Property and Professor Macpherson." *Political Studies* 24 (1976): 397–422.

Harrington, James. "Aphorisms Political." In *The Political Works of James Harrington*, ed. J.G.A. Pocock, 761–79. Cambridge: Cambridge University Press, 1977.

– "The Art of Lawgiving." In *The Political Works of James Harrington*, ed. J.G.A. Pocock, 599–704. Cambridge: Cambridge University Press, 1977.

– "The Commonwealth of Oceana." In *The Political Works of James Harrington*, ed. J.G.A. Pocock, 155–359. Cambridge: Cambridge University Press, 1977.

– "A Discourse upon this saying: The Spirit of the Nation is not yet to be trusted with Liberty; lest it introduce Monarchy, or invade the Liberty of Conscience." In *The Political Works of James Harrington*, ed. J.G.A. Pocock, 735–45. Cambridge: Cambridge University Press, 1977.

– "The Prerogative of Popular Government." In *The Political Works of James Harrington*, ed. J.G.A. Pocock, 389–566. Cambridge: Cambridge University Press, 1977.

– "The Rota Or A Model Of A Free State Or Equal Commonwealth." In *The Political Works of James Harrington*, ed. J.G.A. Pocock, 807–21. Cambridge: Cambridge University Press, 1977.

– "A System of Politics Delineated in short and easy Aphorisms Published from the Author's own Manuscript." In *The Political Works of James Harrington*, ed. J.G.A. Pocock, 833–54. Cambridge: Cambridge University Press, 1977.

Harris, Tim. "'Lives, Liberties and Estates': Rhetorics of Liberty in the Reign of Charles II." In *The Politics of Religion in Restoration England*, ed. Tim Harris, Paul Seaward, and Mark Goldie, 217–41. Oxford: Blackwell, 1990.

– *Restoration: Charles II and his Kingdoms, 1660–1685.* London: Penguin, 2006.

Harrison, John, and Peter Laslett. *The Library of John Locke*, 2nd ed. Oxford: Clarendon Press, 1971.

Hawke, Michael. *The Right of Dominion, and Property of Liberty.* London, 1655.

The Heads of Proposals, Agreed on by his Excellency Thomas Fairfax, and The Councell of the Armie. London, 1647.

Hill, Christopher. "Introduction." In Gerrard Winstanley, *The Law of Freedom, and Other Writings*, ed. Christopher Hill, 9–68. Harmondsworth: Penguin, 1973.

– *Milton and the English Revolution.* London: Faber, 1977.

– *Puritanism and Revolution: Studies in Interpretation of the English Revolution of the 17th Century.* London: Secker and Warburg, 1958.

– "The Religion of Gerrard Winstanley." *Past and Present Supplement* 5 (1978): 1–57.

– *The World Turned Upside Down: Radical Ideas during the English Revolution.* London: Penguin, 1972.

Hirschmann, Nancy J. *Gender, Class, and Freedom in Modern Political Theory.* Princeton, NJ: Princeton University Press, 2008.

– *The Subject of Liberty: Towards a Feminist Theory of Freedom.* Princeton, NJ: Princeton University Press, 2003.

Hobbes, Thomas. *Behemoth or the Long Parliament.* Ed. Paul Seaward. Oxford: Oxford University Press, 2010.

– *The Elements of Law Natural and Politic.* Ed. Ferdinand Tönnies, 2nd ed. London: Cass, 1969.

– *Leviathan.* Ed. Noel Malcolm, 3 vols. Oxford: Oxford University Press, 2012.

– *On the Citizen.* Ed. Richard Tuck and Michael Silverthorne. Cambridge: Cambridge University Press, 1998.

– *Writings on Common Law and Hereditary Right.* Ed. Alan Cromartie and Quentin Skinner. Oxford: Oxford University Press, 2005.

Hoekstra, Kinch, and Quentin Skinner. "The Liberties of the Ancients: A Roundtable with Kinch Hoekstra and Quentin Skinner." *History of European Ideas* 44 (2018): 812–25.

Holstun, James, ed. *Pamphlet Wars: Prose in the English Revolution.* London: Frank Cass, 1992.

Honohan, Iseult. *Civic Republicanism.* London: Routledge, 2002.

Honoré, A.M. "Ownership." In *Oxford Essays in Jurisprudence*, ed. A.G. Guest, 107–47. Oxford: Oxford University Press, 1961.

Höpfl, Harro. "James Harrington." In *Oxford Dictionary of National Biography*, ed. H.C.G. Matthew and Brian Harrison, 60 vols., 25:386–91. Oxford: Oxford University Press, 2004.

Horace. *Satires, Epistles and Ars Poetica.* Trans. and ed. Henry Rushton Fairclough. London: William Heinemann, 1926.

Houston, Alan. *Algernon Sidney and the Republican Heritage in England and America.* Princeton, NJ: Princeton University Press, 1991.

– "Republicanism, the Politics of Necessity, and the Rule of Law." In *A Nation Transformed: England after the Restoration*, ed. Alan Houston and Steve Pincus, 241–71. Cambridge: Cambridge University Press, 2001.

Hoxby, Blair. *Mammon's Music: Literature and Economics in the Age of Milton.* New Haven, CT: Yale University Press, 2002.

Hughes, Ann. "Gender and Politics in Leveller Literature." In *Political Culture and Cultural Politics in Early Modern England: Essays Presented to David Underdown*, ed. Susan D. Amussen and Mark A. Kishlansky, 162–88. Manchester: Manchester University Press, 1995.

The Humble Petition of the House of Commons. [London], 1643.

Hunton, Philip. *A Treatise of Monarchie.* London, 1643.

Ince, Onur Ulas. *Colonial Capitalism and the Dilemmas of Liberalism.* Oxford: Oxford University Press, 2018.

Ingram, Attracta. *A Political Theory of Rights*, 2nd ed. Oxford: Oxford University Press, 1994.

Jenkins, Hugh. "Shrugging off the Norman Yoke: Milton's *History of Britain* and the Levellers." *English Literary Renaissance* 29 (1999): 206–25.

Johnston, Nathaniel. *The Excellency Of Monarchical Government, Especially of the English Monarchy.* London, 1686.

[Jones, William, and Sidney, Algernon]. *A Just and Modest Vindication of the proceedings of the Two last Parliaments.* [London], 1682.

Jordan, J.K. *Men of Substance: A Study of the Thought of Two English Revolutionaries, Henry Parker and Henry Robinson.* Chicago: University of Chicago Press, 1942.

Judson, M.A. *From Tradition to Political Reality: A Study of the Ideas Set Forth in Support of the Commonwealth Government in England, 1649–1653*. Hamden, CT: Archon Books, 1980.

– *The Crisis of the Constitution: An Essay in Constitutional and Political Thought in England, 1603–1645*. New Brunswick, NJ: Rutgers University Press, 1988.

– "Henry Parker and the Theory of Parliamentary Sovereignty." In *Essays in History and Political Theory in Honor of C.H. McIlwain*, ed. Carl Wittke, 138–67. Cambridge, MA: Harvard University Press, 1936.

A Just Complaint, Or Loud Crie of all the well-affected Protestants in England. London, 1643.

Kahn, Victoria. *Wayward Contracts: The Crisis of Political Obligation in England, 1640–1674*. Princeton, NJ: Princeton University Press, 2004.

Keeble, N.H. "General Introduction." In *The Complete Works of John Milton*, ed. N.H. Keeble and Nicholas McDowell, 12 vols., 6: 1–129. Oxford: Oxford University Press, 2013.

Kelly, Duncan. *The Propriety of Liberty: Persons, Passions, and Judgement in Modern Political Thought*. Princeton, NJ: Princeton University Press, 2010.

Kelly, Patrick. "'All Things Richly to Enjoy': Economics and Politics in Locke's *Two Treatises of Government*." *Political Studies* 36 (1988): 273–93.

– "General Introduction: Locke on Money." In John Locke, *Locke on Money*, ed. Patrick Kelly, 1–109. Oxford: Clarendon Press, 1991.

Kelsey, Sean. *Inventing a Republic: The Political Culture of the English Commonwealth, 1649–1653*. Manchester: Manchester University Press, 1997.

Kennedy, Geoff. *Diggers, Levellers, and Agrarian Capitalism: Radical Political Thought in Seventeenth Century England*. Lanham, MD: Lexington Books, 2008.

Kishlansky, Mark. *A Monarchy Transformed: Britain, 1603–1714*. London: Penguin, 1996.

Knights, Mark. "John Locke and Post-Revolutionary Politics: Electoral Reform and the Franchise." *Past and Present* 213 (2011): 41–86.

Knoppers, Laura Lunger. "Late Prose." In *A Companion to Milton*, ed. Thomas Corns, 309–26. Oxford: Blackwell, 2001.

– "Headnote." In *The Complete Works of John Milton*, ed. Laura Lunger Knoppers, 12 vols., 2: lxxxviii–civ. Oxford: Oxford University Press, 2008.

– "Milton's *The Readie and Easie Way* and the English Jeremiad." In *Politics, Poetics, and Hermeneutics in Milton's Prose*, ed. David Loewenstein and James Grantham Turner, 213–25. Cambridge: Cambridge University Press, 1990.

Kramer, Matthew H. *John Locke and the Origins of Private Property: Philosophical Explorations of Individualism, Community, and Equality*. Cambridge: Cambridge University Press, 1997.

– "Liberty and Domination." In *Republicanism and Political Theory*, ed. Cécile Laborde and John Maynor, 31–57. Oxford: Blackwell, 2008.

Larmore, Charles. "A Critique of Philip Pettit's Republicanism." *Philosophical Issues* 11 (2001): 230–43.

Laslett, Peter. "Introduction." In Sir Robert Filmer, *Patriarcha and Other Political Works of Sir Robert Filmer*, ed. Peter Laslett, 1–43. Oxford: Blackwell, 1949.

– "Introduction." In John Locke, *Two Treatises of Government*, ed. Peter Laslett, 3–126. Cambridge: Cambridge University Press, 1988.

Lawson, George. *Political Sacra et Civilis: or, A Modell of Civil and Ecclesiastical Government*. London, 1660.

[Lawson, George]. *Conscience Puzzled, about Subscribing the New Engagement*. N.p., 1651.

Lee, Daniel. *Popular Sovereignty in Early Modern Constitutional Thought*. Oxford: Oxford University Press, 2016.

L'Estrange, Roger. *Considerations and Proposals In Order to the Regulation of the Press*. London, 1663.

Levy, Michael B. "Freedom, Property and the Levellers: The Case of John Lilburne." *Western Political Quarterly* 36 (1983): 116–33.

Lewalski, Barbara K. *The Life of John Milton: A Critical Biography*. Oxford: Blackwell, 2000.

Light shining in Buckinghamshire. [London], 1649.

Lilburne, John. *The Charters of London*. London, 1646.

– *Englands Birth-Right Justified Against all Arbitrary Usurpation, whether Regall or Parliamentary, or under what Vizor soever*. [London], 1645.

– *Innocency and Truth Justified*. London, 1646.

– *The Legall Fundamentall Liberties of the People of England Revived, Asserted, and Vindicated*. London, 1649.

– *The Upright Mans Vindication*. [London], 1653.

– *A Whip for the present House of Lords, or the Levellers Levelled*. London, 1648.

[Lilburne, John]. *Regall Tyrannie discovered*. London, 1647.

Lilburne, John, William Wawlyn, Thomas Prince, and Richard Overton. *A Manifestation from Lieutenant Col. John Lilburn, Mr. William Walwyn, Mr. Thomas Prince, and Mr. Richard Overton, (now Prisioners in the Tower of London) and others, commonly (though unjustly) styled Levellers*. London, 1649.

– *An Agreement of the Free People of England*. London, 1649.

List, Christian, and Laura Valentini. "Freedom as Independence." *Ethics* 126 (2016): 1043–74.

Littleton, Thomas. *Littleton's Tenures in English. Lately perused and amended.* London, 1594.

Locke, John. *The Correspondence of John Locke.* Ed. E.S. de Beer, 8 vols., vol. 1. Oxford: Clarendon Press, 1976.

– *An Essay concerning Human Understanding.* Ed. Peter H. Nidditch. Oxford: Oxford University Press, 1975.

– "An Essay on Toleration." In *Political Essays*, ed. Mark Goldie, 134–59. Cambridge: Cambridge University Press, 1997.

– "First Tract on Government." In *Political Essays*, ed. Mark Goldie, 3–53. Cambridge: Cambridge University Press, 1997.

– "Second Tract on Government." In *Political Essays*, ed. Mark Goldie, 54–78. Cambridge: Cambridge University Press, 1997.

– *Two Treatises of Government.* Ed. Peter Laslett. Cambridge: Cambridge University Press, 1988.

– "Verses on King Charles II's Restoration." In *Political Essays*, ed. Mark Goldie, 203–4. Cambridge: Cambridge University Press, 1997.

Loewenstein, David. "Milton's Prose and the Revolution." In *The Cambridge Companion to Writing of the English Revolution*, ed. N.H. Keeble, 87–106. Cambridge: Cambridge University Press, 2001.

– "Gerrard Winstanley and the Diggers." In *The Oxford Handbook of Literature and the English Revolution*, ed. Laura Lunger Knoppers, 327–45. Oxford: Oxford University Press, 2012.

Lopata, Benjamin B. "Property Theory in Hobbes." *Political Theory* 1 (1973): 203–18.

Lovett, Frank. "Milton's Case for a Free Commonwealth." *American Journal of Political Science* 49 (2005): 466–78.

– "Non-Domination." In *The Oxford Handbook of Freedom*, ed. David Schmidtz and Carmen E. Pavel, 106–23. Oxford: Oxford University Press, 2018.

Lutaud, Olivier. *Cromwell, les Niveleurs et la République.* Paris: Aubier, 1978.

– *Des Révolutions d'Angleterre à la Révolution Française.* La Haye: Martinus Nijhoff, 1973.

– *Winstanley: Socialisme et Christianisme sous Cromwell.* Paris: Didier, 1976.

MacCallum, Gerald C. "Negative and Positive Freedom." *Philosophical Review* 76 (1967): 312–34.

MacGilvray, Eric. *The Invention of Market Freedom.* Cambridge: Cambridge University Press, 2011.

Machiavelli, Niccolò. *Discourses on Livy.* Trans. and ed. Julia Conaway Bondanella and Peter Bondanella. Oxford: Oxford University Press, 1997.

– *The Prince*. Trans. and ed. Peter Bondanella. Oxford: Oxford University Press, 2005.

Macpherson, C.B. *The Political Theory of Possessive Individualism: Hobbes to Locke*. Oxford: Clarendon Press, 1962.

Marsh, John. *An Argument or, Debate in Law*. London, 1642.

Marshall, John. *John Locke: Resistance, Religion and Responsibility*. Cambridge: Cambridge University Press, 1994.

Marvell, Andrew. "An Account of the Growth of Popery and Arbitrary Government in England." In *The Prose Works of Andrew Marvell*, ed. Annabel Patterson, Nicholas von Maltzahn, and N.H. Keeble, 2 vols., 2:177–378. New Haven, CT: Yale University Press, 2003.

Matteucci, Nicola. "Dal costituzionalismo al liberalismo." In *Storia delle idee politiche, economiche e sociali*, ed. Luigi Firpo, 6 vols., vol. 4, pt. 2, 13–176. Turin: Unione tipografico-editrice torinese, 1983.

Maximes Unfolded. London, 1643.

[Maxwell, John]. *Sacro-sancta Regum Majestas*. Oxford, 1644.

Mautner, Thomas. "Locke on Appropriation." *American Philosophical Quarterly* 19 (1982): 259–70.

McCammon, Christopher. "Domination: A Rethinking." *Ethics* 125 (2015): 1028–52.

McClure, Kirstie M. *Judging Rights: Lockean Politics and the Limits of Consent*. Ithaca, NY: Cornell University Press, 1996.

McElligott, Gerald Jason. "The Book Trade, Licensing, and Censorship." In *The Oxford Handbook of Literature and the English Revolution*, ed. Laura Lunger Knoppers, 135–53. Oxford: Oxford University Press, 2012.

– "Propaganda and Censorship: The Underground Royalist Newsbooks, 1647–1650." PhD diss., University of Cambridge, 2001.

McElligott, Gerald Jason, and David L. Smith, eds. *Royalists and Royalism during the English Civil Wars*. Cambridge: Cambridge University Press, 2007.

Mendle, Michael. *Dangerous Positions: Mixed Government, the Estates of the Realm, and the Making of the Answer to the XIX Propositions*. Tuscaloosa: University of Alabama Press, 1985.

– *Henry Parker and the English Civil War: The Political Thought of the Public's "Privado."* Cambridge: Cambridge University Press, 1995.

– "Parliamentary Sovereignty: A Very English Absolutism." In *Political Discourse in Early Modern Britain*, ed. Nicholas Phillipson and Quentin Skinner, 97–119. Cambridge: Cambridge University Press, 1992.

– "The Royalist Origins of the Separation of Powers." In *Royalists and Royalism during the English Civil Wars*, ed. Jason McElligott and David L. Smith, 175–91. Cambridge: Cambridge University Press, 2007.

– "The Ship Money Case, the Case of Shipmony, and the Development of Henry Parker's Parliamentary Absolutism." *Historical Journal* 32 (1989): 513–36.

Milam, Max. "The Epistemological Basis of Locke's Idea of Property." *Western Political Quarterly* 21 (1967): 16–30.

Miller, David. "Constraints on Freedom." *Ethics* 94 (1983): 66–86.

Milton, John. "Milton's Commonplace Book." In *Complete Prose Works of John Milton*, ed. Don M. Wolfe, 10 vols., 1:362–513. New Haven, CT: Yale University Press, 1953.

– "Eikonoklastes." In *Complete Prose Works of John Milton*, ed. Merritt Y. Hughes, 10 vols., 3:337–601. New Haven, CT: Yale University Press, 1962.

– "The Tenure of Kings and Magistrates." In *Complete Prose Works of John Milton*, ed. Merritt Y. Hughes, 10 vols., 3:190–258. New Haven, CT: Yale University Press, 1962.

– "A Defence of the People of England." In *Complete Prose Works of John Milton*, 10 vols., vol. 4, pt. 1, 165–1655, ed. Don M. Wolfe, 301–537. New Haven, CT: Yale University Press, 1966.

– "A Second Defence of the English People." In *Complete Prose Works of John Milton*, 10 vols., vol. 4, pt. 1, 165–1655, ed. Don M. Wolfe, 548–686. New Haven, CT: Yale University Press, 1966.

– "The Readie and Easie Way to Establish a Free Commonwealth." 1st ed. In *Complete Prose Works of John Milton*, ed. Robert W. Ayers, 10 vols., 7:353–404. New Haven, CT: Yale University Press, 1980.

– "The Readie and Easie Way to Establish a Free Commonwealth," 2nd ed. In *Complete Prose Works of John Milton*, ed. Robert W. Ayers, 10 vols., 7:407–63. New Haven, CT: Yale University Press, 1980.

– "Samson Agonistes." In *The Complete Works of John Milton*, ed. Laura Lunger Knoppers, 12 vols., 2:69–120. Oxford: Oxford University Press, 2008.

A Miracle: An Honest Broker, Or, Reasons urging a more liberall Loane towards the maintenance of Religion, Law, and the Kingdomes safety in them Both. London, 1643.

"Misotyrannus, Laophilius." *Mene Tekel; Or, The Downfal of Tyranny.* N.p., 1663.

More, Thomas. *Utopia.* Trans. Robert M. Adamsed, ed. George M. Logan. Cambridge: Cambridge University Press, 2002.

More Light Shining in Buckingham-shire. London, 1649.

Morrill, John. *The Nature of the English Revolution.* London: Routledge, 1993.

– *Revolt in the Provinces: The English People and the Tragedies of War 1634–48.* London: Longman, 1999.

Morton, A.L. *The World of the Ranters: Religious Radicalism in the English Revolution.* London: Lawrence and Wishart, 1970.

Mueller, Janel. "Contextualizing Milton's Nascent Republicanism." In *Poetry and Politics: New Essays on Milton and His World*, ed. P.G. Stanwood, 263–82. Binghamton, NJ: Medieval and Renaissance Texts and Studies, 1995.

Nalson, John. *The Common Interest of King and People: Shewing the Antiquity and Excellency Of Monarchy, Compared with Aristocracy and Democracy.* London, 1677.

Narveson, Jan. "Libertarianism vs. Marxism: Reflections on G.A. Cohen's 'Self-Ownership, Freedom and Equality.'" *Journal of Ethics* 2 (1998): 186–218.

Nedham, Marchamont. *The Case of the Commonwealth, Stated.* Ed. Philip A. Knachel. Charlottesville: University Press of Virginia, 1969.

– *The Excellencie of a Free-State.* London, 1656.

– *Interest will not Lie. Or, A View of England's True Interest.* London, 1659.

[Nedham, Marchamont]. *Mercurius Pragmaticus*, no. 9, 9–16 November. N.p., 1647.

– *Mercurius Politicus*, no. 69, 25 September–2 October. London, 1651.

– *Mercurius Politicus*, no. 88, 5–12 February. London, 1652

– *Mercurius Politicus*, no. 92, 4–11 March. London, 1652.

– *A True state of the case of the Commonwealth of England, Scotland, and Ireland.* London, 1654.

Nelson, Eric. *The Greek Tradition in Republican Thought.* Cambridge: Cambridge University Press, 2004.

– *The Hebrew Commonwealth.* Cambridge, MA: Harvard University Press, 2010.

– "Liberty: One Concept Too Many?" *Political Theory* 33 (2005): 58–78.

Nelson, Scott A. *The Discourses of Algernon Sidney.* London: Associated University Presses, 1993.

Neville, Henry. "Plato Redivivus: or, A Dialogue Concerning Government." In *Two English Republican Tracts*, ed. Caroline Robbins, 61–200. Cambridge: Cambridge University Press, 1969.

A New Engagement, or, Manifesto. [London], 1648.

A New Plea for the Parliament: and the Reserved Man resolved. [London], 1643.

Norbrook, David. *Writing the English Republic: Poetry, Rhetoric and Politics, 1627–1660.* Cambridge: Cambridge University Press, 1999.

Nozick, Robert. *Anarchy, State, and Utopia.* Oxford: Blackwell, 1974.

Nuzzo, Enrico. *La superiortà degli stati liberi: I repubblicani inglesi, 1649–1722.* Naples: Edizioni scientifiche italiane, 1984.

Olivecrona, Karl. "Appropriation in the State of Nature: Locke on the Origin of Property." *Journal of the History of Ideas* 35 (1974): 211–30.

– "Locke's Theory of Appropriation." *Philosophical Quarterly* 24 (1974): 220–34.

– "The Term 'Property' in Locke's Two Treatises of Government." *Archiv für Rechts- und Sozialphilosophie* 61 (1975): 109–15.

Orr, D. Alan. "Law, Liberty, and the English Civil War: John Lilburne's Prison Experience, the Levellers and Freedom." In *The Experience of Revolution in Stuart Britain and Ireland: Essays for John Morrill*, ed. Michael J. Braddick and David L. Smith, 154–71. Cambridge: Cambridge University Press, 2011.

Otsuka, Michael. *Libertarianism without Inequality.* Oxford: Oxford University Press, 2003.

Overton, Richard. *An Appeale From the degenerate Representative Body the Commons of England assembled at Westminster.* London, 1647.

– *An Arrow against All Tyrants And Tyrany.* [London], 1646.

[Parker, Henry]. *The Case of Shipmony briefly discoursed.* London, 1640.

– *The Contra-Replicant.* N.p., 1643.

– *Jus Populi.* London, 1644.

– *A Letter of Due Censure and Redargution.* London, 1650.

– *Observations upon some of his Majesties late Answers and Expresses.* London, 1642.

Pateman, Carole. "Self-Ownership and Property in the Person: Democratization and a Tale of Two Concepts." *Journal of Political Philosophy* 10 (2002): 20–53.

– *The Sexual Contract*, 2nd ed. Stanford, CA: Stanford University Press, 2018.

Patterson, Annabel. *Early Modern Liberalism.* Cambridge: Cambridge University Press, 1997.

Peacey, Jason. "Henry Parker and Parliamentary Propaganda in the English Civil Wars." PhD diss., University of Cambridge, 1994.

– "John Lilburne and the Long Parliament." *Historical Journal* 43 (2000): 625–45.

– "News, Pamphlets, and Public Opinion." In *The Oxford Handbook of Literature and the English Revolution*, ed. Laura Lunger Knoppers, 173–89. Oxford: Oxford University Press, 2012.

Peltonen, Markku. *Classical Humanism and Republicanism in English Political Thought, 1570–1640.* Cambridge: Cambridge University Press, 1995.

Petchesky, Rosalind. "The Body as Property: A Feminist Re-vision." In *Concerning the New World Order*, ed. Faya Ginsburg and Rayna Rapp, 387–406. Berkeley: University of California Press, 1995.

Pettit, Philip. *Just Freedom: A Moral Compass for a Complex World.* New York: W.W. Norton, 2014.

– "Keeping Republican Freedom Simple: On a Difference with Quentin Skinner." *Political Theory* 30 (2002): 339–56.

– *On the People's Terms: A Republican Theory and Model of Democracy.* Cambridge: Cambridge University Press, 2012.

– *Republicanism: A Theory of Freedom and Government.* Oxford: Oxford University Press, 1997.

– "Republican Freedom: Three Axioms, Four Theorems." In *Republicanism and Political Theory,* ed. Cécile Laborde and John Maynor, 102–30. Oxford: Blackwell, 2008.

– *A Theory of Freedom: From the Psychology to the Politics of Agency.* Cambridge: Cambridge University Press, 2001.

Phillips, Anne. "Feminism and Republicanism: Is This a Plausible Alliance?" *Journal of Political Philosophy* 8 (2000): 279–93.

– *Our Bodies, Whose Property?* Princeton, NJ: Princeton University Press, 2013.

"Philodemius, Eutactus." *The Originall and End of Civill Power.* London, 1649.

Pincus, Steven. "Neither Machiavellian Moment nor Possessive Individualism: Commercial Society and the Defenders of the English Commonwealth." *American Historical Review* 103 (1998): 705–36.

Pipes, Richard. *Property and Freedom.* New York: Alfred A. Knop, 1999.

Pitkin, Hanna Fenichel. "Are Freedom and Liberty Twins?" *Political Theory* 16 (1988): 523–52.

– *The Concept of Representation.* Berkeley: University of California Press, 1967.

A Plea for the Parliament. London, 1642.

Pocock, J.G.A. *The Ancient Constitution and the Feudal Law: A Study of English Historical Thought in the Seventeenth Century,* 2nd ed. Cambridge: Cambridge University Press, 1987.

– "Authority and Property: The Question of Liberal Origins." In *Virtue, Commerce, and History: Essays on Political Thought and History, Chiefly in the Eighteenth Century,* 51–71. Cambridge: Cambridge University Press, 1985.

– "England's Cato: The Virtues and Fortunes of Algernon Sidney." *Historical Journal* 37 (1994): 915–35.

– "Foundations and Moments." In *Rethinking the Foundations,* ed. Annabel Brett, James Tully, and Holly Hamilton-Bleakley, 37–49. Cambridge: Cambridge University Press, 2006.

– "Historical Introduction." In *The Political Works of James Harrington,* ed. J.G.A. Pocock, 1–152. Cambridge: Cambridge University Press, 1977.

– "Machiavelli, Harrington and English Political Ideologies in the Eighteenth Century." In *Politics, Language and Time: Essays on Political Thought and History,* 104–47. London: Methuen, 1971.

– *The Machiavellian Moment: Florentine Political Thought and the Atlantic Republican Tradition*. Princeton, NJ: Princeton University Press, 1975.

Pocock, J.G.A., and Gordon Schochet. "Interregnum and Restoration." In *The Varieties of British Political Thought, 1500–1800*, ed. J.G.A. Pocock, 146–79. Cambridge: Cambridge University Press, 1993.

A Political Catechism. London, 1643.

Priestley, Joseph. "The Present State Of Liberty in Great Britain and Her Colonies." In *Political Writings*, ed. Peter N. Miller, 129–44. Cambridge: Cambridge University Press, 1993.

Proceedings in Parliament 1610. Ed. Elizabeth Read Foster, 2 vols., vol. 2. New Haven, CT: Yale University Press, 1966.

Proceedings in the Opening Session of the Long Parliament: House of Commons. Ed. Maija Jansson, Jennifer Klein Morrison, Alisa Plant, and Shawn Smith, 7 vols., vol 1. Rochester, NY: University of Rochester Press, 2000.

Puritanism and Liberty Being the Army Debates (1647–9) from the Clarke Manuscripts with Supplementary Documents. Ed. A.S.P. Woodhouse, 2nd ed. London: Dent, 1974.

Raab, Felix. *The English Face of Machiavelli: A Changing Interpretation, 1500–1700*. London: Routledge and Kegan Paul, 1965.

Radzinowicz, Mary Ann. "The Politics of *Paradise Lost*." In *Politics of Discourse: The Literature and History of Seventeenth-Century England*, ed. Kevin Sharp and Steven N. Zwicker, 204–29. Berkeley: University of California Press, 1987.

Rahe, Paul A. "Machiavelli in the English Revolution." In *Machiavelli's Liberal Republican Legacy*, 9–35. Cambridge: Cambridge University Press, 2006.

– *Republics Ancient and Modern: Classical Republicanism and the American Revolution*. Chapel Hill: University of North Carolina, 1992.

Raymond, Joad. "In 1649, to St. George's Hill." *Huntington Library Quarterly* 75 (2012): 429–46.

– "John Streater and the Grand Politick Informer." *Historical Journal* 41 (1998): 567–74.

– "Marchamont Nedham." In *The Oxford Handbook of Literature and the English Revolution*, ed. Laura Lunger Knoppers, 375–93. Oxford: Oxford University Press, 2012.

– *Pamphlets and Pamphleteering in Early Modern Britain*. Cambridge: Cambridge University Press, 2006.

[Rous, Francis]. *The Lawfulness of obeying the Present Government*. London, 1649.

Runciman, David. *Pluralism and the Personality of the State*. Cambridge: Cambridge University Press, 1997.

– "What Kind of Person Is Hobbes's State? A Reply to Skinner." *Journal of Political Philosophy* 8 (2000): 268–78.

Russell, Conrad, *The Causes of the English Civil War*. Oxford: Clarendon Press, 1990.

– *Unrevolutionary England, 1603–1642*. London: Hambledon Press, 1990.

Russell, Conrad, ed. *The Origins of the English Civil War*. London: Macmillan, 1973.

Ryan, Alan. "Locke and the Dictatorship of the Bourgeoisie." *Political Studies* 13 (1965): 219–30.

– "Locke on Freedom: Some Second Thoughts." In *Traditions of Liberalism: Essays on John Locke, Adam Smith and John Stuart Mill*, ed. Knud Haakonssen, 33–53. Sidney: Centre for Independent Studies, 1988.

– *Property and Political Theory*. Oxford: Blackwell, 1984.

Sabbadini, Lorenzo. "Popular Sovereignty and Representation in the English Civil War." In *Popular Sovereignty in Historical Perspective*, ed. Quentin Skinner and Richard Bourke, 164–86. Cambridge: Cambridge University Press, 2016.

Sallust. "The War with Catiline." In *Sallust*, trans. and ed. John C. Rofle, 1–129. Cambridge, MA: Harvard University Press, 1931.

Salmon, J.H.M. *The French Religious Wars in English Political Thought*. Oxford: Clarendon Press, 1959.

Sampson, Margaret. "Property in Seventeenth-Century English Political Thought." In *Religion, Resistance, and Civil War*, ed. Gordon Schochet, 259–75. Washington, DC: The Folger Institute, 1990.

Sanderson, John. "The *Answer to the Nineteen Propositions* Revisited." *Political Studies* 32 (1984): 627–36.

– "Philip Hunton's 'Appeasement': Moderation and Extremism in the English Civil War." *History of Political Thought* 3 (1982): 447–61.

– "Serpent-Salve, 1643: The Royalism of John Bramhall." *Journal of Ecclesiastical History* 25 (1974): 1–14.

Sauer, Elizabeth. "Milton's *Defences* and the Principle of '*Sanior Pars*.'" In *The Oxford Handbook of Literature and the English Revolution*, ed. Laura Lunger Knoppers, 445–61. Oxford: Oxford University Press, 2012.

Scott, Jonathan. *Algernon Sidney and the English Republic, 1623–1677*. Cambridge: Cambridge University Press, 1988.

– *Algernon Sidney and the Restoration Crisis, 1677–1683*. Cambridge: Cambridge University Press, 1991.

– *Commonwealth Principles: Republican Writing of the English Revolution*. Cambridge: Cambridge University Press, 2004.

– "The Rapture of Motion: James Harrington's Republicanism." In *Political Discourse in Early Modern Britain*, ed. Nicholas Phillipson and Quentin Skinner, 139–63. Cambridge: Cambridge University Press, 1993.

Seaberg, R.B. "The Norman Conquest and the Common Law: The Levellers and the Argument from Continuity." *Historical Journal* 24 (1981): 791–806.

Sechler, Michael J., and Janelle Greenberg. "'There Is Scarce a Pamphlet That Doth Not Triumph in Bracton': The Role of *De Legibus et Consuetudinibus Angliae* in Stuart Political Thought." *History of Political Thought* 33 (2012): 25–54.

[Settle, Elkanah]. *The Character of a Popish Successour, and what England may Expect from Such a One.* London, 1681.

[Sexby, Edward, and Silus Titus]. *Killing Noe Murder.* [London], 1657.

Shanks, Torrey. "The Rhetoric of Self-Ownership." *Political Theory* 47 (2019): 311–37.

Sharp, Andrew. "John Lilburne and the Long Parliament's Book of Declarations: A Radical's Exploitation of the Words of Authorities." *History of Political Thought* 9 (1988): 19–44.

Sidney, Algernon. *Discourses concerning Government.* Ed. Thomas G. West. Indianapolis, IL: Liberty Fund, 1990.

– *Court Maxims.* Ed. Hans W. Blom, Eco Haitsma Mulier, and Ronald Janse. Cambridge: Cambridge University Press, 1996.

Simmons, A. John. *The Lockean Theory of Rights.* Princeton, NJ: Princeton University Press, 1992.

Sirluck, Ernest. "Milton's Political Thought: The First Cycle." *Modern Philology* 61 (1964): 209–24.

Skinner, Quentin. "Classical Liberty and the Coming of the English Civil War." In *Republicanism: A Shared European Heritage*, ed. Martin van Gelderen and Quentin Skinner, 2 vols., 2:9–28. Cambridge: Cambridge University Press, 2002.

– "Classical Liberty, Renaissance Translation, and the English Civil War." In *Visions of Politics*, 3 vols., 2:308–43. Cambridge: Cambridge University Press, 2002.

– "Conquest and Consent: Hobbes and the Engagement Controversy." In *Visions of Politics*, 3 vols., 3:287–307. Cambridge: Cambridge University Press, 2002.

– "The Context of Hobbes's Theory of Political Obligation." In *Visions of Politics*, 3 vols., 3:264–86. Cambridge: Cambridge University Press, 2002.

– "Freedom as the Absence of Arbitrary Power." In *Republicanism and Political Theory*, ed. Cécile Laborde and John Maynor, 83–101. Oxford: Blackwell, 2008.

– *From Humanism to Hobbes: Studies in Rhetoric and Politics.* Cambridge: Cambridge University Press, 2018.

– "History and Ideology in the English Revolution." In *Visions of Politics*, 3 vols., 3:238–63. Cambridge: Cambridge University Press, 2002.

– *Hobbes and Republican Liberty.* Cambridge: Cambridge University Press, 2008.

– "Hobbes on Persons, Authors and Representatives." In *The Cambridge Companion to Hobbes's Leviathan*, ed. Patricia Springborg, 157–80. Cambridge: Cambridge University Press, 2007.

– "The Idea of Negative Liberty." In *Philosophy in History: Essays on the Historiography of Philosophy*, ed. Richard Rorty, Jerome B. Schneewind, and Quentin Skinner, 193–221. Cambridge: Cambridge University Press, 1984.

– "John Milton and the Politics of Slavery." In *Visions of Politics*, 3 vols., 2:286–307. Cambridge: Cambridge University Press, 2002.

– *Liberty before Liberalism.* Cambridge: Cambridge University Press, 1998.

– "On the Liberty of the Ancients and the Moderns: A Reply to My Critics." *Journal of the History of Ideas* 73 (2012): 127–46.

– "On Neo-Roman Liberty: A Response and a Reassessment." In *Rethinking Liberty before Liberalism*, ed. Hannah Dawson and Annelien de Dijn. Cambridge: Cambridge University Press, forthcoming 2021.

– "On Trusting the Judgement of Our Rulers." In *Political Judgement: Essays for John Dunn*, ed. Richard Bourke and Raymond Geuss, 113–30. Cambridge: Cambridge University Press, 2009.

– "Surveying *The Foundations*: A Retrospect and Reassessment." In *Rethinking the Foundations*, ed. Annabel Brett, James Tully, and Holly Hamilton-Bleakley, 236–61. Cambridge: Cambridge University Press, 2006.

– "A Third Concept of Liberty." *Proceedings of the British Academy* 117 (2002): 237–68.

Smith, David L. *Constitutional Royalism and the Search for Settlement, c. 1640–1649.* Cambridge: Cambridge University Press, 1995.

Smith, Nigel. "Gerrard Winstanley and the Literature of Revolution." In *Winstanley and the Diggers, 1649–1999*, ed. Andrew Bradstock, 47–60. London: Frank Cass, 2000.

– *Literature and Revolution in England, 1640–1660.* New Haven, CT: Yale University Press, 1994.

– "Popular Republicanism in the 1650s: John Steater's 'Heroic Mechanicks.'" In *Milton and Republicanism*, ed. David Armitage, Armand Himy, and Quentin Skinner, 137–55. Cambridge: Cambridge University Press, 1995.

Sommerville, Johann P. "The Authorship and Dating of Some Works Attributed to Filmer." In Sir Robert Filmer, *Patriarcha and Other Writings*, ed. Johann P. Sommerville, xxxii–xxxvii. Cambridge: Cambridge University Press, 1991.

– "English and Roman Liberty in the Monarchical Republic of Early Stuart England." In *The Monarchical Republic of Early Modern England: Essays in Response to Patrick Collinson*, ed. John F. McDiarmid, 308–20. Aldershot: Ashgate, 2007.

– "Ideology, Property and the Constitution." In *Conflict in Early Stuart England: Studies in Religion and Politics, 1603–1642*, ed. Richard Cust and Ann Hughes, 47–71. Harlow: Longman, 1989.

– *Royalists and Patriots: Politics and Ideology in England, 1603–1640*, 2nd ed. London: Longman, 1999.

Sreenivasan, Gopal. *The Limits of Lockean Rights in Property*. Oxford: Oxford University Press, 1995.

Steiner, Hillel. *An Essay on Rights*. Oxford: Blackwell, 1994.

St John, Oliver. *The Speech or Declaration of Mr. St.-John, His Majesties Solicitor Generall*. London, 1641.

Stone, Lawrence. *The Causes of the English Revolution, 1529–1642*. London: Routledge and Kegan Paul, 1972.

– *The Crisis of the Aristocracy, 1558–1641*. Oxford: Clarendon Press, 1965.

Streater, John. *A further Continuance of the Grand Politick Informer*. [London], 1653.

[Streater, John]. *A Glympse of that Jewel, Judiciall, Just, Preserving Libertie*. London, 1653.

– *Observations Historical, Political, and Philosophical, Upon Aristotle's first Book of Political Government*, no. 2, 11–19 April. London, 1654.

– *Observations Historical, Political, and Philosophical, Upon Aristotle's first Book of Political Government*, no. 7, 30 May–6 June. London, 1654.

– *Observations Historical, Political, and Philosophical, Upon Aristotle's first Book of Political Government*, no. 11, 27 June–4 July. London, 1654.

Suárez, Francisco. *Tractatus de legibus ac Deo legislatore*. Ed. Luciano Pereña, Pedro Súñer, Vidal Abril, César Villanueva, and Eleuterio Elorduy, 8 vols. Madrid: Consejo Superior de Investigaciones Científicas, 1971–2010.

Sullivan, Vicki B. *Machiavelli, Hobbes, and the Formation of a Liberal Republicanism in England*. Cambridge: Cambridge University Press, 2004.

– "Muted and Manifest English Machiavellism: The Reconciliation of Machiavellian Republicanism with Liberalism in Sidney's *Discourses concerning Government*, and Trenchard's and Gordon's *Cato's Letters*." In *Machiavelli's Liberal Republican Legacy*, ed. Paul A. Rahe, 58–86. Cambridge: Cambridge University Press, 2006.

Taft, Barbara. "Appendix 1: Walwyn's Canon." In *The Writings of William Walwyn*, ed. Jack R. McMichael and Barbara Taft, 527–38. Athens, GA: University of Georgia Press, 1989.

Talisse, Robert B. "Impunity and Domination: A Puzzle for Republicanism." *European Journal of Political Theory* 13 (2014): 121–31.

Taylor, Charles. "What's Wrong with Negative Liberty." In *The Idea of Freedom: Essays in Honour of Isaiah Berlin*, ed. Alan Ryan, 175–93. Oxford: Oxford University Press, 1979.

The Subject of Supremacie. London, 1643.

Thomas, Keith. "The Levellers and the Franchise." In *The Interregnum: The Quest for Settlement, 1646–1660*, ed. G.E. Aylmer, 57–78. London: Macmillan, 1972.

Thompson, Christopher. "Maximilian Petty and the Putney Debate on the Franchise." *Past and Present* 88 (1980): 63–9.

Thompson, Michael J. "The Two Faces of Domination in Republican Political Theory." *European Journal of Political Theory* 17 (2018): 44–64.

Tierney, Brian. "Dominion of Self and Natural Rights before Locke and after." In *Transformations in Medieval and Early-Modern Rights Discourse*, ed. Virpi Mäkinen and Petter Korkman, 173–203. Dordrecht: Springer, 2006.

To the Right Honorable, the Commons of England In Parliament Assembled. London, 1648.

Tuck, Richard. *Natural Rights Theories: Their Origin and Development*. Cambridge: Cambridge University Press, 1979.

– "A New Date for Filmer's *Patriarcha*." *Historical Journal* 29 (1986): 183–6.

– *Philosophy and Government, 1572–1651*. Cambridge: Cambridge University Press, 1993.

Tucker, Josiah. *A Treatise Concerning Civil Government, in Three Parts*. London, 1781.

Tully, James. *An Approach to Political Philosophy: Locke in Contexts*. Cambridge: Cambridge University Press, 1993.

– *A Discourse on Property: John Locke and His Adversaries*. Cambridge: Cambridge University Press, 1980.

– "Property, Self-Government and Consent." *Canadian Journal of Political Science* 28 (1995): 105–32.

Tyranipocrit, Discovered with his wiles, wherewith he vanquisheth. Rotterdam, 1649.

Van Parijs, Philippe. *Real Freedom for All: What (If Anything) Can Justify Capitalism?* Oxford: Clarendon Press, 1995.

Vernon, Elliot, and Philip Baker. "What Was the First Agreement of the People?" *Historical Journal* 53 (2010): 39–59.

Vox Plebis, or, The Peoples Out-cry Against Oppression, Injustice, and Tyranny. London, 1646.

Waldron, Jeremy. "Enough and as Good Left for Others." *Philosophical Quarterly* 29 (1979): 319–28.

– *God, Locke, and Equality: Christian Foundations of John Locke's Political Thought*. Cambridge: Cambridge University Press, 2002.

- "Locke, Tully, and the Regulation of Property." *Political Studies* 32 (1984): 98–106.
- "Pettit's Molecule." In *Common Minds: Themes from the Philosophy of Philip Pettit*, ed. Geoffrey Brennan, Robert Goodin, Frank Jackson, and Michael Smith, 143–60. Oxford: Clarendon Press, 2007.
- *The Right to Private Property.* Oxford: Clarendon Press, 1988.

Wall, Steven. "Freedom, Interference and Domination." *Political Studies* 49 (2001): 216–30.

Wallace, John M. "The Date of Sir Robert Filmer's *Patriarcha.*" *Historical Journal* 23 (1980): 155–65.
- "The Engagement Controversy 1649–1652: An Annotated List of Pamphlets." *Bulletin of the New York Public Library* 68 (1964): 384–405.

Warwick, Philip. *A Discourse of Government, As Examined by Reason, Scripture, and Law of the Land.* London, 1694.

West, Thomas G. "Foreword." In Algernon Sidney, *Discourses concerning Government*, ed. Thomas G. West, xv–xxxvi. Indianapolis, IL: Liberty Fund, 1990.

Weston, Corinne Comstock, and Janelle Renfrow Greenberg. *Subjects and Sovereigns: The Grand Controversy over Legal Sovereignty in Stuart England.* Cambridge: Cambridge University Press, 1981.

Wilcher, Robert. *The Writing of Royalism, 1628–1660.* Cambridge: Cambridge University Press, 2001.

[Wildman, John]. *Putney Projects.* London, 1647.

Williams, Gryffith. *Jura Majestatis, the Rights of Kings Both In Church and State.* Oxford, 1644.

Winfrey, J.C. "Charity versus Justice in Locke's Theory of Justice." *Journal of the History of Ideas* 42 (1981): 423–38.

Winstanley, Gerrard. "A Declaration to the Powers of England." In *The Complete Works of Gerrard Winstanley*, ed. Thomas N. Corns, Ann Hughes, and David Loewenstein, 2 vols., 2:1–30. Oxford: Oxford University Press, 2009.
- "Englands Spirit Unfoulded." In *The Complete Works of Gerrard Winstanley*, ed. Thomas N. Corns, Ann Hughes, and David Loewenstein, 2 vols., 2:161–70. Oxford: Oxford University Press, 2009.
- "Fire in the Bush." In *The Complete Works of Gerrard Winstanley*, ed. Thomas N. Corns, Ann Hughes, and David Loewenstein, 2 vols., 2:171–234. Oxford: Oxford University Press, 2009.
- "An Humble Request to the Ministers of both Universities." In *The Complete Works of Gerrard Winstanley*, ed. Thomas N. Corns, Ann Hughes, and David Loewenstein, 2 vols., 2:253–77. Oxford: Oxford University Press, 2009.

– "The Law of Freedom in a Platform." In *The Complete Works of Gerrard Winstanley*, ed. Thomas N. Corns, Ann Hughes, and David Loewenstein, 2 vols., 2: 278–404. Oxford: Oxford University Press, 2009.

– "The Mysterie of God." In *The Complete Works of Gerrard Winstanley*, ed. Thomas N. Corns, Ann Hughes, and David Loewenstein, 2 vols., 1:255–312. Oxford: Oxford University Press, 2009.

– "The New Law of Righteousnes." In *The Complete Works of Gerrard Winstanley*, ed. Thomas N. Corns, Ann Hughes, and David Loewenstein, 2 vols., 1:472–600. Oxford: Oxford University Press, 2009.

– "A New-yeers Gift for the Parliament and Armie." In *The Complete Works of Gerrard Winstanley*, ed. Thomas N. Corns, Ann Hughes, and David Loewenstein, 2 vols., 2:107–60. Oxford: Oxford University Press, 2009.

– "A Watch-Word to the City of London." In *The Complete Works of Gerrard Winstanley*, ed. Thomas N. Corns, Ann Hughes, and David Loewenstein, 2 vols., 2:79–170. Oxford: Oxford University Press, 2009.

Wolfe, Don M. *Milton in the Puritan Revolution*. New York: T. Nelson, 1941.

Wood, Ellen Meiksins. *Liberty and Property: A Social History of Western Political Thought from Renaissance to Enlightenment*. London: Verso, 2012.

Wood, Gordon S. *The Creation of the American Republic*. Chapel Hill: University of North Carolina Press, 1969.

Wood, Neil. *John Locke and Agrarian Capitalism*. Berkeley: University of California Press, 1984.

Worden, Blair. "Classical Republicanism and the Puritan Revolution." In *History and Imagination*, ed. Hugh Lloyd-Jones, Valerie Pearl, and Blair Worden, 182–200. London: Duckworth, 1981.

– "The Commonwealth Kidney of Algernon Sidney." *Journal of British Studies* 24 (1985): 1–40.

– "English Republicanism." In *The Cambridge History of Political Thought*, ed. J.H. Burns and Mark Goldie, 443–75. Cambridge: Cambridge University Press, 1991.

– "Factory of the Revolution," *London Review of Books* 20 (1998): 13–15.

– "Hobbes and the Halo of Power." *New York Review of Books* 56 (2009): 40–3.

– "James Harrington and *The Commonwealth of Oceana*, 1656." In *Republicanism, Liberty, and Commercial Society, 1649–1776*, ed. David Wootton, 82–110. Stanford, CA: Stanford University Press, 1994.

– *Literature and Politics in Cromwellian England: John Milton, Andrew Marvell, Marchamont Nedham*. Oxford: Oxford University Press, 2007.

– "Marchamont Nedham and the Beginnings of English Republicanism, 1649–1656."
In *Republicanism, Liberty, and Commercial Society, 1649–1776*, ed. David Wootton,
45–81. Stanford, CA: Stanford University Press, 1994.

– "Milton and Marchamont Nedham." In *Milton and Republicanism*, ed. David Armitage, Armand Himy, and Quentin Skinner, 156–80. Cambridge: Cambridge University Press, 1995.

– "Milton, *Samson Agonistes*, and the Restoration." In *Culture and Society in the Stuart
Restoration: Literature, Drama, History*, ed. Gerald MacLean, 111–36. Cambridge:
Cambridge University Press, 1995.

– "Republicanism and the Restoration, 1660–1683." In *Republicanism, Liberty, and
Commercial Society, 1649–1776*, ed. David Wootton, 139–93. Stanford, CA: Stanford
University Press, 1994.

– "Republicanism, Regicide and Republic: The English Experience." In *Republicanism:
A Shared European Heritage*, ed. Martin van Gelderen and Quentin Skinner, 2 vols.,
1:307–27. Cambridge: Cambridge University Press, 2002.

– *The Rump Parliament, 1648–1653*. Cambridge: Cambridge University Press, 1974.

– "'Wit in a Roundhead': The Dilemma of Marchamont Nedham." In *Political Culture
and Cultural Politics in Cromwellian England: Essays Presented to David Underdown*,
ed. Susan D. Amussen and Mark A. Kishlansky, 301–37. Manchester: Manchester
University Press, 1995.

[Wren, Matthew]. *Considerations on Mr. Harrington's Commonwealth of Oceana*. London, 1657.

INDEX